HISTORY OF
GREEK CULTURE

JACOB BURCKHARDT

HISTORY OF
GREEK CULTURE

Translated from the German by
PALMER HILTY

With 80 halftones and many line drawings

FREDERICK UNGAR PUBLISHING CO.
NEW YORK

Translated from
the abridged version (1958) of the two-volume
Griechische Kultur by Jacob Burckhardt
published by Safari Verlag, Berlin

Printed in the United States of America

Library of Congress Catalog Card No. 63–14065

ABOUT JACOB BURCKHARDT

Jacob Burckhardt, the Swiss historian of culture, was born in Basel in 1818. After a tentative start in theology he turned to history and literature, doing advanced work in Berlin and Bonn, where he was greatly influenced by German scholars, including Leopold von Ranke. Upon completing his studies he became a university lecturer at Basel in 1844.

The impressions gained from two trips to Italy turned Burckhardt from romantic to classical art and culture. After publishing studies in the history of art and culture, he was called to a professorship at the Swiss Federal Institute of Technology in Zurich in 1855. That same year saw the publication of his *Cicerone, eine Einleitung zum Genuss der Kunstwerke Italiens,* (*The Cicerone: An Art Guide to Painting in Italy,* 1855), intended as a companion for travelers wishing to understand and enjoy the masterpieces of Italian creative art of the *trecento* to the *cinquecento*.

In 1858 he accepted a professorship at the University of Basel and a post at the Teachers College, also in Basel, and filled both positions until 1893.

In 1860 Burckhardt published his *Kultur der Renaissance (Civilization of the Renaissance in Italy)*, in which he depicted the rise of the modern state and the development of the *uomo singulare*. Thereafter he restricted his literary labors to elaborating university lectures. The wealth of his manuscript legacy was published as *Griechische Kulturgeschichte (History of Greek Culture,* 1898–1902, two volumes) and *Weltgeschichtliche Betrachtungen (Reflections on History,* 1905). In the present volume, translated from an abridged edition of *History of Greek Culture,* material of interest largely to specialists alone has been omitted.

In his *History of Greek Culture* Burckhardt did not glorify Greek history; rather he attempted a thoroughly realistic picture of ancient Hellas with its many tangled and unsavory developments. Without detracting from the enduring worth and splendor of Hellenic art and thought, he unflinchingly depicted the weaknesses of the Greek systems, especially the sad state of Athenian democracy. The task he set himself he described in part as follows:

> It is my aim to keep alive interest in ancient Greek culture. No glorification is intended, nor do I wish to prettify. But the great

world-historical position of the Greek mind and position between the orient and occident must be made clear. What the
Greeks did and endured they did and endured differently from
all other peoples before them. Where others lived and acted
from dull compulsion, they were free, spontaneous, original, and
aware. Hence in their activities and capacities they appear to be
essentially *the* gifted race of men, subject to all the mistakes and
sufferings of such a people.

In the world of the intellect the Greeks pushed to limits of
accomplishment which mankind must not fail to appreciate and
aspire to, even when it cannot equal the Greeks in achievement.

Greek accomplishments were such that posterity has had no
choice but to study the Hellenic way of life. Those who withdraw from this endeavor will be stranded in the backwaters of
culture.

Looking with dismay on the leveling tendencies of the nineteenth century, Burckhardt took refuge in the beauty of the world of Hellenism, which
became the home of his soul and whose heroically tragic philosophy of life
he made his own. What he said about the gradually fading frescoes of
Leonardo's *Last Supper* is equally appropriate to the tragic destiny of the
Greeks: "The most beautiful art on earth must perish, and death delights
most in devouring that which is most glorious in the world of man."

Burckhardt admired the Greek character because it developed toward
a higher type of man capable of meeting the severe demands of an aristocratic way of life. The aristocratic Greek strove for noble excellence in his
competitive sports, created the popular ideal of practical wisdom, and stood
his ground in the never-ending battle with the tragic *amor fati:*

> High over the heads of men destiny sits enthroned,
> The tirelessly ripening harvest of their own sowing.

Consequently he stressed the virtues of the Greek *agon,* a contest without any utilitarian motives, invigorating life in the sense of a sound mind
in a healthy body. The Greek system of education, rooted in the nurture of
the body, produces a joy in life and harmony in culture, and demands a
certain degree of fulfillment in life on earth.

The historian thus fastened his gaze on the panorama of historical time,
thereby escaping the danger of fruitless ideological speculation. In his works
he studied politics and culture from a unified point of view. Those who feel
some inner kinship with Hellenism may find significant values in Burckhardt's *History of Greek Culture.*

P. H.

CONTENTS

Part I

STATE AND NATION

Part II

THE FINE ARTS

Part III

POESY AND MUSIC

Part IV

ON PHILOSOPHY, SCIENCE, AND ORATORY

ILLUSTRATIONS

At the end of the book

ix

*Plates numbered 48, 57 to 62, 64 to 78, and 80 are
from photographs by Alinari-Art Reference Bureau.*

PART I

STATE AND NATION

Chapter One

THE POLIS

All beginnings are lost in obscurity, including those of a race or people. Still, the social foundations of Greek life, namely, marriage and the family and property rights, appear to have been present already in pre-Hellenic times; they were certainly present among the Hellenes and Greco-Italic people before they differentiated into sub-groups. They must have been shaped by a primal religion which bestowed a central role on the ancestral cult as well as on the hearth. Ancestor worship also imposed monogamy, found in Greece at the very beginning, as evidenced by elaborate marriage rites and the severe punishment adultery entailed. And, likewise, the right to own land was causally related to veneration of the hearth and graves.

According to Diodorus, the hearth taught man the art of building houses. Originally, Greek houses were separated from each other; there were no rows of houses with partition walls between them. The family burial site was located on one's own land; therefore, this property could not be alienated. The duties deriving from ancestor worship also imposed the right of inheritance. The son inherited the land, the daughters being left out. But, to guarantee the continuation of sacrifices to the dead, daughters as inheritors were married to the next of kin, and adoption was permitted. Paternal power must have been very comprehensive.

In historical times the *genos*, i.e., the racial community in the old sense, was present only as a vestigial remnant, surviving nowhere in its original form. The genos appeared as a recollection, as an awareness of a common ancestry, and in a communal worship of the dead, the grave site being the only property held in common. The relation of the later lines of descent to the ancestral lineage remains in question; the accession of slaves and hired hands also had a complicating effect on the racial groupings. The interrela-

3

tion of the racial stocks and tribes baffles conception and is purely hypothetical. We simply cannot tell whether families formed *phratries, phratries phylae,* and *phylae* tribes, or whether, on the contrary, the tribe was first and it broke up into phylae, phratries, and sub-groups. Whether it was a process of subdivision or of amalgamation cannot be ascertained.

In any event, a remnant of gray antiquity towers like an ancient mountain peak above alluvial plains—the phylae. The marked changes in the social structure and in the usage of words have here, as elsewhere, greatly encumbered our grasp of the original affairs.

The population of the Doric states tended to be composed of three phylae —Pamphylians, Dymaneans, and Hyllosians. Pamphylus and Dyman were sons of King Aegimius and grandsons of Dorus, while Hyllus was the son of Heracles, who once helped Aegimius in combat against the Lapithae. This third branch must somehow have been the favored one, for it provided the leaders, the Heraclidae, under whom the Dorians set out on their renowned migrations and laid the foundation of states.

In Attica, and likely also in other Ionic states, there were four phylae: Geleontes, Argadeis, Aegicoreis, and Hopletes, heroes who were ostensibly the sons of Ion. Antiquity supposed that these names stood for various modes of life—roughly, landowners, tradesmen, shepherds, and a knightly nobility. Not until subsequent historical times did each of the phylae comprise eupatrids and ordinary citizens of every sort. The phylae became elective bodies and, after Solon's constitution, each one contributed one hundred members to the council. It can not be determined whether the phylae in their early stages lived each in a separate place or not. Later, to be sure, they all lived together; it sufficed to know to which phyle one belonged. The names of the Athenians who fell at Marathon were recorded on the gravestones set on the large burial mound, according to phylae and, indeed, according to the new ones with which Cleisthenes replaced the old ones.

Are we to say that originally the Dorians were divided into three phylae and the Ionians into four? Or rather that the Dorians took their rise from the combining of three phylae, the Athenians from the combining of four? A fiery smelting process inconceivable to us gives rise to a race of people, whose individual states quite consistently reflect their common origins.

Originally, phylae were based on descent rather than occupation, as suggested by the examples adduced, for later phylae were artificially created in new settlements. When misfortune befell Cyrene, Demonax was called from Arcadia to restore order; he created three phylae out of the main components of the population: the first of emigrants from Thera and their neighbors, the second of men from the Peloponnese and Crete, and the third of men from the islands.

In its three original *tribus* Rome perhaps possessed a far older arrangement than it realized, namely, proto-Greeks and Italians living together, as may well be supposed they did in that area. It is commonly agreed that, although tradition makes Ramnes, Tatian, and Luceres centuries [subdivisions of tribus] instituted by Romulus, they were originally names of tribus. In Rome, indeed, there flourished a counter legend, according to which three population groups came together in the city only many years after it had been founded—Latins, Sabines, and some Etruscans. Dionysius of Halicarnassus, born a Greek, was the only one to detect that all three tribus were native there and that those who came later, Sabines and whoever else, were subsequently incorporated among the tribus already existing.

Cleisthenes may have divided the four phylae of Attica into ten in order to equalize matters. The four old phylae which Solon used as a basis may well have become lopsided in power during the agitated century between Solon and Cleisthenes. Such arrangements are veritable Janus heads; one face turned toward ancient processes and foundations from which the whole complex descended, the other turned toward the basis of representative government in states and hence often altered and deliberately reshaped.

Before the Greeks, the Phoenicians had already founded *poleis,* i.e., city communities, city states, with bodies of laws. The power of the kings was limited by a council whose membership apparently was made up of the chiefs of privileged families. These city states were able to settle colonies that copied the organization of their mother cities. These *poleis* differed from the ancient royal strongholds of the Orient, which in each nation represented the central point of the whole; they differed from the gigantic army encampment of the Assyrian dynasties on the Tigris, differed from Babylon founded as a common stronghold for property and the gods, differed from the three alternating residences of the Achaemenids, differed from the great mercantile centers associated with oriental trade, and from the temple cities of Egypt: essentially, they were civil strongholds.

Would the honor of the Greeks suffer if one assumed that the Phoenician *poleis* influenced them? In many other respects the early impact of Phoenician culture on Greek life is recognized; we may assume that Thebes was originally a Phoenician city on what later became Boeotian territory. At all events, the Greeks must have had early knowledge of the cities along the Phoenician coast and of the colonies they planted.

For a long time they lived in the form of a multitude of smaller and larger tribes under chieftains called kings. Single tribes or their royal members must have taken over or built cities and citadels here and there. Thucydides supposed that the ancient cities, both on the islands and on the mainland, were built at some distance from the sea because of piracy. For only later, with the rise of Greek shipping, there were built strongly walled cities on the coasts and on the headlands, for commerce and defense against neighboring powers. Mycene and Tiryns are much older than any polis.

But, in that ancient period, people making up a tribe lived mostly in hamlets. It is not known whether these settlements were politically organized and how they were officially represented in the tribal government, nor to what extent common shrines and customs and mutual self-defense tended to unite neighboring settlements. If the people had access to strongholds in their communities or territories, they must have used them as common citadels, as refuges against pirates from land and sea. The ancient Sikanians in Sicily lived exclusively in fortified places on elevations, because of pirates. Still, it is said *they lived in hamlets*, although the term poleis is already in the offing for these settlements.

The ancient Greek tribes must have somehow been possessed of stronger impulses than the other Indo-Europeans. Their subsequent vitality and energy was, as it were, prefigured in the migrations, settlements, and intermingling of the old individual groups, which must often have been on the move for long periods. Accounts of these events are quite numerous but so tangled and confused that they only occasionally serve for a precise historical reconstruction. Every little clan has its own migration legends, whereas among the Germanic tribes only broad outlines were known. The Greeks are keenly aware of their origins and their settlements, even though they express this awareness in myths. They personify their past by means of tribal heroes who flee and later achieve new dominion; they weave these legends into the general body of myths. The legends, graves, and cults centered about these heroes are an earnest of the strong vitality later expressed in the poleis. Bards recited heroic lays; in addition, a more general body of poetry, at once genealogical and ethnographical, might arise, like that of the *E(h)oiae,* Homer's catalogue of ships, and similar epic material. These migration legends set no limits on the exploits the tribes perform, and children and children's children recount these exploits with defiant exultation.

The polis is the definitive form of the Greek state, a small independent state comprising a central city and surrounding territory; it tolerated no competing stronghold and no independent citizenry. The Greeks never thought of the polis as having developed gradually, but only as the product of a single creative act. Greek fantasy teems with notions of cities being founded full-fledged and, as whim had no part in shaping these cities, so the life in them is wholly under the aegis of necessity.

The Greeks had, above all, a city-state outlook. When the Achaeans, driven out of the southern Peloponnesus, settled in their new locality in Achaea on the bay of Corinth, they could certainly have established a unified state; indeed federation was at hand, but they had no penchant for it. Instead, they established twelve poleis where the Ionians had hitherto lived in hamlets scattered over twelve little districts, and actually their communal activities rarely went beyond periodic sacrifices and festivals, as those in the sacred grove of Zeus at Hamarion not far from Aegae. And the Ionians, who had fled from the Achaeans, went under Athenian leadership to the west coast of Asia Minor. There, they naturally founded a series of twelve poleis.

To maintain rule over larger territories and not expose individual settlements to perpetual struggle against invasion, either a Spartan militarism or an exceptionally favorable location was necessary, like that of the people of Attica. Attempts to federate into larger groups succeeded only temporarily, in wartime; they were never lucky or powerful enough to achieve permanence. In the long run the hegemonies of Sparta and Athens aroused terrible hostilities, and whoever has learned to know the polis will know how uninclined it was to treat fairly its weaker allies, however expedient it might have been to do so. The clue to the whole unhappy history of Boeotia lies in the perpetually repeated attempts to embrace that territory in a federal union.

In creating the polis, the vital elan takes the form of the so-called *synoikismos,* the joining together of hitherto separate settlements in a fortified city—on the sea wherever possible. The motives of commerce, material prosperity, and the like would only have created a *polisma,* a *ptoliethron;* but the polis is something more than that.

Without question, the Dorian migration was largely the external motive force that gave rise to the polis. Both, those who migrated and those who were able to ward off the invaders, were ripe for an organization that promised increased permanent power in defense as well as attack, constituting the real purpose of their existence.

When people lived in hamlets, say seven or eight to a district, they were exposed to tribal hardships, but their way of life was more innocent than later. They had to defend themselves against pirates and land robbers, but still they carried on as peasants. Now, polis began to compete with polis for existence and political power. And without doubt more land was cultivated originally, for when people concentrated in a city they began to neglect the outlying acres within their bounds. *Synoikism* may well have been the beginning of the laying waste of Greece.

Political thought of a later age has depicted the *synoikism* of the people of Attica as having been brought about in mystical times by Theseus. He first dissolved the *prytanies* (presidencies) and archonships in the twelve settlements into which Cecrops had gathered the people of Attica for the sake of safety, and then permitted only one *buleterion* (council hall) and one *prytany* in Athens. The people might live in the country on their holdings, but henceforth they had only one polis which Theseus was able to hand down to descendants as great and powerful, since everybody paid tribute into a common treasury. This was the ideal desired everywhere, and the whole of Greek life pressed toward this, its final form—the polis—without which the higher Greek culture is inconceivable.

To be removed from his ancestral graves must have spelled a misfortune for the Greek. For then he either had to neglect his ancestral rites or perform them only with difficulty; at any rate he no longer had the ancestral burial site daily before his eyes. Being forcibly removed to a new place of residence was an act that caused more sorrow and grief than any other, even in the entire later history of the polis.

Accounts of the founding of cities are numerous. In the Peloponnesus, Mantinea, already mentioned in Homer, became a polis through the uniting of five communities. Only after the Persian Wars was Elis made into a city out of several communities. During the Peloponnesian War, the Mytileneans wanted to transplant all the inhabitants of Lesbos into their own city; whereupon the people of Methymna appealed to Athens and so prevented the whole venture. In 408 B.C. Lindus, Ialysus, and Cameirus voluntarily united to establish the magnificent city of Rhodes destined for a truly splendid future; it is not difficult to imagine, however, with what feelings the people abandoned their age-old cities.

During the Peloponnesian War, Perdikkas II of Macedonia persuaded the inhabitants of the peninsula of Chalcidice to forsake their coastal towns and settle in Olynthus, a migration that likewise entailed withdrawal from Athenian hegemony. The state of Argos was especially notorious for having carried out *synoikism* by use of force, even though it was done for the sake of strengthening its position against Sparta. In the face of an enemy like Sparta, Epaminondas himself knew of no better stratagem except to persuade a goodly number of weak little Arcadian settlements to move together into a large center, Megalopolis. The inhabitants of Trapezus, refusing to join in the colonization of Megalopolis, were attacked, and they fled to the city of Trapezus on the Euxine. After the battle at Mantinea, many wished to leave the *Megalopolis* but were forced to return and remain in the large city by the rest of the Megalopolitans with Athenian help. Part of the abandoned settlements later lay fully deserted while some of them became villages occupied by Megalopolitans who cultivated the adjacent land.

Why were smaller places not left to carry on as country towns represented by elected officials in the council of the polis? Simply because in the long run they would not have been content to remain towns but would have exerted all the power they possibly could to remain independent and so become poleis themselves.

Perhaps only the entirely new city of Messene was founded with great cooperative enthusiasm. Here Epaminondas did not have to coerce surrounding communities; he merely had to appeal to descendants of Messene (who had scattered throughout the Greek world but had recently returned) in order to get them to build a new capital. Those who had been without a country for several generations and even for centuries, now had a homeland. On the other hand, very many poleis were founded by high-handed tyrants and overlords. The Sicilian tyrants, even the best of them, ruthlessly mingled peoples in poleis already established. They supposed that they could be sure of the loyalty of poleis only when they had removed half or more of their populations and brought in outsiders, even mercenaries, as replacements.

Gelo, meritorious in other respects, razed Camarina and brought its inhabitants, along with over half the population of Gela, the people of Megara Hyblaea, and of other Sicilian cities, to Syracuse, where he gave the upper classes citizenship but sold many of the commoners into slavery abroad, for he distrusted the masses. He appointed his brother Hiero tyrant of Gela. Hiero transferred the inhabitants of Catana to Leontini and peopled the empty walls of Catana with five thousand Syracusans and as many Peloponnesians. He wanted ready troops to defend the strategic city and also looked forward to being honored some day as the heroic founder of an eminent polis. Later Dionysii and Agathocles caused some of the most frightful exterminations and new racial mingling in Sicily.

A tyrant like Mausolus forcibly gathered the inhabitants of six cities into his Halicarnassus. This amounted to three-fourths of the eight cities of the Leleges, and we are not told to what extent the people might have regarded the transference as a benefaction. In the history of the diadochi, the newly founded cities in the Orient and in Egypt above all claim attention; and not to be overlooked are the violent deportations, the racial commingling, and the renaming of famous old cities these diadochi carried out in the ancient Hellenized territory of western Asia Minor.

The establishment of a polis was the great, the decisive experience in the whole existence of a tribe. Even in cases where people continued to cultivate the fields, in time their rural way of life became predominantly urban nevertheless. And men who had been farmers became politically minded when living together. But the significance of the experience was reflected in legends about the founding of the city and its delivery from great dangers in the past. When Heracles was driving his cattle through Italy, he met Croton, who wanted to help him. But Heracles in the dark of night mistook him for an enemy and killed him; later he recognized his mistake and honored him greatly by building a city named Crotona around his grave site.

Where there was no monument honoring the past, veneration went to some shrine such as a spring. At Haliartus in Boeotia the stream Lophis took its rise from the blood of a boy cut to pieces by his father at the behest of the Pythian priestess, who during an unrelieved drouth commanded him to kill the first living being he met. At Celaenae in Phrygia, a chasm opened which swallowed many houses and people. Pursuant to an oracle that the most precious offering should be hurled into the chasm, gold and silver were tried but did not help; then the heir to the Phrygian throne mounted his horse and spurred it into the chasm, whereupon it closed. At times, the acquisition and deposition of relics, such as bones of a person long dead would suffice for the founding of a city. For instance, when the Athenians under Hagnon definitely founded Amphipolis, he secretly sent some people to the country of Troy to fetch the remains of Rhesus from his burial mound. Possibly, also, human sacrifice was later replaced by a more innocuous rite, the *telesm,* consisting of the burial of secret objects.

The real center of a polis was the agora, the public square. The little ancient towns consisted only of an agora, on which were situated the *prytaneum,* the council chamber, the courthouse, and one or more temples. The agora also served for sports and popular assemblies. But even when facilities for one or more of these functions were richly provided for elsewhere, the agora still remained the heart of the city. "Market place" is a very inadequate translation, for wherever people built towns they included market places. But agora is the noun form of the verb *agorein,* to assemble; very often it also signifies an assemblage, regardless of the place.

On this Aristotle helpfully provides us a very clear distinction. He demands an agora for the free men, where nothing may be bought and where no farmer or laborer may enter except on command of the authorities, and another agora for the purpose of buying and selling. In coastal towns people tended to locate the public square near the harbor; at least that is what the Phaeacians did whose whole life was arranged with a view to comfort. Here, in the presence of ships, surrounded by temples, offices, monuments, shops and exchanges as thick as they could stand, the Greek was exposed to *agorazein,* an activity not to be translated by one word of any other language. Dictionaries give *to traffic in the market place, to buy, to talk, to deliberate,* etc., but cannot reproduce the combination of business and conversation mingled with delightful loafing and standing around together. It is enough to say that forenoon got the well-known designation —the time when the agora is full of people.

When a crowd of idlers arose in a city, it routinely developed as the public square crowd. In the sixth century B.C., Cyrus the Great is already said to have told the Spartan envoys: "I have never yet been afraid of men who have a special meeting place in the center of their city where they gather and cheat one another on oath."

If any man has ever been greater than his place of residence, surely that man was the Greek. The living polis with its pride of citizenship was a much grander product than all its walls, harbors, and magnificent structures. Aristotle classified man as being by nature a political creature. In an eloquent passage of his *Politics,* he contrasts the Greeks with two kinds of barbarians—the natural man of the north and the man of culture in Asia—

Ariadne as wine server
Silver coin from Histiaea on Euboa

and accords them the advantages of both: the courage of the one and the intelligence of the other, so that they are not only free and in possession of the finest polity, but also able to rule over all others as soon as they establish a state.

Monuments of a not unpleasing kind decorated agoras; in the agora of Thuriae, the eminent man Herodotus was buried. Indeed, in later times a forest of altars and statues of famous men almost cramped the public square of Greek cities. A monument to the grisly recollection of a human sacrifice was nearly always present. Among people other than Hellenes, a similar saga may now and then echo about the walls of a stronghold. The touching song the Serbians sing about the founding of Skadar may well reflect Greek influence.

A characteristic narrative branch of poetry and prose was devoted to the history or to the myth of the founding of cities. Illustrious names like Mimnermus of Smyrna, Cadmus of Miletus, Xenophanes of Colophon are numbered among those who recounted such native legends. In addition, Xenophanes deserves our gratitude for recording the bold wanderings of the Phocaean fugitives until their founding of Elea. These early stories laid the foundation of later Greek historiography.

Rights of man were not recognized in antiquity, not even by Aristotle. He regarded the polis as a community of free men; *metics* (residents of foreign birth) and especially the masses of slaves enjoyed no political rights; whether, beyond that fact, *metics* and slaves were human beings was not spelled out. Indeed, as time will show, the duties imposed on citizens were not commonplace, and not just anybody would do.

Here it was above all a matter of quality; accordingly limits were imposed on the quantity. Infants born crippled and ill formed were not, according to Aristotle, to be brought up; and his view becomes intelligible when one reflects on the wretched lot a cripple had among the Greeks. But, as we know, many infants were abandoned because their parents could not or would not care for them, and Thebes, which forbade this practice, was cited as an exception.

The mode of life a polis was obliged to maintain was characterized by the word *autarkeia*, self-sufficiency; a very obscure word to us, it was fully comprehensible to the Greeks. This self-sufficiency required arable land to grow the necessary foodstuff, trade and industry to provide modestly for the remaining necessities, and an army of *hoplites* comparable in strength to that of the neighboring, usually hostile, polis.

Aristotle speaks on this subject as plainly as we could wish. As soon as a polis became overpopulated, it could not maintain itself. The greatness of a city was dependent on the number of its citizens. It could not be upheld by its horde of workers (*banausics*) if there was a paucity of hoplites. To administer justice and to perform their official duties with merit, citizens had to know each other and the character of the people.

As to optimum size, a city should be large enough to provide for the necessities of life yet small enough to be within eyeshot. And it appears that ten thousand was regarded as the proper number of mature citizens for a city to have. Heraclea and Trachinia and Catana (renamed Aetna after a new colony was established there)—all had this number; by way of illustration, we may also mention the popular assembly of ten thousand in Arcadia.

In recent times, apart from philosophical and social thought, it is essentially the individual who demands a state advantageous for his own purposes. For the most part, all that he demands really is security, so that he may freely develop his potentialities. To this end he gladly makes well-defined sacrifices, though the less the state bothers him otherwise, the more content he is. The Greek polis, on the other hand, starts with the whole, which precedes its parts. From an inner logic we may add this: It is not only a matter of giving preference to the general over the particular but also of preferring the permanent over the momentary and transitory. The polis demanded that the individual not only take part in campaigns, but be ready to sacrifice his individual existence for it is to the whole that he owes everything, including the security of his very existence, then enjoyed by a citizen only within his own city's limits, or at most within the range of its influence.

Whoever governs or is governed here is the citizen of the polis. To govern means, more precisely, to serve on the tribunal or to hold an office. As a rule, the citizen realizes all his capacities and virtues within the state or in its service. The entire Greek spirit and its culture are most intimately related to the polis, and of the poetry and art created during the flowering of Greek genius the loftiest by far was not created for the enjoyment of individuals but for the public, i.e., the community.

The magnificently moving knowledge of these views comes to us in part from the greatest Greek poets and in part from the philosophers and orators of the fourth century, who no longer were able to capture prevailing sentiments and rather dwelt on those that should have obtained.

The native city is not only home, where one is happiest and whither one is drawn, but also a mighty being, lofty and divine. Above all, one owes it one's life in battle, thereby merely repaying the polis for one's keep. Now and then Homer grants the Trojans, and especially Hector, the most ecstatic patriotic sentiments, and the elegiac poets, in the few works that have survived, dwell often enough on patriotic subjects. But Aeschylus is the most powerful witness. In his *Seven Against Thebes* the speeches of Eteocles combine the belief in the citizen's highest duty to sacrifice himself for the homeland with the noble emotional tone befitting the king and defender. In his own epitaph, Aeschylus mentions only his courage, saying nothing about his poetry.

> Of his prowess the grove of Marathon can tell
> And the long-haired Persian who learned to know it well.

But in the end it is the polis, not the individual, who gets credit for the mighty deeds of valor, and this polis was the victor at Marathon and Salamis, not Miltiades and Themistocles. And, to Demosthenes it was a symptom of decline when people said that Timotheus had captured Corcyra and that Chabrias had defeated the enemy in the naval battle at Naxos. At all events, the most deserving hero owes more gratitude to his country than his country owes him.

In the *Suppliants*, the splendid choral ode of the Danaids overflows with blessings gratefully bestowed on hospitable Argos. But Aeschylus reserved his finest tribute for his native Athens in the last great choral ode of the *Eumenides*. In the dialogue with Athena the goddess assuages the wrath of the Furies by recounting the honors they would receive if they dwelt in Attica. Only one writer in antiquity was able to produce mightier notes of this kind. Aeschylus wishes and prays; Isaiah, in his vision of the future Jerusalem, prophesies and envisions his prophecy as fulfilled.

Furthermore, the polis exerts an educative force. It is not only the best of nurses, the watch and ward of the boy playing on the soft ground, sparing no pains to care for him, but it also trains the citizen throughout his whole life. It sponsors no schools, although it fosters the conventional instruction in music and gymnastics. One cannot neatly categorize the many-sided cultural influences affecting the whole citizenry: choral songs at festivals, the sumptuous rites of worship, the architecture and works of art, the drama and recitations by rhapsodists.

The participation in state government, either as an administrator or a concerned subject, made living in a polis a continuous educational process.

During its more prosperous periods, the city-state exercised powerful social controls by conferring honors on the individual until abuse of this practice induced the more intelligent to forgo the laurel wreaths, acclamations by heralds, and other honors. In time the whole preceding history of a praiseworthy city came to be one of the strongest inducements to excellence. "Nowhere," Xenophon said, "are the deeds of forebears grander and more numerous than in Athens" thereby inspiring many people to emulate these virtues.

Thus the polis represents an image for the highest heroism and dedication under a collective will, forging its way out of rural beginnings by means of action, suffering, and passion; hence the polis must rigorously define the requisites and obligations of its active citizens who have to be a part of this power.

Such poleis embrace a kind of happiness and unhappiness totally different from that of cities of other times and nations. Only the most impetuous city republics of the Middle Ages ever attained this level of living and suffering, and even then for short periods only.

This also explains the essentially violent nature of the polis. In spite of all its leagues and compacts, the polis, as a rule, is externally isolated. Often it is joined in life-and-death contests with its nearest neighbor, and so is exposed to the terrible arbitrament of fortune on the battlefield.

Within its own realm the polis is most fear-inspiring for the individual if he is not willing to lose himself completely in it. The modes of coercion it freely resorts to are death, dishonor, and exile. There is no appeal beyond the polis, and no escape, for the fugitive abandons all personal protection.

Supreme power, lodged in the state, curtails individual freedom in every respect. Worship of deities, feast days, and myths take their origin from the polis; the state is likewise a church invested with the legal right to prosecute for impiety, and this combined power completely overshadows the individual.

He owes the polis military service; in Rome till he is forty-six, in Athens and Sparta for life. The polis has complete power over him and his property; it can even set a price on certain goods. In short, the individual has no security of life or property over against the polis and its interests. And this servitude to the state exists under all constitutions, but most oppressively in democracies, where under the guise of working for the state and its interests villainous demagogues could interpret in their own way the principle "the state's interest is the supreme law."

In addition to being a religion in itself, the polis encompassed the other forms of religious practices; and the fact that the community as a whole took part in sacrifices and festivals made for a strong sense of unity among the citizens quite apart from the laws, the constitution, and public dealings of the citizens with each other.

When the polis began its decline, it was no longer satisfied with the worship of deities, even in the special sense of heroes and guardians of cities, and it deified itself as *Tyche* [Fortune] with the high crown. A sentence of Pindar throws remarkably clear light on this transition.

> O Tyche, savior goddess, daughter of Zeus the deliverer, I beseech you to hover about mighty Chimera! You direct the fleet ships by sea, the darting battles by land, and the gatherings where men take counsel.

The *Tycheum* was perhaps not the largest, but often it was one of the most elegant temples of a city.

In time, however, the goddess *Tyche* no longer sufficed, for when victorious in battle, most cities could not refrain from humiliating the conquered, or from idealizing themselves as *Demos*. And this at times was done in such a monstrous form as the placing of a statue in the agora at Sparta, which can have come only out of the most wretched period of that state. And since *Demos* was customarily represented in a shape proper to the so-called "good daimons," he became in time the subject of an active worship.

As an ideal whole, the polis appears in another sense and in another form, namely, as a *nomos*, which comprises in one term both the laws and the constitution of a state. The loftiest expressions are used to praise the law and the constitution as the invention and gift of the gods, as the soul of the city, and as the guardian and keeper of every civic virtue. The laws are the *rulers of cities,* and Demaratus the Spartiate tried to make Xerxes understand that his countrymen have a ruler, this ruler being the law, of which they stand in fear more crushing than the Persians in fear of their great king. Hence, the lawgiver stands out as a superhuman being, and the glory of a Lycurgus, a Solon, a Zaleukus, or a Charondas was reflected upon persons living considerably later. For instance, around the year 400 B.C., Diocles of Syracuse codified the laws, and after his death was accorded the fame of a hero and honored with a temple.

Above all, the *nomos* (law) was not meant to serve the temporary interests and moods of the individuals, or submit to the casual whims of the majority. The retention of the old laws was praised at least in theory; one recognized in the customs and usages dating back perhaps to the founding of the city the basic strength, of which the laws were only the expression. In some states, the boys had to learn the laws by heart according to some melody or cadence, not simply as a learning device but rather to preserve the laws unchanged. *Nomos* has the twofold meaning of law and melody.

On the other hand, ancient records tell us that, having drawn up a code of laws for the Athenians, Solon bound them by a solemn oath not to repeal any of them during the ten following years while he was away on his travels. But soon thereafter they experienced a grave political crisis and in the end changed his constitution, making it fully democratic. Many other Greek poleis had similar experiences and, despite their initial code of laws, most colonies suffered turmoil and had a stormy history. The full-fledged democracies were perpetually subject to the craving for revision. According to Aristotle, law was no longer sovereign in a democracy, rather it was the crowd.

The Greek conception of the state completely subordinated the individual to the general polity but, as will be seen, it also developed the tendency of pushing him onward very forcefully. In conformity with this idealized conception, the prodigious powers of the individual should have realized themselves fully in the community and become its most vivid expression. But in deed and in truth, Greek freedom was modified by the ubiquity of the state. Not even in religion could the individual find refuge from the state. Moreover, he could not be sure that the gods were good and merciful. Individuals and parties ruled over religion in the name of the polis.

Whoever in antiquity considered himself entitled to sovereignty, or only aspired to it, hesitated at nothing in respect to his competitors and opponents, not even at annihilation. In these poleis, all political punishment, whatever the guilt of the vanquished, took the form of vengeance and obligatory execution. This will become clear when we see that the punishment of the ostracized and executed was extended to their children and, in a way, to their forebears, whose graves were desecrated. The Hellenes recognized clearly two alternatives: either we destroy them, or they will destroy us; and they acted inexorably on this principle.

That those who killed tyrants were signally honored, provided they escaped with their lives, and often even after death were honored with public monuments and worshiped as heroes, is so well known as to leave no room for doubt. The result was that some obscure murderer, subsequently found to have been a scoundrel and a traitor, like Phrynichus in Athens (411 B.C.), would receive citizenship as a public benefactor, be publicly crowned with a wreath at the Greater Dionysia and other festivities. The slayers were acclaimed, whatever their motives or personal worth.

Since the polis was the real and the loftiest religion of the Hellenes, wars fought for the polis took on all the horrors of religious wars. Every break with the polis disrupted the life of the individual. Consequently, people bemoaned a civil war as the worst, the most frightful, and most godless of all wars, thoroughly hated of gods and men. Unhappily, this knowledge never brought about peace. No one at that time could openly say that the fictitious goal (of unbounded citizenship) overtaxed the powers of human nature in the long run, but it was obvious that men of ability secretly lost heart and increasingly shunned public office. A system of philosophical ethics arose which severed its ties with the polis and took on a universal human scope. Epicurus and his school stripped the polis of its feverish deification, reducing it to a compact for mutual security. The desire of the polis to survive at any cost was to prove itself in times of terrible suffering. The guilty individual, Isocrates says, *may die before retribution overtakes him, but the poleis, endowed with deathlessness, must endure the vengeance of men and gods alike.*

Chapter Two

THE POLIS IN ITS
HISTORICAL DEVELOPMENT

1. Kingship

No doubt the oldest heroes were kings. They engaged in their contests and adventures alone, without any followers to support them; as a rule, they would have found troops superfluous in the kind of battles they fought. Finally, there dawn those kingdoms the rulers of which the earlier and later Greeks could envisage with clarity. Athens of Theseus, Thebes of the Labdakides, and Argos-Lacedaemon of the Atrides. The royal dynasties are in part foreigners; the myth cycles reveal that foreigners, sometimes even fugitives, with great ease became kings, as for instance the Heraclidan kings of the Dorians, who with their ancestor Heracles, were Achaeans. But the history of Greece is not unique in recounting such occurrences. It was generally assumed that in primeval times sovereignty was exclusively in the hands of kings. That was the only kind of rule conceivable among the tribes as long as they were moving about and migrating. But even when a tribe settled down, the royal sway might well have continued for quite a while.

Sovereignty, as shown by Homer, was woven together of peculiar strands: out of genuine primeval memories, lofty epics, and some traditional features, of royal rule deriving from the post-Dorian age of Homer but in his day falling into desuetude already. The typical old, resplendent personal attributes of the epic kings were thoroughly clear and familiar to the Greeks. These kings stemmed from Zeus and were invested by him with the scepter and the privilege of command, judging, and sacrificing at the head of the tribe. Now surrounded by a festive court and a council of the eldest, then accompanied by charioteers, heralds and rhapsodists, they are unforgettable personages.

18

Having matured in their political development, the Greeks, to be sure, came to be a little more critical with regard to the existence of those heroic personages. Thucydides tried to ascertain the taxes and income to which these lords were entitled. Aristotle ventured to reconstruct precisely the origins of these kingdoms, but, in doing so, betrayed his inability to conceive of a state as arising except as a result of reflection and volition of a group, that is, by a definite founding. He supposed that those men were elevated to kingship who benefited the people in war, united them into a state, enlarged the territory of the state, or otherwise promoted the means of their livelihood; or such men as were elevated to kingship by a powerful minority or aristocratic caste to protect them against the demos. Men invested with such kingship had power of life and death over individuals on campaigns only and, in contrast to tyrants, who ruled over unwilling subjects, they held office for as long as their constituents were content.

In Greek mythology, heroes acquire dominion by doing away with horrid individuals and monsters. In Minos, however, in addition to the king of Crete and other islands, there is the Minotaur demanding his toll of human flesh. Perhaps there is also an Asiatic moon god, to say nothing of the judge in the underworld, the conqueror extending his exploits to Sicily, and the jealous master of Daedalus. It is quite possible that for a time unity obtained among islands of the sea, while sheer plurality marked the mainland. The dominant position of Crete in the whole Aegean Sea, and also its size and population perhaps fitted Crete to bring about this unity.

The Heraclidae symbolized the formation of new migrant kingships, originating out of leadership in war among the wandering Dorians. In the next few centuries, occasionally even in decades, these kingships were reduced to only a few, while the long extant aristocracy took over the reins of power, forming the earliest stage of the real polis. It would be wasted effort to try to ascertain precisely the course of events in Greece; still, we get a few clues from Homer who witnessed ancient heroic as well as post-Dorian kingdoms dissolve. The Achaean army encamped before Ilion had the appearance of a somewhat stormy democratic agora. This agora was just as *man-ennobling* as the battles were; i.e., the individual had found a stage where he could assert himself. Later, when the confused turmoil occurs at the ships Odysseus threatens the rabble-rousers with his scepter and cries out to them his famous words about the worthlessness of the rule of the many, until order is restored in the assembly. Thersites gets up and rants, truly presaging Greek demagoguery to come. Kings desiring to make an impression get along best by using meekness and tact. The just ruler so brilliantly portrayed by Hesiod had achieved his ends with gentle words; for this purpose his eloquence, the gift of the Muses, serves him especially well.

Finally the dynasties declined and fell outright. Disunity in the family, incompetence and arrogance of the royal sons, if there were any, generally provided the occasion. Priam said of his own sons, after the best of them had perished:

> These the war has swallowed; the scapegraces only are left me,
> Liars are they all and cadgers and delicate dancers,
> Robbing the people they revel in the fat of the lambs and the
>   kids.

There is something atavistic and legendary about a people killing their king to placate the wrath of the gods. Even if they had wanted to spare the rest of the dynasty, doing so would have gone against the grain of a well-known proverb: *A fool is he who kills the father, leaving the son alive.* The Arcadians ceased to have kings after stoning two, both named Aristocrates —the grandfather for the rape of a priestess of Diana, the grandson for treason causing the defeat of his Messenian allies. However, no one lightly decided to kill a king, for as Homer's Amphinomous, the most thoroughly decent of all the suitors, says, "It is dreadful to slay a royal race" (*Odyssey* XVI, 401).

The kingship sometimes ceased because of some other atrocious deed. The Messenians had no more kings after Aristodemus committed suicide; only a general [*strategos*], with unlimited power in wartime. On the other hand, the ancient Athenians exploited the sacrificial death of Codrus to make it appear unseemly for another to succeed so worthy a king. The *eupatrids* degraded his son Medon to a mere lifetime *archon*, while his other sons and bastards led settlers to Ionia. Aristotle sums up the course of events as follows: The kings had become despicable and guilty of hybris, committing some outrage possible only for a tyrant but not for a king with his powers limited. Thereupon dissolution readily followed, for when men no longer want them, kings simply cease to exist; but the tyrant rules over unwilling subjects. In addition, mutiny may well help to topple royal rule.

New officials took over the several functions hitherto in the hands of the king. In Athens and elsewhere, the person in charge of the solemn state sacrifices retained the title *basileus* (king). Now and then the chief judge was also called a *basileus*.

In his *Panathenaikos,* Isocrates (p. 258 ff.) supposes that under their ancient kings, unencumbered by the abominable deeds of other dynasties, the Athenians attained to the virtues of justice and sobriety and that, consequently the republic, the introduction of which he ascribes to Theseus, could assume its most pre-eminent forms. At the time when kingships were being abolished, a new royal dynasty was founded: the Temenids in Macedonia, of which Herodotus gave such a poetic account. At that time, no one had any premonition of the events Greece would have to endure under the descendants of this new dynasty.

The rule of the aristocrats which succeeded the kingships was relatively weak, proving to be merely a transitional stage. Its prospects were best in areas where a migrating Dorian tribe of close-knit solidarity was able to subdue an alien people and, as a peer group, maintain hegemony over them. The most important state of this nature will now engage our attention.

2. *Sparta*

> Woe to you Spartans abhorred by all mortals,
> Lords of Lacedaemon, filled with false counsel,
> Masters of lies, contriving misfortune,
> Compliant, untruthful, and double-dealing,
> You ruffians, sully not with murder on murder;
> Your hearts, are they not set on shameful lucre,
> Your tongues on lying, your minds on betrayal?
> Perish, you.

Thus Andromache of Euripedes cries out her laments over Sparta, and Attic orators enlarge upon this theme. It was the ineluctable destiny of Sparta, curt of speech and careless of writing, that Athens, which pre-eminently wielded the pen in Hellenic matters, should establish the reputation of her mortal enemy. The first man to report circumstantially about Sparta, Herodotus of Halicarnassus, is accused of having become churlish toward Sparta because of his long stay in Athens. Thucydides on the other hand remained heroically, almost incomprehensibly, objective, and finally there were some Athenian converts who glorified Sparta. The earliest was Tyrtaeus, in the seventh century, and in the fifth and fourth there was Xenophon, the most zealous and influential of them all.

The greatness of this politico-social structure is twofold. To a certain extent, Sparta was the most perfect embodiment of the Greek polis, and, at the same time, it formed a counterpoise to all the rest of Greece, differing partly in origin and partly in development. Since, at the end of the fifth century, Sparta came out victorious in the great crisis involving all Greece, it continued to enjoy its victory for thirty relentless years. Spartan splendor dazzled people far and wide and survived subsequent misfortune. The lower the later Sparta sank, the more its earlier history was glorified. Sparta had been more envied even than loathed, and many another polis would have liked to become like Sparta save for other forces, mainly those of individualism and democracy, which proved insuperable.

Those Dorians who, during the great migration around 1100 B.C., pressed into the valley of the Eurotas, appear to have dealt moderately with the Achaeans whom they subjugated and with other racial remnants such as the Leleges, Minyas, etc., whom they found there. Subsequently, perhaps being at loggerheads among themselves and threatened by those whom they held in subjection, they introduced radical changes in the ninth century, providing an exceedingly strong organization for themselves and permanent slavery for the Achaeans. This change is personified in Lycurgus to whom, as in Athens to Theseus, a whole chain of developments is ascribed, though many of them palpably belong to later periods. This did not bother the ancient minds in the least. For them Lycurgus is Sparta with all its arrangements and modes of life. For four hundred years he is claimed to be actively present at the most varied occasions. The question has often been raised whether he was not a divine rather than a human being. Reports are not wanting in later periods that he visited Egypt, Libya, and went as far as India, pursuing his comparative studies, though Crete is supposed to have served him as a model. (Herodotus I, 65).

The rise of Sparta was especially hard on the peoples it subjugated. For them the only choices were enslavement, expulsion, or extermination. The Achaeans remained in some of their cities, doubtless unfortified, while the Dorians took over others completely. As for the rest, the cities Homer still knew as flourishing, the reader may take Pausanias as a guide and wander about their ruins. He will find that here a cult of Kore [Persephone] still survived and nearby an *Eleusinion* (temple of the Eleusinian Demeter), and that there lay the ruins of an Achaean city, perhaps called Cyparissa. The rise of a new power has never been a mild process, and Sparta became such a power to all around it. It was able to force the whole civilized world to acknowledge it until the twilight of its day, so great is the spell of a powerful will on later millennia, even when sympathy is lacking.

It seems that the decisive event can only be conceived as having come about abruptly and suddenly. The Dorians were strong enough to bring about a new distribution of land, one of those *anadasmoi,* taking place everywhere, and to keep the largest and best part for themselves, including nine thousand lots entailing all rights and duties and remaining inalienable in toto. The subjugated people, composed entirely of fellow Hellenes, fell into two classes: the *perioeci,* who got their own land to till consisting of thirty thousand lots of actually poor land, and *helots,* who had to farm the land of the Dorians, seven families to each Dorian lot. It was no small task to hold this mass of people in continuous dependence during those centuries when tyrannies and democracies were taking root throughout all Greece. But the problem was solved, and the best proof of the unquestioned power of the

Dorians or Spartiates was the fact that when they waged war they took along great numbers of *perioeci* and helots, even as high as three times their own complement, who bore arms and transported provisions.

In the campaign at Plataea there were at least seven helots for every Spartiate. To be sure it would have been dangerous to leave them at home while their masters were away, and thus taking them along on military campaigns did not prove that the Spartiates trusted them. As workers and traders the *perioeci* were indispensable to Sparta. They were allowed to own chattel property in addition to their land. It is, however, only fair to mention that, in Athenian opinion, the *perioeci* in relation to their masters were virtually on a par with the helots, and that their souls were not less in bondage than those of slaves. Attempts also have been made to soften some of the harsh traits traditionally ascribed to the life of the helots. It may well be that on the lots (estates) of the Spartiates which they had to till, the helots were able to live rather full lives after having met their quota of produce. Weaklings would have been useless in war. Still, they remained slaves, though not by purchase but by birth. They could get married and have some family life, yet, to be bred to slavery was utter wretchedness in the eyes of the Greek. The Spartiates permitted no traffic in slaves, thereby enjoying great economic and moral advantages, but toward these erstwhile fellow Hellenes they maintained a hard and steady rigor unmitigated by any kindly feelings such as Greeks elsewhere at times were wont to show toward slaves bought from Scythia and Asia. The dishonorable state of the helot was driven home to him not by distinctive dress but by a regular yearly flogging, administered without reason, and by ridicule after he had been made drunk. If, however, a helot attempted to rise above his slavelike status, he was put to death and his master punished for not having kept the overweening fellow in his place. And if they became too numerous, the masters unleashed against them the so-called *crypteia*, which meant going out at night and killing off as many as necessary. At a critical juncture of the Peloponnesian War, two thousand of the ablest helots bent on freedom were singled out and done away with.

On this foundation, the Dorians erected their new existence, and did so with the continuing advice of the Delphian Apollo. For hundreds of years, the royal couriers traveled regularly between Sparta and Delphi. In the end one suspects they did so at Spartan rather than Delphian initiative, and that Delphi gave its oracles at Spartan entreaty. Neither party cared a fig what the fancy of the other Greeks might conjecture about this intercourse, and so disregarded it.

Every Greek polis attributed a high degree of sanctity to its constitution, the *nomos* as set down in words. But in Sparta even the various laws of

Lycurgus are called *rhetrai*, divine edicts, oracles (not compacts as had been interpreted). Tradition has preserved but a few of these because Lycurgus left no written constitution and, least of all, as Plutarch remarks, essays about politics and ideal republics, as Plato and Zeno did. He left, instead, a working state for which he is given full credit. This great man who re-established the state enjoyed not only hero worship, as did other founders and lawgivers of poleis, but also divine worship, complete with temple and sacrifices. Even so, as Aristotle testifies, the honors accorded him fell short of his merits (Plutarch, *Lycurgus* 31).

We shall not try to unravel how many of the old traditions were retained and how many innovations were introduced during the great decision of the ninth century. There persisted the Heraclidan *dyarchy* of two kings, derived from the period of the Dorian migration. This *dyarchy* was politically weak because of its duality—its separate ceremonies, funerals, annals, etc., and its prohibition against intermarriage, which might have otherwise become the rule, resulting in marriages among relatives and a consequent degeneration of the race. At the same time, the state maintained the principle of hereditary kingship, making it hard for the ambitious to strive for dominion. The dynastic families had a reputation for inborn military genius, acquired from the accumulated tales of all kinds of exploits ascribed to various Heraclidae.

In addition to the kings, there was a *gerousia,* a council of elders with twenty-eight members, perhaps once the dominant power in the state. Since the introduction of the five member cabinet of the *ephors,* however, it was in charge of daily affairs only. The manner of their selection is not clear. Aristotle thought it was childish and complained that one had to seek votes for the post. Other writers, seeing in Lycurgus a statesman who selected wisely from models and created original legislation, are enraptured at the way he arranged for the calming influence of the *gerousia* to steady the impetuous kingship, making it at the same time a barrier against the dangers of a developing democracy. Finally, there was the periodic popular assembly composed of all male Dorians thirty years and over. The assembly accepted or rejected by acclamation the proposals made by the kings or the *gerousia.* But if the members of the *gerousia* deemed the assembly's decision to be faulty they could reject it and dismiss the assembly.

The Dorians were above all an army perpetually ready for war, holding the Peloponnesus in subjugation or state of siege and threatening beyond its borders as far as they could. At the time of its political reform, Sparta presumably had nine thousand adult members, each of whom received one lot. According to a surviving record, it was at one time a polis of ten thousand, but they probably numbered a great deal more later, and the families may have felt crowded on the land that was their lot. Why did these overcrowded families not hurl themselves at some neighboring, less powerful, tribe of fellow Hellenes which was treating its subjugated natives humanely, thereby constituting a standing reproach and maybe even posing a threat to Sparta? After having subdued pockets of resistance in the valley of the Eurotas (Amyclae, etc.), the Dorians did make their great advance, and while other Hellenes were sending out colonies, Sparta took possession of Messenia.

When, at the outbreak of the first Messenian War, 743–742 B.C., someone asked King Polydorus whether he wanted to wage war on brothers, he said, "All we want is land not yet distributed, that is, not yet divided by lot for our people." Naturally, the Dorians did not lay waste either farms or buildings as the Greeks usually did, since they regarded the land as already their own. They distributed the land by lot among their own people and reduced such of the natives as were not killed, sold, or driven out, to serfs on their farms. The newly acquired lands must not have sufficed for the excess Spartiate population, for soon thereafter a large group of penniless young Dorians, the so-called Parthenians (Justin. III, 4), had to be sent out of the country and occupied Tarentum. Throughout this whole war, the oracle at Delphi sided with the conquerors.

An insurrection of the Messenians sparked the Second War (685 B.C.–?), when for the first time there is a decline in Spartan fertility, for the Spartiates are said to have complemented their diminished ranks by using helots not only as armor-bearers but also as line soldiers. They also had to resort to diplomacy. In the end Sparta won, all the Messenians unable to escape becoming helots, and Spartiates remaining in sole possession of Messenia. At home the Spartiates had to eke out their dwindling army and did so, significantly enough, not with *perioeci* but with helots. Later they enfranchised these, endowing them with full citizenship.

Thus straitened, the Spartans could not take over more land for themselves or their helots and had to be content with maintaining supremacy and hegemony over the masses already subjugated. Now began that period of Sparta remarkable for the resourcefulness in maintaining its status. This is the Sparta ancient authors spend so much time in describing—an organization compelled to assimilate serfs in order to defend itself against the enslaved, to ward off external dangers, and to impress fear and admiration on the rest of the Greeks. If at the time of the Persian Wars the Spartiates still numbered eight thousand, as Herodotus assumed maybe somewhat optimistically, they were scattered in the valley of the Eurotas and in Messenia; at any rate they decreased rapidly soon thereafter. It is almost certainly correct to interrelate the rise of the *ephors* with this state of events.

Already during the First Messenian War, as is well known, *ephors*

were appointed to act as deputies for the absent kings, especially in administering justice. But at the beginning of the sixth century a change of state organization must have taken place, extending the power of *ephors*. The five *ephors* were no longer appointed by the kings but chosen by the people at a yearly election. Their office was invested with a religious aura such as not even the kingship had, and they were allowed to observe the heavens

Tile painting

to enable them to bring charges against the kings when deemed necessary.

They did not rise in deference to the kings; in fact, the only honor the latter enjoyed above those of the other citizens was that they did not have to respond to a summons until issued the third time, whereas everybody else had to rush posthaste across the *agora* at the first beckoning of an *ephor*. Every month they swore mutual oaths, the kings that they would uphold the constitution, the *ephors* that in the name of the state they would be loyal to the *dyarchy*, which would of itself remain true to its oath.

At first glance, one is tempted to suppose that this change was introduced to keep a king from becoming a tyrant; it seems, however, to have resulted from the general course of events, because it was expressly specified how a derelict king could be tried by a Great Commission consisting of the *ephors,* the *gerousia,* and the other king or *dyarch.* Even though the *ephorate* was designed to curb the ambitions of gifted aspirants to become autocrats and of demoted individuals to start a revolution, it was one of those Damocles swords which a whole ruling caste suspends over its own head. Hence also the tremendous exertion toward equality in conveniences and ways of life as well as toward preventing accumulation of chattel property or its devaluation. How beggarly the *sycophancy* [professional informing] of the democracy shows up by comparison!

The *ephors* did not proceed according to laws and statutes but at their own discretion. They did not let a guilty official finish his term, as elsewhere in Greece, but could remove him from office at once, imprison him, and have him put to death. They could convene and preside at the popular assemblies and receive ambassadors. In war all essential controls passed into their hands. They arranged the campaigns, corresponded with the army leaders by means of the famous ciphers (*skytale*), and limited the authority of the kings nominally in command, by means of advisers assigned them. Later two *ephors* accompanied each king. The people, i.e., the high caste, were fully at ease amid all this because they elected the *ephors* every year, thereby having things well in hand.

The nearest historical parallel is probably the Council of Ten in Venice, likewise elected every year by the whole ruling class and also endowed with plenary powers. Whereas in Venice it was necessary to secure the state only from attempts at tyranny, from conspiracies by impoverished *nobili,* and from external dangers, Sparta, in time, had to face not only its impoverished Dorians but also the formidable internal threat of the *perioeci* and helots. Venice permitted the submissive ones to keep their property; Sparta deprived them of the larger and better part of it. Venice was loved by the subjects of its city and territory; Sparta was abominably hated. Fundamentally, Venice desired only enough power to assure its safety, but Sparta pursued an aggressive foreign policy, on principle, craving the dependence of the rest of the Greeks lest they disaffect the Dorian serfs.

The *ephorate* no doubt helped substantially to shape the new, cunning Sparta into a singularly high order of the accomplished Greek polis, with full equality in customs and culture for all its citizens, with the greatest possible restrictions on private life, with an abundance of leisure, contempt of money-making, and single-hearted devotion to all that upholds the freedom of the state. It was said that every polis strove for the common ideal of all the Hellenes, *kalokagathia,* the ideal of physical and intellectual excellence, but the state of Sparta existed for its sake exclusively.

This accomplishment rested on the fact that the family, the child and its nurture, and the whole subsequent life of the individual were far more rigorously subordinated to the common welfare than anywhere else in Greece. This regime produced a type of people that veered off sharply from the other Greeks, hardly being able to hold intercourse with them. Other states had to use force to discourage people from leaving, but Sparta did not because the Spartiate was ill at ease abroad unless he appeared as a victorious warrior. Defiance rang in the proverb: Sparta was allotted to you as a home, crown it with honor! On the other hand, it was not hard to keep foreigners away without prohibition; none went there unless forced to, and then left as soon as they could.

Marriage was strictly regulated, ostensibly for eugenic purposes. These included bodily exercise for girls to make them as strong and healthy as possible. On closer examination, however, marriage appears to have been saddled with a curse, which was to be removed by all sorts of laws and usages. Lycurgus, we are told, decreed that the breeding of children should be a matter of common interest to the "worthy" people and that, therefore all "empty" jealousy was interdicted. It was supposed that by this arrangement the offspring would stem not necessarily from any given husband, but from the most excellent.

The child then, in fact, was to belong to the caste rather than to a particular couple. The communal education, described countless times, began early and accompanied the Spartiate throughout his whole life. Each age level controlled and watched over the next one below it; at no time were the people without anyone ruling over them. Exercising and hardening their bodies, engaging in calisthenics and athletic contests, and stealing crops filled the period of youth. It would scarcely be possible not to see that all this was deliberately brutalizing. Before the altar of Artemis Orthia, a divinity inspiring madness and murder, whom none had the courage to hurl into a fire, bloody floggings were carried out, an exception in all Greece and a veritable school in ferocity, as were also the bloody athletic contests engaged in by the *ephebi* [young men, 16 to 20, in training for military service]. The goal of all education was to give the future warrior and overseer of serfs the skills he would need and to inure him to the privations he would have to undergo. Consequently, gymnastics that were popular in all the rest of Greece had only a limited scope in Sparta. And so, in spite of the fact that it was in charge at Olympia, Sparta had but few Olympic victors and, up to the time of Herodotus, one only, King Demaratus, won the four-horse chariot race. One did not learn to read and write; one's education was altogether oral or musical.

The reports on the so-called *mothakes*, children of helots, are highly significant of the Spartan view of their own education and its political tendency. Certainly not in the early periods, but later when the inequality became glaring, there arose the custom of letting the rich Spartiates keep companions from among the *perioeci* or helots, and these shared in their education and particularly in gymnastics. Lycurgus, i.e., the Spartan state, fully enfranchised them and, indeed, it was the wisest thing that could have been done, for these *mothakes* not only had taken part in gymnastics but also had heard and seen as much as any citizen of Sparta. A number of the most famous Spartans—Callicrat Callicratidas, Gylippus, Lysander—were *mothakes.*

The Spartiates then actually enjoyed that lifelong abundance of leisure, i.e., freedom from work, which was such a precious ideal for the rest of the Hellenes, still preoccupied with the popular assemblies and court sessions which had fallen into disuse in Sparta. The Spartiates engaged in no gainful occupation, going out occasionally to inspect the family estate and taking liberties with his neighbor's chattels (animals, equipment, helots, etc.). Gold and silver were not in circulation; iron money had to fill the actual needs.

When not at war, the Spartiates, according to Plutarch, spent all their time in dancing, festivities, pleasure, hunting, exercise, and discourses. This overlooks only one thing, the everlasting need for armed patrols, to keep the Lacedaemonian and Messenian helots and *perioeci* from getting restive. Even those who lingered in Sparta itself were always armed to meet an uprising at any moment. This was the only purpose of the celebrated common mess, *syssitia,* shared by a club of fifteen (just as it was the purpose of the *andreia* in Crete). Social intercourse, shaped by the *symposium* (banquet) and the *agora* in other cities, took the form of a more or less witty guardroom and a school for mockery in Sparta; of course one could withdraw from this mockery, but it was considered more prudent to put up with it.

The Spartan diet consisted of a dark broth, a solid and nourishing dish that was even prepared for the gourmets in Athens. The Spartiate most likely dined better than the middle-class Athenian did. In only one respect did he make a severe sacrifice: wine was doled out to him very sparingly because the safety of the state depended upon a vigilant sobriety. No exception was made even at the Dionysian festivals when, at Athens, drunks were hauled home in wagons and, in Tarentum, the whole city got inebriated, for the danger of conspiracy was greatest precisely at festivals of this sort.

In reality, people constituted an army and their state was that of an armed camp. The number of soldiers who set out on a military campaign was a state secret, and after a victory one could not easily find out how many had fallen. After a defeat it was altogether impossible, unless there was an *Epaminondas* present who discovered it nevertheless. After the battle at Leuctra, he ordered the Lacedaemonian allies to gather up their dead first and thereafter the Spartans to get theirs. Not until it was learned how few the allies had lost did the thousand remaining corpses have to be Spartans or *perioeci*.

It was the Spartan custom to eulogize family members fallen in battle, and for the mothers to pronounce heroic sentiments, an unusual collection of which may be read in Plutarch (*Apophthegmata Lacaenarum*). It was also found necessary to have in reserve for those who had "trembled," i.e., faltered in battle, an award of dishonor, *atimia*, conveying ridicule of cowardice. But after *Sphacteria* one proceeded more cautiously with *atimias*. Soon thereafter the state found it expedient to impose heavy fines instead.

Sparta's position in the Hellenic realm of the beautiful is most extraordinary. These people, made deliberately narrow-minded, bent on equality in their mode of living and on keeping down the subjugated castes, were Greeks all the same, and for revering their gods they needed art in the same broad scope as their kindred did everywhere else. The Spartan state was at times wealthy enough to adorn its temples most splendidly. One could not expect Spartans to engage in the plastic arts. Even the rest of the Greeks regarded the greatest masters in sculpture as *banausics,* simply because they could not see anything noble in manual labor, though it be linked to a sublime transport of the spirit.

Spartan symbolism surprises one with some unhandsome features. They represented their god of war in fetters to insure his fidelity, whereas Athens expresses the same idea more appropriately with the wingless victory goddess. The Spartans also represented Aphrodite in fetters, to symbolize faithfulness in wedlock, which, in the light of what was said above, was a poor subject to call attention to.

However, such things may be amply offset by the many accounts of the poetry and music cultivated in Sparta. It is inviting to learn that the city engaged in worship of the Muses and had a temple for them, and that the kings sacrificed there before going into battle. The Spartans marched on campaigns not only to the blare of trumpets, but also to the accompaniment of flutes, lyres, and harps. Thaletas of Crete is associated with Lycurgus. The melody and rhythm of his songs, which were dignified and soothing, was conducive to obedience and harmony. Then, around the time of the Second Messenian War, there appeared Terpander of Lesbos and Tyrtaeus the Athenian.

Terpander, who increased the number of strings on the harp from four to seven, was called during a time of great unrest because the oracle had said that reconciliation would attend his playing the harp, and indeed, all hearing him embraced and were moved to tears. In the few words of his that have survived, he praises Sparta "where bloom the spears of young men and the clear-voiced Muse and justice in the market place." In Tyrtaeus Sparta got a poet not only gifted in composing songs but also skilled in *paraenesis* (a branch of poetry stimulating heroic virtues) beyond anything Sparta could produce. Though his activities in Sparta were mostly legendary, significant remnants of his elegies have been preserved, and hence we know how the poetic language of Athens sounded in the service of Sparta and in scorn of its victims.

Toward the end of the seventh century, Alcman, born in Lydia but reared and emancipated in Sparta, composed in the Doric dialect. We are assured that "the not too mellifluous tongue did not dampen the charm of his songs." Famous poets later avoided Sparta, and later musicians such as Timotheus did not always enjoy their sojourn there. Still, in Sparta, music was and remained strikingly in the foreground of life and also had its place of honor in campaigns and at feasts. Carefully the usage of the old songs was preserved and learned by heart. This body of songs included all the different kinds of older choric poetry. Music and poetry must have touched life daily in connection with gymnastic and martial dances. Allegorically, Sparta was even represented as a woman with a lyre.

But none of these things prove that the Spartans had more musical talent or enthusiasm than the rest of the Greeks did. At that time music was still a therapeutic art. A later writer, but one who possessed various authentic old documents, sums up the whole phenomenon in the following words:

> The Spartans understood nothing about music, for they were more concerned with physical exercise and weapons. When they were ailing in body or mind, or were otherwise afflicted, needing the help of the Muses, then, following the advice of Delphi, they brought in strangers to serve as doctors, or priests to offer propitiatory sacrifices.

Thereupon the *poets* are listed, beginning with Terpander. No doubt, poetry and music played a most important role, and Alcman ventured to say: "Skill on the harp glides ahead of the sword," but by and large "the Spartans of all men treasure least poetry and the glory to be won by it."

Instead of literature, the Spartans cultivated pithy, sententious brevity, brachylogy, described by the generic term "laconic." They purposely cultivated this style from early days on. Since they felt they could not measure up to the other Greeks in fluency, the Spartans deliberately stressed brevity, perhaps not without sensing what sheer rhetoric and grandiloquence would eventually lead to in other poleis. The political style of Spartan orators we learn from non-Spartan reporters, the most important of whom is Thucyd-

ides, but he sheds no light on it either, because he himself constantly strives
for an astounding brevity.

It is hardly necessary to say anything about the special coloring which
Greek religion assumed in Sparta. One deferred to Delphi as to a permanent
authority in cult matters; but the festivals in honor of the gods were
peculiarly an expression of the way of life in Sparta as perhaps nowhere else
in Greece, inasmuch as they had no gathering for the sake of trade or politics, no *symposium* or *agora,* no popular courts and no assemblies. Because
of the July and August festivals of *Carnea, Hyacinthia,* and moon phases
the Spartans postponed the most important military campaigns and, though
engaged in war, they observed the appropriate cult rites with painstaking
care. The behavior of a Cleomenes or Pausanias incontrovertibly shows that
cramping superstitions ruled in Sparta, the price paid for narrow-minded
and narrow-hearted education. It is also shown in the way Lysander could
count on Spartan superstition, whereas the leading classes in Athens at that
time already discarded such attitudes. In Sparta superstition and the exploitation of superstition alternate with each other.

There remains only to examine as briefly as possible the results achieved
by this state and these people, such as they manifested themselves in the
course of time. We have already seen that the Spartans could not helotize
the Peloponnesus beyond a certain extent. They took Tegea from the
Arcadians and Thyreatis from the Argives, but for the rest, they had to content themselves with hegemony over as many Peloponnesians as possible,
thus securing their military allegiance. In the course of the sixth century,
the Spartans suppressed in many places a form of government that seemed
intolerable to them—tyranny—and did so not only in the Peloponnesus (the
Cypselidae in Corinth and the Aeschines in Sicyon) but also on various
Aegean islands and on the coast of Ionia. But when they intervened against
the Pisistratidae in Athens, they meddled in matters they did not understand,
and everything they proposed to achieve ended in failure. Athens became
democratic and increased in size and power. Then, says Herodotus, Sparta
had to accept a double misfortune: they had driven out people with only
their shirts on their backs, people who had been their guests, such as
Hippias, and received no thanks from the Athenians for it; they understood
that only tyrants could keep Athens weak and in proper submission to Sparta.

In the Persian Wars, Sparta conducted itself with blind egoism and
abandoned the rest of the Greeks in cold blood, supposing that it would be
able to get the mastery of the Peloponnesus with Persian consent. Spartans
purposely arrived too late for the Battle of Marathon; at Thermopylae they
deliberately sacrificed the small troop under Leonidas that honor might
redound to Sparta without exposing its main force to the risk of defeat. The
determined maneuvering it took to bring about the Battle of Salamis against

the willful opposition of Sparta is detailed in Herodotus. At the beginning of the campaign of Mardonius, the Spartans supposed that they could leave the rest of Hellas in the lurch and retire idly behind a fortified wall across the Isthmus of Corinth. However, Chileos of Tegea shrewdly got the Spartans to see that if Athens and Persia should combine, they would find other ways to enter the Peloponnesus. And so, at the eleventh hour, Sparta made the most crucial decision of its entire history, namely, to throw in its whole armed might against Mardonius. With the victory at Plataea, Sparta won back the dominant position it had lost in Greek affairs as a whole.

Until well along into the sixth century the Spartans all appeared to have achieved a remarkable uniformity, being possessed of only one thought, one law—to increase the power of Sparta. Later, however, we learn of single powerful individuals all in revolt against the limitations and privations imposed by the laws of the land, indeed in a barely disguised rage against all and everything.

Already in the sixth century, there appears the formidable figure of King Cleomenes whom the *ephors* were apparently unable to withstand effectively. On one occasion he did refuse a bribe, but that such things were a matter of daily discussion in his house is revealed on another occasion when his little daughter Gorgo, eight or nine years old, admonished, "Father, you had better go away or the stranger (it was Aristagoras) will corrupt you." His conduct was manifest iniquity, perpetrated against gods and men, mingled with abominable superstition. He bribed the Pythian oracle against his colleague, Demaratus; and at every enterprise consulted the embalmed head of a companion he had murdered. His flight, his attempt to stir up the Arcadians, his return, insanity and suicide, sound, in the account of Herodotus, like a bad dream.

The Spartans feared his intrigues in Arcadia, but even so, they used questionable judgment when they recalled him to occupy his throne again. Pausanias, his successor, was likewise made up of superstition and wickedness. As a Spartan commander who had won the battle at Plataea, he was perhaps beyond all control. In his rancor against the Spartan state, he promised to free and enfranchise even the helots if they would revolt and help him to turn everything upside down. For plotting with the Persians to subjugate all Greece, including Sparta, to the great king of Persia he drew a short sentence of imprisonment and was set free again, for money, no doubt. The second time, he was found guilty of further dangerous and incriminating intrigues and the *ephors* had to arrest him, but a hint from one of them enabled him to flee to the temple of Athena Chalkioikos [of the "Bronze House"]. Here he met his end, probably because any attempt to rescue him would have raised too much hue and cry.

He had fled into a small room in the temple. The *ephors* walled up the doors, putting sentries around, to starve him. When he was on the point of dying, they carried him out, still breathing, but he died soon after. The victor of the battle at Mycale, Leotychides, having been sent on a campaign to Thessaly, took a bribe and got caught with a sleeve full of money. In consequence, he died a fugitive in Tegea. Nevertheless bribery continued to be the way to get things done in Sparta, and certainly not only when it involved kings, who anyway were watched too closely and, as a rule, were quite powerless. In order to put off the outbreak of the great war, Pericles later allowed ten *talents* a year to flow to Sparta, seeing to it that all the influential persons were given due consideration. But one thing became clear to the Spartans: Their commanders ran great danger of succumbing to temptation when abroad on long and important assignments. It was probably for this reason that the Spartans soon lost their dominant influence over the Greeks, permitting the Athenians to assume theirs again.

The real state of affairs came to light after the great earthquake in 468. A general revolt of helots in Lacedaemon and Messenia occasioned what is called, not without reason, the *Third Messenian War*. With the aid of their Peloponnesian allies, the Spartans emerged masters again, but only after waging war for nine years. At the bidding of an oracle from Delphi the Spartans had to allow their adversaries to withdraw, in accordance with an agreement, instead of annihilating or at least enslaving them. This marked a distinct decline in power for the Spartans, although they managed to stay in control of their own affairs.

The campaigns the Spartans undertook outside the Peloponnesus in the years immediately following were almost like required acts of piety, such as rendering help to tribal kin in Doris and later to Delphi against Phocis. In Boeotia, Sparta would have liked to strengthen Thebes as an equipoise to Athens; it aided in the victory at Tanagra and once even marched its Peloponnesians to Attica. But all this was done in a rather perfunctory way and without zeal. At the close of the so-called Thirty Years' Truce, Sparta was willing to maintain the status quo and was afraid to endanger it through war. It lent a deaf ear to the complaints its allies raised against Sparta's neighbors, refusing to believe them. There is no doubt that the money the Athenians secretly sent as bribes did its work, although a realistic appraisal of affairs also played its part.

Sparta had its principles, as King Archidamus phrased it in Thucydides. Sparta never underestimated an enemy and never counted on his making mistakes; i.e., it was never carried away by enthusiasm, as Athens was, with its popular assembly. Sparta was under the control of a strong government. So when the Peloponnesian War finally broke out, Sparta could formally declare its intention to free Hellas, and it decidedly had on its side the sympathy of the larger number of Greek states. During the first half of the war the Spartiates were kept in readiness in the Peloponnesus, and sent out allied soldiers under Spartan command wherever possible. In 425, at Sphacteria, 292 soldiers, among them only 120 of the ruling caste, surrendered to the Athenians, an event of the greatest significance. The reputation of Sparta, however, soared again under the command of Brasidas, one of the few sympathetic figures of his caste. The leaders of the Spartiates disliked him, however, and failed to give him adequate support. The Spartans welcomed the Peace of Nicias (421 B.C.) which enabled them to smooth over the national crisis, at least for the time being. Anyway, during the years of this so-called peace, Spartan importance seemed to wane, and the Athenian and democratic influences to gain in the Peloponnesus.

The Sicilian expedition of the Athenians and its outcome definitely gave the Spartans a breathing spell. In the second half of the war, the Peloponnesus was safe, and the Spartans, advised by Alcibiades, were able to launch heavy attacks on Attica. By promising King Darius Nothus the Greek cities of Asia Minor they got money for their indispensable fleet and the help of his satraps. With the victory at Aegospotami and the surrender of Athens under the most abject terms, the war ended, and for three decades Sparta enjoyed supremacy over all Greece.

During the later years of the war, the directing of the Spartan state and its politics was less in the hands of King Agis than of a council of able Spartans controlling the *ephorate*. Members of this council must have selected the generals, each worth an army, who led hosts of allies and mercenaries as though they were Lacedaemonians. On this expedition to Asia Minor, Agesilaus had only thirty Spartiates, really only a council of war. At first glance it seemed that Sparta's hegemony had an advantage over Athens' former rule, craving neither ships nor money, only subordination. In reality, however, Sparta heaped up thousands of *talents* from the payments made by its subject nations, and whether it recruited men without using force cannot be known. For the time being, the Spartans materially strengthened their dominion by aiding those political parties which they had put into power. These satellite parties, and the *sycophants* aping them, prated of Sparta as being the "teachers of Hellas," a phrase Pericles had used to eulogize Athens.

Still, closer inspection showed that deep and incurable evils seriously threatened this state. Consider the man who admittedly was the chief tool and spokesman of this state, Lysander. What a remarkable figure! He combined the wickedness of the Spartiate, who is at heart in revolt against the order of his own polis, with the viciousness prevalent in the rest of a Greece brutalized by the Peloponnesian War. He understood the most despicable club life as thoroughly as any Athenian. He surrounded himself with obsequious informers and adulatory poets, and had sacrifices offered to himself as to a god. As it was said of Alcibiades in regard to Athens, so it was said of him: Sparta could not endure a second Lysander. However, of the two, Alcibiades will remain the more sympathetic figure. Lysander intrigued outrageously against his own state in order to become king, not merely by inciting the *perioeci* and helots, but by trying to stir up the Spartiates themselves. The crude deceptions he resorted to with the help of oracles to accomplish his ends do not induce one to form a particularly high opinion of the intelligence his countrymen had shown in these matters.

Private property had begun somewhat to sap the strength of Spartan life since the Peloponnesian War, but now it was irresistibly expanding, and, in direct consequence of it, the ruling caste declined swiftly and dangerously.

The Peloponnesian War had brought the Spartans into far closer contact with the rest of the Greeks and their customs and conceptions than any war ever had; moreover, the ties with Persia had brought great wealth into Spartan coffers. The formerly closed system just fell apart, and evidently the state no longer paid attention to the amassing of wealth by individuals. Some have lamented that the degeneration began with the otherwise very deserving Gylippus who had removed three hundred *talents* from state money pouches, not knowing that in each pouch was a note telling him how much silver it contained. But thieves who dipped into the treasury had long been about. Permitting the accumulation of private property was the decisive development. At the same time, great changes were made in the disposition of the parcels of land originally allotted to the Spartiates. These hereditary estates were very important as a basis for the ruling caste, and should have been protected in every way possible. Wealthy persons named powerful individuals in their entailments, excluding their own relatives. These fell into indigence and dependence that unfitted them for noble aspirations. They envied and hated the rich possessors. Thus, some Spartiates remained nobles, while the rest became plebeians.

If only the Spartiates had been numerous! Right after the Peloponnesian War, however, on the occasion of the conspiracy of *Kinadon,* the Spartiates were counted for tax purposes as only a hundredth part of the populace. The *perioeci* and helots, as well as the half-breeds that had developed in time, frankly admitted that they would have liked to eat the Spartans raw. Up to the battle at Leuctra, Sparta, in the heyday of its misdeeds, was still the most powerful and renowned state of Hellas, though it had one of the lowest citizen rolls. A state and society in such straits may collapse in a day. Sparta might well have developed into a tyranny, perhaps even one of unusual strength. The appearance of Agesilaus thwarted this development.

Without any prospects of ascending to the throne, he grew up among ruffians, doubtlessly witnessing and fighting in the latter part of the Peloponnesian War. In 398 Lysander promoted him, a mature man, to the throne over the head of his nephew, Leotychides, in a manner hardly justified. Agesilaus must have judged his own and Sparta's position with penetrating sagacity. His determined will enabled him to renounce greed, pleasures, and tyrannical bearing typical of the unrestrained Spartiates. He wanted to be as good and great a king of Sparta as circumstances permitted.

In the very first year of his reign occurred the conspiracy of Kinadon (397 B.C.), which revealed the foremost weakness of Spartanism. Agesilaus may have felt that it was no longer a matter of restitution but only of prolonging the status quo, and this was possible only if the forces at hand were kept on the move. One might best try to cover up the evils with daring, and Agesilaus was indeed among the rulers of all times the ablest at glossing things over. He showed the highest respect for all the external forms and for the whole state ceremonial, and was almost childishly humble toward the *ephors*. In addition, he was religious by nature and once he gave his word he kept it—altogether a different man from the contemporary Attic statesmen and army commanders.

Lysander stood at his side at the beginning, hoping to control him. He obtained for him the command of the army pitted against the satraps in Asia Minor. The Spartans broke off relations with the Persians, to whom they were indebted for their final triumph in the Peloponnesian War. For two years (396–394 B.C.), Agesilaus marched an army hither and thither in Asia Minor, penetrating as far as Phrygia. The army consisted of two thousand *neodamodes*, newly enfranchised helots, and eight thousand allies augmented by occasional recruits. Xenophon, who a few years earlier had led a Greek army amid quite different dangers into the East, now spent a longer period at the headquarters of Agesilaus. He later wrote an admiring account of this campaign, praising Agesilaus as a real Spartan. Others who had surveyed this campaign judged that Agesilaus and his army had achieved nothing great or praiseworthy. This campaign simply brought to light the rottenness of the Persian dominion, a fact known for a long time. But Greek life had likewise fallen into decay, and it was by bribery that King Artaxerxes Mnemon was able to bring about the Corinthian War against the Spartans.

When the *ephors* recalled Agesilaus by means of a *skytale* [secret scroll], he obeyed immediately and, without making any fuss, gave up his alleged Asiatic plans of advancing upon Ecbatana and Susa. They praised his action as marvelous. Indeed, Sparta was no longer accustomed to such obedience. Yet it is a question whether Agesilaus was not indeed glad to be relieved of his adventure. Back in Europe again, he gained a victory at Coronea due mainly to his resolute personal boldness, then returned to Sparta as plain and unassuming as ever, without a shadow of that dangerous arrogance others had returned with from their exploits abroad. And if the hundred talents he gave to the god at Delphi was indeed a tenth of his Asiatic booty, then he had enriched the Spartan treasury by nine hundred talents, remaining poor himself.

But he, above all others, had to know that even victories could hold dangers for the Spartans, for they were so few in number. After having brilliantly vanquished Corinth, the heavy-armed Lacedaemonian infantry set out to return to Sparta, but Iphicrates and his mercenaries attacked and killed several hundred of them. Thereafter, Agesilaus, leading the rest of his soldiers home, had to use all his cunning to disguise the sorry state of his army so that the Arcadians would not jeer at them. When Conon and Pharnabazus, serving as Persian admirals, ravaged the coast of Laconia and restored the walls of Athens with Persian money, Spartan sentiment was all for making an alliance with Persia again, whatever the cost. Antalcidas, who negotiated and signed the peace, belonged reputedly to the opponents of Agesilaus, who had to approve the peace anyway because he had promised to weaken Thebes by declaring autonomy for all the states, including those of Boeotia (387 B.C.).

The bold stroke by which Phoebidas captured Thebes with Spartan soldiers was approved by Agesilaus in such a way as to imply that he had secretly ordered this attack. The aggression of Sparta against Thebes raised the wrath and urge for freedom of all those suffering under Spartan domination. And when, after three years, Thebes was freed by a revolt under Pelopidas and Epaminondas (382 B.C.), and formed an alliance with Athens, Sparta was incomparably worse off than before it had garrisoned Cadmea, the citadel of Thebes. At this time, however, Agesilaus led no campaigns because of a protracted illness. When he did so again, his campaigns were no longer brilliant and consisted mostly of devastations.

After Thebes and her allies had quarreled for several years, becoming more and more belligerent, and the people under Spartan hegemony more and more discontented, a general peace conference was called at Sparta, at which Epaminondas appeared and made the deepest impression. Xenophon takes no notice of the main scene; but, if Plutarch's account is accurate in at least its main outlines, then, in effect, Agesilaus crudely declared war on the Thebans, supposing, as did the rest of the Greeks, that he had concluded a peace and isolated Thebes (372 B.C.). He is clearly responsible for the battle at Leuctra even though not he but Cleombrotus commanded the Spartan army.

The Spartans staked everything on this one battle, as they had done at Plataea, but those days were gone. The battle at Leuctra was a blow from which Sparta never recovered; it was a terrible loss of blood for the Dorian ruling caste however one looks at the figures; even if of the thousand Lacedaemonians that perished only a small part were Dorians, still the four hundred Spartiates whom Diodorus mentions were absolutely more than the Spartans could afford to lose. Then too, after winning a smashing victory with its six thousand soldiers, Thebes, hitherto isolated, was able to head a powerful alliance against Sparta, while the Spartan hegemony was rocked to its very foundations.

Then there unfolded the further consequences of this defeat. Sparta stood condemned, and was bereft of its main historical achievements when Arcadia withdrew and Messenia, hitherto regarded as crushed, became an independent state again (369 B.C.). All this happened while Epaminondas and Pelopidas were in the Peloponnesus with their newly-won allies and moved into the vicinity of Sparta. Agesilaus did not dare to oppose this flood tide with his soldiers in open combat. First and foremost he had to defend the city, and he turned a deaf ear to the taunting challenges of his enemies. He saw how old Lacedaemonian men, whose heroic minds were celebrated in so many beautiful maxims, cried out in grief and trudged about in confusion, and how those famous Lacedaemonian mothers lost their heroic calm and behaved like madwomen when they heard the tumult and saw the watch fires of the enemy. By sheer presence of mind he dispersed two hundred men, probably desperate Dorians, who had occupied a fortified part of the town where the temple of Artemis stood. Later, when fifteen of these had been apprehended, he ordered their execution by night. Other Spartan citizens met clandestinely in each other's houses, planning a revolution. These too were taken and secretly put to death. At this time also, *perioeci* and helots who were in the army ran away to the enemy in droves. During the period of greatest stress the Spartans freed a thousand helots to keep them from defecting with the others. Sparta undeniably owed its deliverance to the king, and the following year its first new success to his son, Archidamus. The father and a procession of Spartans went out to meet the victor with tears of joy, whereas formerly no display was made over victors or heralds of victory. Had Sparta had a democratic popular assembly, jury trials, orators, and *sycophants,* it would probably have staged a bloody trial.

Agesilaus lived to see rich Messenia become independent while he was king. His life was touched by one last splendor when he succeeded in rescuing the city of Sparta out of the very hands of Epaminondas. On this occasion, king and city fought with desperate courage, and various individuals performed heroic deeds. The death of Epaminondas at Mantinea removed Sparta's greatest threat, and, amid the general confusion in Greece, it could have collected itself and recovered somewhat. But now it was Agesilaus himself, this embittered old graybeard, who kept Sparta out of a general peace, at least a nominal one, and alone carried on another war to reconquer Messenia (361 B.C.). But when this attempt failed, Agesilaus gave the appearance of being insatiably bent on war so that even his followers tired of him.

His expedition to Egypt, which had revolted against Persian domination, was a retaliatory act upon the Persian king who had declared himself for Messenian independence. Agesilaus' exploits on the Nile do not belong here. When this eighty-four-year-old hero died in the Port of Menelaus on the African coast, he was on his way home, planning to take up the cudgels again, this time against Arcadia.

If, at this time, the abler people everywhere in Greece turned ever more away from the state, in Sparta this turning away took the form of absenteeism, especially among the kings, simply because they could not bear to stay at home in their wretched country. As often as they could they would gather a troop of mercenaries and take up service abroad, where they occasionally disgraced themselves. One of the most meritorious of these kings was Archidamus IV, a son of Agesilaus. Before going to the aid of the Tarentines, he and his wife Deinicha are known to have accepted bribes from the temple treasury at Delphi. The murmuring Spartans had to endure the domination of Philip of Macedon over Greece and, after the battle at Chaeronea, suffer the most abject humiliation on their own territory. In the following years it was their consolation to serve in no Macedonian army camp, to ignore every congress, and not to contribute anything to anybody. The strutting days of Sparta were past recall, and when Antipater defeated the revolting Peloponnesians at Megalopolis, Sparta expressly exonerated from dishonor its soldiers who had fled from there as Agesilaus had done after the battle at Leuctra.

It was the wantonly insulted royal scion Cleonymous who had called Pyrrhus into Lacedaemon, and the heroic rescue of the capital by King Areus and his son Acrotatus was one of the last moments of glory for this decrepit state. Afterward both perished in war with the Macedonians and Megalopolitans. For decades thereafter the history of Sparta is obscure, until the deeds and destinies of the kings Agis and Cleomenes turn it into tragedy one last time before the end of the Dorian state of the Heraclidae (236–222 B.C.).

Both of these kings, their family and entourages, had the good fortune to be written up in sympathetic accounts which served Plutarch as documents. The reputation of Cleomenes in particular will live even though the darker traits stressed by Polybius and others retain their veracity.

The Spartan state was to get an entirely new foundation by nothing less than a revolution from above. When one learns that there were left only seven hundred Spartans, i.e., Dorians able to bear arms, and that among these only one hundred had inherited and owned land, one is astonished that after all the defeats and humiliations they were able to dominate their subjects as long as they did. Now, through a massive admixture of *perioeci* and a redistribution of land, there was to rise a powerful, capable upper class. By means of unscrupulous conquests and alliances, it was to achieve the respect of its neighbors and perhaps even renewed dominion over Greece. Such a revolution was a distinct possibility at a time when redistribution of boundaries, annulment of debts, and annihilation of opponents were the order of the day elsewhere in the Greek states. As to the dangers of political change, the Greeks, with their abundant energy, were not inclined to avoid them for lack of naïve recklessness.

Agis planned to amalgamate the Dorians with a large majority of those *perioeci* and strangers who were already accustomed to Spartan life, provided they were people of choice character, and to settle them on 4,500 parcels of land allotted to them in a certain area of Lacedaemonia. He also wanted to divide the rest of the land into 15,000 allotments for the remaining *perioeci* capable of bearing arms. The 4,500 were obviously to hold the power in the state, but after having replenished the ranks of the ruling class, the 15,000 would not have been much inferior.

However, this *coup d'état* succeeded only in driving out temporarily the opposing *ephors* and the other king of the *dyarchy*; an uncle of Agis had treacherously sabotaged the plans for reform because he wanted to retain his landed property. Reaction set in, and Agis died in prison. His widow became the wife of Cleomenes, the son of the other king, and she secretly won him over to the cause of her first husband. The rest was accomplished by Sphaerus, one of those Stoics who after that time appeared quite often as the mentors and confessors of political idealists.

As a nominal king under the suspicious *ephors*, Cleomenes had to wage war to assert his rights, and did so fighting the Achaean League, a union of greatly weakened poleis representing official Greece as distinct from Macedonians, tyrants, and rapacious Aetolians. To do this, he was unhappily forced to rely on mercenaries from Tarentum and Crete, while he broke up the Spartans into small groups and distributed these as far as possible to keep them impotent. He could begin his *coup d'état* in Sparta only by marching home at the head of a mercenary army (226 B.C.). Thereupon, having slaughtered the *ephors,* he demolished their houses, and banished eighty people.

Cleomenes addressed the assembled people, announcing that debts would be canceled, the land newly distributed, and the mercenaries given a pension. A portion of the latter were declared Spartiates so that the city and its territory would not have to run the risk, because of its small population, of falling prey to the Aetolians and the Illyrians. It would be hard to conceive a shakier political foundation than that of the Heraclidan king at the time.

Thereupon Cleomenes, his closer following, and finally all other citizens, yielded their possessions, which were then re-allotted. It is recorded that there were four thousand heavily armed soldiers again, a number Cleomenes achieved by giving the franchise to a good many more of the ablest *perioeci* than the number of Dorians in the plans of Agis. He is reputed to have restored the customs and ways of life set up by Lycurgus, but in his short and troubled reign he can hardly have accomplished much. He had to rush into a new war to safeguard his reign and chose to attack the Achaeans.

His initial success brought about an alliance hitherto considered impossible between two opponents—the Achaean League and the Macedonians under Antigonus Doson. For his part, Cleomenes was actually an ally of the Aetolians and hoped, though in vain, for help from Ptolemy Euergetes of Egypt. In addition, he enjoyed in various Achaean cities the fickle sympathy of the populace, which hoped for a Spartan deal, i.e., a redistribution of land and a cancellation of debts, at that time the customary rallying cry for a revolt. After protracted fighting, treated in much detail by Polybius, Cleomenes was crushed at Sellasia and, after a brief farewell, left Sparta for Egypt. In their account of the end of Cleomenes and of his men in Alexandria, Polybius and Plutarch have raised an eternal monument to the last Dorian Spartiate.

In whatever happened in Laconia from now on the first question is: What racial tribe was involved? For at the Battle of Sellasia, according to reports, the entire Lacedaemonian army of six thousand, composed of Dorians and very many *perioeci*, was wiped out, save for two hundred survivors. Among the free people in the valley of the Eurotas the Dorians thereafter can have formed only a negligibly small part.

Now it was a foreign army that invaded Sparta, and Antigonus Doson, in a hurry to get home, addressed the people most graciously and left them to themselves, not tampering with their conditions. In all Greece, however, it was a time of general decay. The whole endeavor of Cleomenes was of the kind that thrives on victories abroad but wilts in the face of defeat. Penalties finally attached to being the inheritors of ancient Sparta, with their cocky attitude and tradition of crime. From the rest of Greece rampant democracy, with its lusts and violence but also with tyranny in its repulsive later forms, rushed like a storm over a Sparta unable to muster any resistance.

At some time equality was proclaimed for everybody. There is some question whether the helots were also included, although no clear mention is later made of their servitude. Perhaps it was in these dreary times that there was erected a gigantic statue of *Demos* towering in the vicinity of the agora.

Ephors, now without doubt Achaeans, combined into competing factions and more than one was murdered by their colleagues or by the so-called demos, who then elected new ones. Murder cut down the *gerontes,* old men, and even the temple of Artemis Chalkioikos [bronze house] and her altar no longer offered protection to the victims. One of the last scions of the Heraclidae, a certain Lycurgus, was advanced by bribery and elevated to kingship in the *dyarchy* while still a child. Twice he was driven from the throne and twice he returned. In the meantime, the old lust for vengeance flared up in renewed wars against Messenia and Arcadia. A Macedonian king invaded Laconia again and plundered and devastated the country, though he was unable to capture Sparta itself. Then, after King Lycurgus, or rather after his son Pelops, came Machanidas, the first Spartan ruler who might be called a tyrant because he disposed of the *ephors* and ruled autocratically. His only possible aim being conquest, he went out against Peloponnesian states with mercenary troops whom he could not hope to pay unless it be by thoroughly plundering the wretched cities of the Peloponnesus. The Achaean League at that time just happened to have the good luck of possessing a capable leader and general, Philopoemen, who with his own hand slew the tyrant in open battle near Mantinea (207 B.C.).

But tyranny survived. Nabis the terrible, of unknown origin, usurped the supreme power (206–192 B.C.). He was regarded as one of the worst of that disreputable lot the Greeks called tyrants. At this time the Greeks intervened in the war between the Romans and King Philip the Younger of Macedon, and so were drawn out upon the high seas. But what is important in all this is not so much the alliances Nabis formed, now with Rome and now with Macedon, as his rule in Sparta, which he could enforce with some consistency during his fourteen years in power. In his campaigns during which he took and held Argos, he may well have been able to supplement his mercenaries with soldiers drawn from his own people. For his other deeds of violence he sought hardened criminals, the scum of far and near.

Nabis was in collusion with the pirates of Crete, and he protected the highwaymen, murderers, and temple robbers that slunk around in the Peloponnesus when they were in trouble. He practiced extortion with refined instruments of torture, and concentrated most perseveringly on exterminating all Dorians who might in any way become prominent.

Dorians in his view included the whole upper-class group of Cleomenes, all the rest of the Dorians, as well as the distinguished Achaeans. The wars of Nabis belong to the history of the Achaean League and Roman politics, and it is a disgrace that the great T. Quinctius Flaminius conquered him several times but let him slip out of his grasp on orders from above.

During that time the Spartan state was also deprived of its southern part, i.e., its seaports; this area, later known as Free Laconia, was under the protection of the Achaean League. In this campaign against the Achaean League, Nabis received aid and recruits from the Aetolians, likewise dissatisfied with the Romans. The commander of these recruits began by murdering the tyrant, and amid the tumult that followed, the Achaeans under Philopoemen entered the fray and forced Sparta to join the Achaean League and the people to accept Achaean education and customs, dropping those of Lycurgus. This latter severity was not only pointless, but it also evoked the stiffest resistance by the people who, though Achaeans, prized the old Dorian way of life much more highly. The rest of Spartan history is a sorry tale. A demagogue, Chaeron, brought about such terrible confusion by redistributing the land again and committing murders that Achaea intervened once more (about 180 B.C.). Sparta carried repeated complaints to Rome, but Rome left these matters deliberately in suspense. These conditions contributed to the Achaean War, which put an end to the Achaean League and many other Greek doings, once and for all.

Indeed, the Dorian race must have virtually disappeared, especially after the bloodletting of Nabis. Among all the people mentioned with Philopoemen in the writings of Livius, hardly one can have been a full-blooded Dorian, nor were there any among the exiles. On the other hand, all the non-Dorian Achaeans and the half-castes who lived well or ill in the Eurotas valley, had adopted the Dorian way of life as far as they could and imitated the behavior of their vanished rulers, at least in externals. The Dorians had been models of elegance to whom the rest looked up with envy and hatred. Nothing now kept these people from living in the Dorian ways, and outsiders liked to regard their way of life as genuine and original.

A craving for glory was one of those mysterious traits which most clearly distinguished the Greeks from other peoples. By the time their state and possessions had slipped from the hands of the Dorians, the image of splendor left by their ancient forebears had long become a force in Greek life in general, and numberless individual traits thereof had impressed themselves upon the whole Greek nation. Those who now tilled the soil and trod the earth of Lacedaemon regarded this heritage, from the primeval myths down to the memory of the last Cleomenes, as though it had always been not only their possession but their own creation.

3. *Subservient People in Other Poleis*

The main end of life for Sparta had been to keep the serfs in their place, in particular the non-Dorians and Messenians in the Eurotas valley. This outlook shaped the whole internal life of Sparta and materially helped to determine foreign policy. Undoubtedly, the Dorian migration had laid the foundation of a number of similar power structures elsewhere. Many powerful poleis had reduced to servitude the people living around them—subjugated Greeks or half-barbarians—but no other polis was able, as Sparta was, to orient its whole national and international life with a view to perpetuating this system. None of them lacked severity toward their serfs, but all of them lacked persistence and drive for the indispensable harmony and equalitarianism within the leading caste.

Documents about these matters for the periods in question are very meager. Still, the erstwhile master-serf relations were well-nigh or completely forgotten and already scarcely understood. They persisted with some clarity only on Crete and in Thessaly, and one can only conjecture to what extent the subjugated people elsewhere were half-free or still serf, part owners, hereditary tenants, bond servants or day laborers on the lands attached to the manors. Without civil rights and governed at the discretion of the polis, they apparently were not in a position to attract the attention of the chroniclers.

As to Crete, the designations transmitted to us give some clue to the different gradations of servitude. At any rate, when the island was Dorianized, it took on modes of life bearing much resemblance to those of Lacedaemon, and even though a political pluralism arose and the Cretan cities fought with each other, none of them called upon the serfs of the other cities to revolt. For, in general, the obedience of the serfs on the island seemed assured by the absence of any immediate neighbors.

In Thessaly, the so-called *penestes* were the ancient native Perrhabic and Magnesian people who yielded themselves as servants to the invading Thessalians so as to remain on the old accustomed clod of soil. In exchange for stipulated produce of the land, the Thessalians promised they would neither kill nor remove them. Some of these *penestes* were wealthier than their overlords, as now and then serfs were in recent Russian history because the ruling caste had lived in riot and revelry. Anyway, the lords of Thessaly and Crete exerted no pressure, as did Sparta, in seeking to force all the countries around to adopt the Spartan army system and oligarchical government in order to keep the subjugated peoples from getting restive. Also, neither Thessaly nor Crete aspired to be the teachers of Hellas.

Since the eighth century, the colonies owed their rise in part to the desire of the subjugated and oppressed people to flee from their poleis. But, having landed on some foreign coast, they acted no differently than their homeland oppressors, though to be sure toward barbarians or half-barbarians, who in turn became subject peoples without civil rights, though retaining the privilege of owning property.

Now and then this relationship is said to have come about in a friendly manner. When Heraclea was established in Pontus, the Mariandyni living in that area voluntarily accepted the rule of the Heracleotes in exchange for the guarantees of shelter and of not being sold abroad. Byzantium, on the other hand, treated the Bithynians as Sparta did the helots, and around Syracuse the Callicyrians or Cillicyrians were in similar servitude.

Aristotle rejects the whole system: A state relying on subjugated people cannot maintain an even keel. When treated gently these people become insolent and want equality with their masters; treated harshly they become malicious, treasonable, and upon occasion join with the underprivileged groups in the city itself. The Callicyrians did this when they made common cause with the Syracusan demos and were driving out the landholders until Gelon came to their aid and overthrew the Callicyrians, using the occasion to make himself master of Syracuse.

In spite of their moderate treatment, the *penestes* repeatedly rose in revolt when their Thessalian masters were at war with their neighbors. Aristotle finds it at least desirable that the enslaved people should be barbarians and not of the Greek race. In addition, he also indicates what changes were being brought about: More and more non-Greeks were bought as slaves and put out to farm land around a city-state.

4. Slavery

That golden age when, according to writers of later comedy, no slaves yet existed, must be sought in a very early age. As far back as tradition reaches, slaves have always existed in the countries around the Aegean Sea, where capture of and traffic in slaves were so easy and where the Phoenicians had been the teachers and precursors.

Homer attired slavery in a peculiar greatness in two figures: Eumaeus, who resists robbers and outlaws despite his own status as a piece of property, and the glorious Eurycleia. Homer, it is true, is concerned only with royal courts and great leaders. It is hard to determine to what extent Hesiod in *Works and Days* regarded farm hands as slaves; without a doubt, however, the poet viewed honest farm work not as *banausic* but as beneficent. Apart from the subjected people just considered, it is likely that farming was almost exclusively in the hands of free people as late as the ninth century.

At the other end of the scale, the possessing classes came to despise work and workers, acquiring that anti-*banausic* attitude which regarded the noble athletic games as the only worthy purpose of life. This aristocracy somehow got possession of the best land, now and then of all the land within the city-state territory, and got the landless free men to farm it for them. But these menial farm hands may have preserved the memory of better days their fathers once enjoyed while still living in hamlets, before the merciless polis was founded.

Once colonizing was in full swing, many doubtless went along to escape serfdom and bondage. And the readier the colonies were to supply slaves, the easier the gaps in the ranks of farm labor were to fill, for these colonies lay mostly on coasts where captured slaves from the interior were traded off. In wars of Hellenes against Hellenes, the victors killed the grown men and sold the wives and children, apparently abroad. When they spared the men, they did not keep them as domestic slaves but to work the mines, or held them for high ransom.

Since many regions were fully dependent on slave labor, war was too irregular and uncertain a source for supplying the need; only trade assured regularity. To keep an adult Greek captive as a slave in one's home was surely hard and dangerous. In most instances we find that the slaves kept in the homes or in the fields were of barbarian origin.

In rural areas where people lived predominantly in hamlets, laborers remained free for quite a while; among the Locrians and Phocians the younger members of the family customarily served the older or the first-born one. They did not keep slaves until shortly before the holy war of the fourth century. When a polis fully developed its potential, it did so by means of slave labor. And whoever, as a free man, worked on farms or in the city for wages found the idea of citizenship out of his reach. Indeed, the free man could hardly find any market for his services because the slaves and *metics* [resident aliens] filled the need. Such a fellow preferred looking for work from day to day to being under a pledge, which to him would have been a kind of servitude, in that it made him feel dependent.

Where and in what states did slaves first come to be the servants in households and the workers on farms and in handicrafts? When and where were galleys first manned by slaves? Large enterprises exploiting masses of workers, like mines for instance, presumably were always operated by slave labor.

Slaves came from a variety of sources. Scythians, Getaeans, Lydians,

Phrygians, Paphlagonians, Carians, Syrians filled Greek homes and farms. Cautious buyers tried to get each slave from a different nationality, which was easy to do where only three or four were used. It is not certain whether the barbarian slave dealers drew more upon their own people or upon war captives or on slave-hunting to supply the market.

During the heyday of Greece, even a highly cultivated Hellene could become the slave of another Greek falling into the clutches of a powerful enemy or a pirate. Once one had become a slave, citizenship or high birth availed naught. Phaedo and Plato both suffered this fate, the former in his youth, the latter when already a famous philosopher. Both were redeemed. Now and then a second owner might speculate on the chance of redemption. Diogenes remained with his buyer Ceniades of Corinth, later obviously voluntarily.

In the fifth century, the average price for an ordinary slave was two *minas,* the mina being worth a hundred drachmas. In the fourth century one and one half minas was regarded as reasonable, showing that the supply was steady and plentiful. Else more slaves would have been raised at home to supplement the purchases abroad. But breeding slaves was not considered profitable; indeed, wedlock among slaves (little more than concubinage and barely tolerated by the masters) was not considered expedient, unless it was desired to attach the better slaves by means of their children to the service of the house and to its welfare.

One did not expect much of slave children. The yearly attrition was reckoned at ten per cent, and one naturally wished to keep one's slaves as useful animals. One saw one's friend suffer hardships or perish without being much concerned; but one took one's slave to the doctor and nursed him, if he died, one lamented and regarded it as a loss.

We may ask what happened when a region became so impoverished that it could no longer afford to buy slaves, and especially when the number of free-born laborers dropped as they became more loath to work. Most likely the country soon turned into a waste.

Later on, Cappadocians, Phrygians, and Lydians usually did the baking because of their skill in it. On large estates a slave was made an overseer of the others, and from among the female slaves one became the stewardess who was carefully instructed and treated gently and discreetly. Aristotle supposed that one should respect and deal fairly with slaves entrusted with the more responsible jobs, while giving the ordinary ones plenty of good wholesome food. Larger households needed doorkeepers to check on things carried in and out. A slave no longer useful for other work might well have handled this.

The slaves of Sophocles' father were all builders and braziers, those of

Isocrates' father were all flute makers. Some workshops might employ hundreds of slaves, depending on the business and the condition of the times. In mines, there were many thousands of slaves, being the property either of the state or of a private owner. The citizens grew concerned about the wretched existence of these slaves only when they threatened to become dangerous. A document one wishes Xenophon had not written glowingly portrays to the Athenian citizens how profitable it would be to employ more slaves in the silver mines, for with ten thousand they would take in one hundred talents a year, and by sufficiently increasing that number they could all live without working.

As if the number of slaves in the homes and on the fields of Attica were not enough, Xenophon thinks the state should have at least three slaves in the silver mines for every citizen, a good sixty thousand at that time; then Athens would be even more orderly and more efficient in war. These proposals are just as foolish as the encouragement given to resident aliens or *metics,* who were to be lured to Athens in great numbers. How costly it would have been for Athens to live on this kind of income! A single unlucky battle taking the lives of many citizens would have enabled the *metics* to become masters of the state already undermined in the literal sense.

These *metics* were Lydian, Phrygian, and Syrian in origin, as were many of the slaves; in part they may have been the offspring of slaves who had been freed, and a number of household and silver-mine slaves who presumably also were freed. Xenophon finally wonders whether approval of his proposals should not be sought in Dodona and Delphi, and if approved, under the protection of which gods they should be carried out.

It is hard for us to think of Greece as harboring amid four to five million free men twelve million slaves, nearly all of foreign extraction (Hellwald); of Attica as having four times as many slaves as free men (Curtis), to say nothing of individual industrial cities like Corinth where the free men comprised about one tenth of the population; the state of Corinth is supposed to have had 460,000 slaves and Aegina fully 470,000.

Nobody has ever been blind to the great dangers all this slavery involved. To be sure, the mobs which at times took over whole cities were not slaves as the word used to describe them suggests, but suppressed natives. The big slave wars in Sicily really took place under Roman rule when the system of latifundia had enormously increased the number of slaves. Concurrent with the second uprising in Sicily, the slaves in the mines of Attica, now grown into many myriads, revolted (about 100 B.C.), and having killed their guards and seized the Acropolis at Sunium they proceeded to lay waste the land.

The greater the number of slaves in a state, the more severe was the discipline and the more urgent the desire for escape and vengeance. In every war, people feared that large masses of slaves would burst their shackles. More than twenty thousand slaves, mostly skilled craftsmen, hence the more valuable ones, ran away from their Athenian masters, hard pressed by their defeat in Sicily and the occupation of Deceleum by King Agis and his Spartan troops. Strategy in war included provoking the enemy's slaves to revolt; hence everyone who could somehow manage it would remove his slaves along with the rest of his family over the border for safety when an enemy threatened to invade. The victor at a naval engagement freed the galley slaves and fettered their masters.

Even in time of peace, the nation had to bear the consequences of the fact that all free men in the more highly developed cities and country districts spurned work with all their might. As will be seen, there existed in some places better and more comfortable conditions, but in Attica one knew that as a rule the slaves were malevolent toward their masters. Basically, a slaveholder was protected by the nearness of his neighbor who also owned slaves. Says Plato:

> The citizens serve each other as voluntary bodyguards. Rich townspeople who have many slaves live without fear because the whole city is ready to come to the aid of every single individual. But if some god should transfer an owner of fifty slaves along with his family and all his property out of the city into a wilderness where no stranger would come to his help, what fear he would have that his slaves would dispatch him. He would have to be nice to some, making them promises and freeing them without any cause; he would be the flatterer of his thralls or their sacrificial victim.

A slaveholder whose slaves knew of a wrong he had committed could look upon himself as the most unhappy of all men, being their lifelong hostage and in no position to punish them, no matter what they did; on occasion they might have been liberated for informing on him. It follows that an intelligent slave was even regarded as dangerous, and especially so when tainted with the mentality of free citizens.

The fact that the slaves were barbarians or semi-barbarians a priori qualified the treatment they received. This fact also induced Plato and Aristotle to class them in a low theoretical rank even though their motive is not expressly phrased. That Aristotle was gentle and kindly disposed toward them, as is evident from his last will and testament, redounds all the more to his honor. The slaveholders steeled themselves against pity for the hordes they surrounded themselves with, whose life admittedly was worse than death. Laws prevented the master from deliberately killing and raping his

slaves, perhaps less for their protection than to keep him from brutalizing himself; otherwise he could discipline and mistreat them any way he wished.

A misfortune for all slaves was the very presence of that most wretched class, the mine slaves, who for centuries were ill treated in any way human beings could be. They were provided only with the things needed to keep them alive and in some strength; when not at work, they must have been permanently shackled. Even ordinary slaves were often shackled, not for reasons of discipline but to prevent their escape.

That a slave preferred to be a drudge on a farm to being a menial in a city household was no doubt due to his generally rural origin, and under a sensible master his lot was as bearable as any he could expect if he were to return home. The shepherd slave was probably treated just as well as a hired hand today, because the care of animals depended so much on his good will.

The shepherds of Sicily and lower Italy mentioned by Theocritus were slaves without doubt, but still they, like the farm slaves of Xenophon, had their own property, including sheep and goats, and were able to make pretty gifts. Arcadians gave lavish entertainments to which they invited both masters and their slaves, serving them the same dishes and mixing their wine in the same bowl [*krater*]. Now and then the masters served the slaves at feasts and played dice with them. When the Greeks learned about the Roman Saturnalia, where such was the custom, they found it was a thoroughly Hellenic feast.

The common way of dealing with slaves, according to Xenophon, was to check exuberance through hunger, banish indolence by whiplashes, forestall flight by fetters, and stealing by locking up everything that could be.

Following the Peloponnesian War, the slaves of Athens were bold and free in their demeanor. Their frocks were like those of the *metics* and poorer citizens, so that one could hardly tell them apart because they all had pretty much the same shabby appearance. Often they were better off, thanks to their property, which, to judge by the later comedies, must often have been quite considerable. After the defeat at Chaeronea, the populace at Athens was intent on freeing the slaves, enfranchising the *metics*, and restoring their honors to the dishonored.

At the time of Demosthenes, the slaves were more boldly vocal than the citizens in many cities; it appears that they also attended the theater, now and then took part in the Attic mystery rites, and when partisan spirit ran high, they even pushed their way into the popular assembly.

In highly cultivated Athens, however, the slave could at any moment be most bitterly reminded of his true status. *Some*, says Plato, *do not trust their slaves at all and so goad and whip them much and often, whereby they really enslave their souls*. Moreover, there was also the judicatory torture of slaves, to which one must suppose the Athenians resorted rather often. In lawsuits, even in civil suits, a litigant could submit his own slaves to testify in his behalf under torture or demand that his opponent bring his slaves into court to testify against him under torture.

In connection with his demand that the slaves of his victim Leocrates be tortured, the orator Lycurgus, whose coarse emotional appeals tell us so much about court procedure in the fourth century, calls the torture of slaves by far the most just and appropriate means for getting at the bottom of a case in court. Leocrates refused and thereby supposedly betrayed his bad conscience, as if a humane disposition and kindly feelings for his slaves could have played no part. Perjury and bearing false witness were rife in Athens at that time. To be sure, once torture of slaves became legitimate in court proceedings, it was merely a matter of time before torture could be applied to non-slaves.

The slave remained a commodity, and occasional favors tossed him were only apparent; as for example, putting him as a pedagogue in charge of the children, until they were well along in adolescence. We must also remember that the duty of the pedagogue was essentially negative, that is, to guard and defend the child, while the teachers proper were free men, and especially that, while it was possible to hire a free man as a teacher for a while, particularly if he was a fellow citizen, it was very hard to keep him long, because he was not accustomed to, and hence not fit to live in, this kind of dependence. To pick from a few or many slaves the one best suited for the task should have been fairly easy over a course of years; no doubt mutual trust and attachment obtained between some masters and slaves, as attested by various epitaphs to outstanding slaves, as also to faithful nurses who were likewise bondwomen.

On the whole, slaves who had been freed were not in good odor. It is self-evident that when bad and ungrateful slaves were freed, they hated their master above all people because he had known them in their servitude. In the newer Attic comedy, the freed slave appeared rather frequently as an accuser in court (without doubt against his master), as though the enjoyment of free speech consisted in lodging accusations, and what was typical in comedy must have been commonplace in life. The slave so vexatiously freed in Lucian's *Timon* must no doubt be relegated to the days of Imperial Rome, as well as Trimalchio in Petronius.

Of course there were instances when a slave was given free rein for having mastered a particular skill in a handicraft, skills appearing occasionally but not necessarily as hereditary in a free Greek family.

And finally, it is self-evident that slaves performed all special routine work which the state, particularly the highly organized Athenian state, had to have done. They were the secretaries, lower officials, policemen, etc. The ambitious free man wanted nothing to do with a little office; he was either going to be a demagogue or starve. A man of the demos snatched only at such offices as promised to line his pockets.

5. *The Greek Aristocracy*

Things were simplest in the wake of the Dorian migration when a victorious tribe took possession of the best land and established itself as the ruling aristocracy (Sparta). We may take it for granted that elsewhere the aristocracy developed out of an earlier nobility surrounding a king, or out of such people as had grown wealthy enough to keep horses, or from those especially skilled in war, or even out of a single former royal family (Corinth), and that this aristocracy owned the most and best land, and that it usurped sacerdotal offices and legislature, misusing jurisdiction to the point of selling debtors abroad as slaves (Athens).

The aristocracy was powerful as long as it remained numerous and possession of land was the one deciding factor. The Greek aristocracy never mastered the art of amassing chattel property and exploiting it for itself; by contrast, that of the Phoenician cities appears to have succeeded in this very well. It has already been suggested that the dispossessed citizens formed the main body of the emigrants to the colonies and that slaves were bought to fill the labor requirements.

In the large Greek cities in Asia Minor which had once been colonies, and elsewhere, aristocracy took the form of timocracy [rule by the rich]. Probably this happened in part from deliberate reflection and may have rested on a kind of compact. The duration of the rule of aristocracy, or of the tyranny alternating with it, depended, as will be seen, on the time it took the opposing forces to come into their own. Altogether aristocracy was in power for three or four centuries. In spite of many hostilities and fights on both coasts of the Aegean Sea, this age was one of peace and quiet in comparison with the following. The nobility felt that it comprised a superior caste in the nation; it had not yet become fashionable to use one's peers for personal advancement and then to turn around and destroy them, and this we must keep in mind in connection with that age.

This nobility was not only a political but also a social force which exerted an influence on later Greek culture long after the mansions of nobility had fallen into ruin. The great legacy of the aristocratic period to the nation was *kalokagathia,* that wholly individual fusion of a moral, aesthetic, and material dedication to an idea which we can only intimate, not define sharply; and indeed, the moral and aesthetic accent is rather on the *kalos*, the material on *agathos*, as already in Homer the *agathoi*, the genteel and rich, were contrasted with their inferiors.

That fusion, accomplished in the youthful dawn of a people, was to survive in the mind for as long as there were any Hellenes. Philosophers strove in vain to give a new meaning to *kalokagathia*; the most powerful democratic forces in the poleis could not wipe out this concept, however, and all the elegant speeches about the natural nobility of inner worth left no lasting impression. Belief in noble lineage persisted.

In a way, the life of the aristocrats carried on the heroic age; weapons, bodily exercise, and banquets made up the life of these *nobly excellent* people, insofar as it was not taken up by the state, by sitting on juries, or in performing the rites of worship. A high point of this aristocratic life consisted in sports and especially in horse racing and chariot racing at the celebrated centers of competition. Noble man had made the noble animal, the horse, his companion which accompanied him in war and in sports; the word horse was incorporated in so many family names that this animal was obviously the aristocrat's favorite possession. The keeping of horses was the mark of nobility, and the aspirations of a man who could well afford it and take part in chariot races at the great festivals were of all men's the proudest and most fitting.

To what extent the nobility carried on the intellectual life of the nation can be only hazily determined; tradition deals more kindly with the tyrants at whose courts art and poetry tended to forgather. In turn, aristocratic states had an abundance of privileged individuals who as a group constituted the ideal of Greek life within their centuries: a common government in the state, skill in warfare, splendor in competitive sports, and noble leisure for all these. With them, there began that agonistic mentality, that spirit of competition among equals, which in countless ways permeated all thought and action of the Hellenes.

We hear most about the aristocracy when it was in dissolution in various ways and from various causes, just as we do about the reign of the kings when in decline. It deteriorated when it was no longer able to discipline itself. It turned into an oligarchy by forming a nucleus which usurped not only the power but also the greatest wealth and most important state offices and began to rule in a violent and greedy manner.

Members of the aristocracy failed, as in Sparta, to sustain the ancestral estates as prescribed by various old codes of law. Younger scions of the family became a dangerous element in the state when they were landless or the estate was split up into too many little holdings. Amid violent brawling within the caste, a dangerous number of impoverished aristocrats arose who were keenly aware of their noble ancestry but without the means for living in the noble style. The primary condition for caste survival, however, was that the opportunity for such living be made available to the greatest possible number, because privileges can thrive only when its interested defenders are numerous.

Money and chattel property, industry and trade, thrived better in the hands of the common people. Merchants, industrialists, and shipowners emerged from the ranks of craftsmen and seamen. And as these lower castes —besides the noble *hippeis* [horse owners, knights]—began to assemble armies of *hoplites* for war and to keep their galley slaves constantly ready to sally forth, eventually they had to become the masters of the city. They were no longer bound to their lords through piety because they had become as skilled as anyone else in the art of political argumentation, which at that time produced good or bad constitutions in hundreds of colonies.

The enslavement of debtors was judicially sanctioned and rigorously applied, chiefly by the *eupatrids* in Attica, a procedure as dangerous for themselves as it was cruel and severe. They had enslaved a great many debtors and even sold some into slavery abroad. Members of the demos heavily in debt often had to sell their children. The alleviation Solon brought about in this respect is as important as his constitution.

Exploiting this debtor's code and committing acts of heinous violence could swiftly cause upheaval, introducing tyranny or democracy. Introduction of the latter used to cancel debts, redistribute the land of the rich, free farm serfs and give them equality in the sovereign municipality, forcibly marry off daughters of noblemen to commoners, etc. Theognis, who had experienced all this in Megara, describes circumstantially the grief and resentment of those who had been ruined.

Sending out colonists in large numbers demonstrably failed to save more than one aristocracy from destruction; in fact, such actions may have indirectly contributed to it by increasing the trade with the colonies and thereby the chattel property and the number of inhabitants of the mother city and the defiance associated with this population growth. Miletus, which sent out seventy-five colonies, had to endure terrible crises.

The aristocracies that Aristotle knew were not traditional aristocracies surviving into his day but temporary oligarchies having arisen chiefly in reaction to democracies and also as puppet supports of Sparta. The aristocrats were no longer of the old nobility but of the wealthy who had seized the polis in self-defense. Oligarchs of this kind tried to heap the burden of the state on others and to keep for themselves its dignities and its profits. In his second *Rhetoric* [Rhetorica ad Alexandrum] Aristotle gave later oligarchs some good advice on how to endure. But we do not know whether his advice was followed or whether, in the face of constantly renewed pressure from democracy, it helped any in the long run, even if it was followed.

That earlier, primeval aristocracy represented not merely caste rights or interests but a philosophy of life and a moral system. Pindar, who celebrated this aristocracy, when in most poleis it had lost or was about to lose its grip on the helm, is in a certain sense an abiding memorial to its way of thinking.

6. *The Tyranny*

Aristotle regarded tyranny as an evil offshoot of monarchy and hence treated only its bare essentials, there being no reason to investigate it more thoroughly. But he had no justification for being so brief, for tyranny was unavoidably a part of the Greek concept of the state, and in every talented and ambitious Greek dwelt a tyrant and demagogue.

Above all, one is not to suppose that the kingships developed into tyrannies, nor does Aristotle say they did. Of the very few examples that seem to indicate they did, not even Pheidon of Argos or Arcesilaus III of Cyrene pass muster, as will be seen. Tyranny is much more the lethal disease of the aristocracy. If, when threatened by internal strife, an aristocracy is able to find a temporary umpire, as the nobles of Lesbos did in Pittacus and the patrician *populus* of Rome did in their dictators, then it can still save itself. The tyranny which rises from the masses in the name of the ruled is far more dangerous. It is an anticipated democracy by one man.

Since the polis has unlimited power over its citizens, it possesses it also when personified by a tyrant, who arrogates no more power to himself than the polis exercises at all times anyway, and the citizen may be really no worse off under a tyranny. Often tyrants ably represented their poleis, and the fact that tyranny was widespread over the whole Hellenic world in the seventh and sixth centuries proves that it must have filled some need. It seems obvious that in the course of time conflict arose between the tyrant's rule, which in many cases had become a personal affair, and the wishes and desires of the various classes of the population.

Moreover, the success of this system depended on the personal ability of the individual in power. One may not judge this system by the assertions of later times, when democracy had generally won out and when the tyrants still flourishing were some of the most vicious, like Alexander of Pherae, Clearchus of Heraclea, Dionysius the Elder and Dionysius the Younger.

Tyranny usually started with an aristocrat, perhaps a demoted half-breed like Cypselus, or an Olympic victor in the full flush of his popularity like Cylon; the high-ranking priesthood might also assist as it did the House of Gelon; a commander of a lucky campaign or an occupant of a powerful office might be tempted to seize absolute rule. Somehow one had to achieve a degree of popularity and catch the eye of the people as a future helper, for crowds or bribery pave the way to tyranny.

Bribery might take a very mild form. Peisistratus, a leader in the Megarean War, popular already, was open-handed and threw wide open the portals to his gardens and his estates, thereby rising to the summit of power. Nor did men ambitious of tyranny despise the succor of religious superstition; one even obtained or forged an oracle of Delphi. When Peisistratus usurped power the second time he pulled the well-known trick of driving a tall Greek woman in a chariot to Athens as the goddess Athena, who advised the people to welcome Peisistratus back.

All sorts of coups d'état were used to seize power, depending on the exigencies and the opportunities at hand. The actual seizure tended to be a bloody affair, since it was not merely a matter of changing a government but also of avenging wrong suffered and of cutting off a possible reaction. Phalaris made himself tyrant of Agrigentum in 565 B.C., hardly twenty years after it was founded, by fortifying the Acropolis, on which he as general contractor was building the temple of Zeus, and then, when the people had gathered at a Thesmophoria festival, sallying forth with his workers and killing the males. Two generations later, Theron subjugated the same town after giving the money, entrusted to him for constructing a temple to Athena, to mercenaries kept secretly in readiness.

Polycrates seized Samos at the festival of the goddess Hera in 536 B.C.; his accomplices, marching in the procession, fell upon the others with daggers, while he with the rest of his followers seized the strong points of the city. Members of the overthrown party who survived the uproar had no recourse save hasty flight, or, if lucky, unmolested withdrawal.

On assuming power, the tyrant inevitably had to cancel all debts, since he could not possibly have posed as the legitimate successor to the aristocracy he had partly banished, partly exterminated; although we are expressly told that now and then a decent tyrant held the land and sold it back to those he had banished. Matters no doubt ran their own course when the usurper represented a tribe hitherto downtrodden, as for example, the tyrants of Sicyon; they helped the Ionians to rise over the Dorians again and to take over the council, court, and municipal offices, thus becoming again the ruling people. And while it is not specifically mentioned and is not likely that the Dorians were dispossessed, no doubt the Ionians exploited their advantage by taking over the best land.

Whatever may have been to the advantage of the hitherto suppressed elements, the tyrant would have fulfilled his mission in the eyes of these people as soon as he had secured that advantage for them. To live henceforth as free men no doubt appeared possible to them even without him. Thus he had to learn how much easier it is to seize power than it is to hold it. The freed masses who assisted him by active participation or passive nonintervention were likely to expect or demand a general felicity never found anywhere on earth; in fact, he could hardly even satisfy their most reasonable expectations. He could stay on top only through force; the visible expression of this was the bodyguard of spearmen set up at first against attempts by the deposed to assassinate him but later continued as a protection against the people.

In Greece, those recruited as bodyguards will most likely have been of Grecian stock. Perhaps for the first time in Hellenic history we find here an army detached from the polis and available for any purpose; these *doryphors* [spear bearers] are the forerunners of those powerful mercenary armies of the fourth century.

But there now appeared bold and highly gifted individual tyrants who tried to make a break into the general Greek view of life by praising work, trade, and gainful activities, hitherto all under a curse among the Hellenes.

First, we must mention a peculiar Janus head, Pheidon, King of Argos (about 660 B.C.), stemming from an old line of the Teminids and perhaps thrown into the company of tyrants by a single unscrupulous act. He had seized the management of the Olympic festival and thereby become very popular among the Argives. This ruler, one of the few hereditary ones, an offspring of the Heraclidae, was zealous for trade and commerce, set up standard weights and measures, and probably struck the first Greek coins.

Perhaps more noteworthy and more widely known are the regulations set up by Periander, the second tyrant of Corinth. The city had long been famous for trade and industry and at least the *Bacchanids,* as Strabo reports, had ruthlessly exploited the emporium [trading place]. What he now went about doing had no doubt a political purpose and served to protect the state; in addition it appears also to have had an economic and educational tendency.

He was warlike and constantly on campaigns; he built *triremes* and ruled on both seas, likely because Corinth had to move outward to maintain itself. Whether he used mercenaries is uncertain. He also sent out settlers to establish colonies, not just to get rid of disaffected elements or to provide for sons and bastards, but to assure loyal outposts for his little realm. But, above all, he seems to have subjected his capital to a sharp and considered discipline, something it urgently needed. The Greeks had recently begun to make contact with Egypt, and possibly reports of that country and its caste system stirred him not to let the activity of Corinth go on its own, but to regulate it. The egoism of an ordinary tyrant would hardly have been so far-sighted: He did not allow just anybody to settle in Corinth, he interfered with the purchase of slaves and with their idleness, he always managed to find them some work, and loafers on the *agora* were punished. The reason that had been adduced for the last measure was to quell conspiracies hatched in idleness, but that was not likely his main purpose. Finally, he set up a board to restrain people from spending beyond their income. It is very clear that he shuddered at the proliferation of a big city and that he had no ambition to keep watch over a gigantic mass of people. Hence Corinth was to rise above a life of unrestrained enjoyment, and if he forbade lavish banquets, as is asserted, then he did so less because they might have been centers of conspiracy (dangerous conspirators need no such occasions) than because they might well have degenerated into immoderate revelry.

The Corinthians were to be industrious and relatively equally prosperous *banausics* [artisans] protected externally by the might of the state. The ruler had no need to fear such people and may have even regarded their interests as his own. That the purchase of slaves was only curbed, not stopped, admits of various interpretations: as to house slaves, the oriental pomp and host of luxury slaves were to cease; as to factory slaves, the rise of excessively sprawling industries and the concomitant overgrowth of the city were to be halted.

Periander ruled Corinth without collecting any direct taxes, making do with collections at the ports and market place. Polycrates of Samos, who climbed to power much later and much more wickedly, and pursued an impulsive and quixotic course in politics, nevertheless hoped to win the Samian masses by capturing many islands and mainland cities, by plundering friend and foe and then sharing the prizes of war with the people, and by expanding the trade with Egypt. It was certainly popular to see captives of Lesbos dig the whole moat around the wall of the capital. Every mother who had lost a son in war he put under the care of a rich Samian: *I give you this one to be your mother.*

Peisistratus got Athens into his power while a great political and social upheaval over Solon's constitution had by no means subsided but was still in full flood; in many respects he appears to have conceived his duties much as Periander did: the Athenian state protected externally by his power, by alliances, and by strongholds abroad, and internally secured by labor and trade. He returned the people who had been attracted by the magnet of the city and were lounging around there, back to their farms: *Why are you idle? If your harness team died, accept another from me and go to work! If you have no seed, I shall give you some.* In addition he had a genuine taste for the magnificent, a decidedly fascinating personality, and a brilliant intellect.

Many cities jointly supported him with money the third time he seized power in 541 B.C., showing that they must have had a high confidence in his success and significance for Greece. The chief tribute he and his sons exacted of the Athenians was an income tax of only 5 per cent, with which they adorned the city and defrayed the cost of their wars and sacrifices; to be sure we are not told that the people voted to pay this tax, but unless they had been in favor of it it would have been hard to collect.

Tyrannies of this sort are the exact opposite of the Spartan ideal, which was abundance of leisure and of the *kalokagathia* of the aristocrats, which some tyrants might pre-empt for themselves, attending the great athletic festivals. Some, like Phaedon, might even compel games to be held under their supervision, or institute new games, as Periander allegedly instituted the Isthmian games and Cleisthenes the Pythian games, insofar as these were not already centers where *agonistic* festivals of the Muses were held.

It was of course inevitable, and for such clever men foreseeable, that their subjects, to the extent that they were free, would through trade and industry develop security and a spirit of independence which might finally overturn the tyranny. Perhaps they relied on the hunch of the people that only pleasure and profit suffer through the abolition of tyranny. Something more, however, than mere calculation lived in these communities, namely, the image of some kind of aristocratic or even democratic polis. The gold-and-gilt statue of Zeus set up at Olympia by Cypselus, the marvelous fountain of Theognis at Megara, the *Olympieum* [temple of the Olympian Zeus] of Peisistratus, the debt to him and to his sons for collecting and redacting Homer and perhaps for promoting the Attic Theater, the body of useful artificers Polycrates gathered about him at great expense, the useful animals they imported—all these could not avert the relatively premature downfall of these tyrants. And yet the most famous poets of that age sought out these courts and praised them, and we find Arion with Periander, Ibycus and Anacreon with Polycrates, Simonides and Anacreon with Hipparchus, to say nothing of the Sicilian tyrants of the fifth century with whom Simonides, Pindar, Aeschylus and Bacchylides were present either personally or in their songs. In cordial frankness, Pindar teaches us that these poets were not necessarily flatterers.

We have such fragmentary information about the older Ionic and Aeolic tyrants at Ephesus, Miletus, Cymae, etc., that we cannot possibly get a sure and consistent notion about either their rise and fall in relation to the aristocracies, or the nature of their rule, which according to legend was very harsh.

The great and general danger threatening every tyranny, as already said, lay in the desire of the free men or the aristocrats to be the polis. However brisk private life and all its enjoyments, and however mild the political and police control might be, people did not want to be ruled from above, and were especially vexed at the tyrants for trying to get them to engage in useful work. The Greeks were not disposed to live in mere little Carthages or to turn Persian in city after city, which is precisely the danger they faced in states without a citizenry. In the meanwhile, these tyrants, obviously alert to the threat, formed a kind of alliance among themselves and wished tyrants might take over other cities.

Almost from the outset, Sparta, for reasons given above, was hostile and dangerous; moreover, tyranny had no built-in safeguards. The Greeks noted, above all, that the dynasties had a short duration, as though it were willed so by a higher power. The oracle knew this ahead of time, and later the saying was:

> Divinity does not allow tyrannies to reach the third generation,
> but fells them like pine trees or strips them of their sons; of all
> the tyrannies only that of the Cypselides, that of Hiero, and that
> of the Leuconides on the Cimmerian Bosporus passed on to the
> grandchild. (Aelian V. H. VI 13.)

The tyrants ruled more severely toward the end because their opponents became bolder and more aggressive. These opponents may have been the old suppressed parties surviving abroad in the form of children or grandchildren or only in the form of this or that powerful family. The Alcmaeonidae in exile were still rich enough to adorn the temple at Delphi, committed to them, with Parian marble instead of travertine and to bribe the Pythia to take sides against Hippias, inducing this oracle to prophesy to the Spartans that Hippias would perish. The house of Periander came to an end in 581 B.C. when conspirators of the nobility murdered Psammetichus, his grandson and successor. Furthermore, they demolished the palace of the tyrant, abolished the Cypselidae, and emptied all the family graves.

The later chroniclers were usually content to let the tyrant perish by some act of personal revenge, supposedly given higher sanction by ethical or political motives. Aristotle treats this subject in much detail and says that the tyrant provokes the attack by some crime, i.e., *hybris,* linked with some shameful misdeed; he adds that the three chief motives for this liberating act are hate, contempt, and love of fame. The assassination of Hipparchus carried off the ablest of the Peisistratidae; Hippias got away unscathed, though a few years later his death brought that dynasty to an end. Some hereditary tyrants also voluntarily abdicated out of a sense of decency. Less edifying is the story of Aristagoras, who laid aside his rule of Miletus while at the same time delivering up his fellow tyrants in their respective cities.

Most remarkable events occurred on Samos after Polycrates was nailed to a cross in Magnesia in 522 B.C. He had left Meandrius, his private secretary, in full charge of the island. Meandrius, however, did not want to rule but merely to save his skin after having compromised himself by taking over a priestly office. It was nothing uncommon for the priestly offices associated with the kings in heroic times to continue under the aristocracies, e.g., the *archon basileus* in Athens.

When the reign of Polycrates suddenly came to an end, Samos was thrown into an uproar. Meandrius, who had set up an altar to Zeus the deliverer and had marked a sacred precinct around it, announced to the popular assembly that he was not taking over but instead proclaimed equality of rights, asking for himself only six *talents* and the hereditary priesthood of his sacred shrine; thereupon the people, wildly threatening vengeance, clamored for an accounting of his office. Now, reflecting that if he did not become tyrant another would, he recklessly seized despotic power.

The mantle of tyranny passed either, as in this case, to a new tyranny, or, as in Athens, to a democracy long since taking shape; or, as elsewhere in the sixth century, to some kind of aristocracy.

The Sicilian tyrants comprised a special group. Unhappily, we are but ill informed about those that appeared before the fifth century. In his great historical opus Diodorus, at the time of Augustus, dealt very circumstantially with the vicissitudes of his lovely and unfortunate native island, working with sources that were quite excellent. That part of the history covering the early period in question was in books six to ten, now lost.

Having settled Sicily with colonies, the Greeks effectively ruled over the native Sicanians, Sicelians, etc., from the eighth century on; the Phoenicians held only three cities in the northwest. In the several Greek poleis, tyrants arose almost at the beginning, like Panaetius in Leontini who won over the foot soldiers against the rich and the horse riders and, after butchering these off, seized the rule in 680 B.C. We have already discussed Phalaris and Agrigentum, although after him the city appears to have become an aristocracy under legitimate leaders. But toward the end of the sixth century tyranny rapidly increased, as though it were a matter of course, and all this happened without any necessity of strengthening national defense, in fact, even before any Carthaginian army was on the island.

The internal confusion these tyrants exploited in coming to power derived from the inequalities among the people; the descendants of the original colonists owned the land or most of it (whether Dorians, Ionians, or some other racial group), and maybe they pre-empted all the civil rights in the state, excluding submerged immigrants and the original native population which later had been enslaved.

The people managed to get rid of a tyrant and perhaps a second one, as for instance in Selinus where Pythagoras, with the aid of Euryleon, a Spartan adventurer, overthrew the tyrant and then killed Euryleon at the altar of Zeus in the agora soon after he had usurped the tyranny. Gelo treated human beings and cities like inanimate commodities and sold members of the demos he had subjugated abroad into slavery. This was the only way for him to go about it if he wanted to establish a large state with Syracuse as its capital, for the individual cities on their own would never have put their hearts into any such scheme; left to themselves they would have remained republics or tyrannies, but already Carthage was approaching, a terrible confederate for such as had hoped to remain independent at all costs.

Through his mighty victory on the banks of the Himera in 480 B.C., Gelo emerged as the savior of the Greek nation and was subsequently able to render account and submit his resignation to the popular assembly, but the assembly refused it amid wild acclaim. When dying, he was able to install his brother Hiero as his successor (478 B.C.), and the latter continued, as indicated above, to mingle and transplant peoples in madcap fashion.

Theron, of Agrigentum, with whom Hiero scrupulously kept the peace, carried on in the same way in his little domain. Both dynasties supposed that they would achieve a sense of security only by recruiting powerful mercenary armies, which were garrisoned in Syracuse, Agrigentum, and in annexed cities, or even made into citizens of these places. Hiero's was a harsh and money-mad reign, and that intellectual pursuits could have lent some luster to it he never properly understood. At death he left the rule to a brother with a reputation for truculence; in a short time he was tossed out by a revolt but was permitted to go freely to Italy.

The disturbances in the democracy were so violent in Syracuse that they inevitably led to internecine hostilities, the consequence of which was the famous Athenian intervention (415–413 B.C.). The victory of the Syracusans, even though with Spartan help, saved them from Athenian intentions of selling them into slavery. This Sicilian campaign also threatened Carthage, however indirectly, thereby arousing her, and when Athens was fatally crippled, Carthage decided to throw everything she had into the capture of Sicily. After Silenunt, Himera, and Agrigentum had fallen most lamentably (408 B.C.), Dionysius arose as a tyrant in Syracuse (405–367 B.C.) wallowing in turmoil; intrinsically his reign was typical of the newer tyrannies sprung from democracies.

Meanwhile, events on the island ran the following course. After all that had happened a voluntary alliance of free cities against Carthage was impossible. Dionysius posed as the protecting shield of Hellenism against the Hamitic barbarians, and he impressed the powerful Greek cities on the mainland and the rest of the Hellenes until it became clear that he was not trying to annihilate the Carthaginians but purposely spared them so that he would remain indispensable for those whom fear of Carthaginian slavery drove into his arms. In treaties with the Carthaginians he ceded great old cities to them, declared others under tribute to them, and brutally subjugated the rest for himself.

He turned some of these over to brutal mercenaries to massacre the inhabitants and to settle the area themselves. He sold the inhabitants of other cities into slavery or transferred them to Syracuse, the only large city under despotism which after varying reigns of terror finally enjoyed peace and quiet in the later decades of Dionysius' rule. He razed a number of poleis because he could not have held them in check and so merely ruled over these territories; and furthermore, he prevented revolt by setting up a secret police (Plutarch *Dion* 29) to spy on the people. He undertook expeditions to southern Italy and to Etruria to plunder cities and temples in order to replenish his finances. He removed many sacred treasures, including a golden mantle from a statue of Zeus, observing with humorous mockery, "You see how the immortal gods favor sacrilege."

When Dionysius died in 367, he imagined that he was leaving an iron-clad tyranny to his son, and such it was as far as the finances and the military might were concerned, for he was supported by four hundred *triremes,* ten thousand infantry recruits, ten thousand cavalry men, and several myriad of *hoplites.* His family affairs, however, might well have caused him worry. After his first wife had perished miserably in a revolt in Syracuse, he had a double wedding on the same day, marrying Doris of Locri and Aristomache, daughter of Hipparinus of Syracuse. The former bore him three children, the latter four. He married half-brother to half-sister without any fear of consequences, e.g., his son Dionysius by Doris to his daughter Sophrosyne by Aristomache; he also married a daughter by Aristomache to a younger brother of hers, Dion. It was obvious that these relations would lead to rivalries.

And now the tyranny was to pass on to his son, still very young, whom his father had carefully sheltered from associating with persons unsuited for the future tyrant, but had failed to endow him with the qualifications appropriate to that office. Beside him stood the remarkable figure of Dion, who had happened to land in this environment, but who possessed such peculiarly strong and characteristic qualities of Hellenism that he is worth a closer scrutiny.

As the brother-in-law of Dionysius the Elder and as an eyewitness of the cruel destiny of the Sicilian cities, he should have despaired utterly, fled, or committed suicide. The situation in Syracuse was actually such that any undoing or even relaxing of the tyranny would have unleashed the enslaved and brought about a wild turmoil. Now, Plato had been known by reputation in Syracuse for quite some time. Dion invited him to come from Tarentum and presented him to the tyrant. Although Plato barely escaped with his life, he succeeded in imbuing Dion with his political ideals and with blind hope.

We do not know precisely what plans Dion had in mind for the individual cities; still a hazy image of an aristocratic state modeled on Laconia and Crete hovered before his eyes, and all his activity shows that he was convinced he could improve conditions in the cities, even the very worst of them. He lived in hopes of inheriting the tyranny some day to do away with it. As long as his brother-in-law lived, he had only to perform his commands, which were neither mild nor just, and by marrying his daughter he gave earnest of good behavior. When Dionysius the Younger succeeded to the tyranny, he received excellent advice from Dion and was enthusiastic about him, but courtiers whose objectives were indirectly promoted by Dionysius' gruffness and dogmatism (deprecated also by Plato) soon persuaded him to beware of Dion's guardianship.

At any rate, Dion managed to have Plato urgently invited to Syracuse a second time; it was supposedly his secret hope that through his influence Plato would soften the despotic ways of the tyrant and turn him into a regent with respect for the laws; or, if this failed, he would unsaddle Dionysius and turn the city over to the Syracusans, for even though municipal democracy was little to his liking, tyranny was even less so.

Plato came and in a short time seems to have won the enthusiasm of Dionysius and his court, but at the same time the opposition party was very active. It won out and had Philostus, the historian and representative of the theoretical and practical politics of tyranny, recalled from the exile imposed by Dionysius the Elder. It also succeeded in letting fall into the hands of the tyrant a highly compromising letter it had forged, ostensibly from Dion to the Carthaginian government, in which he promised them a favorable peace if they would turn to him. The tyrant put him on a boat and transferred him to Italy without giving him an opportunity to defend himself. Officially he was not in exile, only absent, and he regularly received his money, enabling him to live in a grand style, all of which does honor to Dionysius.

Dion went to Athens and Plato followed soon after; there he spent his time mostly in the Academy. At the recommendation of Plato, he associated with Plato's nephew Speusippus and deliberately cultivated charm and a pleasing character. He went to other cities and associated everywhere with the best and politically most astute, i.e., the adversaries of the current exponents of democracy. Various cities decreed him honors and the Spartans conferred citizenship on him, for they had enjoyed Syracusan help in the war against Thebes, although after the battle at Leuctra that aid had little significance. He was also initiated into the Eleusinian mysteries, his sponsor being Kallipos, his Athenian host, who later murdered him.

All this aroused the distrust and envy of Dionysius, who cut off his further supply of money. Dionysius, however, wanted Plato back by all means and even applied to the Italian Pythagoreans for support. Since he made every concession to Dion depend on Plato's reappearance, the philosopher decided to make a third journey to Syracuse. But here his employment was so fruitless, and after a year his relations with the tyrant so tense, that he had trouble making it back to Athens unharmed. One gets the impression that Dionysius invited Plato as a scheme to keep Dion on his good behavior.

Without any consideration whatsoever Dionysius now sold Dion's property, took away his wife and married her to another man, and debauched his younger son so that Dion hardly had any choice except to attempt forcibly to overthrow the tyranny. Speusippus and most of his other friends in the Academy encouraged him, although Plato held back, and in Sicily the news must have spread that Dion was expected to return. The virtuous Dion had no recourse now save to recruit an army of mercenaries, for of the thousands who had fled from Syracuse only twenty-five had the courage to support him.

At first others secretly recruited for him on the island of Zacynthus, including politicians and philosophers who enlisted for him the seer Miltas, a former student at the Academy. When these mercenaries discovered the aim of their campaign, they were shocked and were kept from disbanding by the prospect of being leaders of Syracusan soldiers rather than being ordinary soldiers themselves and by the spectacle of Dion's wealth displayed in a gigantic sacrifice to Apollo.

They embarked, and after being whipped around by a storm, put to land at Ecnomus in southern Sicily. At that time Dionysius was in Italy. Having been joined by inhabitants of Syracuse and by people who had fled or been transferred from Agrigentum, Gelo, and Camarina, Dion marched unmolested to Syracuse. Since the garrison at Epipolae had been lured away by a false report, he made his entry without bloodshed. The foremost citizens went in solemn procession to meet him, and his heralds announced that he was coming to overthrow the tyranny and to free the Syracusans and the rest of the Siceleotes.

The opposition party held out in the castle where they were joined eight days later by Dionysius. Even though Plutarch forgets to mention it, the fighting in and about Syracuse inevitably must have started the dissolution of the Syracusan government and gradually ushered in those terrible conditions that Timoleon found later.

While his soldiers were besieging the Acropolis, Dion was constantly harried by demagogues, and this created great unrest among the vile and unhappily mingled populace of Syracuse. The favorite was a certain Heracleides, a Syracusan fugitive who had already worked against Dion on the Peloponnesus. This Heracleides arrived with seven *triremes* and some other ships in the harbor of Syracuse, right after Dionysius' company of soldiers had sallied forth from the castle and been repulsed, an engagement in which Dion had distinguished himself, and right after Dion had publicly read a letter from Dionysius wherein he had used threats and promises in an effort to compromise him. Heracleides appraised the situation at once and decided to undo the tyranny on his own.

Through his demagoguery and by stirring up suspicions against every step Dion had taken, he succeeded in getting the populace to elect him *nauarch* [commander of the fleet] against the will of Dion. Nevertheless, after the people had taken the franchise into their own hands and voted him in, Dion found it inadvisable to remove him. Then Heracleides succeeded in destroying a small flotilla under Philistus who was bringing Dionysius reinforcements from Japygia, and the populace began to find Dion's mercenaries superfluous and to expect everything from Heracleides. He, however, did not succeed in capturing Dionysius, which would have pleased the populace most. Indeed, Dionysius rejected an offer to capitulate to the Syracusans lusting after his blood. With his most important and most valuable possessions, he managed to sail away unobserved to Italy, leaving his son Apollocrates in charge of the castle.

Precisely his failure to intercept Dionysius prompted Heracleides to promise the people fulfillment of their utmost desires; hence he instigated Hippo, another ambitious contender, to call upon the demos to share in a redistribution of the land, since equality of possession was the root of all freedom and impoverishment the root of all slavery. Dion's protests against these proposals foundered on the resistance put up by these intriguers.

Heracleides persuaded the people to withhold the pay of Dion's mercenaries and to elect generals inimical to him. When these plotters tried to draw troops away from Dion by offering them Syracusan citizenship, he decided to leave the city and take his mercenaries to Leontini. As he was departing, the insolent mob assailed him. He pointed out that the enemy still held the castle and tried by bloodless feints to hold the crowd off, but they persisted in attacking until finally he had to meet force with force.

The Syracusans became more and more reckless, and having vanquished a fleet under Nypsius sent by Dionysius they caroused until deep into the night. The generals did not dare to discipline the drunken crowds. Suddenly, at the head of barbarian mercenaries, this same Nypsius pressed into Syracuse killing and robbing. The only hope lay in Dion and his troops; so, having stewed for quite a while in their own hot shame at having to acknowledge their blunder, the confederates and knights spoke up for recalling Dion. The deputation to Leontini reported tearfully the general reversal of sentiment, and Dion led it to the popular assembly in the theater where, on his recommendation, the people voted to pull up stakes and march to Syracuse.

But in the meantime Nypsius withdrew to the Acropolis. The demagogues had a breathing spell, and succeeded once more in turning the crowd against Dion, thus preventing his entry into Syracuse. It took another and much more frightful attack by Nypsius to show that Dion was indispensable. Dionysius, having despaired of regaining his tyranny, desired that this office should be buried in and with the city, and must have sent new orders to Nypsius to let the city go up in a general conflagration. Hence Heracleides had to implore Dion to come in all haste. Appearing as a savior and god and his mercenaries as brothers and fellow citizens, Dion, after hard fighting, succeeded in driving the foe from the Acropolis and in extinguishing the flames.

How insecure his position still was would soon appear. While the rest of the demagogues had fled at Dion's victory, Heracleides had eloquently commended himself to Dion's magnanimity, and Dion pardoned him, much against the advice of his friends, who thought he should turn over the evil and envious man to his mercenaries. Heracleides in turn proposed in popular assembly to make Dion commander in chief of land and naval forces. The best people were for it, but nothing came of this proposal because the bulk of the lesser folk did not want to part with an admiral pleasing to them. Dion had to be content with the people giving up their resolve to redistribute the land.

But now Heracleides exploited the unpopular decision not to redistribute the land. At Messina, whither he had sailed, he incited his soldiers and sailors against Dion as being ambitious for the tyranny. At the same time he concluded a secret agreement with Pharax, a Lacedaemonian leader of mercenaries in the service of Dionysius, stationed in the vicinity of Agrigentum. The treacherous insinuation that Dion was concerned only with prolonging his command forced him to fight under unfavorable conditions.

While he was about to launch a second attack, Heracleides returned to Syracuse with his fleet to shut him out of the city again. Dion managed to get into the city with his cavalry just in the nick of time, but was not powerful enough to reject a reconciliation with Heracleides, mediated by Gaisylus, a Spartan adventurer who in the meantime had arrived in Syracuse. Heracleides had to swear solemn oaths which, if broken, Gaisylus was to avenge. A better guarantee for his subordination was the resolution of the

Syracusans to disband their fleet as useless, expensive, and constantly tempting the admirals to revolt.

And now finally the time came when Apollocrates was forced to surrender the Acropolis because of hunger and dejection and to flee with his mother and sister in five loaded *triremes* to his father, Dionysius. Great jubilation reigned in the city, and Dion was once more united with his sister Aristomache, his son, and his wife Acete, whom he took back, deeply moved, despite her enforced marriage to another. He rewarded his friends and helpers richly and established himself modestly.

Plato wrote to him that all the world had its eyes on him, but he is said to have had his eyes fixed only on the Academy, and to wish it would approve of his prudence and restraint in the conduct of his affairs. Despite Plato's warning he refused to give up any of his dignified aloofness and be more affable and friendly with the people.

He was now faced with the task of drawing up a constitution, and his ideal was a monarchy along Spartan lines, i.e., a mixture of democracy and monarchy, with aristocracy holding the crucial balance of power. It appeared impossible to attain this goal as long as Heracleides was around, for he was again engaged in intrigue. He refused to take part in a session of the popular assembly on the grounds that he was only a private citizen, and he also grumbled because Dion had not demolished the Acropolis and dishonored the grave of Dionysius the Elder. He insisted that Dion should send for co-workers and co-regents from Corinth.

Earlier in life Dion had maintained that no evil in man is so deep-dyed that repeated kindness will not remove it, but the behavior of Heracleides made him alter this view. At least, he permitted those who had long been intent upon it to assassinate Heracleides in his home. Dion then accorded him an honorable funeral, at which he addressed the army, explaining that the city could not have had peace as long as they were both active in it.

Since the demos now had no acknowledged leader, a new aspirant arose from among the men in his immediate entourage in the person of Callippus, the Athenian, who felt he might try for the rule of Sicily as the prize of battle. This dubious friend, who reportedly got twenty talents from the Carthaginian enemies for murdering his host, suborned some of Dion's mercenaries for his own cause and himself related to Dion what these soldiers said or allegedly said. Dion then charged Callippus to go and talk disrespectfully about him to the soldiers so as to ferret out the evil-minded ones. In this fashion Callippus discovered the vicious elements useful to him.

If anyone told Dion about Callippus' slanderous talk, he said nothing inasmuch as he had himself ordered him to do it. But Callippus began spreading the rumor that since Dion had lost his son he was thinking about naming Apollocrates, Dionysius' son, as his successor, and suspicion about him grew apace. But Dion, whose mind had been gloomy since the assassination of Heracleides, which he regarded as a foul blot on his life, said he was ready to die and would gladly submit to the cutthroat rather than live in continual fear of friends as well as enemies. Finally, when Callippus perceived that the women of the family were suspicious and wary of him, he quieted them with a fearful oath. But he saw that he would have to act quickly.

While Dion was banqueting in a hall with some friends, the conspirators surrounded him and barred the doors and windows. Then the Zacynthians, obviously Dion's mercenaries suborned to murder him, pressed in, fell upon him and, being unarmed, for all who entered the house were searched, tried to strangle him. Dion defended himself and the struggle lasted long, for neither his friends inside nor those outside had the courage to help him since all wanted to save their own lives by waiting to see who would come out on top. Finally a Syracusan handed a dagger through a window to a Zacynthian and thus they cut Dion's throat as if he were a sacrificial animal. Aristomache and Arete were imprisoned, and Callippus seized control of the government.

After Dion was murdered, his followers bestirred themselves and executed some persons unjustly taken to be his murderers. The very same people who had declared Dion a tyrant now praised him as a savior and deliverer; nor could Callippus prevent them from giving him a magnificent funeral and honoring him with a monument.

Nepos, who apprises us of Dion's subsequent popularity, also tells us something deliberately suppressed in documents which are enthusiastic for Dion, namely, that after the death of Heracleides, Dion divided the wealth of his recognized opponents among his own mercenaries without scruple and, when in need of more, he subjected even his friends to tribute. This captivated his army but alienated the respectable citizens. Although he did not aspire to be a tyrant, he could not dispense with tyrannical methods if he wanted to stay in power at all. For this reason, the people adjudged him an insufferable tyrant, and he was severely criticized also by those whose opinions he valued.

Callippus, we read, began with a brilliant reign but lost Syracuse in only ten months, when he marched out to capture Catana. Thereupon, having to leave Sicily, he went to southern Italy where he finally occupied Rhegium, but lacked money to pay his soldiers. He is supposed to have been murdered with the same dagger that cut down Dion. The government of Syracuse passed to Hipparinus, son of Aristomache and half-brother of Dionysius, then soon after to Nysaeus when Hipparinus was murdered, and finally to Dionysius himself who returned to the capital from Locri where he had been tyrant.

At the same time there arose in various cities lesser tyrants in league with the now nearby Carthaginians. Timoleon of Corinth then came to Sicily and drove all the tyrants, including Dionysius and the Carthaginians, into the western corner of the island. Again fugitives returned, Greek colonists poured into Sicily, and democracies were established in relatively populous cities. But not long after Timoleon's death, disturbances and disorder arose similar to those following the departure of the old tyrannies.

Twenty years later there came into power Agathocles, who seems to have combined the tyrannical might of a Dionysius with the grandiose daring of a military commander and adventurer. This ghastly but fascinating figure gives the impression of having embodied the intellectual and moral strength but also all the forsworn wickedness of later Hellenism. Hardly another character in history evokes such admiration and loathing. At seventy-two he ascended like another Heracles a pyre, having been poisoned at the instigation of a grandson.

In contemplating the history of Sicily we descend from one circle to another as in Dante's hell. The poleis put up a most fierce resistance to Agathocles to preserve their autonomy; their will to live had not yet been bled to death. But in the third century plundering mercenaries, individual tyrants, and Carthaginians rampaged about madly, no one recognizing a possible deliverer in Pyrrhus.

What Hiero II, elevated by the soldiers of Syracuse, might have accomplished in the long run remains uncertain. It was about time the Romans, after initial enmity, took him over and the island also, however wretched the lot of the island subsequently was as a Roman province. The specifically Greek poleis perished, but the Hellenic element, the rest of the Greek nationality, was saved from the Africans.

The last tyrannies were those of the later Antigonid period, but we prefer here to limit ourselves to those in Greece (Elis, Sicyon, Argos, Megalopolis, etc.). As long as the democracies were able to devour the wealthy, to cancel debts, and to redistribute the land, they needed no tyrants. Under tyrants the spoils of division went to the mercenaries instead of to the people, but strife, impatience, and iniquity caused the rise of democracies nevertheless.

Such tyrannies, however, can hardly be called governments, using as they did any and all means to preserve themselves. Now they were supported by the Antigonids and now again harassed and abandoned. Corinth alternated between tyrants and Macedonian garrisons. The Achaean League made it one of its chief duties to get rid of these tyrants.

But when events were propitious tyrannies kept emerging with the first demagogue or adventurer adroit enough to turn the trick. The upheaval at the beginning was the mildest step. Next, the rich were inevitably banished or killed and their property given partly to the tyrant's followers, partly to his mercenary guards. The men of Gaul were everywhere regarded as the only reliable mercenaries. The *diadochi* enlisted them as the only recruits to be relied on for victory, and whenever they could afford them the tyrants made the most of this valuable race of men.

Murder and confiscation, however, sufficed for only a short time to nourish this host. To arm and endow the proletariat would have furnished questionable support. The tyrant who had granted a redistribution of land was not needed to keep the banished and fugitive folk from making an incursion. Another man served equally well in his place, as the rapid upheavals of office amply proved. It was in the nature of things that nothing could satisfy the greed of the state-supported crowds who therefore constantly provoked new political upsets.

No wonder that milder tyrants, with little or no blood on their hands, thanked the gods when they were able to turn their weary power over to the almost equally weary Achacan League. Others, who had committed some heinous deeds, lived in deadly fear of *doryphors* [spearmen], weapons, gateways, and trapdoors, and even so they succumbed to murder.

Now and then, we are told, philosophers instigated and carried out these assaults, for with the death of other potential aspirants, philosophers found themselves at that time taking a more active part in public life. After decreeing the most abominable proscriptions, the tyrant Abantidas of Sicyon supposed he could still discourse with philosophers in the agora, but he was killed by them and their adherents, very much as Clearchus of Heraclea was. This time, as it so frequently happened, they merely changed tyrants. But when democratic conspirators succeeded in killing the tyrant in his home or even at an altar to the gods in the agora, they proclaimed that the citizens were free, destroyed the castle, and ignominiously butchered the family or let them commit suicide. It was an old practice to take the most frightful vengeance on the tyrant's wife and children, to wipe out the dynasty.

Among other accomplishments, Aratus, leader of the Achaean League, was able to liberate his native Sicyon. Early in the morning the theater was packed until the herald appeared and announced in behalf of Aratus that the citizens were free. There were citizens who took their spectator role literally. When this same Aratus was battling a tyrant around Argos, the Argives sat quietly and looked on impartially, as though it had not been a matter of their freedom but merely that of judging events at the Nemean games. Severely wounded, Aratus had to withdraw this time. He then laid waste to Argolis, which helped neither his cause nor theirs. (This is not the place to deal with the fortunes of democracy at that time.) Before Rome stepped in and prevented further mutual extermination, Sparta suffered what was likely the most frightful of all tyrannies at any time, outside of Sicily, that of Nabis (206–192 B.C.).

At the time of the Roman emperors, when one could survey the entire line of Hellenic tyrants, Lucian summed up in the figure of his Megapenthes all those conventional traits of the later and purely evil tyrants which the orators had popularized. Elsewhere, Lucian discloses the admiration the Greeks had for everything not inherited but achieved by personal determination and energy. Historical research should always pay attention to the uninhibited wishes expressed by wags in the poesy of bygone peoples. We need only listen to Lucian's *Samippus: I would not want to be a hereditary king like Alexander or Mithridates, but become one as a brigand with thirty trusty fellows until there are five myriads of us, and then conquer Greece or over- run Asia.* (cf. Lucian Navigium 28 and Kataplus.)

7. Democracy and Its Development in Athens

All deliberate reflection on state politics tends to make for equality in the broadest sense. To how many human relations this equality will be extended depends on the circumstances. Kingship and aristocracy rested on original conquest and on unmistakable authority; tyranny on actual seizure with the pretense of seeing to the interests of all against the exploiting few. Now we shall look at Greek states where reflection was not only actively but inevitably determinative at their very founding.

These were the colonies. Here for the first time the Hellenes applied their natural talents to setting up new political institutions, taking the various elements and forces into consideration. They did not proceed in a brute fashion, but considered fairly the different constituents comprising a colony. Here the office of lawgiver takes on a new meaning. Whereas Theseus and Lycurgus are mythical, that is to say personal embodiments of social and political developments, now there arise individuals delegated by the group to draw up laws and constitutions. Such were the famous Greeks Charondas and Zaleukus. On some occasions the oracle at Delphi would send an "arranger" to a lawless colony, such as Demonax of Mantinea who was sent to Cyrene.

In the mother country the same forces and desires were active, though only in reshaping the state from an aristocracy or tyranny into a democracy. On the dividing ridge of time we find Athens with Solon (594 B.C. seq.)

who arranged matters so that the whole citizenry could vote for the nine *archons*. Eligibility to this office, however, did not extend to owners of chattel property but was limited to wealthier landholders who in fact were mostly of the traditional nobility.

It is an honor to Athens that it not only produced such a man but also trusted and obeyed him, at least during the transition period. This can be explained only by the inner maturity this highly gifted people had attained under the rule of the *eupatrids*. To be sure the tyranny of Peisistratus and his sons followed, but then after Cleisthenes there came a period of rapid transformation leading to a full-fledged democracy. It would be well to center our attention now on Athens.

First of all we meet with a clear insight that it is not feasible to turn over the government of the state to all citizens indiscriminately, whether they want it or not. At all events, subsequent leaders of the state sought to provide the widest possible participation in state affairs by the citizens. These could now annually elect the Senate of five hundred, fifty representatives from each of the ten *phylae,* fifty of whom held office for thirty-five days at a time. Moreover, they could select the Popular Court of five thousand which was subdivided into several chambers and which was now ready to give a hearing to all appeals. At the same time, the number of citizens was increased by enfranchising foreigners and *metics*. Euboea was conquered and divided into four thousand parcels on which Athenian citizens were settled by lot.

We cannot fully ascertain to what extent Cleisthenes and his followers continued or determined policy which Athenians, once committed to, would not relinquish. Every Athenian who was a citizen in the full sense of the term was considered qualified for every office, and hence members of the Senate were subsequently no longer elected but chosen by lot. This procedure eliminated both continuity of personnel and the formation of a class of functionaries, and at the same time all advantages and disadvantages accruing from a system of tenure.

Each man to whom the lot fell was examined by the Senate as to his life and character, his behavior toward his own family and in society, his participation in military campaigns, his record of law obedience, etc., but not as to his knowledge or special ability for the office. If one's answers were inadequate or if anyone raised any complaints against him, the Senate either turned the case over to a popular court or decided the matter itself.

At all events, this period, with democracy standing on its own feet, differs in one main particular from the age of the Peisistratidae: in the former period the finances were in the hands of the government, in the latter they were entrusted to ambitious men who knew how to exploit the state. Aristides, however, stands out as a remarkably honest man among them.

Themistocles may have been great and capable, yet he regarded it as perhaps his main achievement to have augmented an inheritance of three talents into a hundred, or at least into eighty. From the beginning finances were in the hands of cliques, and they continued so as long as one can historically pursue their internal workings. For the personality of Themistocles, Herodotus found a tradition already fully established. Athens saw itself delineated in him, hence his brilliant patriotic recklessness in the Persian War, and other individual traits putting one in mind of Alcibiades. He had

Victor with flutist and village elder
Vase painting

spurred on the demos against the highborn, inciting it to impudence. He reaped a golden harvest on the side by despoiling those who had had Persian sympathies during the war. What did he want to use all this money for? Did he have a *coup d'état* in mind? From the fate of Miltiades he could well have surmised that in the Athenian democracy his luck could not hold forever. He had himself been instrumental in ostracizing others.

It appears to have been impossible in Athens to introduce a government of the few that would have provided freedom for everybody, that is, an oligarchy based on an equality of rights as envisaged by Thucydides. Abuse of power would have been inevitable, and Thucydides himself said that a democratic system is necessary to give refuge to the poor and bridle the rich. The Greeks understood how to combine equality of citizenship with political inequality. To protect himself, the poor man had to have the right to be a voter, a judge, and a magistrate.

What with the enormously increased power of the polis, even the lowliest had to insist the more urgently on being a part of it. All the power formerly exercised by the kings, the aristocrats, or the tyrants now had passed into the hands of the demos which amplified and extended the pressure brought to bear on the life and soul of the individual. The demos was far more restless and jealous in the exercise of power. Especially noteworthy are the measures it took to protect itself against the influence of talented individuals—the procedure in electing army generals and in applying ostracism.

So that no one individual might become too powerful, there was a high command in wartime composed of ten generals elected yearly, one from each of the *phylae* the troops of which he was to command. There was a supreme commander heading this staff of generals, but the office rotated daily among them. Fortunately, at Marathon Aristides gave the good example of letting Miltiades alone assume the supreme command. Yet three generations later Alcibiades was to warn in vain that one man alone commanded the Spartan force.

When ostracism was introduced, it was done allegedly to forestall tyranny forever. Every year the Senate inquired whether there was ground for banishing any citizen. If six thousand votes were cast against anyone, he had to leave Athens for at least five or even ten years, and this at a time when life beyond the protective borders of the state was hazardous in the extreme. Banishment was justifiably equated with punishment by death. In the fifth century the distinguished Athenians and a number of lesser ones were ostracized or threatened with ostracism. Here was manifest the ingrained hatred, not of the mob—the mob admires the unscrupulous ambitious unless it is incited against them—but by those who are impotently envious of excellence and unique abilities.

Ostracism was devised as a barrier to ambition. In all the history of the world, mediocrity has never again displayed a similar flash of genius; it barricaded itself behind popular feeling. Thus ostracism was applied as soon as a man began to gain public confidence, a thing this state ruled out on principle until it blindly accorded this very confidence to the demagogues.

> "The demos, haughty of spirit and made confident by its late victory at Marathon, was envious of anyone of more than common fame and reputation. Ostracism was not a punishment of any evil deed, but was speciously described as a way of reprimanding and chastising pride and excessive power, while in fact it was a decorous way of relieving and satisfying feelings of envy," as Plutarch justly observed on the occasion when Aristides was banished.

The Persian Wars were timely, coming in good season. Athenian democracy appeared to have stood the test. It received its lasting consecration at Marathon where its *hoplites,* and at Salamis where its seamen, won victories over the Persians. As a result Athens achieved hegemony over the Delian League. Sea power appeared above all to be intrinsically linked to democracy, and people in the Piraeus were even more demotically minded than those of Athens. *What a goodly thing freedom is,* says Herodotus. *As long as the Athenians were under tyrants, they were no better in warfare than their neighbors, but once they had thrown off the yoke of tyranny they became by far the best fighters in the world* (V. 78).

But not only the demos had attained a keen perception of its power; the rich natural resources of Athens fostered powerful individuals in those extraordinary times despite all the ingenious devices of distrust. *The democratic republic can do without able leaders even less well than oligarchy can, but it can endure them no better either* (Ranke). Miltiades died in prison, and Themistocles, after playing a game with Athens that still dazzles and dizzies the reader, ended up as a guest of the great king of Persia. However, the Athenians continued to expand and consolidate their empire and to carry out most audacious naval operations, even assisting Egypt in her revolt against Persia. Twenty to thirty thousand citizens assumed this tremendous burden, having more and more to devote themselves fully to public duties, while *metics* and slaves (three hundred to four hundred thousand?) did the work.

They levied three kinds of taxes: first, the military tax, for the maintenance of the army and navy which not only protected the single states within the empire, for these contributed their share in taxes, but also defended Athenian interests elsewhere; second, the tribunal tax, since Athens did not want the wealthy to sit on tribunals and since Athens also served as a court of appeals for member states of the Delian League (some days nearly a third of the citizens were sitting on juries); third, the assembly tax, for the maintenance of the whole administrative machinery, for internal and foreign affairs alike were openly debated and run by the assembly, even though a popular statesman might hint at secret doings and speak of certain monies being expended on essential purposes, like bribing Sparta, etc.

The most demoralizing tax, however, was the *theoricon* [theater money], doled out to the poorer citizens for theater tickets, for celebrating festivals and games, and for sacrifices and public meals. The waste caused by this tax was relatively as great as that at the most sumptuous courts, and later wars were lost for lack of money because this sacrosanct tradition could not be abolished. In addition, Athens was being adorned with the most glorious buildings and art works, and simultaneously had become a great trading center.

Pericles, responsible for most of the taxes just mentioned, delivered a famous funeral oration wherein he portrayed Athenian power and the beauty of its life as though these had blossomed forth like a flower, the Athenians achieving easily and as a matter of course what others gained only by hard work. This optimism, seen in a perspective of several thousand years, is all the more deceptive because Pericles spoke cleverly and modestly.

For the benefit of subsequent ages, those few short decades of full Athenian glory were fated to come about not merely to give birth to the most noble of Greek creations, but also to provide some understanding of the unbounded capacities of Greek genius. When enthusiasts for Hellenism wish that the days of Greek splendor might have endured longer, they are indulging in idle daydreaming, for the general conditions were already so delicately keyed that any change could have brought about nothing less than destruction.

The Athenians had not only their very real qualities and capacities but also their evil passions. In addition to his manner of schooling them, Pericles was also forced to humor their greed with pleasures of all sorts—not to satisfy it would have been impossible. Had he been as rich as Cimon, he could have made use of his own means, but he had to use public funds instead. Moreover, the terribly jealous ambition of the Athenians turned them against their teachers and made them try to supersede them. Even Pericles himself was so attacked in his last years from all sides that he might have regarded the outbreak of a general Hellenic war as at least desirable. The years were gone when he could *subdue the haughty and encourage the faint-hearted.*

Then too, the citizens had become unsettled owing to the endless popular assemblies and court sessions, for most of them lacked the calming effect of daily work. We need only listen to the second oration of Pericles:

> We are hated, as all are who have taken it upon themselves to rule over others, and for the sake of great ends we must face the fact that those who rule are envied. Our rule is indeed a tyranny. It may have been wrong to seize it, but it is no longer in your power to let it go, for then vengeance would break in upon you.

The *Report on the State of the Athenians* tells with frightening clarity how oppressive the burden of this rule was on the subject states. When the states comprising the empire chafed this much under Athenian hegemony, then nothing could come of the *Panhellenic Proposal* of Pericles, which incidentally does not reflect the otherwise astute politician. He tried to convoke a congress of all European and Asiatic Greek states *for the purpose of peace and communal matters,* a pleasant sounding project one would have liked to pursue in greater detail. Inevitably, however, it remained a pious wish because Sparta, as could have been foreseen, opposed it.

It was frankly admitted that at the start of the Peloponnesian War, Sparta had the sympathy of more Greeks than Athens did. In this war Athens lost untold treasures, not only in money but also in capable, courageous, self-sacrificing men. But, right after this calamity, Athens embraced demagogues like Cleon, who tripled the tribunal tax to provide a livelihood for the poor and to win their allegiance, but made enough on the side to pay off a heavy personal debt and amass a fortune of fifty talents. Later Athens was bewitched by its own brilliant Alcibiades, in whom and in whose Sicilian expedition this highly favored race displays its inward feverishness, one of the most remarkable spectacles in history. This war ended in the shocking subjugation of Athens by Sparta and the rule of the Thirty Tyrants.

The internal unrest accompanying this war came to the fore in terrible struggles between the democrats and the rich or powerful. In Athens, too, these two forces came to blows. Since the days of Themistocles all Athenian parties had formed clubs (*hetaeries*), as did also the chief leaders at their headquarters. Though they seem to have disappeared at the height of Pericles' reign, now they came to life again and resorted to every trick of the trade.

In 411 B.C., a coalition of all anti-democratic clubs, by recourse to the most aggressive means, succeeded in imposing an essentially oligarchic constitution, even though it lasted only a few months. In the next five years we find the Athenian oligarchs fully matured and firmly intent on their course of action. Though many Athenians would have liked to move out to the colonies, the democracy showed contempt for the emigrants, much as the French Revolution did. However, it had taught every capable Athenian of every party, including its own, to be thoroughly independent in spirit. This became apparent for the first time in the person of Alcibiades.

By far the greater number of the oligarchs, be it noted, helped to smash the last resistance to Lysander, thereby promoting the downfall of their native city, but every victory of Athens would have been a victory for the demos. They had fully determined upon ridding Athens of industry and of her dependence on the sea while restoring the landed aristocracy. After the surrender, they seized the power and set up a reign of terror under the Thirty Tyrants, who executed fifteen hundred people and announced a redistribution of property.

Athens was thoroughly defeated, but this appears less serious than the fact that the yawning gap in its population, gradually brought about by the war, was filled by such inferior stock. The royal mantle that formerly draped a demos exercising imperial rule now hung slouchily about a figure shrunk to skin and bones. Since Athenians, accustomed to spending much time in jury duty, missed the appeals from confederate states and felt suspicious, as the defeated generally do, they haled Athenian citizens into court all the more freely. One of the first victims was Socrates.

Amid the changing personnel in these offices the secretary was the only really permanent and experienced person and inevitably had the greatest influence on the conduct of affairs, yet often he was only a state slave. The state of Venice never fell into such dependence on its secretaries. The Athenians, highly skilled at correcting what they had botched at the beginning, issued an edict prohibiting the same person from holding a secretarial office for more than two years. It would pay us to examine how the Greeks went about the highly important matter of codifying their laws—those of Solon, and thereafter the extremely great number of other laws, some of them conflicting with each other.

As we know, Athens had no lack of wise old laws and cited them with praise. The Athenians did not rescind the old laws, but kept on adding new ones and thus let the chips of contradiction fall where they would. The scandal of admitting wholly contradictory laws in court finally became so intolerable that a codification became essential. This task, bandied from commission to commission, finally fell to a nondescript functionary, Nicomachus, born of a slave, who not only procrastinated the matter from year to year but also deleted genuine laws and forged others, both for money. Before he could be brought to trial, catastrophe overtook Athens at Aegospotami.

After the state was reorganized, a larger board and a special committee were appointed to codify the laws. Through influential protection Nicomachus again managed to be put in charge of the project. He dragged it out for another four years and then sought to make himself popular by devising new laws relating to cult rites, necessitating resplendent sacrifices.

As soon as a people, at least of our race, emerges out of barbarism, they demand something more than state organization and public life; they desire the privacy of an undisturbed home and independence in the realm of thoughts and feelings. To a certain extent, Sparta succeeded in reducing the members of the ruling caste to no more than political entities; elsewhere, and especially in Athens, the polis, by urging the individual onward, encouraged him to develop his personality as far as possible and to acquire private property and the philosophic outlook associated with it. The demos also craved to share in this wealth, and effectively levied tributes upon the rich.

Almost to the time of the Peloponnesian War, men were bent on being generous—partly from conviction and partly from ambition. Cimon continually made all kinds of amends for his wealth. But it was not until conditions became really bad that exploitation of the rich began in earnest and was severely felt, as we learn from many statements. This development was possible only because the wealthy could not leave, or if they did, they faced the same or greater hazards abroad.

Had the public contributions [*leitourgias*] demanded of the wealthy been only for needs of the state, not a word would be said—quite in the spirit of antiquity, and apart from taxes, often quite high, these public contributions really included only the *trierarchia,* the obligation to outfit triremes according to the demands of the time. But many additional outlays were expected which were not voluntary gifts, such as equipping indigent citizens for war, dowering daughters for marriage, or assuming funeral expenses. Other taxes were for the entertainment of the people, especially the *choregia,* a tax defraying the expenses for dramatic choruses and lyric choruses employed in divine worship and at festivals, along with dancers, flute players, etc.; the so-called *gymnasiarchia* and its expensive subdivision, the *lampadarchia,* indeed, the expense for contests of every sort; also the equipping of representatives to festivals at shrines abroad; finally, providing hospitality for numerous members of the phylae or of a particular demos.

It was not a question of volunteering or of choosing by lot; the ten phylae selected their fellow citizens who had to assume their respective obligations of defraying the cost of the regular yearly events as well as the cost of the special events. It was not advisable to attempt to escape this onus, and in the Peloponnesian War the wealthy trembled at the hatred which their refusal to contribute might provoke. For a long time, the traditional view prevailed that these public contributions were honorific and no one could lightly disregard the good will of his countrymen; this sense of duty was so strong that many exerted themselves beyond their capacities. If a man like Plato could not afford a *choregia,* he preferred raising the funds from his rich friends to withdrawing from the obligation. But if someone was rich and lucky enough to sponsor a winning chorus, he received a tripod as a prize and built a sacellum (little sanctuary) on Tripod Street wherein to house the award.

One may say that the money the rich would otherwise have squandered in gratifying their ease was largely expended on great works of art to delight the people as a whole, a signal honor to the Athenians; the coercion involved, however, tarnished, as it were, such acts of grace. The Athenian state had the power to tax at will property owners and industrialists in exchange for the security (limited, to be sure) that it afforded them and in time found it conveniently democratic simply to designate those who were to pay heavier taxes or to dole out money to the people directly.

The reign of the Thirty Tyrants was terrible in principle and in practice, but the bearing of the earlier Athens was such as to lend the Thirty Tyrants a shimmer of justification. Lysias appropriately comments on these hideous conditions. The surviving adherents of the Thirty could say: This is what we tried to make impossible forever, but now it is upon us again. Things like the exploitation of the rich ran their course, for a time, with impunity, until one fine day they hit rock bottom. Beginning with the Macedonian period, the *Panathenaeans* [splendid public festivals] took to simplicity again. Later Athens was manifestly poor and subsisted by catering to foreigners.

The reason for this change in behavior on the part of the demos was not far to seek. The Athenians who had turned from honest labor to spending their time in assemblies and court sessions suffered now from a warped and prurient imagination, like idlers who think of nothing but eating; their greed shaped their notions of booty and accruals from offerings.

It goes without saying that others cheated on taxes and withdrew from their appointed tasks whenever they could; still, being Athenians, they knew they risked denunciation and prosecution. By and large, we can recognize the guilty in the prosecutors and hence will have to scrutinize the popular court, the heliaea, divided into ten sessions, known for their severity. The Athenians were all the more eager to sit on these tribunals, after Cleon tripled the pay of the judges, really one of the most corruptive measures ever taken.

Instead of appealing to ancient documents, it might suffice to let Aristophanes' Philocleon tell about the delights of judgeship in his own very engaging manner. Here we can be certain that every trait is drawn from life and that this dreadfully commonplace fellow represented thousands of others just like him.

> What great fun it is to lord it over all and to be feared by the vociferating culprits and their families! From the moment I leave my bed, men of power come forward and offer me obsequious welcomes. And the accused, oh what tricks and flattery they use to secure my benevolence. Some tell me anecdotes or relate a comic fable by Aesop. Then a father, trembling as before a god, beseeches me not to condemn his son. Is this not a great power which can disdain wealth and spread fear?

The Attic sense of justice was poor, truth without much effect; persuasiveness meant everything. It was common practice to sway judges by dragging forward young children and having them prostrate themselves and wail and weep with one accord, or by having influential members of a party intercede. One could tell the court things which no judge would tolerate today. The brief account of Hermogenes in Xenophon sums up the situation: *Athenian judges moved by oratory executed many who were innocent and freed others who were criminals.* Henceforth, in the whole ancient world efforts in oratory were devoted to achieving results before tribunals. This art of swaying judges had its beginning in Sicily and was soon applied in courts everywhere. Besides, it came to be used for impressive momentary effects in public oratory.

In Athens the stage for public oratory was the famous popular assembly which, as in all democracies, had usurped the duties of the Senate and had largely come to act as the government. The judgment we may pass on the popular assembly is really a comprehensive judgment on the history of Athens. In comparison with that of other poleis it is relatively favorable. After the restoration following the rule of the Thirty Tyrants, this assembly, though having its ups and downs, remained the living organ of the state, and whereas in other states the bloodiest crises were repeated, Athens invariably took the way of deliberations and resolutions, whatever the issue. This assembled demos was regarded as a living organism and came to assume the standing of an ideal in the visual arts, though it was treated less respectfully by the writers of comedy, and in Plato, on one occasion, it was a large beast the study of whose passions and caprices constituted political wisdom.

As to the tone of the deliberating assemblies, the members knew how to comport themselves with dignity. Expressions like the following were customary: *The people of Athens, the highest authority in charge of everything in the state and empowered to do whatever it desires.* In the same building, beside the Senate chamber, was a chapel dedicated to Zeus Bulaios and to Athena Bulaia, where the senators stopped for prayer before entering the chamber; they sacrificed to the welfare of the democracy.

These people, among whom perjury was rampant, supposed they could accomplish something by making all Athenians regularly take an oath against the enemies of their democracy before the Dionysus festival. If a man universally hated was murdered, the city became jubilant and crowned the murderers with laurels, whatever sort they might be. In 408 B.C., the Athenians declared the murdered Phrynicus a traitor and crowned—not the murderer, who was only a slave of Hermon, but Hermon himself and his accomplices. Soon thereafter, in connection with this scandal, a certain Diocleides contended that the assassination had been meant to destroy the demos. For this allegation he was placed on a chariot, driven to the *prytaneum,* and banqueted there. Later he admitted that he had lied.

Although the character, volition, and destiny of the Athenians form in these matters an inseparable pattern, future ages will always be tempted to argue with them. In the heat of passion, this state not only made decisions resulting in the most destructive follies and violent brutalities, but also rapidly used up or frightened away its men of talent. For succeeding millennia, Athens has been significant not as a political state but as a cultural force and wellspring of intellect of the highest order.

We may say, for instance, that in the Peloponnesian War the impetuosity of the assembly and the most heroic courage in battle were expressions of one and the same emotion, and that from time to time the people did have their moments of moderation and wisdom. But at the frenzied trial of the admirals after the naval victory off Arginusae, the populace shouted: *It is unbearable that some would curtail the power of the demos.* Only a year later lamentation was to strike Athens with all its might.

We will now discuss what influences had swayed this public body. Until the end of the Peloponnesian War one may blame on occasion the oligarchs and their secret malevolence for favoring an upheaval which indeed later had come about. After the restoration of the Athenian state, two types of men tried to prevail upon the assembly and the popular court—the public orators (rhetors, demagogues) and the sycophants. We may well presume that they had their following of claquers, hissers, and perjurers.

Orators long continued to recite in the grand old manner of rhetoric. Andocides could still venture to say: *Not those who pursue their private ends lend greatness to the polis but these are made great and free by those who concern themselves with public matters.* Sadly we know who at that time concerned themselves predominantly with public affairs and why they did so. Despite all their patriotism and distrust of the unpredictable demos, the Athenians were open to the charge made long since that many of them sought, by hook or by crook, to enrich themselves at the expense of the state.

When Themistocles repeatedly said he shuddered at the thought of having to mount the speaker's rostrum, he did so not only because he knew the Athenians were fickle but also because he feared that those who knew how he had amassed a fortune while in office would blackmail him. If one ponders how many were diverted from productive work, what demands in taxes and contributions [*leitourgias*] were made upon the individual, how pervading the distrust which killed all sense of honor, and finally how venturesome the spirit of the Athenian was, one will fully appreciate the famous saying: *The speaker's rostrum is a golden harvest.*

Men made use of or held their tongues in amassing wealth by graft in state offices, in army posts, and in foreign service, all obtained through the art of demagoguery, by gifts from allies as long as the empire was large, by accepting bribes in courts, or by dipping one's hands into the public till. Outsiders without influence, mostly indigent but equally covetous, often pictured these gains too glowingly and the misdeeds too darkly. *Whoever enriches himself at the expense of the state,* the saying ran, *robs temples, graves, and friends, will commit perjury and treason, forswear himself as a judge, and accept bribes as an official.* At any rate, corruption was profitable and widespread. Proof of this lies in the remarkable reputation enjoyed by honest finance officials like Lycurgus.

The trials that dealt with these matters, like those of the army generals of the fourth century, accused not of embezzlement but of bribery by the enemy, were judged not on their merits but by the pressure and influence the plaintiffs and defendants could muster. The act of threatening an important person with a lawsuit passed among the people all too lightly as the mark of genuine patriotism and statesmanship, as if these acts were not routinely repeated; often an accuser covered up his own peculations by provoking indignation against others.

Many times it was quite clear that certain Athenians turned favorable suits for peace into decrees for prolonging war because they could profiteer from the turmoil. The people should also have surmised that even well-intentioned generals would secure themselves against Athenian folly by arranging ties abroad. The distrust, revealed by the unremitting prosecutions, though justified now and then, was a disease by its very nature and incurable, because regarded as a sign of health. When Lycurgus, who for many years had been a blameless treasurer, lay on his deathbed, he had himself carried to the *bouletereum* to render his last accounts. No one raised any objections except a certain Menesaechmus whom Lycurgus refuted. Then he was carried home to die. But when Menesaechmus repeated his charges, the sons of the dead man, so often crowned with wreaths and also honored with monuments, were cast into prison and freed only when Demosthenes issued a stern warning.

The operation of this system called forth the whole nimble host of sycophants; slander became recognized as a regular profession. To be sure, the Athenian system could no more dispense with this sort of aid than the Spanish Inquisition could do without its informers. The polis, like the royal rule in Spain, had become deified, turned into a religion, resorting to extreme measures to subdue even the slightest deviation. In a short time, the system became dependent on these extremes.

Fear of the sycophants kept numerous people from leaving the polis and from shirking their many onerous duties or from plundering the public funds even more shamelessly than they did. If anything proves that here the idea of the state was allowed a sway far beyond the limits compatible with normal human nature, it is the unabashed acceptance of this social evil, this reliance on terrorism, still in as full bloom a hundred years after the Peloponnesian War as before and continuing into the period of the Diadochi until the times of the Romans. Indeed, once a state attaches no shame or disgrace to the leveling of slanderous charges, then at all times and among all people denouncers are bound to appear.

Only Greek democracy—in the fullest sense, only Athenian democracy —ever frankly admitted this practice and elevated it to a principle of government to which all citizens of wealth and consequence were subject. The rabble found no fault with this practice, fully congenial and comprehensible to it.

I am a witness in court cases appealed from the islands, a sycophant and an uncoverer of guilt. Work does not agree with me; my grandfather already was an informer, a character says in Aristophanes. But the writers of comedy need not concern us seriously, because they are tempted to caricature the figure of the sycophant and obviously enjoy doing it; on the brink of such a quagmire one may prefer to limit oneself to factual statements.

The sycophant puts on patriotic airs, wants to assist the polis and *the established laws,* he wants to ferret out whether the citizens are living up to the demands of the state in all respects. He was liable to a fine of one thousand drachmas if he failed to win one fifth of the judges' votes, and of another thousand drachmas if he withdrew his accusation. However, he could easily get one fifth and probably more of the complaint judges in the *heliaea* to support him. If he happened to draw a fine, as a rule he never paid it. At the time of Lysias, there was a certain Agoratus with an accumulated debt of ten thousand drachmas, but he sat as a judge, was a member of the popular assembly, and haled many into court for all sorts of alleged crimes against the state.

This conduct of affairs kept the innocent, especially if they had any wealth, in a state of perpetual terror. Throughout his whole life, Nicias trembled at the sycophants; how this essentially determined the destiny of his army and of himself has already been related. Xenophon's Isomachus, this paragon of excellence, is everlastingly denounced. A most instructive advice is that which Socrates gave to Crito, likewise constantly persecuted —to hire a counter-sycophant. Crito was fortunate enough to find a highly qualified person in Archedemus who inspired terror in the sycophants and was then employed by Crito's friends and honored, i.e., the honest men had to take this serviceable rogue in to dine with them. The Thirty Tyrants killed and drove away many sycophants; later, however, the breed spawned rapidly again.

The Spanish Inquisition fully achieved its purpose with its information system because the informers, with rare exceptions of nefarious extortion, were thoroughly in sympathy with the aims of the Inquisition. The Attic state was less fortunate in its sycophants, for they cared nothing about the outcome of the trials, only about being bought off. Voluntary poverty was the best insurance, though not to everyone's taste. A sycophant might well inject himself into the examination a man chosen by lot had to undergo to determine his fitness for office. From there on, it was a lifelong threat hanging over any man possessing enough wealth to invite blackmail; perennially a brood of extortioners was about demanding hush money.

The innocent were most vulnerable to extortion to escape court scandals, which all decent people tried hard to avoid and even the sycophants shied away from. If a case went to court, the sycophant received only a small portion of the fine; settling the case out of court was much more lucrative. If he dropped the case in court before it went to judgment, he often had his forfeit of a thousand drachmas handsomely repaid. If even this last stratagem did not work, a sycophant would prosecute the case in court, but precisely where wrong should have found redress, namely, in the court, there the sycophant most likely applied himself with greatest success.

After the death of Alexander, the aged Aristotle was accused of impiety by this dangerous and inane breed trying to fleece him, whereupon he went to Chalcis and put himself under Macedonian protection. He wrote in jest to Antipater that he could not remain in a city where, as in the garden of Alcinous, there stood fig upon fig (*sykon epi syko* [*sykon* being the first root of sycophant]).

It would be erroneous to suppose that in time these sycophants lost their hold just because determined orators had exposed them hundreds of times and because the people had seen through their wiles. Demosthenes tells about Sephanus, the protector of the prostitute Neaera, who lay in wait in his own home trying to catch someone making indecent advances to his alleged wife and daughter, so as to practice extortion on him. Demosthenes on one occasion told the judges: *You have punished no sycophant as he deserves but always content yourselves with listening to them as if the safety of the demos depended on having many accused and many sycophants.* One saw them scurrying in the market place like adders, or like scorpions with their stings raised looking for victims they could plunder.

In spite of this sort of assistance Athens lived on as a state, thereby proving its extraordinary vitality. If one could but clearly grasp in its entirety the evil sycophancy carried in its wake, one would be genuinely startled.

But this Athens with its dubious system of justice loved to have its tribunals impose hard and spectacular punishments, as other poleis did for that matter. Every transgression, whatever other consequences it may have entailed, was regarded as a threat to the state, as a lessening of its safety. Accordingly, every trial tended to have political overtones, and since the polis actually was or intended to be the real religion of the Greeks, punishments took on the nature of vengeance for sacrilege perpetrated against the highest deities. This explains the extraordinary severity—death penalty besides fines and *atimia* [dishonor]—attaching to the judgment in cases even of minor infractions.

Athenian courts were generous in meting out other punishments too, especially *atimia*, applying it for a limited or an indefinite period, sometimes linked with confiscation, and on occasion allowing the first comer to maltreat the victim. Lawsuits involving impiety took on a senseless vehemence precisely because the polis initiated them. Nowhere else existed such a ridiculous disproportion as between the vengeance for offending or disbelieving in the gods, and the ethical and theological fecklessness of those same gods. The most horrid punishment, refusal of burial rites, had to be included in the penalties imposed upon those found guilty of crimes against the state.

In 411, when the oligarchy of the Four Hundred fell, Antiphon was executed as a traitor and his corpse thrown across the boundary.

In this context belong the many execrations pronounced in the name of the state which, though fundamentally a lay structure, behaved like a church. Myths and history reveal how terribly people dreaded being cursed, particularly by their parents. And, once pronounced, curses were taken to be objective forces beyond recall. Preposterous, of course, was the notion that an execration pronounced by a polis against its enemy should have the same effect in reality as in myth; it was simply an imitation.

The oaths taken to make alliances binding were also very pathetic. When Aristides swore an oath to validate the alliance between Athens and its confederates, he tossed a red-hot iron into the sea, so as to say that the curses should retain their power until the iron would float. It would seem more sensible to make a compact binding for a perilous hour only, as when during the war with Mardonius, Aristides ordered the priests to invoke curses on all who might desert the alliance or have any dealings with the Persians.

These conditional curses had parallels in others invoked on oneself to assert innocence and analogues in threatening psephisms [measures carried by vote], to bind the future by decreeing *atimia* or death for anyone henceforth who should propose a motion opposing something already approved. It is utterly ridiculous for a party in power to suppose it could thus bind future generations, although in fact this kind of psephism did precede democracy to which one would be inclined to attribute it.

The *eupatrids* [hereditary aristocrats] had already decreed the death penalty for anyone who should propose an attack on Salamis. One may observe that, by and large, the more unreasonable some resolution was, the more vehemently the polis defended it as perfect and sacrosanct.

To the foregoing should be added the curse invoked on fugitive persons *in contumaciam.* As they stood facing the west, priests and priestesses uttered oaths and waved purple garments in accordance with ancient rites. This curse was pronounced on Alcibiades after he had been condemned to death in absentia and his property confiscated. Later, when Athens had to welcome him back as if he were a protective deity, the demos commanded the venerable priests to revoke the curse; Theodorus, the hierophant [official expounder of rites of worship and sacrifice] explained hereupon that he had not really pronounced any execration on Alcibiades except one to take effect in case he harmed the state.

The many punishments had their counterpart in honors and rewards the state conferred, although the same state permitted the unscrupulous ambitious to plunder on a vast scale and either could not or would not protect the virtuous citizens.

Athens, like the other poleis, regarded the bestowal of its citizenship as a precious gift reserved for the select few. The only examples of mass induction into Athenian citizenship occurred when the Plataeans who had escaped alive and the slaves who had proved their loyalty in the naval battle off Arginusae were enfranchised. It took six thousand votes cast secretly to validate induction into Greek citizenship.

Since clever orators more than once had managed to mislead the demos, the proceedings could be contested in court. Those granted citizenship could not become archons or priests. However, wreaths were freely bestowed, as was the title *benefactor of the people,* the right to sit in tribunals and on the front seats at festivals, and to claim precedence in court hearings. These honors were inexpensive and conferred according to the mood of the moment on all kinds of people, including singers, guitarists, jugglers, and ball players.

A special mark of honor was the right to banquet in the prytaneum, sometimes decreed for life and on occasion made hereditary. These lifelong banquet privileges were especially conferred on Olympic winners with their undoubtedly blest appetites, also on deserving statesmen, victorious generals, public benefactors like the physician Hippocrates, and other meritorious persons.

It seems the fourth century was especially spendthrift in this respect. During that time the granddaughter of Aristides was granted the privilege of banqueting as lavishly as the Olympian winners. The descendants of Harmodius and Aristogeiton and others who had killed tyrants belonged also to this patently colorful crowd.

Athens alone of the poleis never canceled debts nor redistributed the land. Still, around 400 B.C. little Attica was said to have had ten thousand landowning citizens and only five thousand non-owners. Besides the citizens, there were the *metics,* working hard and paying conscientiously their poll tax and other taxes imposed on them. If they failed to pay the poll tax they could be sold into slavery. These *metics* were, of course, inclined to favor continuity of the democratic system among the people under whose rule they lived. The Thirty Tyrants had killed the rich metics, probably not merely for the sake of their money but also to suppress this caste as a whole in order to promote the ideal of an Athens without trade and independent of the sea.

8. Democracy Outside Athens

The great difference between the Greek cities and Rome was that in Rome the affluent proprietors developed better means to protect themselves than they did in Greece. As soon as the people in Greece had achieved equality and no longer had to fight for their rights and principles, there began a struggle between the rich and the poor, in some cities with the introduction of democracy already, in others after a shorter or longer period of moderation.

In the early years of tribal rule this anguish was unknown. It was the equality of rights that had made the people keenly aware of the inequality of means. Reaching some degree of equalization by means of work, which the wealthy needed done and the poor could have done for pay, was impossible because of the anti-banausic attitude toward work. The poor discovered that being lords of the ballot they could become lords of the resources as well. In Athens and elsewhere they reimbursed themselves for sitting in the popular assembly and in court. Then they sold their votes, especially as judges, exacted all sorts of *leitourgias* [contributions] from the rich, resorting to arbitrary confiscation of property and banishment. Outside Athens, they canceled debts and overthrew governments.

These first measures of redress only heightened their sense of insufficiency and hence their greed. Men lost all respect for the rights to property, and each measured his rights only by his so-called needs, in reality a euphemism for greed. To achieve their goals they needed merely a momentary majority at the polls. Everywhere there were revolutions and counter-revolutions, everywhere only factions at the helm of government, but there was neither loyalty nor civil obedience except when pressure was brought to bear, and even then subversion was always latent in people's minds.

Aristotle dealt with these class conflicts at great length. He wrote at a time when the different principles of government had been tried out in all their various shadings. He had a low opinion of the oligarchies of wealth still trying to maintain themselves here and there. For they misused their power even more than the democracies did. His considered view was that the many have more insight and capacity for rule and that they can be better than any single individual, provided that as a throng they will not be too submissive. He admitted that the moderate form of democracy most pleasing to him did not exist anywhere; also he knew that any attempt to set up a real democracy would founder because those capable of using the necessary force could not be won over to do so.

He regarded as real citizens only those who could bear arms, and thought that popular assemblies should approve or disapprove accounts rendered, amend the constitution, and determine highest policy in war and peace. They should not, he thought, engage in discussions but only vote pro or con or, when dissatisfied, send the measures back to the officials. The authority, he believed, should be vested in officials either elected or chosen by lot; their tenure should be long and their power should be strictly limited, because great power linked with short terms of office tends to corrupt. He demanded above all that these representatives receive no pay, for only then would the indigent give up trying for these offices and the government thus come into the hands of the wealthy and the learned.

Aristotle held that a democracy would thrive best in a state composed largely of farmers too poor to sit too often in the assembly and hence content with casting their vote and with listening to accounts rendered. In such a polity, the well to do could fill the offices blamelessly and without being put under pressure. He thought those old laws to be useful which limit the size of land holdings and make them hereditary. Where there was a market crowd, a popular assembly should never be convened without men from the countryside. Since an assembly tended to shape the government and since the ways and habits of the market place crowd were fickle, an assembly needed the steadying balance afforded by the country people.

Being able to do what one wanted to constituted freedom and equality, in the view of Aristotle. In a polity providing these, the three branches of government—the legislative, the executive, and judicial—would be in the hands of the many. As soon, however, as popular decrees took the place of laws, a kind of mob rule would supplant the government by law; the demos would become a despot composed of the many and, ruling by force over its betters, would be thus merely another tyranny. Whereas the tyrant issued edicts, the many would resort to psephisms. The flatterer was to the tyrant what the demagogue would be to democracy. The demagogue would spur the people to give his decisions precedence over the laws and would enhance his own stature by bringing all issues directly before the people.

The many wanted either not to be ruled at all or so ruled that they would also rule in their turn (VI, 1); moreover, the offices and appointments would now be made sources of personal gain, being no longer provisional duties from which one would gladly withdraw to return to his private affairs (III, 4).

So that all might have their turn, tenure was to be as short as possible (VI, 1) and offices still permanently occupied were to be either abolished or their tenure shortened; nor were offices to go to the same person twice, save posts in the army. The crowd composed of *banausics,* small shopkeepers, and day laborers roaming the city was always ready for an assembly (IV, 5). Only when the state is too poor to pay those attending the assemblies will the people be willing to let the Senate rule, but as soon as the state can pay, the assembly will strip the Senate of its power, usurping all authority for its own.

In populous democracies this vicious circle running its course would end in maltreatment of the rich and respected. Instead of having fewer assemblies and shorter court sessions, the crowd would assemble more frequently and demand more pay. When the customary revenues proved insufficient, the people would raise additional funds either by direct taxes or by graft in corrupt courts and by the activities of sycophants. Aristotle added that as a consequence many democracies have toppled (VI, 3). No surplus in the national treasury was ever to be doled out to the proletariat, a practice he compared to carrying water in a sieve; aware of this and desiring more the demagogues would repeat their appeals for public handouts. But the interest of the possessing classes demands that the many be not too poor and be provided work. Aristotle also found further similarities between the government of tyrants and that of the extreme democracies, e.g., the almost limitless license allowed to slaves, women, and children, and the general indifference to the excessive liberties people took.

At that time the most frightful conflicts raged in many areas of Greece between the supporters of democracy and the still existing men of power—the aristocrats and the wealthy—the former comprising the Athenian party and the latter the Lacedaemonian party. The word oligarchy must not be limited to a class consisting of only a few; clearly it often included thousands, indeed the whole property owning caste. This became evident in the terrible events on the island of Cercyra; Thucydides put the number of noblemen killed at one thousand, Diodorus at fifteen hundred. And yet, even fourteen years later the demos was in fear of the surviving fugitives, so that it freed the slaves and enfranchised foreigners. In Argos, a thousand young men of the wealthy class, skilled in the use of arms, overthrew the democracy and formed an aristocracy, though for a short time.

Upon coming into power the demos, in its earliest period, had already divided the property of the nobility; now it applied the principle of the equality of all free men in persecuting and exterminating the upper classes and the wealthy.

> Ofttimes the demagogues, desiring to flatter a crowd, threatened
> to divide the properties, or to exact so heavy a toll that the
> wealthy fought back hard enough to overthrow the democracy.

Sometimes a defeat in battle sufficed to overthrow the rule by the demos as it earlier had sufficed to end an aristocratic regime. Naturally, victorious oligarchies of various states joined together in alliances; under the aegis of Sparta oligarchies of other states received help against the demos. But wherever the democratic forces were not driven out the oligarchies, by the very logic of survival, had to maintain the strictest party rule: offices and posts went exclusively to those who had actively fought the demos or had returned after having been expelled.

The two parties never managed to reach a working partnership, or, if so, only for a passing moment. Aristotle said (IV, 9): *Regardless of which party triumphs, no common polity is achieved, for the victors seize power as the prize of victory and set up either an oligarchy or a democracy.*

Democracy largely prevailed in Greek cities, especially after the Battle of Leuctra, when Sparta no longer was able to protect itself, to say nothing of assisting other oligarchies. The means the demos relied on to stay in power was repeated mass murder. About the time of the Battle of Leuctra, the mob in Argos clubbed to death twelve hundred citizens and even their own leaders when these counseled moderation. Thereupon horror really broke loose; prolonged warfare with more powerful neighbors, yearly devastation of their territory, and then regular executions of rich and respected citizens, which was done with a joy rarely felt in killing foes.

The only forms of political constitution recognized were democracy and oligarchy. We have explained above why tyranny did not thrive on Greek soil. Although Aristotle regarded democracy as safer and more enduring than oligarchy (IV, 9), nevertheless he found that the condition of all the states was deplorable.

The popular assemblies everywhere had reduced government to momentary expediency and caprice. Their resolutions had no bearing whatever on their previous decisions; in fact, they undermined their legislation. Savagery and treason, rife everywhere, were often abetted by the grossest effrontery. *Crude, ignorant boors, insolent in their power, sneered at the judges of athletic contests, abused the chorus leaders at the Dionysia, and insulted the army commanders and gymnasiarchs.*

But ever and again *evil and ambitious rhetors and demagogues sought to equalize the haves and the have-nots.* If a man had squandered his inheritance, the polis might burst into a passion as if he had robbed it of its own prospects, its own rightful dues. The Abderites dragged their illustrious fellow citizen Democritus into court on grounds of having squandered his patrimony, but set him free when he read them his *Diakosmos* and his piece

Concerning the Things in Hades, explaining that these were what he had spent his wealth on.

Even as the Athenians used confiscation in quite normal times to improve their finances, this method was used often enough elsewhere. Foreign ships were simply taken as prizes with the proviso of later restitution in kind; the rich were stripped of their silver on the spur of the moment and given iron tokens instead to be redeemed later. If, on the occasion of a revolt, the well to do found themselves in prison, they were subject to extortion and exile and could consider themselves lucky to escape with their lives.

When Timoleon came to Sicily, the Siceliots trembled most of all at anything connected with the speakers' rostrum and the agora because all the tyrants had sprung from there, but all Timoleon could do was set up democracies. Nothing else grew on this soil until the day of the great monarchies. Because so many Greek cities and nearly all colonies were situated on the seacoast, mutual intercourse and exchange of ideas on politics and philosophy were facilitated, keeping alive a spirit of innovation. *The sea is a teacher of evil,* sighed Plato, and Cicero, in a long and eloquent disquisition, elaborated further upon this theme.

Men of culture and refinement who by their virtues might have been able to support public administration, withdrew into private life out of timidity, and after the middle of the fifth century let the management of the government fall by default into the hands of the most brazen and evil scoundrels. Railing against this never helped any, not even in antiquity, when from the fourth century on this tendency of men who had attained a certain level of thought and culture to flee from public life became the rule. When the mobs stormed the poleis they fleeced, exiled, and killed many of them as oligarchs and in any event threatened and limited their continued existence as a caste. Now, however, the men most important for the world and its culture were no longer statesmen or those who paraded as such but men of the spirit in its broadest sense.

One prefers to bypass the later period of the democratic polis, especially that after the Battle of Chaeronea, for it was a chain of cause and effect leading to mutual extermination and to the desolation of Greece, until it was taken over by the Romans. However, history aiming at factual presentation cannot avoid this sorry tale of affliction.

The chief evil of democracy was that it had become imbued with an anti-banausic attitude so that equality of rights was coupled with an aversion to work. This enabled the indolent to turn the polls and the courts into a permanent threat against the propertied class. It was an insane misuse of majority power in a matter which inevitably had to split the majority group again into yet another majority and minority. Although real oligarchs had long since ceased to exist, the populace continued calling its victims by that name. These events, as Polybius showed, ended in countless catastrophes for the cities, in perpetual warfare of polis against polis, and in growing impoverishment that heavily reduced the use of slaves. Hence, later on their journey through Greece, Strabo, Plutarch, Dio Chrysostom, and Pausanias had to wander through many a desolate area with its cities in ruins.

9. The Enduring Quality of City Populations

Three characteristics distinguished the city populations of ancient Greece from all later ones: a strong inner cohesion, at least of the prevalent majority; an abhorrence of external subjugation; and a willingness to be transplanted. No people of later times could have said with Themistocles, as he did before the Battle of Salamis when Xerxes was threatening the city, that as long as Athens had two hundred ships full of people, she had a polis and a mightier one than did the Corinthians, and if driven by necessity, they would sail for Siris in Italy (Herod. VIII, 61). Only in reference to this willingness for resettlement is it possible to understand the suggestion the Peloponnesians made after the victory at Mycale, that the people of the Ionian cities be removed to Greek cities which had held with the Persians (Herod. IX, 106). In this light also one can understand how during wartime a citizenry could act on a suggestion to leave their city as a pledge to a foreign people in order to return to it later.

The resettlement of entire cities by tyrants in fifth century Sicily was abnormal, but when the citizens assembled again after their cities were freed, they were capable of making similar decisions themselves, as they had done in the events at Leontini. Everywhere, Greek bodies of citizens bore up under destinies which no recent ones would endure precisely because these latter are merely individual citizens, not a body of citizenry in the ancient sense.

Armies operating far from home might upon occasion cohere into a citizenry. In the Sicilian campaign, Nicias, the Athenian general, could tell his troops after the disastrous battle in the harbor: *Consider that you constitute a polis the moment you settle down, wherever it be.* In the Anabasis, the Greeks felt themselves to be an army camp community, however dissimilar their origins, and Xenophon seriously considered founding a polis with them on the Pontus.

A remnant of an exiled citizenry might, after many decades, return to its original city, as the Plataeans sojourning in Athens did after the peace of Antalcidas, and when the Thebans drove them out again, they were returned by King Philip thirty-six years later, following Chaeronea.

The Messenians furnish by far the best example of the rejoining and consolidation of a whole people driven into exile; they appear not to have developed a sense of being a polis until they were driven from their homes. Some of them were scattered abroad at the time of the First Messenian War, but others, at the time of the Third, were granted free passage abroad at the command of the oracle at Delphi. It is to be remembered that this second group had not only been abroad for about a hundred years, but had already been treated like helots for a good two hundred before that. Still, they responded to the call of Thebes and returned from all corners of the earth to establish their new state with New Messene as its capital. After all that time, they still maintained their customs and dialect, whereas today the second generation of non-English speaking immigrants to North America commonly forgets its mother tongue. And no holy temple drew these Greeks home as it did the Jews after the Babylonian exile.

But Greece was afflicted by parties and groups of citizens who, having fled or been exiled, held together with might and main and waited for the hour of return at all costs. The fugitive is one of the best known figures in Greek mythology; one fled or was driven away because of deliberate or accidental murder, and every princely court during heroic times sheltered its fugitive. The words the tragedians put into the mouths of fugitives they borrowed from the frightful experiences of their own century. In *Oedipus at Colonus,* Sophocles has both Oedipus and Polyneices utter curses against their homeland as Sophocles may well have heard them uttered. Aeschylus certainly felt horror at the fugitive returning and attacking his native city.

The polis everywhere had begun to carve living chunks out of its own body, and by the mid-part of the fifth century central Greece was teeming with exiles. At Coronea a large host of fugitives—Boeotians, Euboians, Locrians, and of whatever other origins they were—helped defeat the Athenians. Often it was an empty hope that heartened the fugitive, yet it did offer him a semblance of joy in life.

Theognis therefore bemoans the fugitive (V, 209) but also warns his Cyrnus not to befriend a fugitive (V, 333) because the same man, having returned home, customarily does an about-face. The real curse upon him was his bitterness and his longing to return home by whatever means. Not for nothing was there the saying that linked *the fugitive and the godless.* The fugitive not only wanted to regain his old home but knew that as a rule he could do so only by use of the most overt force, effectively deposing those in power. Be it enough to say that they were Greeks striving with Greeks for mastery. Alexander's colonies in Asia may well have attracted a great many of these wandering fugitives. Perhaps it was better for these unfortunates to settle in Asia than to return home.

The fatal demonic power of the returned fugitives became apparent in Thebes, for instance, shortly after the news of King Philip's death. These fugitives arrived by night and imitated the liberation of the Kadmeia from Spartan occupation forty-three years earlier by killing the commanders of the Macedonian garrison. Now they were able to rouse everybody with the cry of *Freedom!* in the popular assembly—old and beautiful words, according to Arrian. With the most flippant defiance the Thebans rejected Alexander's offer of pardon and began shooting at his men; since there were among the fugitives such as could not expect mercy, they whipped the people into a fighting mood.

When Alexander stormed the city, he had only to turn it and its inhabitants over to the rage of its neighbors, the inhabitants of Plataea, Phocis, and other places, who destroyed it with deliberation. The Macedonian king found it hardly necessary to burden himself with the destruction; he simply let the Greeks go after Greeks.

Chapter Three

OBJECTIVE CONSIDERATION OF THE FORMS OF THE STATE

The Hellenes could not establish a polis without providing a forum for deliberation, and at once there came into being an agora with its inevitable consequences: debates dealing with every single political question of the day and with the affairs of the state as a whole. The earliest poets, Hesiod with his admonitions and Tyrtaeus with his challenging appeals, range from the hortatory to the prophetic; Solon already voices detached reflection. After mind and tongue had been fully set free, not only the poets apostrophized, glorified, and scoffed at the polis in every manner, but statesmen spoke on the situation of the polis in broad and illuminating discourses, historians steeped themselves thoroughly in political views, and philosophers favored the state not only with their reflections but elevated it to an object of poetic meditation while tending actually to withdraw from the polis themselves.

These Hellenes examined not only their own poleis, and it was from them that we learned all that we knew about the constitutions of other ancient nations, from Egypt to Persia and Carthage, until as late as the nineteenth century, when archeological discoveries made additional contributions to our knowledge. Polybius gave us the most valuable and concise account ever made of the Roman state in the days of its greatness. Only the Greeks clearly visualized and compared everything.

The same year that Aristophanes staged his *Clouds*, there appeared the earliest political memoir surviving anywhere on earth, *On the Athenian State,* falsely attributed to Xenophon. An Attic oligarch—Critias or whoever it was—presented in icy detachment the working details of Athenian democracy, showing that, evil though the conduct of this government might have been, it was thoroughly appropriate to the ends in view.

In describing political situations and in establishing proposals, Thucydides achieved a sure and perfect mastery in his debates and speeches, and it is irrelevant whether they came from him or from those to whom they are ascribed. In his *Hellenica*, Xenophon gave us an account of the incomparable life-and-death contest in oratory [logomachy] between Critias and Theramenes. Soon the known orations on the Attic state and tribunal were to begin.

In his *Cyropaedia*, Xenophon limned an ideal king educated in Socratic ethics and thereby indirectly criticized Greek democracy in its decline. Even though it was not altogether to his liking, Xenophon admired Sparta and thought that it exemplified the best attainable state for Greece. Although Plato had early been repelled by the actual conduct of Attic state affairs and consequently had refused to take any part in them, he was for a long time nevertheless unable to shake off an urge for political activity.

He had the notion that only true philosophy could serve as a standard of right and wrong in private and public life and that misery would burden mankind until the philosophers became kings and filled the chief offices, or until the kings and top officials in the poleis became philosophers. It was obviously futile to try to get the Athenians then in power to become philosophers, but to try to persuade a single mighty ruler to turn to philosophy seemed to Plato to be worth the attempt. And so the man who had to stay aloof from Athenian politics went three times to advise the tyrants of Sicily, and each time had to flee for his life.

Plato even believed that his own utopias could be realized. In addition to the idealized image, given in *Timaeus* and *Critias*, of a primeval Athens nine thousand years ago and modeled substantially on Egypt, Plato developed two comprehensive polities, one absolute, the other moderate, as it might be realized on earth.

The first book, *The Republic (Politeia)*, besides its formal literary excellence has enduring historical value owing to the vast amount of information it gives about contemporary conditions in Greece. This work is unique in disclosing the most profound motives and true intentions of the polis. *The Republic* demanded that the men of the two upper classes—the rulers and guardians—completely abdicate their individuality and submerge themselves in the communal life, giving up their private property, as well as eating and living with their wives. The children would not know their parents and would be reared as public wards from infancy. This showed most plainly how the ideal of the polis could harden the heart of even a choice spirit.

The Republic excluded the productive classes—farmers and industrial workers—that is, the masses, from participating in the affairs of the state, relegating them to the role of servants. At that time, however, the masses in

Greece had the hilt in their hands, and it was unrealistic to believe that they would let go of it.

Nearly every utopia advocates the common possession of property. Two reasons made it impossible to introduce this innovation. To acquire private property, so as to indulge in personal enjoyment, was one of the chief ambitions of the Greeks at that time, corroding even a good many Spartans whose city the Republic resembles more closely and draws on more fully than it does any other Greek state. Moreover, people had learned somewhat to counteract the unequal distribution of wealth by periodically plundering the rich. Furthermore, the local guards stationed in barracks and naturally possessed of a high sense of duty, cut a sorry figure when pitted against the powerful mercenaries that pillaged the poleis at that time. Finally, the whole Republic, with its system of built-in safeguards against all innovations and with its caste divisions, each having its prescribed duties, contrasted most strikingly with the free and rich development individualism found among the Greeks contemporary with Plato.

But the most dubious element was the government of the whole scheme. According to Plato, early selection and careful nurture were to produce a superior class of rulers, all of which is hard enough to conceive of as happening smoothly because, after all, they were Greeks, but when they were supposed to be philosophers to boot, the reader may well begin to smile.

In his last years Plato contrived a limited utopia in his *Laws,* a work traceable in its main outlines to no other thinker and recognized already by Aristotle as written by him. This moderate ideal, devised with a view to easier practical application, was fundamentally as impossible as the *Republic,* precisely because it likewise flies in the face of the Greeks' nature, indeed of human nature itself. The *Laws* did not require having women and property in common; it stipulated an agricultural community with 5,400 parcels of land distributed by lot and removed as far as possible from the sea, for which all Greeks languished.

Plato presented the details of this state so minutely that he betrayed his desire to make the inward and outward life of the individual absolutely subservient to the polis. Man was not only to be barred from the sea, which brought so many vile and variegated customs, but also from his own imagination so that the whole community would have to *say and sing* the same thing for a whole lifetime.

Although poesy had commonly played a great role in Greek education, it was to be strictly confined to very narrow limits, and art and religion were to be hieratically kept in their niches. Significantly, the government was not to be in the hands of a committee of philosopher-rulers but was to be under a single *lawgiver,* permanently installed, a universal protector, rewarder, reprimander, a moralist and a controller of all property, expenditures, and business of the people. This lawgiver was naturally in need of a host of officials to help him discharge his duties. Still, Plato justifiably suspected that disaffection would rear its head; to forestall this, he allowed no one to travel, and those who might have been abroad were to say that everything was better at home.

The keystone of the *Laws* is an optimism imposed by force. We hardly need the criticism of Aristotle to realize how utterly impossible the fantasies of these two books really are and how directly they cut athwart the actual conditions obtaining among the Greeks. Plato had a coercive streak in him and imparted it also to some of his students, for wherever they attained influence in a state they tended to be despotic and denunciatory.

The chief grievance posterity can lodge against his two books is their program to freeze Greek culture. To be sure, the development of Greek culture was implicitly connected with the decline of the polis, and that development has greatly concerned mankind ever since and has played a most important role in world history. In neither of his utopias did Plato evince any grasp of the future or influence it in the slightest. He voiced the ancient original intention of the polis, and his proposals, insofar as they touched on reality at all, were essentially attempts to revive forms that had become outmoded for good reasons.

Plato's contemporaries and later philosophers, following his lead, elaborated a number of utopias, some of which Aristotle enumerated. Subsequently the Stoics Zeno and Chrysippus wrote theirs. But in the meantime it had become fashionable to put these utopian accounts into the mouth of some mythical character in a never-never land, as Theopompus did in the discussions of Seilenus with Midas.

Fanciful travel tales became popular, describing some marvelous region far away and interweaving desirable political and social features. The work of Hecataeus of Abdera, a contemporary of Alexander the Great, on the Hyperboreans might have been an ideal polity consistently developed. Euhemerus' account of the blessed island of Panchaea is hardly more than a pompous Cockaigne. The island off Ethiopia to which Jambulus paid an imaginary visit is not much more interesting than that of Euhemerus, though it does come to grips with some political concepts.

Even though Plato may have stood alone in expecting to see his utopias realized, nevertheless all creators of utopias must be presumed to have some desire to influence practically the political and social views of their contemporaries. Aristotle stands in lone splendor over against them all. He knew more about the real state than all the rest did; his great work treating the *constitutions* of 158 different states is extant only in fragments. But his

Politics (teaching about the state) is preserved. Its value lies not only in its general definitions, in its prevailing Greek view of the nature and purpose of the state, or in its wealth of information about current Greek practices, but also in the recognition that various root forms are all justified and in the parallel study of the various modifications these root forms had undergone. In consequence the world views politics to this day in part through the eyes of Aristotle and uses some of his expressions in discussing it. It may hence be assumed that his school and later philosophers, whose numerous works on the state we know only by their titles, contributed significantly to propagating his views and others similar to them.

But since the days of Antisthenes already, the Cynics had set themselves apart from the polis by using the privilege of poverty and sneered at it with all their cunning. They were at home everywhere, and everywhere they were strangers, a living indictment of a free state now prey to despotism as were the *Sufis* of the ruined sultanates in the medieval Orient. Finally Epicurus appeared, resolving the dilemma at least in theory, by conceiving the polis as a mutual compact for safety's sake, man no longer existing for the sake of laws but laws for the sake of man. But of course no insight of individuals, however penetrating, could prevent the gradual dissolution of the Greek state ostensibly enjoying freedom but actually rocked by persecution and internal crises.

It is a law of nature that all forces reach their full and conscious development in opposition to and in contest with each other. Hence, a fully developed political power is a paramount condition for all outward and inner growth and the indispensable stay for the climbing vines of culture. For a relatively long time, the Greek poleis accomplished great things in culture. And finally Greece in her glory hurled back the Persians in their thrust to the west and thereby probably helped to shape the outward destiny of mankind.

It was not the poleis though, but Alexander, who conquered Persia, and he did it while they were conspiring against him. There remains only to judge the other fortunes and misfortunes the poleis brought upon themselves, and we might well say that in the long run the polis in its internal and external development tended predominantly to make the citizens unhappy.

The polis not only developed individuals into personalities, but it also spurred them violently onward, at the same time demanding complete self-renunciation. In the end it was not the polis that determined policy but the masses that happened to gather at the assembly, not with a view to higher principles but to satisfy their greed, which unfortunately was insatiable. One may well get the notion that in the whole history of the world hardly any power anywhere had ever paid so dearly for its life and strife as the Greek polis did. These unhappy events certainly caused posterity to suffer incalculable loss, however abundant the contributions of later Greeks may have been, particularly in the visual arts.

We should deeply lament if we could envisage in its entirety all that the Greeks destroyed by slaying outstanding men, by intimidating others and driving them into mute private life, by disrupting the continuity of noble families, by suppressing refined conviviality and by abetting self-seeking domination through the misuse of public oratory.

Chapter Four

THE UNITY OF THE GREEK NATION

1. Internecine Warfare and the Forces of National Unification

Because the Greeks always had been politically pluralistic and remained so as long as possible, their ability to develop a powerful unified culture is ample proof that originally they derived from a unified nation. The Greeks offer the remarkable drama of an old and persistent enmity among many small branches of one and the same nation so that, viewed panoramically, this spectacle already appears somewhat uniform, as it were, forming a single group for the eye.

In the heroic age the hero stormed castles and, having killed the lord, either married his daughter or carried her off as a slave. The earliest invading Greeks, however, when unchecked, were outright pirates; various figures merged the pirate and hero in one. In those days, the dissension among the kin was expressed symbolically: Eteocles and Polyneices struggle with each other already in the womb. In addition, the myths teem with deliberate and involuntary murder, and the spleen of that age consisted essentially in wandering about because of some such murder.

The *Odyssey* consistently takes piracy, i.e., sudden landing and plundering, for granted, even on the part of its most praiseworthy heroes. Menelaus rather freely admitted (IV, 82.90) that he had acquired his treasures largely by pillage; Nestor quite naïvely imputed a similar course of action to Telemachus (III, 72), and when the suitors arrived in the underworld the shade of Agamemnon surmised among other things that they were killed while stealing cattle, just as he himself had earlier been suspected of doing (XI, 400).

Odysseus above all was mighty in piracy; he ravaged the Thracian

Warrior with shield and arrow at bay
Interior of a cylix

coastal city of Ismarus, killed the men, and carried off the women and rich plunder, dividing it *equally* among his men (IX, 38). It never occurred to him to ask himself what harm he had suffered from the Cicones. He supposed he could recoup what he had lost to the suitors by raiding of his own (XXIII, 358). In his considered conduct of life, he goes on killing and robbing without any qualms (XIII, 259; XIV, 262; XVII, 425).

The whole Cyclops story was nothing but a reflection of the wicked primeval dealings between crafty sea robbers and wild shepherds (IX). Polyphemus, who finally perceived with whom he was dealing, was the savage shepherd caricatured as the sea folk knew him; cannibalism was attributed to him as it was to the Laestrygonians (IX, 116.124), which may have been historically true.

Other heroes stole cattle with a view to proffering bridal gifts to royal daughters. An interesting tale dealing with piracy tells about Butes and how the host of men he had gathered about him on the island of Naxos stole women from the various coastal areas. Two chiefs quarreled over the beautiful Pankratis and killed each other; so she fell to a third man. The heroic age had one good quality: it did not systematically lay waste whole regions, i.e., destroy the plantations or farms; destruction of this kind was reserved for the Greeks in the days of their cultural refinement. Armed robbery by land prevailed among some of the more backward tribes. The Ozolians, Locrians, Aetolians, and Acarnians still followed that old way of life up to the fifth century.

Exclusiveness, ill will toward all other poleis, especially the neighboring ones, was not only a dominant feeling but almost a mark of civic virtue. Antipathies among modern cities, which derive mostly from economic causes, give no notion of the rancor, secret or manifest, which Greek cities harbored for each other. The least harmful aspect of this ill will was the sarcasm and calumny periodically indulged in; the worst was the extermination of one's neighbor, as Argos had destroyed Mycenae.

One of the greatest merits of the aristocratic age was that, on the whole, it preserved peace and evolved the agonistic virtues as an outlet for its ambitions. Violent outbreaks of hatred between the poleis have their beginning in the restless fifth century. Although the awareness of a common bond among the Dorian or Ionian tribes determined in part which side a polis took in the great upheavals, such as the Persian or Peloponnesian wars, yet, as before, no quarter was given to one's closest neighbor and the nearest tribal kin. The Lacedaemonian Dorians exterminated the Messenian Dorians with a vengeance merely because they coveted their land.

He who has learned to know the harshness of the polis toward its own suppressed parties and has seen how the polis oppressed people of old Greek stock in its vicinity, will see in its external conduct simply an extension of the same logic. The more feverishly tense life became in the fifth century polis, the more frequently it engaged in external warfare, the shorter were the intervals of peace and the more unreliable became the treaties. More and more, the single state became aware that all other states were in life-and-death competition with it, and comported itself accordingly, so that the period of the highest cultural achievements coincided with the most atrocious executions.

Listening to the Greeks, one would suppose that humane codes sacredly observed governed the conduct of victors in war: not to raze cities, to spare people who yielded with outstretched hands, to free prisoners for a stipulated ransom, to permit the enemy to bury its dead, to respect the honor of young women, etc. In time, the nation even came to imagine that Hellenism and humaneness were synonymous, and already at the capture of Ilium the victors, in allegedly Hellenic fashion, had granted each person permission to carry away his dearest possessions, whereupon Aeneas had taken his household gods and his father with him.

According to myths, the murder of strangers took place only in countries far away; for all that, the Greeks rather frequently murdered their own at home. Those alleged humane practices were adhered to, when they were, for purely practical motives—fear of vengeance and hope of ransom. Sparing a temple while annihilating the people around it rather takes on for us the character of a deliberate sacrilege. The horrors reported hereafter took place in part at the time of Phidias, Iktinus, Zeuxis, and Parrhasius, with all its subtleties of conversation and choric meters. When the tragedians, as is well known, confuse Mycenae and Argos, that means little because in the year 468 B.C. the Argives had sold part of the Mycenaeans as slaves, scattered the rest abroad, and laid the city as well as Tirynthus in ruins.

All ancient peoples regarded it as an immutable law that the vanquished and their goods became the property of the victor. But the small Greek cities living next to each other as sovereign states were animated by the sweeping egoism of doing not only what was essential to their survival but whatever in a wider sense appeared desirable and convenient besides. Sparta expressed this view unequivocally through the mouth of the dreadful King Cleomenes when he attacked Argos without the slightest provocation: *Whatever harm one can do an enemy takes precedence over all justice before gods and men.*

The other poleis also committed shocking iniquities, not especially in the heat of passion but deliberately, out of so-called necessity, and not only against enemies but also against such as it seemed advantageous to victimize, not only because of compelling motives of war but because of political odium. The Greeks continued to act as if the Hellenic supply of men were inexhaustible and as if Persia and the world of barbarians were no longer a constant threat.

The documents on the destinies of Plataea and Melos have been indelibly preserved. The heroic remnant of the besieged Plataeans surrendered on condition that Spartan judges would try them; five such judges appeared with secret instructions to pronounce the death sentence on them as a favor to Thebes, which might be useful to Sparta in the Peloponnesian War. These same Thebans had destroyed Plataea earlier, at the time of Xerxes, and were to do it again after the scattered fugitives had returned to the city after the peace of Antalcidas.

It was Macedonia that restored Plataea permanently. But the philosophy that might makes right found its consummate expression in the callous way the Athenians demanded submission of the Melians during peace and neutrality, knowing full well that this act would provoke opposition which inevitably would lead to the destruction of the weaker party. In point of fact, when the Melians were starved into surrender, the Athenians killed the men, sold the women and children into slavery, and colonized the island with Athenians. But woe to Athens, the great polis, if ever it fell into misfortune and had to remember how it had treated the weaker states.

Commonly the victors completely destroyed a city they vanquished, not sparing even the temples and the graves; sometimes they carried off the statues of the gods. Or they might let old or unique temples stand, as Alexander had done after the conquest of Thebes. Out of the usable material left after they had totally destroyed Plataea the Thebans built a temple to Hera and a caravansary two hundred feet square; they leased out the land of the Plataean state. At other times, the ruins of the city and the surrounding territory were dedicated to a temple found there, thus effectively forestalling the restoration of the city.

The victor had to prevent the rebuilding of a city come what may, for since the sites of cities were often well chosen, one could easily foresee that the people panting for revenge were eager to rebuild, and would do so unless they were prevented. One means to achieve this was the solemn imprecation, a very ancient custom, Strabo supposes, because Agamemnon already had laid the city of Ilion under a curse.

If the victors let the city stand, they had to resettle it with new inhabitants; but even if they destroyed the city, they still did not dare let the old population survive lest it return to its former habitation. They had either to kill or enslave their captives. If they enslaved them, they either sold them somewhere or used them as their own slaves at home. If they murdered even women and children, as the Byzantines and Chalcedonians did when they marched through Bithynia in 415 B.C., they did so because they had enough slaves already and had no prospects of selling them to advantage.

After conquering Mitylene on Lesbos the demos contented itself with executing the thousand guiltiest sent to Athens and with distributing nearly the whole island to Attic *cleruchies* [military colonies to safeguard strategically important points], demolishing the walls, and confiscating their ships. When King Philip reduced and razed Olynthus, an Olynthian traitor served as assessor in selling his fellow Olynthians; there were also Greeks who accepted Olynthian slaves as presents from King Philip. Most of the Athenians captured at the end of the Sicilian expedition perished in Syracusan stone quarries where they were detained awaiting sale; only a small number was saved as a favor.

At the slightest difficulty the victors might slay their captives so as not to have to feed them any longer. Alcidas, a Peloponnesian admiral, dispatched for the same reason some unarmed men even though they had not raised a finger against him and had been forced into an alliance with Athens.

In the course of the Peloponnesian War, Athens, having no money to pay thirteen hundred Thracian mercenaries, sent them away with the general injunction to harm the enemies of Athens. They made a sudden attack upon the completely unarmed and undefended city of Mycalessus in Boeotia, plundering homes and temples, murdering young and old, including women and children, all the boys in a school, even draft animals and everything alive. Granted that they were bloodthirsty Thracians; still, they were led by an Athenian, Diitrephes, who must have known very well where he was taking them.

The requital came with Aegospotami. The Athenians had resolved, if they won, to cut off the right hand of every prisoner they took. A short time before they had hurled to death the crews of two triremes, and Lysander, who now presided at the trial by the victorious allies, with his own hands killed the Athenian general who had issued the order for that atrocity. The Spartans and their allies executed all three thousand Athenian prisoners.

The Spartans, however, would not consent to the destruction of Athens as demanded by the Corinthians, Thebans, and others. They withheld their consent not for the high-minded reason they adduced, that a Hellenic city which in past crises had done so much for Greece should not now be reduced to slavery, but rather on the shrewd calculation that it was best not to provoke a last desperate struggle and that the destruction of Athens would only make Thebes the more formidable.

It was already a sort of clemency when the inhabitants were only driven out of a city, as the Athenians drove out the Aeginetans in 427 B.C. because it appeared safer to have Athenian colonists living on the island, although the Aeginetans had been paying tribute to Athens for thirty years. The subsequent events, however, are instructive. When the Athenians later took the Peloponnesian city of Thyrea, where Aeginetan fugitives lived, they brought them to Athens and killed them because of long standing enmity, i.e., the Athenians merely proved thereby that they had not been able to annihilate them all in 427. After the fall of Athens, Lysander returned the surviving fugitives; it will come as no surprise that the Aeginetans henceforth did not allow any Athenian to set foot on the island.

At Salamis, Aegina had fought the Persians in a most glorious manner and like Athens had also been a city famous for its art. The envy of the powerful neighbor, however, had demanded first the oppressive subjugation and then the expulsion of the Aeginetans. Similarly, the glory the Mycenaeans had won in the Persian War led to their destruction in that it had provoked the envy of the Argives.

The Hellenes knew one another and knew that defeat in war meant not only subjection to a power stronger politically and militarily, but also total destruction, for the victor would take possession of all property, appropriate the territory, and kill or sell the inhabitants. Since the downfall of the polis meant the destruction of all citizens, its defense took on the character of protecting the communal existence of the city as well as the personal existence of the individual, and the more turbulent the times and the more frequent the trials of destiny became, the more certainly the polis could rely on each citizen to be a fighter and the more determined was its defense.

The systematic devastation of enemy territory deserves a closer look. All people in all ages resorted to devastation as a means of inflicting injury on an enemy. In the Middle Ages in Europe, open villages were destroyed to impoverish the lord they were attached to and so to force him to yield; to this end, houses were burned, farmers killed or dispersed, the cattle—if not killed already by the owners—and all the rest of the property stolen.

Among the Greeks pillage and devastation were nothing out of the ordinary either. It was a different matter with the destruction of trees, which went far beyond the aims of the war and really stemmed from an inveterate and irreconcilable hatred. Cleombrotus, a later Spartan king, put himself under a heavy cloud of suspicion when he refrained from laying waste Boeotia. Agesilaus, likewise on a campaign in Boeotia, ordered his confederate troops to devastate the land and to chop down the trees. When they would not properly carry out his orders he revoked them but had the soldiers move their camp several times a day so that they used up as much timber in setting up new barracks as they would have destroyed at his commands. The devastation Agesilaus caused in Greece added up to a frightful total.

Could no one among the outstanding thinkers and patriots grasp the historical implications of this kind of warfare and give the nation a timely warning? There were such people and warnings enough if one had only cared to listen. Lysistrata, in Aristophanes' play of the same name, tells the Athenians and Laconians:

> Using the same consecrated water, you as kinsmen sprinkle in common the altars at Olympia, Thermopylae, Delphi, and other places too many to name; yet you destroy your fellow Hellenes and their cities, and all the while barbarians are near at hand.

But Plato, to his eternal glory, speaks the plainest words in his *The Republic:*

> Should Hellenes be allowed to enslave the people of Hellenic cities? Should they not rather prevent others from doing this? Should they not make it a custom to spare the Hellenic race lest the barbarians enslave them? Should they not be forbidden altogether to keep Hellenes as slaves? One should also not pillage those who have fallen in battle, but should permit the enemy to gather their dead for burial. Furthermore, no arms (of defeated Greeks) should be hung on display in temples. Hellenes

should not ravage the land of the enemy, cut down the trees, and burn the houses, but should take only the year's crop. Fighting among Hellenes is not war but a disease, for by nature they are friends. The term *war* applies properly only to fighting between Hellenes and barbarians, for they are by nature at odds with each other. Hellenes should act toward barbarians as they now act toward one another.

Where individuals thought, spoke, and wrote so nobly, posterity will not spare severe judgment on a people that persevered in acting meanly, and especially so because exceptions among leaders did occur: "Epaminondas and Pelopidas," Plutarch says, "never killed or enslaved the population after capturing a city." Referring to the time around the beginning of the second century B.C., Plutarch also says:

> As diseases appear to lessen when the body weakens, so conflicts waned among the Greek states as their wealth diminished. But right up to the time of the Roman rule, one Greek city would occasionally pounce on another to rob it of its last crumb.

But far beyond this late period and even in the time of the Roman emperors, Greeks kept the memory of victory over other Greeks alive by every means possible. The less they had been able to overthrow or destroy an enemy permanently, the more lavish they made their *tropaeum* marking a victory over this enemy, so as to nettle him the more. The centers where the greatest communal festivals and divine worship took place were crammed with mementos of Greek victories over other Greeks.

In Olympia, the Elians set up a *tropaeum* for repelling a Spartan attack, and in the temple of Zeus, directly under the Nike of Paeonius, hung the golden shield of the Lacedaemonian confederacy commemorating their victory at Tanagra over the Argives, Athenians, and Ionians. For their part in the battle at Sphacteria the Messenians of Naupactus dedicated a goddess of victory on which, however, they did not inscribe the name of the conquered out of apprehension—for they were Spartans.

But even in the days of the Roman emperors Delphi, above all, was the monumental museum of Greek hatred for Greeks, of mutually inflicted suffering immortalized in the loftiest works of art. This museum was almost perfectly intact while Greece was filled with ruins and waste, the guilt for which rests not with the Macedonians and Romans but with the Greeks themselves. The only Greek city whose temples were not adorned with spoils of Hellenes and the anathemas of kindred dead but with the weapons of barbarians was Corinth. These weapons bore the inscription: *The Corinthians and General Timoleon delivered the Hellenes dwelling in Sicily from the Carthaginians and they dedicated these gifts to the gods.*

The cities, to be sure, maintained among themselves shorter and longer periods of peace, often resting on treaties. During these periods they carried on a brisk trade and intercourse which required that the resident aliens be granted a certain security. Because of their traveling about, whether for trade, attending festivals, or going on pilgrimages, the Greeks developed a system of hospitality which established for them the reputation of being an especially hospitable nation.

Homer provided illustrations of the unerring tact of the Greeks in these matters. The claim to hospitality deriving from their grandfathers made Diomedes and Glaucus halt their combat; they exchanged weapons and resolved thenceforth to avoid each other in battle. Indeed, a general warning was issued against contests between men having mutual claims to hospitality.

And the poor were protected; Nausicaa and Eumaeus said that the stranger and starveling belong to Zeus. In the early period of the polis, Hesiod proclaimed that those cities will flourish which pronounce a *just* verdict on the stranger as well as on the native. Later, this was no longer taken as a matter of course, for the Greek abroad had to have a local representative to support him in court and to assure his safety in general, which along with other usages in connection with *proxenia* remains unexplained. (*Proxenia* was a compact of friendship between a state and a foreigner.)

If one cannot well perceive the unifying bond of the Greek nation in the antagonistic relations of the poleis to each other, one nevertheless expects to find it in their common religion. As a common cultural element of the highest order religion certainly exerted a unifying force; it carried within it a powerful system of concepts that was shared by the people as a whole. In addition, there were the majestic communal temples, festival places, and oracles where on solemn occasions continental and colonial Hellenes forgathered and became aware how great the nation was; at such times these places appeared to be an intensified Greece.

The great festival seasons were accompanied by a divine truce in war and sometimes on such occasions minor conflicts were settled altogether. The divine truce of Olympia and the holy neutrality of Elis have their own history. However, these festivals did not prevent real wars; in fact, they hardly interrupted them. People did not wish to forgo the old custom of coming together for sacrifices, athletic contests, and markets. The Olympic festival also provided an orderly chronology, for parallel to it local chronology, with special year and month designations, continued everywhere. Apollo at Delphi counseled Greeks at war with Greeks, and his shrine, as said above, was richly adorned with monuments of mutual hatred.

More even than religion, the cycle of heroic myths provided a common tie for the entire people, for its great epic poetry had taken on the character of a common possession. What a tremendous wealth of flowers wafted

Athena with Poseidon and Dionysus
Thyrrhenic jug

together from all quarters until these enchanted fields of myth were luxuriating!—that was something men lost sight of as soon as the epic cycle shaped the great national image, mirroring its feelings, reflections, and ambitions.

Though the semblance of the Oedipus, Agamemnon, and other cycles might appear among other races, the Greeks endowed them with their own unique characteristics and richly varied forms. These myths directly exerted a unifying effect by the fact that their heroes, in addition to their special local activities, assembled for a common enterprise which presented an ideal of collective Greek unity.

The voyage of the Argonauts and the Calydonian hunt present formative stages of these myths in a restricted geographical area. Later these myths were amplified so as to include heroes and men from all tribes, until finally they undertook the expedition to Troy. Thucydides regarded this in all sincerity as the first great Panhellenic venture and as a manifestation of the will of the nation as a whole.

As the heroes were the earliest glorified personalities, so their herald Homer was the earliest intellectual celebrity, universally recognized among the Hellenes; admittedly, he became the chief means used in educating the Greeks from childhood on. After Homer the Greek world became truly one; there are Greeks where there is a recollection of heroes. The beauty of these heroic legends touched and captivated the Latins, the primeval kindred of the Greeks in the west, and the wings of Greek art and maybe also their poesy carried rich treasure even to the dullish Etruscans.

As the unity of the myths conferred a high order of unity on Greek life, so this unity was gradually strengthened by their whole culture, which distinguished the Greeks as such by an abundance of common modes of life of all kinds, without which they would have regarded existence as a misfortune and which brought them together time and again despite all mutual antipathies. This culture complex was powerful enough to assimilate or expel backward elements at home and to turn the barbarians around the Greek colonies and in their interiors into half-Greeks who were at least eager to understand Greek culture. The Greek language above all had truly wonderful national characteristics.

In the early days there emerged, out of the diverse dialects, the language of epic chants understood and craved everywhere, the noblest vehicle for the legends and myths of the gods, the world, and the heroes. Whoever knew Greek became a man set apart from all others, and whoever spoke a good Greek became a Hellene, for he was fit to be one. And finally, the whole Greek existence was animated by a spirit we shall learn to know by the term agonistic in the broadest sense. In time a conscious mode of education was based on this concept, and when grammar, gymnastics, and cithara [lute] playing dominated the youth in the cities, everyone early understood what this Greek life was all about.

2. *Greeks and Barbarians*

The contrast that made the Greek aware of being Greek was the non-Greek, the barbarian. The concept of barbarianism is a remarkable and many-sided one, deserving careful study. The later Greeks, poets, and orators presupposed that among other qualities barbarianism included especially brutality, perfidy, treachery, and were naïvely blind to the fact that in all these traits the Greeks themselves easily matched the barbarians. Finally, the concept of barbarianism ought not to be determined by aversion, for this had been mutual.

All peoples that regarded themselves as constituted by divine law displayed contempt for all other peoples, and the higher castes, wherever they existed, shunned the lower. The Egyptians in particular regarded the Greeks as unclean and surely not only because they ate beef, as Herodotus supposed; the Greeks returned the compliment by preening themselves on their taste for wine as opposed to the Egyptian for beer. The Greeks had the advantage in that they experienced at least no physical loathing and had no purity laws to observe in relation to barbarians, thus feeling unencumbered in their observation of the world abroad.

How the concept of Hellenism gradually evolved can best be explained by the Greek views on the Trojans. Homer did not make the slightest distinction between the customs and religion of the Trojans and the Achaeans. But on fairly archaic vases the Trojans wear Asiatic costumes, and in the Aeginetan groups Paris may be recognized by it. Thucydides regarded them distinctly as barbarians; occasionally Herodotus insulted them as being such; Strabo hardly cared to apply Greek etymology to Trojan place names any more, and Lucian called Paris a barbarian and foreigner at a time when its art forms were no longer distinct from those of the Phrygian Atys and the Persian Mithras.

According to a famous passage in Aristotle, the Greeks found themselves between two kinds of barbarians: those of the north in Europe—brave and free but incapable of ratiocination, of the arts, of establishing a state or exercising rule; and those of Asia—reflective and civilized but feckless and hence enslaved.

The first kind, and especially the numerous Scythians posing a military threat, appear in the fourth book of the *Histories* of Herodotus, who perceptively yet distinctly outlined their customs and those of similarly half-civilized people. The Scythians resented it very much to be referred to as living in bondage. Martial people of this sort, particularly if they could sweep others into their wake, must have felt a boundless exhilaration and overwhelming vitality. Their bondage was that of heart and soul since it was a tribal constraint. However free the individuals in their saddles might have felt, still they had only one group will, much like animal communities; in all their activities, customs and religion, they maintained one and the same level, and did so by force, if need be, for as soon as the whole nation failed to act in complete uniformity, it weakened and may have disintegrated; it rightly sensed that it amounted to something only as a collective entity. The uniformity of thought and behavior of such barbarians revealed itself also in other respects. Whereas the Greek developed his individuality in all sorts of athletic contests, these peoples lacked every understanding of agonistic competition.

Their riding matches were nothing but collective exhibitions of military strength; they staged sham battles, even very bloody ones, as the Gauls did at their armed wassails. War put the barbarians in a mood of higher exaltation, and they waged it in most instances for no reason at all, being impelled to it blindly, as it were. Herodotus reports that the Scythians took their census by counting collected arrowheads. Once a year in each district they held a communion at which every warrior who had killed an enemy could dip his cup into the common wine bowl. Among the Sauromats a young woman could not marry until she had killed an enemy.

The Scythians had shrines of the war god everywhere, and every year they sacrificed droves of animals and prisoners of war, though they did not sacrifice all prisoners as the Greeks did, but only every hundredth man.

The profusion and discernment of Herodotus' observations leave the reader curious nevertheless about matters which the man of Halicarnassus did not observe and discuss, and one is tempted to deplore that he never met with the contemporary Celtic and Germanic tribes at all.

The other kind of barbarians from which the Greeks knew themselves to be distinct were the highly civilized Asiatics whose culture was older and whose technology and ancient lore much richer than their own. Here too the most profound difference was that, while the Greeks were individually developed, the Asiatics were kept in dependency not so much by their collective actions as indirectly by a caste system and absolute despotism. We know the character of the Egyptians chiefly from the Greek conception of it, but this was probably not entirely wrong. In spite of the tremendous achievements the world of culture owes to the Egyptians, and in spite of their intense national pride, it appears that the single individual was morally ground down by servitude.

The usages, symbols and anxiety inspired by ancient religious fears turned the life of the Egyptian into a hard servitude; in addition his whole life, both occupational and political, consisted of unremitting duties. In the *Histories* of Herodotus, there is reflected the general mood of the embittered slave who derives some satisfaction from slandering and vilifying his overlords. The ideal of life was crafty knavery, which in the saga of Rhampsanit, for instance, came in for such high honors.

As is well known, the Greeks took remarkably little notice of the empires of Babylon and Assyria while unknowingly they derived so many things from these cultures. The nearest barbarian people and empire was that of the Lydians, which they knew intimately and had some sympathy for, either because of an earlier close kinship or because of Lydian similarity with Greek life and religion.

On the other hand, they felt nothing but anxiety and odium for the Persian Empire, a latecomer taking over an empire of formerly free nations that had been first subjugated by the Assyrians and then by the Medes. With the exception of Cyrus and Darius Hytaspis, the Persian dynasty produced no rulers of distinction but some villainous characters and one dangerous traitor, Cyrus the Younger. Between their new conquests, these Persian kings were constantly putting down revolts in outlying countries whose property and sanctuaries they had violated.

In their open and glorious struggle with this Persia, the Greeks became the more aware of the existing contrast between themselves and the barbarians. This made the ignominy all the greater when after the Peloponnesian War Artaxerxes Mnemon, whose court was the scene of gruesome atrocities, got his hands into Greek affairs again. But in the meantime many Greeks had learned to know the essential weakness of this imperial colossus, as well as the weakness of the Persians. In the important closing chapter of his *Cyropaedia,* Xenophon showed how the empire had come to confuse appearance with reality and how the old forms of life were outwardly retained though they had become thoroughly hollow.

With the Battle of Arbela the Persian dynasty ended. But when Alexander had come to the Jaxartes River and met rugged barbarians there, the so-called Scythians who shot their arrows across the river to let him know the mettle of the men he was facing, he realized the difference between these men and the Asiatics. Wherever the eastern satrapies resisted him, they did so not in defense of the Persian Empire but because they were proud people, like the Bactrians, who had joined the Persians voluntarily.

Over against the Scythian and the Asiatic stands the Greek, individualistic, emancipated from racial and caste ties, constantly competing with his kin in contests [agones], ranging from athletic encounters at the great festivals to self-assertion in his polis, from the wrestling mat at Olympia to the agora, the courts [stoas] of his native city, and to the competitions determining superiority in song and the visual arts.

The Orient is not agonistic, if for no other reason than because a rigid caste system cannot acknowledge open competition in the lists. The Greeks on their part would not tolerate a barbarian even to be present at their contests. Even Alexander, King of Macedon, an ancestor of Alexander the Great (489–454), a Grecophile, had, when he wished to attend the Olympic games, first to prove that he was a Temenid and so of Greek origin. Furthermore, the man from the Orient was sober-minded in his behavior and did not laugh except perhaps at the jugglers; he ventured to express his wit only allegorically in the dress of a fable.

Instead of discourses at a symposium [drinking together] the Orient, according to Greek notions, only knew hard drinking, so that wherever this habit made inroads into Greece it was referred to as a barbaric influence. Finally, the conviction established itself that only the Greeks responded to reason and the barbarians to force.

The gods of the Greeks were more beautiful than those of the barbarians for whom the divine was not ennobled humanity but something expressed allegorically and slavishly through amalgamation with animal forms, the multiplication of limbs, or ritual raiment and gestures. Powerful priesthoods and the stolid minds of the populace had long since come to a permanent understanding on these matters.

The Greek gods were also more clever than those of the barbarians, just as the Greek was smarter than the barbarian. Even the barbarians regarded the Greek gods as cleverer than their own. In some measure the ancient sanctuaries of the Orient were prepared to foretell future events; unfortunately, these sanctuaries were also paired with astrology. But only the Greek gods pronounced oracles in the full sense of the term, and even Lydians, Phrygians, Italics, and on occasion Carthaginians consulted the oracle at Delphi. Foreign peoples made gifts to Hellenic temples not merely for oracles received but out of genuine reverence. The secret offering that periodically arrived at Delphi from the land of the Hyperboreans may remain a riddle, but it was well known that the throne of Arimnestus, an Italic king, was the earliest barbarian votive offering found among those at Olympia. All this made the Greeks feel they were especially devout, and among them particularly the Athenians. The Greek laymen felt a priestly superiority over people of other cultures because they really knew how to associate with the gods. This notion was revealed very clearly in that strange Delphic oracle during a famine: The Athenians should make vows for Hellenes and barbarians.

As Greek colonies began to dot the near and far coastal regions of the Mediterranean and the Pontus, they often subjugated the barbarians in their vicinities, but much more frequently these latter took up voluntary intercourse with the Greek colonies and received from them the necessities of life, as well as knowledge and noble adornments of Greek culture, as is evident from the adoption of the Greek alphabet by the Celts of Gaul.

After the Ethiopian dynasty fell in Egypt, Psammetichus opened Egypt to foreign trade and commerce once more, which resulted in an economic revolution, a sudden rise in trade and in the population census. The warrior caste withdrew from Egypt into Ethiopia 200,000 strong; though they would have been able, one should think, to hurl these intruders back into the sea, it appears they were thoroughly perplexed by the arrival of the Greeks. Surely these soldiers would not have relinquished their ancient rights to their homeland merely out of chagrin for having been slighted in a campaign of the king against Philistia, or because their privileges had been curtailed.

That they did not revolt against Psammetichus was perhaps because they respected in the foreign-born innovator the sanctity of kingship; nevertheless they remained obdurate to his pleas for their return. Perhaps they were sardonically delighted to see him now protected only by foreigners and at their mercy. With their withdrawal ancient Egypt passed away, unable to withstand the volatile Greeks, and the people, at least in lower Egypt, submitted completely, to the point of producing a mixed race, the so-called "interpreters." It is undeniable that with the penetration of Hellenism and the increase of trade and industry the vitality of the ancient Egyptian nation and culture began to wane.

A few telling facts will serve to show the influence the Greeks had on the Persians. As long as it was in the ascendant, Persia as a world monarchy did not hesitate too long to subjugate, among many other nations, also the Greeks, and to hold them in protracted subjection. Attempts by the Greeks to break away from this empire led Datis, Xerxes, and Mardonius to undertake their great campaigns against Greece with their well-known outcomes.

In the meantime, at the Achaemenid court, Greeks had quite clearly become the most interesting personages. Atossa, the daughter of Cyrus, preferred slave girls from Laconia, Argos, Attica, and Corinth, and her husband Darius heard a great deal of the famous athlete Milon of Crotona. Gradually there appeared at the Persian court, or in proximity of the kings, men like the physician Demokedes, who was treated with high respect but in reality prevented from leaving; Histiaeus, King Demaratus of Sparta, the poet Onamacritus, and others. All of these took part in important state affairs and upon occasion became more influential even than the satraps and the king's relatives.

Indeed, Histiaeus was executed under torture at the order of satraps, lest he again become powerful with the king in spite of all he had done against Darius. And later there appeared at the court of Xerxes and of Artaxerxes the very man who had put to death the Persian herald sent to ask for earth and water in token of submission to the Persians but who during the war itself had had to keep an access open to Persia, the most illustrious of all fugitives—Themistocles. His letter to the king is the typical letter of a Hellene to a barbarian, who would not receive another such letter from anyone in his whole empire. Having learned as much as he could of the Persian language in the course of a year, Themistocles appeared before the king in person.

He was a man of unmistakable natural genius. Without studying a subject in advance, or pondering over it later, but only using his native intelligence, he had the unerring ability of reaching the right conclusion quickly on any matter at hand and excelled all others in forecasting what would happen. He could admirably explain anything he undertook, and he saw more clearly than others whether a venture would turn out well or ill. By the power of his genius and with but brief reflection he was able in the highest degree to do the right thing on the spur of the moment. This was something all the king's relatives, satraps, and magicians could not equal.

Who knows what power these Greeks might have acquired at the court of the great kings of Persia if they had worked with a view to that end, instead of merely wanting to use the power of this court as a means to a safe return to Greece. Greeks long considered it impossible to lead their armies on a campaign into these distant eastern countries. "Leave Sparta before sunset," Cleomenes commanded Aristagoras who wanted to unfold a plan for marching on Susa, "for you will never earn the gratitude of the Lacedae-

Lance fight of pygmies with cranes
Vase painting, British Museum

monians by proposing to take them on a three months' journey from the sea."

In the days of their glory, the Greeks stressed heavily the contrast between themselves and the barbarians. For this reason, Herodotus is the more significant since he acknowledged that the barbarians had accomplished many great things and had reported them objectively before the rhetoricians took over. Euripides, on the other hand, played up to the prejudices of his Athenian audience in a most repulsive fashion. His Odysseus reproaches the barbarians for neither honoring their friends nor showing respect for those fallen in battle; in his *Orestes,* he vents cheap Greek feelings of superiority at stereotyped barbarians, as cowardly, servile, and fearful of death, all of which was allegedly typical of the Phrygians. The more gladly therefore do we listen to Brasidas, a knowledgeable man who had faced the Illyrians in battle before and now described their manner of fighting just before engaging in another battle. Hardly anywhere else will one find the strength and weakness of these primitive barbarians described so well and as briefly as in this address.

It was regarded as the most sorrowful misfortune conceivable for a polis to become barbarian, be it by sudden overthrow or by gradual penetration by foreigners. Greek cities subject to the Persian Empire fell into this category, as when Ephesus was being overrun by foreigners in about 408 B.C., when Persians quartered there and Lydians rapidly infiltrated, until Lysander appeared and by redirecting commerce, establishing shipyards, and other measures, again assured predominance to Greek life.

When a number of splendid Greek cities in Italy were irretrievably lost to the Samnites, Lucanians, and Bruttii, the inhabitants of Poseidonia, later Paestum, were also subjugated. They changed their language and other endeavors, we are told, but they still celebrate one of their Hellenic festivals at which they gather and recall old names and customs; then they lament and weep together, later to go their several ways again.

In the fourth century the emphasis on the contrast between Hellenes and barbarians was much subdued, perhaps because the Greeks themselves had suffered untold atrocities in the meanwhile at the hands of Greeks and because the earlier Greek feeling of national superiority had been broken. Among the philosophers it was significantly Antisthenes, founder of the school of Cynics, who relentlessly condemned the polis and who was first to make light of the old ideals, though he himself was only a half-Hellene, his mother having been a Thracian.

To prove that hard work was no evil, he cited Herakles among the Hellenes and Cyrus among the barbarians, the same Cyrus whom also Xenophon about this time portrayed as a man ideally educated for kingly duties. It is extraordinarily significant that he used a barbarian not only as an example but also as a paragon in ethical questions. For Plato, Egypt was a primeval source of the spirit and an ideal in more than one respect. Since Alexander, Greek views on these matters changed completely, because large countries in the east accepted in part or completely Greek as the language for conducting many of their activities.

It may be an exaggeration to say that the sons of the Persians, Bactrians, and Gedrosians had recited the tragedies of Sophocles and Euripides, but the Hellenized Near East up to and beyond the Euphrates represented a genuine expansion, not so much of the Greek nation as of its cultural domain.

Philosophy especially suffered a veritable invasion, as will be detailed in a different context. It is said that Anacharsis the Scythian was attracted to philosophy already in its early stages, and Mithridates, a Persian nobleman, the son of Rhodobates, was one of Plato's admirers. Now, however, Hellenic wisdom broke through national confines, much as the Pythagorean women had overcome the inequality of sex, and much as the slaves trained to be philosophers had obliterated social distinctions.

The Stoics taught the doctrine that Hellenes and barbarians were equal in that they were the children of the same gods. A hundred years after Alexander, Eratosthenes could say:

*They are wrong who say that mankind is divided into Hellenes
and barbarians; one had better distinguish men according to excellence or depravity, for many Hellenes are morally corrupt and
many barbarians morally noble like the Indians and Aryans, and
also Romans and Carthaginians with their remarkable political
organization.*

From here it was but a short step to the glorification of the barbarians.
This was in part motivated by a longing for inchoate conditions of life, a
longing found at times in the late and highly refined periods of every culture, and it is significant that one expects to find such conditions in lands
far away. At that time it was fashionable to single out the primitive people in
Homer and Aeschylus, like the glorious Hippemolgoi, the law-abiding
Scythians, or the Abioi, a fabulous tribe of the north and the most just of
all peoples, for even in early antiquity men knew the central portions of
the world so well that they sought goodness and happiness on its margins.
Such notions gradually turned into rationalizations. The barbarians were
supposed to have profound religious insight; in the temple of Asclepius in
Aegium a Sidonian contended in the presence of Pausanius that the Phoenicians understood divine matters better than the Greeks did. Whereas formerly the fabulous Hyperboreans had been credited with a prodigious piety,
now barbarians in general were praised for their piety, in contrast to the
growing godlessness of the Greeks. Finally, the barbarians were considered
to be morally superior; the late Greek thought of his own nation much as
Machiavelli did of the Italians. And the inevitable conclusion was that if
the barbarians were depraved, the Greeks had corrupted them.

3. *Hellenic Pathos*

After the foregoing, it may be possible at this point to evaluate in some
measure the quality of Panhellenic experience as differentiated according
to the times and people involved. At the time of the Persian Wars, the
Athenians spoke out clearly and magnificently, as they had every right to do.
The reply they made to the Spartan envoy right after they had rejected
the proposals of Mardonius, the speech of the Athenian messenger to the
ephors, and the oath of the Greek army on the isthmus before the Battle of
Plataea, are enduring monuments to their glory.

Language and lineage, shrines, divine worship, and mode of life the
Hellenes had in common. Likewise their reverence for Zeus Hellenius, horror of betraying Hellas in any manner, craving liberty more than life, the

promise never to destroy any of the cities which had joined in the fight—all this bears ringing testimony to the loftiest sentiments. Even the vows the Corinthian hetaerae made for the welfare of the Hellenes are not to be taken in jest, as they were by later people, but as the solemn mood of a sublime moment.

Then there came the time when the interests of Greece were halved into the hegemonies of Athens and Sparta. Pericles appealed too late to the sentiments of the past and too late he tried to convene a congress of all Greek states for peace and concerted action among the Hellenes, to restore the temples the Persians had destroyed, and to make the sacrifices they had vowed side by side. A nod from Sparta prevented this congress.

Once Athens had deliberately altered its entire history so as to present itself as having been the benefactor of Greece from the very beginning, poets and orators took up and repeated this idea over and over again; the catastrophic outcome of the Peloponnesian War did not affect these claims in the least. Now and then, a general Panhellenic sentiment echoes from Attic tragedy in the name of all Greeks. Herakles could say of himself: *Am I from Argos or Thebes? I boast not one city alone, for every citadel of the Hellenes is my home.* For a short time in the fourth century the ideal of Panhellenism flowered in the person and mighty deeds of Epaminondas, an ideal he was not alone in cherishing. But future prospects were not propitious for these men; they were not able to make this Panhellenic sentiment prevail. After Alexander's death, when the Greeks justifiably revolted in the so-called Lamiac War, the Athenian demos sent out to other cities the following call to arms: *Athens always held that all Hellas was a common fatherland for all the Hellenes; now it behooves us all together to hazard life and limb to set us free.*

Unhappily, many in Athens itself opposed this war. Only a halfhearted revolt was staged, ending most lamentably; the Macedonians occupied Athens and altered its constitution. As Hellenism took on a wider historical scope, it lost its ethical and political significance on the national level and became a major universal cultural influence instead.

PART II

THE FINE ARTS

Chapter Five

THE AWAKENING OF ART

Ultimately the art of poesy of the Greeks constituted their greatest claim to distinction, for in it they achieved their highest pre-eminence over the preceding ages and peoples.

This art is endowed with remarkable endurance, having flowered richly until well into the time of the Roman emperors and having since then outlived much else created by man. Even the earliest archeological finds show a wealth of forms and species pointing to a prolific future. The very oldest art period reflects a great variety of life, especially the multitude of princes and courts of noblemen, many of whom probably sponsored artistic activities, and likewise the local independence and great profusion of religious cults, all of which no doubt contributed very early to agonistic competition.

The occasion was, first and foremost, the worship of deities with its images of the gods and votive offerings of figurines, and then the grave with its funerary imagery and sculptures which at an early time already were meant to be iconic. In addition to all this, there is the liking for adornments so strongly present among the primitives already and stirring them to produce choice artistic objects, and subsequently, in a developing civilization, making full use of power and wealth to find satisfaction.

The finds of Schlieman and other archeologists witness to these archaic artistic endeavors. They dazzle us mainly by the great amount of gold they contain. We call to mind the beaker from Ilium in the shape of a truncated boat, Schlieman's *depas amplikyellon*—men surely drank from both sides of it—and other Trojan vases as well as the great quantities of beaten gold leaf, found in the oldest layers of Mycenae and in the graves on the Acropolis, serving as burial ornaments.

Most important for us is the fact that even the earliest representations of

127

animals (lower sea forms, etc.) and of human beings show a firm style. The life-sized masks made of gold leaf, often with unpleasant but realistic features, are highly significant as being the oldest individual representations of Greek people. The gems employed presuppose the mastery of a highly developed, difficult, and painstaking technique, for the stones used were not only soft stones like steatite and hematite but also jasper, sard, agate, chalcedony, and quartz crystal.

Besides the treasures from burial sites which must be older than the Lion Gate and treasure stores of Mycenae, revealing an advanced and widespread artistic industry in the very earliest period, there are extremely interesting bronze and also terra cotta figurines of human beings and animals, especially horses, found in abundance in the lowest layers of black earth at the pyre altars of Olympia. We may welcome them as the earliest known votive offerings of Greek art; a direct line of descent leads from them to the marvelous groups of the fifth and fourth centuries.

If we add to all this the remains of the earliest architecture: the Cyclopean walls, the treasure houses, the Lion Gate, the earliest examples of architectural planning on Greek soil, we glimpse a potent artistic activity preceding the Dorian invasion. But at the same time we face a large gap reaching from this period to the seventh century.

The description of the two shields in the epic writings of Homer and Hesiod gives a clue to the continuation of Mycenaean art. One may look there into a whole complex mode of delineation not to be thought of as relief work but as inlay of different colored metals. On the shield of Achilles one must imagine, for instance, dark grape clusters, vine stays of silver, a hedge of tin, cattle made alternately of gold and tin, and a field of earth-brown fallow; analogues for all of these have been unearthed at Mycenae, especially the bronze dagger blades having the most delicate hunting scene done in gold filigree. It is, of course, natural that metal works of art would not have endured save under specially favorable conditions as at Ilium and Mycenae; the same holds even more true for wood sculpture whose representatives for us are Daedalus and the Daedalids, and later examples of which are the Cypselus chest and similar objects.

Stone sculpture, though appearing already in Mycenae, developed much more slowly. Since of all antique materials fired clay was about the only one to survive the millennia, we must rely on vases and terra cotta objects to bridge the big gap in Greek art; hence, these are the objects of the most intense archeological research.

Our immediate concern, however, is to establish the positive and negative elements that made Greek art flourish so astonishingly. To be borne in mind above all is the freedom of this art. It is true that long after poesy had clothed the gods with the highest ideality and vitality, the images of the gods remained faithful for a long time to the traditional patterns; in a sense, the conception of the gods was beautiful long before their images became so. Images carved of wood remained in vogue probably for centuries after Homer.

The Greeks had no priestly class, i.e., no permanent power, to impose an untimely and tyrannical pictorialization of the gods and to enforce conformity to this style. This is not simply an instance of negative good fortune; the Greeks could not have had a clergy since they had their polis, which did constrain the artists to glorify the typical rather than the particular so that the style remained consistent without becoming monotonous.

This appears all the more remarkable when we reflect that originally the Greeks, too, possessed the monstrous elements of barbaric or oriental art. Homeric epithets, like cow-eyed applied to Hera, and owl-eyed applied to Athena, suggest a primeval period when Greek gods, like those of the Egyptians, had animal heads; the demonic creatures carved on the so-called "island stones" show the most ghastly animal mongrel shapes. Myths also contained repulsive moments, as exemplified by the births of Pallas and Dionysus, though such elements were severely repressed. The myths themselves tended to discard these elements, but even so the harpies and gruesome demons survived until the time of the Argonauts.

Pan is the only remaining divinity of mixed animal and human appearance; in the nineteenth Homeric hymn, Pan delights the heart of his father Hermes and of the other gods. Possibly, the shepherds had such a strong imaginative conception of Pan's shape that forces which swept away the other mixed forms could not touch him. Other animal intermixtures were not gods any more, only demonic shapes retained in fable.

The plastic arts had to reject the monstrous and strongly symbolic elements, however long and hard the way that led, for instance, from the rough stone Eros found at Thespia to the marvelous creation by Praxiteles. It is conceivable that long after the epic had made the beauty of the gods quite obvious, art still would not venture to present them as beautiful; in other words, men set up rough stones to represent the gods because they felt inadequate to give them the beautiful shapes they were aware the gods should have.

Wherever the hideous element in art survived, it had to be imposed on the Greeks by coercion. When the older wood image of the horse-headed black Demeter burned down in the cave on Mount Elaion, the Phigalians neither replaced it nor continued her feasts and sacrifices until drought and famine struck the land a generation after the Persian Wars and the Pythia counseled them to re-establish the sacrifices and to adorn the cave with divine honors. Thereupon, they zealously renewed the cult and prevailed upon Onatas to carve a new image at any cost. He probably found a copy of the old one or a tradition about it, but he is supposed to have relied mostly on a dream vision of it, i.e., he toned down its more gruesome aspects, undoubtedly.

When not destroyed, other monstrous objects remained, as for instance, the xoanon wood image of the three-eyed Zeus in the temple of Athena on the Larissa acropolis in Argos; according to Pausanias, this image presented Zeus as ruler of heaven, earth, and the sea. Any attempt to beautify this image might well have run into opposition. Likewise, no one in Sparta could have changed their fettered Ares and their veiled Aphrodite Morpho who, with their fettered feet, symbolized fidelity of fortune in war and of women respectively.

Lacking the ideal resources of later times, archaic Greek art employed various items of harsh symbolism even in smaller representations, as shown in the Cypselus chest. The ill-advised theme of Athena rising from the head of Zeus was plastically represented several times, and such a statue once stood on the Acropolis at Athens, but Phidias substituted another motive in the pediment of the Parthenon. Similarly, art as a whole overcame its hideous elements.

Occasionally a light touch of personification helped to represent aesthetically dubious facts; a very ancient statue of Apollo at Delos represented the god with a bow in his right hand and in his left not three musical instruments but the three graces with lyre, flute, and syrinx [shepherd's pipe].

The delight in a richer and more magnificent pictorialization of the gods and in the massive representation of myths awoke in the age after Homer, but we do not know precisely when, why, and from what unfathomable matrix. Art awoke as out of a healthy sleep.

Art had the various technical means at hand. These technical means resided in skills with tools which the old civilizations had long since invented. Since the external requirements for art were met, the Greeks had only to open their eyes and wield their natural powers, which provided some of the strongest promptings to art.

We must also consider the noted beauty of the race, the positive simplicity and beauty of their dress that followed the lines of the body, and the agonistic arts of the gymnasium that soon arose and rapidly developed, providing close anatomical observation.

But the principal factor is really the towering pivotal quality of this race which can only be adumbrated: the combination of freedom and moderation that alone was able to create a living ideal, that immediate respect of each art not only for the gods and men but also for itself. It is that much

Apollo and Artemis in a wedding procession
Vase painting

praised *sophrosyne* [prudence] which during the happier periods of the state exhibited itself as obedience in connection with strong individual development and which unfortunately was all too often wanting in the life of the city. Furthermore, the long period over which Greek art maintained a high degree of excellence is another good indication of the enduring quality of this art. It did not reach a sudden peak as in Raphael and Michelangelo, to degenerate immediately thereafter into mannerisms, with eclectics and naturalists laboriously producing works of art.

Without any slavish rule but in free adoption art was carried from one generation to the next. As already in the myths, art was essentially the reflection of powerful individuals, quite the reverse of what it was in the Orient. First we meet races: the Cyclopes, the Dactyli, the Telchines; then the Hephaestian heroes of art: Daedalus, Trophonius, Agamedes. Early we find names of historical artists to whom tradition ascribes schools of followers; finally, there are free and famous artists active in many cities who also had their schools.

In this way the mythic freedom and varied origins were carried on. Since no one artist or his school was able to draw art as a whole into his wake, art was saved from prostration before genius. The subjective element never predominated; sensationalism, caprice, violent individualism, sudden flashes of genius are totally absent.

Over and over we ask: How did this pure blossom of the spirit arise? How did freedom assert itself amid order, or order amid freedom?

The fact that the Greeks initially restricted artistic representation to temple images and objects of worship would not explain this phenomenon, for piety without an aesthetic sense is no protection against the grotesque, the awkward, and the ugly. Decisive is rather the fact that art began to animate its forms only after poesy had accomplished its task. Longing for living movement stirred early; the gold and silver dogs before the palace of Alcinous and Hesiod's Perseus hovering around the shield of Herakles testify to it. Poetic and popular consciousness had given the gods the highest imaginative beauty of form before art attempted to reproduce it. In this respect art was spared all faltering. This same poesy likewise exemplified the highest order, a style. The older choral lyrics already at hand taught the same lesson.

Theology and the priesthood had nothing to contribute to art because they were not present in the sense they were in oriental nations. What the temple, and in this respect the polis, contributed to art was the monumental will. It posed the highest task well, requiring that the material be precious and seriously treated and that the expenditure for time and place be lavish, as far as we can tell.

Clearly, hieratic influence limited itself to promoting each temple's wish to have nothing less and nothing less lively than the next, thereby arousing emulation which rapidly leveled standards within the various regions of Greek nationality. This influence also stimulated each temple to try to maintain a uniformly high level of excellence in the statues representing the gods, which introduced a salutary element of retardation in the development of art.

Once men had achieved a certain zeal and splendor in honoring a conception of the gods, they clung to this mode. Here, too, prudence, as combining freedom and moderation, influenced the development of art.

Certainly, Greek art quite early had become independent of the demands of religion and the love of conspicuous display by the wealthy. It provided the enormous quantities of representational art the nation demanded, as is evident from the earliest preserved vases to the votive groups during the flowering of Greek art and down to the Pergamum frieze where sculpture really overwhelms the architecture.

We may also mention an exceedingly strong external motive, the application of the contest (agon) to art, expressed in rivalry among the aristocracies, tyrannies, and rich colonies to possess the most beautiful and refulgent art objects; in rivalry among individuals and states to bestow the most magnificent endowments on Panhellenic sanctuaries; in contests between one temple and another to see which would be talked of most, and in the agonistic competition of artists working alongside each other, even though not directly competing for prizes as in dramaturgy. Add to this the important fact that from its very beginning art was confronted with gymnastic contests in full swing, was able to study and observe them, and could create images of gods and men according to these observations.

Chapter Six

THE GENRES OF ART

1. Sculpture

In contrast to the shrines of other nations and religions, the Greek temple had above all the purpose of housing and sheltering the pictorial world of sculpture. The most graceful interplay between architecture and sculpture was achieved in the pediment groups. We should have liked to know how long painting and relief work competed with sculptured friezes on temples. When sculpture finally won the victory and was able to present the central myth of a temple as its noble theme, it created in the pediments of the temple at Aegina, the Parthenon, and elsewhere those marvelous works of composition and light effect in which the beautiful symmetry of the two halves balance each other and rise to a dominant central peak.

In addition there were, as parts of the temple architecture, the external and internal frieze, which the Greeks called animal carriers because of the objects pictured on them, also the *metopes* and the *acroteria* which were decorated with palms, griffins and other mythical animals, and gods of victory and destiny, the whole done with graceful restraint.

The vestibule and the remaining chambers were often filled with votive offerings in a broad sense, ranging all the way from mere captured weapons, mostly shields, to free-standing groups of sculpture. These items included statues of the temple divinity, its attendant divinities, their priests and priestesses, and also of the temple founders and local heroes; in addition thrones, couches, lamps, tables, tripods, altars, steles (burial stones) with incised records, and mementos of all kinds.

In the interior of the temple, which may well have been lighted by an opening in the roof, since the doors hardly admitted adequate light, were many votive offerings. These included the gods dwelling there, sometimes embracing the whole mythical or allegorical relationship of the temple divinity.

Moreover, there were statues of the same temple divinity dating from various periods from the *xoanons* onward, and representing it in the various periods expressed in its epithets; in this respect art had the advantage of being able to portray the different conceptions of the divinity.

There were also sculptured images. But the main object was the temple divinity set on a richly embellished pedestal, rarely placed flat against a wall but so that one could walk around it. This free and isolated mounting of the chief object, not subordinated architecturally to the temple by a niche or as a relief, contributed materially to the development of Greek art. One should bear in mind how Egyptian sculpture essentially clings to the structure; even when the statues are separated from the walls, they are generally so located as to give the effect of being integral parts of the structure.

Occasionally the cult divinity was accompanied by two others; Praxiteles especially loved the trinity. Hence, Demeter is linked with Cora and Iacchus, Apollo with Artemis and Leto, Zeus with Hera and Athena, Athena with Asclepius and Hygiaea, to say nothing of the diminutive figures of temple servants, army generals, and others, at the feet of the main cult figure.

In the vicinity of the temple stood the sacrificial altar, often richly adorned with reliefs, and the other altars; indeed the whole temple enclosure with its propylaea, stoas, and additional buildings and temples of divinities related to the main cult divinity was a place for additional works of art of all kinds. In the temples were also dedicatory plaques with reliefs, mythical graves, rows of gods, statues of heroes, statesmen, famous women, athletic victors, animals, and group sculptures on long or semicircular pedestals—all on a nonuniform scale. There might be even a colossal statue of the cult divinity, like Athena Promachus of the Athenian Acropolis.

Amid all of this there were also sacred plants, springs bubbling, and temple animals running about. These enclosures also contained public halls, the so-called *lesches*.

Leaving the main temple and going down into the city one found smaller temples (sacella) and shrines dedicated to the memory of heroes everywhere. But the greatest concentration of statues and paintings was on the agora and on the stoas surrounding it or on nearby stoas leading into temples or other public buildings. Theaters, stadia, and gymnasiums were full of statuary, and on the outskirts of the town were roads lined with graves, some with elegant little shrines, but none without a monument which with its carvings or relief adorned the tomb as with monumental flower wreaths.

Statues of the gods were found, besides, at sacred springs and in grottos; sacred groves with a temple were often lavishly filled with statuary. It is hard for us to visualize the profusion of sculpture pertaining to athletes and victorious teams embellishing the athletic-game centers. It is as if Greek art had had to produce an untold multiplicity so that future ages seeing the remnants might marvel at the wealth of this nation and the earnest, monumental will it combined with all this expenditure.

A number of external factors account for the relative ease with which this ideal style gained predominance in Greek art. Above all, it was a religious art, and, like every religious art, the Egyptian for instance, it turned away from mere realism and engaged in the quest of the eternal. Its first task was to portray the gods, a task it could fulfill at the outset because popular imagination depicted them with lucid vividness. This art may well have originated in primeval times at the family hearth.

Here men were wont to bury their dead, worshiping them and perhaps, in the very beginning, also the hearth flame. As a consequence of polytheism, a flock of little god figures might gradually have gathered at the hearth, depending partly on the need of divine assistance or in memory of help received and partly on inheritance from relatives. The hearth was also a place where divine images were dedicated.

It is most remarkable that Greek myths make no use of the great quantity of representational art at hand and rarely mention the temple as a structure having an established locality. Homer, in the ninth century, mentions no images, when presumably many were already in existence; the gods themselves appeared to him. It seems the people continued the custom of dedicating images independently of the myths. Now it is important and decisive that the repeated representation of a divinity whom one invoked, or thanked for help, tended to shape the image of the votive offering. The continued dedication of images of the cult divinity would in time gather a heap of these in and around the temple, this practice necessarily tending to beautify and ennoble the style.

For the development of the ideal forms it was furthermore decisive that sculpture carried the banner instead of painting, for it had to accomplish its purpose within a single human figure and so had to restrict itself almost exclusively to form. Here the only natural expression of the spirit is the human body, and the Greeks indefatigably and endlessly exerted themselves to mold in a thousand human forms all things of the mind: gods, men, abstract qualities, localities, natural events, and all that moves the spirit.

To let the spirit speak directly, not only sculpture but other art forms too had from the very beginning to omit the host of secondary details encrusting reality; this presents life under a veil, as it were. But sculpture is driven to simplicity far more forcibly than painting is. Painting may strive for an illusion of reality and be a very effective means to that end, but sculpture never. In this sense, sculpture is substantially the most ideal art, whereas painting, by means of light, background, and abundance of relations can produce an altogether different over-all effect; Rembrandt, for instance, could create an ideal over-all impression by means of thoroughly ugly forms.

The desire to visualize the gods must have been altogether different in Greece than it was in the slavish Orient, above all much more free from compulsion. The fact that poesy had so heavily stressed the glory of the gods had effect, and thus there followed demigods, allegorical beings, the ministering gods, and all the figures of the heroic world.

Since the Greeks were free from repulsive symbolism and able to concentrate on the human form, they could start with nature almost at the beginning and did so, too, as evidenced by the anatomical realism of the earliest archeological finds. The gods were simply idealized human beings. Art had a free hand, and merely limited or simplified costumes and attributes more and more, so as to let character dominate instead. In this art the body was everything; sculpture tells us nothing about the aegis of Pallas, for instance; in fact, it hardly bothers to find out or let us know what it is.

Greek artists sought the truth not only in the individual form but also in posture and gesture; in this quest they were not hobbled by a sacred tradition, as were the artists of the Orient. Before achieving ideality, Greek artists used every means to attain animation, thereby putting an end to traditional concepts. First they put movement into the arms and legs, as seen in the early figures of athletes, differing widely from those of the Orient. To achieve this movement, they limited themselves to experimenting with form, and this exercise—unique in the history of the world—must have done away with the rigidity of statues representing the gods.

It is highly significant that the head remained conventional the longest and, in our judgment, unpleasant and unlovely. After the whole form had reached perfection in variety and beauty of composition, a goodly piece of convention was preserved in the rigid smile which had evidently been regarded as expressing life in earlier sculpture.

In addition to simplifying the attire and attributes of the gods, as mentioned above, the artists also restricted their age to that of youthful appearance, attempting to do so early and conspicuously.

Moreover, we must stress that the juxtaposition of a number of statues of one and the same deity, recognized above as important in that it led to the ennobling of divine statuary, did not cause mere duplication among the Greeks as it did among the Egyptians. It brought multiformity, depending on the different times the votive offerings were made. These statues differed in age, size, material, and in a whole range of postures, gestures, and costumes. In the course of centuries a number of these modes of execution became types because artists imitated them and the Romans handed them down. Among them were preserved not necessarily the most beautiful but those most easily imitated in marble. We are far less accurately informed about the much freer composition in bronze, chryselephantine, and the acrolith technique because their copies survive only in smaller bronzes or on coins.

To be able to represent consummately the spiritual as such, the artist enthusiastically conceived and studied the world of perceptibles as though it were alive, thus making it the most important source of the ideal. They mastered the elements of external life so as to represent the life of the mind with ease. Hence they sought out traits of beauty in a multitude of single individuals. But this average or canon would not have sufficed except for something absolutely unique: that irresistible attraction for the beautiful which will remain an eternal mystery.

The exalted mood of the nation in the fifth century moved the people to accept the ideal in art, and the experience of replacing the statues of the gods destroyed in the Persian Wars contributed to it indirectly. At all events, religion had the least influence. The Zeus of Phidias and other grand statues were created in a relatively irreligious age when Anaxagoras was teaching. The salient point is that the famous masters were able to arouse the will of the people to support them in giving new forms to the Olympian gods.

A Phidias or a Polycleitus could have succeeded in this only by exhibiting models and finished specimens which people could compare with older art works that survived the Persian devastation, like the stately Hera in Argos, the statue of Zeus in Olympia, and some others. After comparing the old and the new, men obviously could not regard the old as beautiful, and after having had the colossal they now recognized grandeur.

These artists astonished the nation by continuously developing ever greater powers in making the gods ever more real and more beautiful. Ever since, all other civilized nations have experienced it with and through the Greeks. The gods of the Greeks have been a canon of beauty in representing divinity and sublimity in all religions, and the Greek ideal of the gods has become a fact of world-historical significance.

Here we encounter the significant fact that, wholly apart from any church, a whole people achieved a consensus in matters concerning the ideal, not because of some religious dogma but owing to a positive recognition of the manifestly beautiful.

These ideal forms are not so much that which is widespread or in general true as that in the life of the mind and the senses which can be generally expressed; hence these forms, though infinite in variety, are the generally beautiful.

For example, we find the face treated by a combination of plastic necessity, or desirability, and physiognomic conviction, so that it may remain doubtful how such a face actually appeared in reality. The contours of the face, in relation to the whole, are somewhat larger than they are in our contemporaries. Clarity, calm, absence of passion, intelligence, and a strong will were perceptibly carved into the broad, round forehead which, together with the straight nose, formed an unbroken line and protruded over the rest of the face.

The forehead with its sharply defined eyebrows was relatively low; a high forehead with the prominent face would require a different skull shape, especially a larger occiput, and the Greeks scorned heads with an almond-like

Athena
Tetradrachma

taper from front to back like those of Canova. The profile of the face harmonized with the profile of the entire head, in a manner quite different from our type today. The eyes were set back but protruding from their sockets; the cornea was convex so as to contribute emphasis to the profile. The upper eyelids were sharply defined. In archaic art the iris and pupil were painted; later, the shadow effect was achieved plastically. The eyelids were given a special shape to express languishment. The corners of the mouth sloped back, making the mouth protrude in profile; the lips were gently parted, the upper one being short. The shape of the lips differed much among the gods. The chin was round, imposing, and rarely dimpled. The ears were fine and delicate.

The hair presented the most diverse forms, ranging from the archaic Assyrian style to the most varied and supple treatment producing most marvelous effects. The ephebi had tight curls, the more riotous satyrs and bar-

barians had tousled hair, and the Aphrodites, from that of Cnidus on, had
wavy hair elegantly gathered. Hera had flowing hair, sometimes delicately
wavy, sometimes gathered in a roll on her head, as did Eros, Apollo, the
Capitoline Venus, and especially Zeus and the water nymphs.

Often diadems and wreaths of grapes, leaves, or flowers gracefully
adorned the hair. The beard also exhibited the whole range of styles, from
Assyrian regularity to the free and grand treatment of Zeus's beard. But hair
is hardly ever like that in reality, whether groomed or ungroomed. The
ancients dealt quite freely with the forms, without, however, diminishing
their viability in the least.

We can say the same for the body, the canons for which varied in different epochs from the solid to the sylphlike, but the forms were always
manipulated with an ideal freedom as was the head, yet retaining their lifelikeness and truthfulness.

The gradations from the gods to the satyrs were gracefully light and
were carried through to the athletes. The satyrs constituted a second class of
beauty and ideality, a world of sensuously cheerful reaching to the maenadic,
and to these belong their counterparts, the sea creatures tending to be more
somber. This did not occur until the fourth century when Praxiteles and
Skopas put the capstone on the art of shaping divine forms.

Here we might call to mind how freely the Greeks represented personification, the so-called allegory. They created winged creatures like Eros,
Nike, and others, infinitely more beautiful than the Orientals did, also the
centaurs, Pans, Tritons, and griffins. These creatures stand before us fully
lifelike, for human and animal forms merge with such enchanting beauty
and lack of inhibition.

Here too we must observe how the momentary is expressed in the outlines of the head, the posture and movement of the whole form—often speaking softly as it were but very significantly of the highest truth and beauty;
we must observe also the shimmer of sadness in the loveliest heads of the
gods, for though the gods be eternal they are not lords of destiny.

These images are completely unconcerned with any spectator; apart
from serving as a focal point in worship, they appear unobserved and
unheard. A look at the pediment statues of the Parthenon teaches us how
the greatest art can embody gracious artlessness.

The raiment is *the thousandfold echo of the form* (Goethe). In their
early period, the Greeks did not exploit the splendor of the fabrics, just as
the Assyrians in their art did not do it either. They dealt with the simple
details of the simple garments of the men and women they portrayed and
did so freely, as beauty in appearance and definition of movement demanded,
so that often one could not follow the flow of the folds. The different tex-

tures, from the coarsest to the finest, were often expressed perfectly and without preciosity of treatment.

Some habiliments, for instance those of the Amazons or of the women of the Parthenon, are noteworthy for their suitability to express movement and composition as well as for their material. These garments were not tailored, for there are no seams and no buttons. They are simple pieces of cloth, square or round (or like butterfly wings?), which become garments only when donned. This kind of clothing was something one wore, something that echoed the outlines of the body, not a sheath for the body like the sacks and tubes we go around in. With its smooth and shadowy parts draping a person, this garment expressed innocently the form and movement of the body.

The abundance of statues representing draped female figures, whether of cult goddesses in temples, of Muses, of priestesses, or others, is especially noteworthy. The long sweep of the garments is unfolded in several layers, in which an inner one at times may shimmer through an outer one, or the head may be half veiled by a part of the garment drawn over it, or a double sash may gird the body and the long *chiton* be tucked up so as to allow ample folds over the bosom, all this presenting a truly marvelous wealth of the most glorious motives.

The gods were often portrayed without any weapons except for helmets, like the Ares-Achilles of the Louvre. Art eschews the inorganic, trusting to illusion for intelligibility.

Above all, this art could take the chance to let the naked body speak for itself. In earlier poetry Aphrodite had her "girdle" and garments made by the Graces and Horae, resplendent in all the colors of spring flowers; now art relied on pure form alone.

With all its freedom, this art nevertheless exercised the greatest restraint regarding capricious flights of fancy. It did not exhibit a single example of repulsive excess. In the fourth century the artists had reached a peak of excellence in representing divine forms; thereafter they repeated and preserved these forms, not only because they found it highly advantageous to do so but also because they could hardly have improved upon them. Greek art renounced the creation of new forms, experiencing instead the art forms at hand as though they were new.

This mode of perception, one of the distinctive mental endowments of the Greeks, as well as their discrimination in respect to the forms, characterized the remarkable concurrence of the Greek views. We shall observe similar traits in respect to their forms of poetry.

Greek artists fashioned not only the ideal but in time they were also portraying the individual, something long since practiced in the Orient.

How many portraitlike reliefs scarcely rising from their background do we not find chiseled in the walls of Nineveh and Persepolis! Egyptian art also created numerous images of seated and standing kings, partly free, partly recessed in the walls, or of tomb steles with their almost free sculpture done in the round, and other works of art like that of the Egyptian scribe in the Louvre. Here the artists had sought, and often attained, sharply individual traits.

But nowhere on earth did the representation of the individual begin as it did among the Greeks. Here the decisive step in portraiture was the representation of athletes, begun in 558 B.C., when the first statue of a victor was set up at Olympia. The essential thing about these portraits in stone is not that they faithfully portray the facial features but that they capture some characteristic movement, perhaps at the moment of victory. The purpose of this sculpture was primarily to portray the individual and secondarily to give substance to the immortal ideal. Sculpting athletes provided artists with the opportunity to develop skill in creating animation and also enabled them to deal with a variety of other tasks. The Amazon was the ideal female athlete.

In the end, the statue of the athlete developed from a monument of an individual into an object of art in its own right, and we marvel at the athletic types later created and repeated purely for the sake of beauty as, for example, the Discobolus, representing the athlete in his most glorious manifestation.

As for the rest of portrait sculpture, we know today that already in quite early times there were statues set up at graves which in a fashion were meant to portray the dead, even though not realistically. It is likely that statues meant for graves had started the trend toward realism in sculpture. When did the polis begin to decree the erection of statues in honor of warriors, statesmen, orators, and poets? We do not know, yet in this field also the Greeks attained the highest accomplishments.

At this point we must also mention the lifelike figures of children and animals, constituting yet another world of artistic interpretation.

And now we turn to the plastic representation of multiple subjects, especially to composition. Here too the Orient paved the way, but Egypt and Assyria lacked the myths and their beautiful diversity. Instead of mythical variety these were ritual and royal chronicles, i.e., enforced narration, bedecking the walls, pillars, and even columns. The artists were expected to give factual completeness and could not avoid constant repetition, the reliefs, stylistically akin to tapestry, flowing into the architecture and spreading over it like a script or ornament.

In representing groups as well as individuals, the Greeks profited by the precursory achievements of their poesy. Thanks to the art of Homer, Greek battles were not fought by divine victors overcoming the forces of darkness but between thoroughly human warriors on an equal footing with each other, whoever they may be. When we read in the *Iliad* how Achaean A kills Trojan B, how Trojan C spears Achaean D in his exposed hips, as he stoops to drag away the corpse to plunder it, and how finally a frightful battle comes to rage about this group, we almost get the impression that Homer deliberately handed down to later art one of the subjects to which we have become accustomed. For he presented Hellenes and Trojans, Lapithae and centaurs, heroes and Amazons, gods and giants, all with the same impartial love.

In order to present this array of objects, art created forms unknown to the Orient. Because a fruitful relation had already existed from the early days between the representations of many figures in battle and the continuous relief or the painted frieze, the relief now went through various gradations until it culminated in the crown of all battles, that between the gods and the giants on the altar at Pergamum. But above all there arose the pediment sculpture and the independent group, like that of the Laocoön or the Farnese Bull.

This impulse to create groups did not confine itself to battle scenes. It depicted also more amiable ones from Homer as, for instance, the group composed of Hector, Andromache, Astyanax, and the servant girl, or Thetis sinking to the ground before Zeus, putting her left arm around his knees and raising her right hand to his chin. As a matter of fact, the whole cycle of gods and heroes cried out for representation, and a whole world of fully developed scenes, some of majestic beauty, must have had a strong influence on the imagination of Greek artists from the earliest days onward.

But even apart from the cycle of myths, according to Homer himself, art very early began to represent animated ensembles and thereby developed the genre picture as exemplified in the tombs of Beni Hasan. Here we call to mind again that the shield of Achilles shows mere genre pictures whereas Hesiod's shield of Herakles intermingles them with mythical elements.

And, finally, in addition to the scenes from myths, the Greeks ventured upon allegorical and political themes in large group sculptures by representing historical individuals linked with their allegorically personified poleis, or with the heroes associated with them, or as Lysander did in the gigantic votive offering for Delphi, by representing the victors conjoined with the gods that grant victory.

To these must be added groups partaking in athletic contests, such as the victors in four-horse chariot races, and groups representing historical events like the monument to Alexander on the Granicus and two of the four large Attalidae group monuments in Athens.

Thus, art may draw from many sources subjects suitable for group representation. The popularity of group sculpture is evident from its earliest appearance on a small scale. Group sculpture had its parallel in mural painting, the popular expression of which was primarily vase painting and engraving done on bronze. Foreign countries, particularly Etruria, eagerly acquired the products created by these techniques.

All polytheistic nations in which architecture and sculpture have flourished, besides representing their gods, attempted from their beginnings to perpetuate the various rites of worship. The piety of the officiating king, priest, or people was made manifest to the nation and to the gods; to the latter no doubt so they would be ever mindful of the needs of the people.

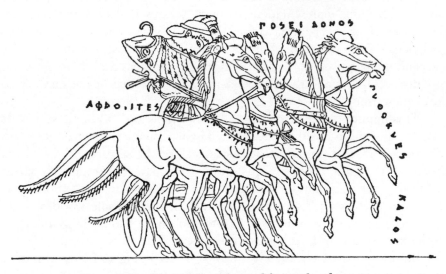

Aphrodite with Poseidon and four-in-hand
Water well decoration

In every sense, man was nearest to his gods at the time he was immersed in ritual worship. Consequently, as already stated, ritual was the main theme of group sculpture in Egypt and Assyria. Religious activity did not appear at all enslaving or repulsive to oriental art but rather a joy; Dionysiac sculpture extracted beautiful motives even out of orgiastic elements.

Statues of priests and priestesses existed in great abundance; many of the extant robed statues probably belonged to this class. If the likeness of the temple divinity was a rather unsightly wooden carving (xoanon), a row of such robed figures might have compensated for the bad effect. This is the way it might have been in the temple of the Eumenides in Achaean Kerynea. Their figures were not big, perhaps they were mere hideous dolls, but at the entrance stood attractive female statues; the people declared that these were priestesses attached to the goddesses.

Festival choruses were immortalized in art, and the greatest achievement of this kind was on the Athenian Acropolis. There was the Panathenaean train of the Parthenon, and on the balustrade of the temple of the Wingless Victory [Nike Apteros] were the Nikes, some leading the sacrificial ox, others preparing the trophy. This was the loftiest interpretation of a temple ritual, the sublimest of all transfigurations of the cultus.

If we were to treat of the smaller and larger ceramic and bronze figures in which sculpture had a kind of second life, if we were to deal with the reduction of reliefs in gems, intaglios, cameos, and on coins, and go on with vases and utensils in precious metals, in bronze, marble, and clay designed in all sorts of shapes and forms, e.g., in their use in candelabras and tripods, or for a variety of different uses, we should find no end.

2. *Painting*

Of the pre-Greek painting only Egyptian remnants have survived, most of them conventional and slavish except the representation of ordinary life in the tombs of Beni Hasan. No information exists on the early art of the Orient apart from the figured rugs of Mesopotamia. Of Greek painting, on the other hand, we have numerous accounts, in addition to murals in the cities at the foot of Mount Vesuvius, some paintings in catacombs, and vase paintings.

When painting was at its height, writers told more about the famous painters from Polygnotus to Apelles than they did about the sculptors. The Greeks must have thought painters more interesting as individuals, perhaps because they were not looked on as banausics as were the sculptors. Later on, drawing became a regular subject in the education of the freeborn.

First of all, there was the monumental painting in the stoas, halls, drawing rooms, and temples, representing themes from myths as well as political ideas and memories. The style of Polygnotus in depicting these motives may have its analogue in the school of Giotto; the style of later painters may have been even more perfectly animated. In the Stoa Basileus in Athens, Polygnotus and his school painted representations of the twelve gods, Theseus with Democracy and Demos, the battle at Mantinea; in the Stoa Poikile, various masters, each following his own bent freely, over a period of time painted scenes depicting a battle of the Peloponnesian War, Theseus fighting the Amazons, events after the fall of Troy, and the battle at Marathon, along with outstanding heroes; in the lateral halls of the Propylaea, they painted many scenes from the legends of Troy, including two illustrious thieves, Diomedes with the bow of Philoctetes and Odysseus with the Palladium,* and a number of portraits and individual figures, like Alcibiades as a Nemean victor, Perseus, Musaeus, and the genre pictures of an athlete and a vessel carrier. Paintings of battles were not limited to Athens. The Artemisium of Ephesus had a sea battle depicting an Eris, and Pergamum displayed a victory over the Celts.

The Amazon Hippolyta in a fight with Theseus
Vase painting

At any rate, painting devoted itself more to historical events than sculpture did; political subjects were fairly common in painting, too.

In the days when drama flourished scenography was a special style of painting which served the rather fantastic tastes of the theater and which was later adopted for decorating houses and palaces. This style appears to have become the fashion for a while; Alcibiades insisted on having it in his residence.

To what extent does Pompeii preserve an echo of all this? The only

* The Palladium, a small wooden image of Pallas Athena (Minerva) fell, according to myth, from heaven upon the citadel of Troy, where it was venerated as a divine pledge of the city's safety. Only after the Palladium was secretly carried off by Odysseus and Diomedes was Troy finally captured by means of the wooden horse.

painting preserved treating of a historical subject is that of the Battle of Alexander. The motives of most paintings are taken from mythology and are also scenographic; individual figures, hovering groups, and other subjects unquestionably reminiscent of the loveliest products of this art form, as are many genre scenes. These were not painted true to life as were those at Beni Hasan, but simply to produce charming scenes. Instead of daily and seasonal tasks we find the pleasing moment; a few people in quiet talk, meditation, a levée, games, a theater scene, etc.

Next to these murals, easel painting (tempera, also encaustic) elicited the liveliest admiration; the famous masters in this field were Zeuxis, Parrhasius, Apelles, Protogenes, Timomachus, and Theon. If their paintings could be made available, they would revolutionize our conventional view of Greek art. These artists strove for an illusion of nature and were uniformly judged by this criterion. They achieved delicate executions by means of color, form, light effects, and foreshortening (Pausias); their best modern parallels would be the Italian realists of the fifteenth century up to Leonardo da Vinci. With the exception of isolated compositions of many figures, these Greeks characteristically executed paintings in which one figure predominated with very few secondary details. In this manner Zeuxis painted a Helen and a Penelope; Parrhasius the Athenian Demos, the simulated madness of Odysseus, and a Philoctetes; Protogenes his Ialysius, working on it for seven years; Timomachus an Ajax, an Iphigenia readied for sacrifice and a Medea just before committing murder.

The intended purpose of painting was quite different from that of sculpture; paintings were made for private possession and came only occasionally and subsequently as votive offerings to this or that temple. This art fitted into Greek homes as larger marble statues hardly could.

In connection with some famous paintings we hear of prices and income. Zeuxis, for instance, charged an admission fee to an exhibit of his Helen. In later times, paintings sold to collectors at enormous prices. According to Pliny, Attalus paid one hundred talents for a painting by Aristides of Thebes; Caesar paid eighty for the Medea and Ajax of Timomachus, to dedicate them in the temple of Venus Genetrix. It should also be mentioned that Demetrius Poliorcetes refrained from setting fire to Rhodes so as not to destroy a painting by Protogenes found in the part of the city he was attacking.

In later times, caricatures and genre pictures like the barber and cobbler shops of Periaceis, still lifes, and the so-called *rhyparographies* [smutty pictures] seem to have gained the upper hand.

Figures seldom appeared in mosaics in Greek times. Hiero the Younger, of the Diadochi period, had a luxury yacht said to have had mosaics on the floors of its elegant rooms depicting the whole story cycle of Ilium. This mode of floor decoration seems to have become fashionable during that time. Nothing further will be said now about the art of drawing, vase painting, and carving chests and mirrors. Be it enough to say that here too Greek art reached the acme of perfection with its lofty ideal of *sophrosyne*.

3. Architecture

The artistic *sophrosyne* of the Greeks is palpably perceptible in their architecture. In the whole history of art the Greek temple is unique in that it stood, by virtue of a deliberate act of self-abnegation, as the most perfect type of which everything else is reproduction and abstraction. Halls, drawing rooms, modest private dwellings, and courtyards are completely subordinate. The motive of the temple is the absolute motive as such. How did the nation arrive at this form?

The essential part of the Greek sanctuary, the sacrificial altar, was not inside the temple building at all but out in the forecourt. The altars, on elevations, mostly dedicated to Zeus, on which the ashes of many sacrifices acccumulated, were not protected by shelter of any sort. At some indefinite time, the inner part of the temple came to be called the *dwelling* of the divinity, and from that point on we may assume that there existed a closed structure, a cella, initially according to legend only a temporary framework like a tent or hut, until art gave this structure monumental form and finally transfigured it most gloriously.

In addition to the many conjectures that will have been made by ancient historians of art, we shall venture one on the origin of the peripteros, an oblong temple with a single row of columns all around it. We believe it was not borrowed from the peripteral temples of Asia and Egypt but was an indigenous product of the Greeks. It probably arose as a timbered hall made of logs at a time when Greece was still heavily wooded. Even if one supposes that the cella was made of stone from the beginning, the hall-like structure around it and the roof were built of timber anyway.

In all parts of the world, the tree trunk is the only conceivable origin of the column or round support. At a time when stone masons were rare and unskilled, the Greeks could have built the hall around the cella only of logs, not of dressed stone columns. Wood beams make it possible to space the columns relatively far apart, and indeed, the large interval of Etruscan architecture derived from this technique.

One may well suppose that the Greeks placed the columns fairly close together, at times even in double rows (dipteral style) if they had plenty of timber. Even when the building was of wood the hexastyle (six columns in a row at the gable ends) may normally have been in double rows. If we inquire what the purpose of the hall really was, we shall find that it was not, as Vitruvius supposed, to offer protection from the elements, but rather to provide a place for displaying the votive offerings numerous in the days of old, especially captured weapons.

The normal wooden temple foreshadowed all the future beauty in the unity of its motive; the cella was the nucleus, the columns and beams were the ideal hall around it, for these lent a marked and solemn emphasis to a relatively small nave. From the very beginning this structure must have been stately and imposing; presumably only the hexastyle was able to invite the shaping powers of the future. This structural form originated and spread in such a way that both the Doric and Ionic styles could equally well evolve from it. This process must be viewed as having occurred fairly suddenly and simultaneously among the Greeks, despite their division into so many tribes.

With the rise of the new temples, the mode of the old structure and its appurtenances silently disappeared, leaving hardly a trace. The peripteros became one of those structural styles which once accepted are safe against future innovations. Arising out of a lofty and mysterious force experienced in an awe-inspiring mood and moment, the peripteros became that universally accepted form of the sanctuary which now and again could attain secular splendor.

First the partial, then the full substitution of stone for wood, except in the roof and ceiling, must have taken place early. In the eighth century, when the Greeks spread out in colonies, the stone peripteros accompanied them as a matter of course, for the oldest temples in Sicily show the new style in a fully developed form. With only the modest material means at hand, this stone technique provided the happiest style of building. Though the proportions were relatively fixed, the dimensions were fluid; consequently, a community could survey and reckon with its resources to plan a temple it could finish in one generation.

The Greeks felt themselves so thoroughly bound to this form that, when they built a temple or a group of them, either in a newly established city or over the years in an old one, they built them all in a similar, indeed almost identical style, never letting the thought of varying the style cross their minds.

We shall not venture any conjecture on specific forms of the original wooden temples or on their colors if any were applied to them, or on the use of drapes and carpets in them, and least of all shall we do so regarding the way stone replaced some of the wooden parts in the temples.

Respect for immemorial usage, awareness of having created something

Pediment group of the Parthenon

unsurpassable of its kind, and a reverent conservatism in art which made even poetry change warily from an old to a new form—these factors inseparably cooperated to achieve the ultimate perfection that was the Greek temple; yet its form answered quite definite purposes only. The temple was different from the hero's grave, corresponding to that of our saint; nor was it a hereditary burial site for the nobility which might have developed a structure comparable to the medieval balcony with a gallery. In it no rites of worship were performed for the people, i.e., no congregation worshiped in it; all the munificent sacrifices were offered on outside altars and only little incense altars could be found inside.

The temple was, as mentioned, first and foremost the dwelling of the divinity, and since the inner sanctum was usually small, increasingly lavish expenditures were bestowed on the external parts. The temple in its entirety was inviting and revealing to the eye, largely because of the transfigured appearance of the wall; consequently a second row of columns was added, making the temple dipteral. Provided space and means were available, temples were characteristically oblong and peripteral, that is, about twice as long as wide, with a row of columns along each side. Temples like the one at Delphi, or with cavern cults, or with two divinities, were exceptional.

The location of the temples was either freely chosen or determined by precedent, i.e., some mythological occurrence. They were frequently located on peaks and promontories, or in sacred groves, sometimes on the Acropolis, in the agora, or next to the harbor, and had courtyards enclosed by walls (periboloi) wherever possible. The temple was set like a votive offering on a stereobate, or base, usually of three layers and hence three steps high; the height of these risers or steps at the larger temples like the Parthenon was too great for practical use and so smaller steps were added in front and other places for convenient access to the raised peristyle.

In front of the temple was the requisite altar, simple in structure though at times splendidly made of fine materials. When the burnt offering was being sacrificed on the altar, the magnificent front door was swung

by Phidias, on the Acropolis

open so that light could fall on the incense altar and the temple divinity. The larger temples also had openings in the roof to admit light; the area directly below was exposed to the weather.

The glory of the temple was completed by the votive offerings placed in the vestibule (pronaos) or colonnade (pteroma) and, in the same magnificent temples, also in the portico (stoa) and even out in the courtyard (peribolos), to which a sumptuous propylaeum (outer court) might afford entrance.

Normally, a temple has a conventional style, which renounces every possibility of change by the integration of diverse structural details.

This principle of purposeful economy establishes nonetheless organic completeness. The Greek temple is in the highest degree true, and therein lies part of its beauty. It represents the most exquisite balance between weight-bearing and pressure-exerting on the part of a horizontal load pressing on vertical carriers (without lateral support through vaulted construction) and expresses this—albeit in two dialects, Doric and Ionic—in a single language of forms.

These styles may have derived in part from Egypt and Assyria; the Greeks may have borrowed some secondary architectonic items, though not before overcoming slavish imitation of motives and converting all reminiscences of the primitive temple into perfect harmony, thus turning the reality of wood into ideal truth.

The column is consummate life, a cylindrical body complete in itself, radiating its force evenly in all directions. Placed at equal intervals from its neighbors and tapering off slightly toward the top, it takes on the semblance of an enduring stability. The slight expansion of the column toward the bottom expresses a vivid inner elasticity, and its fluting reveals an even stronger breath of life, as it were. The height of the column is harmoniously related to the size of the intervals and its strength to the weight it must support. Thus the highest aesthetic and physical truths have joined hands.

The crossbeams are doubled in the architrave and frieze and over them lies the cornice supporting the roof. Here the soft slope of the pediment symbolizes repose, as it were, between contending columns and beams.

The characteristic features of these architectural forms rest, as said above, on common foundations but developed according to two thoroughly autonomous conceptions, the Doric and the Ionic, whose gradual unfolding remains an enigma, though we know that already by 650 B.C. they existed independently alongside each other.

The Doric column has no base and is fluted with sharp-edged grooves, widening somewhat in the middle and tapering slightly toward the top. These columns are about five diameters high and spaced one and one-half diameters apart. The capital consists of one to three necking grooves at the top of the column leading to the echinus, thought of as a vital elastic matter with a variable flexibility, and over it the abacus serving to support the architraves on the column. This abacus is clearly a lingering effect of a board used to support on one column two beams of the architrave where they joined end to end.

This board abacus of the old architecture was preserved in the new to enlarge the supporting surface under the architrave. This architrave consists of stone beams. The frieze on the architrave comprises triglyphs alternating with metopes. Originally the triglyphs were simply boards nailed on the ends of the crossbeams. They were added to the two ends of the structure so as to be carried around all four sides of the temple, thereby raising its height and lending it aesthetic verticality. The crown cornice with other finishing elements topped the frieze.

We also mention the development of the Doric *anta* [a pier produced by thickening a wall at its termination] in the façade of the cella and in the *templum in antis* [whose portico is formed by projections of the two side walls terminating in antas, with columns in between], and the decoration of the ceiling with coffers. Colors were used to set off various parts; the triglyphs were painted blue, the ceiling coffers blue, variegated with red and gold stars; flat surfaces on the metopes and gables were also given color.

In the Ionic style the forms are more autonomous and in their individual beauty more independent of the whole. Many details merely painted on in the Doric order, like the leaves on the molding, the coussinet, etc., are presented plastically in the Ionic. Except in Attica, the Ionic column rests on a square plinth; it always has a generous base on which it is bedded, as it were. Attic architecture found the most beautiful solution for the base, making it round and giving it two swellings and one chamfer.

The shaft of the column is slender, its height being eight and one half or nine times its diameter; the columns are set two diameters apart. The flutings (up to twenty-four) have fillets between them and are hollowed out deeper than in the Doric style. The echinus, set over a decorative wreath, has egg-and-dart ornaments. Upon it lies the double cushion with its volutes from the angles of which flowers depend toward the echinus. The abacus with a beaded profile is gracefully placed. The architrave divided into three planes or fasciae is topped by an ornamental band (taenia) upon which lies the continuous frieze. Above it is a cornice with a dentil band (lacking in Attic structures), and on top of this the curved gutter (*sima*). The antae are more enriched and sprightly than in the Doric order, as are also the ornaments on the walls.

These forms, like the triply divided architrave made of three relatively slender trunks clamped on top of each other, or the cornice with dentil band deriving from serrated boards nailed on the edge of a flat roof, may have their origin not in the heavy oak beams of the Doric style but in more slender trees, perhaps palm trees or others like them, and may go back to Mesopotamia. But when and by what means were these joined to the peripteros to produce a style of expression as marvelous as the Doric? All we can say is that the Orient and the Occident mysteriously worked together to create an incomparably beautiful form.

The Corinthian style is essentially Ionic but has a more ornate capital enriched with leaves and volutes or vines. The acanthus leaves and stalks as presented here grow neither in garden nor field; they belong to a more abstract order, resembling natural leaves only metaphorically. They may have been used in an idealized form as decorations on steles, tripods, etc., long before the Corinthian order existed. The acanthus had long been used as a decoration and the stalk as a symbol of striving. The calyx had no doubt been an old form of support for various things, for it had already appeared on columns in Egypt. In the crowning days of her splendor Greece produced the glorious Corinthian style.

Upon occasion, the Doric and the Ionic, and indeed all three orders, were calmly mingled together in the exterior and the two rows of interior columns. The Ionic columns were used in the interior of the Athenian Propylaea because the greater height demanded the taller and more slender form. The temple of Athena Alea at Tegea had Doric columns outside and Ionic and Corinthian ones inside.

In this architecture the general rules were firmly established although they admitted of endless variations. No two temples had exactly the same proportions, and yet their order and proportions were such that during the years of Doric dominance the naked eye could not distinguish Athenian buildings of this style from those in Sicily. To prevent optical distortion, the columns of the peripteros were tilted slightly inward, their intervals reduced a bit, the corner columns expanded a trifle, and the stylobate and the crossbeams were made somewhat convex.

By such means architecture achieved an almost perfect analogy to the subtlest Greek matrices, verifying almost literally the words of the astrologer in the second part of Goethe's *Faust*:

> The columned shaft and towering triglyph ring,
> Indeed I hear the mighty temple sing.
>
> (Der Säulenschaft, auch die Triglyphe klingt,
> Ich glaube gar, der ganze Tempel singt.)

These same architectural forms were used in profane buildings in a simplified fashion. This tendency began with the relatively minor simplification of the Propylaea of the Acropolis. Commonly, these profane buildings were halls, clubhouses, or stoas, built of columns, beams, pillars, and walls. No new structural principle was introduced until the Diadochi period, which began to combine elements more copiously.

Chapter Seven

PHILOSOPHERS, POLITICIANS, AND ART

Among the innumerable titles Diogenes Laertius preserved of the writings by philosophers not one deals with art. Even the Sophists, who offered opinions on all and sundry matters, skirted the subject of art, save Hippias of Elis who, among other things, spoke about painting and sculpture.

Several times Euripedes mentions that discussions on art had already taken place when Greek culture was in its prime. He does this not only in the first choral ode of *Ion* but also in his comparisons as when Polyxena, before being sacrificed, tears her dress, displaying her breasts like a goddess depicted in art, or as when the chorus in the *Phoenissae* yearns for Delphi, to tarry there and *serve Apollo like golden images of the gods*. But all in all art remained strikingly outside the realm of discussion, discourse, literature, and contemporary poetry. The images of the gods and the stirring myths were the great wellsprings of inspiration for Greek art, that really needed no mediator in the presence of the cult and the contests which it so frequently and sublimely presented. What with a virgin field before them, the philosophers, had they so desired, could have developed detailed and perhaps cramping aesthetics of the creative arts.

However, the most famous masters of the plastic arts were regarded as mere banausics. The historical Socrates constantly went in and out of their workshops to prove to them that they were really nothing but banausics and that they should never venture an opinion or judgment transcending their narrow confines. The Platonic Socrates now and then discoursed with artists, whom he named, but only about external activities never even remotely touching on their art or their peculiarities.

In a sense, philosophy and art were at daggers drawn, the latter glorifying the myths, the former striving to obliterate them from the Greek mind.

Philosophic thought was hostile to the beautiful and the highly imaginative, perhaps regarding itself as competing with the arts; its silence may well have betrayed envy. As is known, the Platonic state allowed no art or poesy or anything else that would make for individual development, except perhaps for that of the philosophers who were to rule the state. Moreover, the widespread nature of the cultus made the numerous pictorial representations of it distasteful to philosophic thought.

The votive offerings heaped up at many hallowed places were a bane to philosophic thought. Moderate people, in the view of philosophy, should make only moderate oblations.

This attitude would have condemned art to external shabbiness and materially reduced its significance. If Plato had had his way, he would not have shrunk from using force to quell its inner development as well.

When Plato composed his *Laws,* Scopas was at the height of his creative activity and perhaps Praxiteles also. Neither had occasion to exchange views with Plato; if they had done so, they might have taught him the lesson that the essence of intelligence consists in the highest development of individual capacities. But through all this, Greek art on the whole remained conservative.

Aristotle was reticent on the subject of the visual arts. The lacuna is noteworthy when one considers the large number and the great variety of his writings, including one on poetics, another on rhetoric, and an important section on music. His *Physiognomica,* still worth while for the artist and the art student to read, shows that he thoroughly understood how to regard the external world as an expression of the soul.

The Stoics reasoned blindly about art much as Plato did.

Critical comprehension and descriptive recording of the different works of art began only in the Alexandrian age and then not among the philosophers. We learn most from the Romans or from the Greeks of Roman times, who show the most reflective comprehension.

Art never reciprocated the aversion of the philosophers, immortalizing them in busts, statues, and portraits more copious than those of any other men except rulers. In the later days of antiquity instruction in the various philosophical systems became obligatory, and wherever the means were at hand the schools acquired portraits of the philosophers, at least of the founders of the several systems.

Seeing events in their proper light, posterity may regard it as the greatest good fortune for the visual arts that the pre-Alexandrian and pre-Roman littérateurs took so little account of art, leaving it fully and freely to its own uncommitted naïvete, whereas poesy was not left to its own devices. At a time when every other subject was frayed by analytic chatter, art had the infinite advantage both in subject matter and conception of being disengaged from all theories and critical orthodoxies and of being able to go its own way.

Art enjoyed the same independence from the politicians in power. Amid the most rapacious and aggressive government, art maintained its integrity and remained steadily occupied with glorious new developments. Religion continually found its highest expression in art; even rather decrepit poleis may well have commissioned Praxiteles and others. The rise of a new power like that of Messene, after Epaminondas restored it, occasioned numerous orders for statues of the gods. Art was not yet at the mercy of the rich, who were constantly diminishing in numbers, or depending on metropolitan exhibits.

In the course of the third century, the Greek city-states declined even before the Romans intervened. Inner unrest, leading commonly to the plundering of the last possessing strata of the population; attacks upon neighboring states with a view to pillage; mad reveling as, for instance, in Boeotia; systematic extermination of the entire ruling class as in Sparta; desolation of the countryside—all these events, as indicated above, marked the downward turn of fortune.

One should expect that no Hellene would have any heart or opportunity left for creating lofty works of art. Beyond Hellas, however, existed large Greek kingdoms where from time to time security and prosperity reigned. In Pergamum, situated in western Asia Minor, a school of sculptors had arisen of whose works until recently only a few, though quite significant, specimens were known. While unspeakable wretchedness ruled in Greece, there arose, either shortly before 197 under Attalus I, or soon thereafter under Eumenes II, the famous altar of Pergamum, over a hundred feet square, the astounding remains of which would alone suffice to make Berlin the world's most famous place for art pilgrimages. [The altar of Pergamum is no longer in the Pergamon Museum, Berlin; it was carried away by the Russians in 1945.]

A relief eight feet high, all around the altar, portrays the battle of the gods and the giants; those parts of it that were raised and are now resting in Berlin are 250 feet long. Naïve, fresh with youth, in tone and treatment much nearer to Phidias than one would have expected, this relief deals with its theme as a lion might with its prey, the most overpowering and most moving theme found in all the myths.

Earlier reliefs presented especially the battles between the Lapithae and the centaurs, the Amazons and fabled animals; here the gods themselves do battle with the semidivine giants, majestically interpreted by the master sculptors as a frightfully sublime storm of attack and defense, all in all by far the most significant expression of the Greek mind known of that period. The names of these artists have not survived while other contemporary events have been preserved in detail; indeed, the only mention of this colossal work is in a minor Latin author assigned to the age of Theodosius.

These sculptors must have been known by name in Pergamum and regarded as quite skilled banausics. Our craving to know the thoughts and feelings of those superb artists would have struck the people of Pergamum as very odd.

PART III
POESY AND MUSIC

Chapter Eight

THE PRIMEVAL AGE

Our task is to recognize poesy as a national force and power, as a mark of a lofty mind of a nation, and to judge the relative significance of its various products. To accomplish this task, we are fortunate in having inherited from antiquity not only the masterpieces themselves but also detailed discussions and analyses of masterpieces, both extant and perished.

Visual art also can help us interpret this poesy. Strictly speaking, this should not be so, for poesy really came earlier and influenced visual art to the extent that, as we have seen, it had already shaped the mythical figures visual art was later to represent. Thus, both dealt throughout with the same factual themes and thus each elucidated what was purely stylistic in the other. In regard to these stylistic matters we only need to recall what we said about art.

Both unite freedom and moderation—*sophrosyne*—here given a distinct meaning in the respect commonly accorded to once-established canons; since both, i.e., freedom and moderation, evolve to style and doctrine, the corresponding precepts become established among the Greeks.

Hence the tremendous wealth of variety within strict limits and order, all of which enables us to compare the great variety in the conception of the gods achieved within strict limits by Phidias and Polycleitus, and in the choral odes. Both are characterized by rich variety erected on a homogeneous base.

On the whole, style dominated for a long time. Even though the polis brought no overt pressure to bear on the poet, he nevertheless clung fast to traditional subject matter and to forms such as they were, for he was a man of the polis, composing for a people impressed by traditional modes and material. This protected both, poet and artist, against all whimsy and repulsive ingenuity.

161

The Greeks did not exclude the freakish and fantastic, which achieved its mature expression in the old comedy but was kept within the strictest limits of an inexorable style. Its parallel in the plastic arts may be found in the blends of part man and part animal (satyr), or of parts of different animals (chimera), always shaped under the exalted laws of beauty. Here, too, style was in full control; caprice was out of place.

A fundamental law common to both visual art and poesy was that the shaping of broad outlines was left largely to the traditions of myths, which having once assumed this role limited themselves to the re-creation of excellent types. The Greeks refrained from inventing new subject matter and instead invested the material at hand with new perceptions and motivations.

Architecture instructs us most lucidly on this matter of a basic law common to all the arts by rigidly adhering to a single type but perfecting it into living excellence.

All Indo-European races are accomplished in poesy: the Hindus, the Persians, the Germanic tribes, the Celts, even the Finns if they may be classed with the Europeans in this context, and the Slavic peoples, especially the Serbians; in their midst are the Hellenes, poetically the highest gifted of all. If we compare the Hellenes with the Latins, we could suppose they separated from their Italic neighbors because these were so prosaic.

Even before the Greeks had permanently settled in their home-to-be, poesy must have been a national force among them, and myth and cult, the great attendants of poesy in its various forms and migrations, must have contributed yeomanly to its development. The rare poetic aptitude of this new nation is evident from the perfection one of these attendants attained; a mythology inherently developed from historical events and personages, rich and varied beyond that of any other nation. This mythopoeic imagination in itself marks a poetic capacity of a very high order.

When bards chant often enough about the early heroes, the populace may acquire the notion of a heroic age filled with tales of derring-do embellished by stories of gods and fabulous beings. In this way, various peoples may have viewed their remote past and broadly idealized it into an age of splendor, listening enraptured to their bards celebrating that bygone age. But a consensus as among the Greeks is found nowhere else; they are the only nation that appears to have concentrated zealously on its myths and developed them homogeneously.

Poesy, being linked with music, is of concern to the singer, who customarily carried the traditions in all countries save those where the priesthood came into power. It is improbable that even in early times poetry, medicine, divine lore, and prophecy were united in one person. Numerous myths, however, testify to the high rank the nation accorded music. If anywhere, then in Greece, everything had to derive from the gods. Every aspect of poesy and music was given some ideal or legendary origin: it was Hermes who invented the lyre, Apollo the phorminx-cithara, and Pan the syrinx or shepherd's pipe. The Muses represented the total range of mind and inspiration. Mount Olympus itself was ever echoing with music and song, and among other songs the Muses sang of the sorrows of mankind.

Music even found a place among the myths of the gods. We are told that Athena threw the flute away when a satyr told her that blowing it twisted her features out of shape. Marsyas took it up and challenged Apollo

Flute player and thyiads
Earthen jug, Santa Maria di Capua

to a musical contest, but Apollo with his lyre triumphed over Marsyas and flayed him. But before this happened to him, Marsyas had instructed the ever young Olympus in music and had invented the music sacred to Cybele, the Great Mother.

The Muses also had their adventures. As long as they were goddesses of springs they were given to love, and Euterpe (or Calliope) had a son Rhesus by the river god Strymon; only later they became immune to Eros. The most important of these myths deals with Apollo and Hermes. Hearing the tortoise-shell lyre, Apollo wanted to have it and let Hermes keep the stolen cattle in exchange for it; while herding his cattle, Hermes blew on a reed pipe (syrinx); Apollo craved it, too, and gave him for it the golden staff with which he had formerly herded his cattle.

Myths of bards, above all Orpheus, paralleled the myths of the gods.

The famous Orpheus, who enchanted wild animals, made rocks and trees move, and touched the hearts of the Erinyes in Hades with pity, may be a pure nature myth; even so, reinterpretation of natural events implied in this myth measures the power song had over this nation.

As for the blind singers whom we must mention, it is to be remembered that as late as the nineteenth century the Serbians still made singers of the gifted blind. We must bear in mind that absence of external distractions may aid mental concentration. This fact helped give rise to the view that a singer with eyesight would be too fortunate and overbearing. Hence there arose also the legend that the singer was born with sight but because he, like Thamyris, rashly challenged the Muses to a musical contest, they blinded him, or that the gods envied and hence blinded him, as they did Teiresias, for revealing too many of their secrets.

We shall not attempt to determine to what extent the bards of primeval times specialized in hymns to Apollo, or to Demeter-Dionysus, or to Cybele. At all events, there is an obscure yet significant recollection linking the origin of song with the ethnologically dubious Thracians and Pieres settled on the northern and eastern slopes of Mount Olympus that was the dwelling of the gods. The foot of Olympus is the birthplace of the Muses, whom Homer always called the Olympians. Musaeus, Orpheus, and also Eumolpus and Thamyris are specifically called Thracians.

Even Hesiod, who calls the Muses Heliconians, says they were born at Olympus and dwell there beneath the peak and go only at times to Helicon, bathing in the Hippocrene and dancing there around the altar of Zeus. Bards of the Thracians and Pieres may well have made Olympus the common home of the gods and linked the dwelling of the Muses with that mountain. Here may be the earliest home of the epic, and here may have taken shape the earliest forms of theogony and the battles of the gods with the Titans.

Hesiod the shepherd became a poet and teacher; his new calling introduces a subtle nuance into the bard's relationship with the Muses. Visiting him at night in his native Ascra, the Muses taught him the glorious art of song at the foot of divine Helicon. They informed him, too, that they could tell him many lies akin to truth but could also reveal to him the truth if they wanted to. After taking this crack at the epic which also accommodates lies, the Muses handed him a twig of the glorious laurel and breathed divine song into him, so that he might know the past and the future and sing of the race of the blessed, the everlasting gods.

The beautiful belief in the Muses began with Hesiod. For him the Muses, i.e., poesy, signified rest from all cares and forgetfulness of evil. But now we must also mention what this nation did to exalt the honor of poesy.

First and foremost, the Hellenes developed a marvelously rich, pliant, and metrically flexible language, the matrix and precondition of poesy as well as of philosophy. One would like to know where and when this language reached its exquisite perfection, which was at once witness and vehicle of poetry. A people possessing such a language has under all circumstances an unfettered and nimble mind, and at the same time such a language will be a sublime instrument for poesy. This language enabled the Hellenes to achieve in both story and description an epic expression excelling that of all other nations.

The great diversity of their life, their many tribes and cities, fostering independent modes of thought, promoted poetry as well as the visual arts. This diversity is reflected even in the earliest extant poetry and the great number of poets to whom it is ascribed. For the Greeks, poetry was self-evidently an expression of the individual. The almost complete absence of servitude in those early days played its part and likewise the relative simplicity of life; in short, the leisure granted to everyone capable of perceiving the world in images and representing it in words and song. The spirit could here be born into flesh as nowhere on earth in our times.

The worship of gods taking on many local variations evoked diversified customs and rites and was not under the thumb of a powerful priesthood that might have made all chants uniform, perhaps complicated or difficult, or that might have regulated it with precepts as Plato in his *Laws* wished them to. Everything remained relatively simple and popular, something an individual priest at a temple could easily master and teach, and something everybody could easily remember. Thus, the Linos song, wherein the people lamented the death of a king's son in early manhood, symbolized the passing of a year, or the paeans to Apollo whereby men summoned up courage to face peril, especially before going into battle, expressed their gratitude after having overcome danger, and where in spring they uttered their hope and trust in a good year to come.

Of this simple kind, too, were the round dances accompanied by harp and lyre, the jolly songs at festival processions accompanied by flutes, and the hymeneal songs and crow songs following them, also the dirges sung by hired singers accompanied by wailing women, which like the hymeneal songs presumably offered opportunity for individual variations. (Crows were esteemed as symbols of fidelity in marriage. Aelian. *Hist. Anim.* III, 9.)

As for the bards of the heroic period, the myths carefully and copiously preserve their memories. *The godlike bard whose songs give pleasure,* together with the diviner, the physician, and the shipwright, to whom we might add the priest, the herald, and the blacksmith, belonged to those craftsmen we should have welcomed as guests, whereas beggars came uninvited. The bards liked best of all to stay at the palaces of princes as long as they could, their task being to glorify the princely forebears.

On the whole, the aristocratic republics were glad when a poet appeared. At a time when the heroic way of life was gradually giving way to an agonistic one in which all and sundry sought for honors in contests, agonistic festivals often spurred poets to excellence. Disregarding Attic drama for the time being, competition played a major role in choral lyrics presented by competing choirs at festivals and divine services, where judges must have presided. In his *Works and Days,* Hesiod shows that bards competed at festivals and games in the times of the kings already. Later, bards and rhapsodes competed with each other at all festivals throughout the lands of the Greeks.

As to the rendition, it is hard to say whether the lyre accompanied the entire song or merely introduced it; in Serbia, the *gusla* does not always accompany the entire song either.

Rhapsody is a comprehensive term implying a stitching together of verses without any marked pauses. The word applies to recitations of quite different kinds of material, i.e., to epic as well as to non-epic, and to verses composed by the poet himself or by others. But the wonderful hexameter could dispense with the lyre, being as it is a kind of song in itself.

The origin of this meter is lost in myth: Phemonoe, the first prophetess at Delphi, or Olen the Hyperborean, the first prophet there, allegedly devised it. Delphi pronounced most of its oracles in hexameters. For a long time this meter was used almost exclusively in lyric poetry, it being the only vessel for poetry as a whole.

The Greeks well knew what they owed to this verse form, adapting itself as it does with unexcelled elasticity to every thought and perception and lending itself so beautifully to onomatopoesis. Aristotle calls the hexameter the most steady and stately of all meters.

Chapter Nine

POESY IN HEXAMETER

1. The Homeric Epos

We have already emphasized that the Greeks had a vital need of keeping their primeval traditions as a comprehensive whole ever present before them. Only the bards had mastered these traditions in a complete and coherent fashion; though they did not create, at least they gave majestic form and harmonious order to Greek beliefs and myths, thus exercising a grand and free dominion over the imagination of these people.

In contrast to the songs of the common folk and simple invocations of the gods, the narrative poetry of the bards had always been an artistic product, i.e., its body of tradition kept growing, thus making it imperative that one begin to cultivate this art as a youth and devote one's life to it. Whether we link the Thracian and Pieres bards with him or not, Homer was far from being the first conscious artist in poetry. His tone and style can only be understood as the outgrowth of an ancient tradition of bards and their schools; in this way only can one explain the flawless mastery of treatment.

This narrative style was most likely created in very early times by distinguished bards or poets possessing both exceptional talent and the purest national consciousness; their followers accepted and transmitted this accomplishment as belonging to the nature of things.

By and large, the genuine bard was indispensable in that he was the one to transmit everything that went beyond daily affairs. He had a most distinguished occupation in life and belonged to a guild whose members traveling about disseminated and preserved the loftier thoughts.

From earliest times songs were handed down orally. Writing was relatively recent, as the fuss Euripedes made over it and the late development

167

of prose attest. That writing was not used at the inception of the epic is evident from the many refrains, repetitions, and recurrent epithets employed,
devices affording the memory time to collect itself. The strongest proof for
us that the Homeric epics were transmitted orally lies in the pleasure they
provide to the listener. Homer's compositions are masterpieces of swift
speech full of vivid adumbrations which in ages of the written word are apt
to be elaborated in tedious detail.

For the bard a prodigious memory was vitally important; Mnemosyne
is not without good reason the mother of the Muses. One should call to mind
that the Vedas and the whole ancient literature of India up to about the time
of Buddha, were composed and handed down orally and that, to this day,
the dedicated Brahmans, except those of Calcutta, still follow in the foot-
steps of their ancestors and learn by heart the whole Rig-Veda (even though
it is available in print) with its thousand hymns and nearly thirty thousand
slokas, containing ritual, doctrine, and laws, all of which are vastly harder
to retain in memory than epic compositions are.

The contents of both Homer and Hesiod suggest that these authors of
great epic poetry had many predecessors. Homer presupposes that all his
heroes and many things relating to them are known; he mentions many
persons in a cursory manner, assuming that his listeners have learned about
them elsewhere. He gives fleeting glimpses of a Heracleid, an Argonaut
composition, and a theogony deviating from Hesiod's. The early state of
poetry, before Homer combined the disconnected fragments into an epic
whole, is perhaps best reflected in the songs of the highly gifted Serbians,
for they present an Iliad *ante Homerum,* i.e., a great mass of poetry as yet
untouched by an epic master.

The great master among the Greeks, of course, was Homer. He beautifully proportioned the parts by appropriate arrangement and subordination,
and by intensifying the motives and characters.

Only a poet of the highest order could have managed Achilles and
Odysseus. We may confidently dismiss the view that the Homeric epics are
only parts of other epics patched together. Indeed, of Homer himself we
know next to nothing. The ancients wrangled about his home, his family,
and the age he lived in. The extant biographies of Homer are mostly fiction;
the most detailed one, falsely ascribed to Herodotus, is a late work remarkable for the way it rallies the reader.

However, we may agree with the literary historians that Homer was an
Ionian living in the ninth century. His precise knowledge of every spot in
Troas suggests that his home was in Asia Minor; he also knew Greece and
was fairly familiar with Ithaca and Pylos, but he saw the islands to the west
through a haze of myth.

"This mighty sway of youthful imagination . . . delineating in great detail the scenes of a heroic age with the merriest cheer and insatiable delight, portraying them in the fairest shapes which exceed all desire to add or detract; the pure joy and light-heartedness with which he plunges into a stream of poetic images and plays and frolics with the gently lapping waves—all these bear witness to the most exalted happiness of heart and mind. Of all the forms poetry has ever appeared in, Homer's has the most objectivity, i.e., complete surrender of the creative powers to the object without any intrusions of the poet's own thoughts, feelings, or personal relations. The mind of Homer is completely native to a sublime and powerful world exempt from all want and need." (*O. Müller, Literaturgeschichte I*)

In antiquity, people quite properly did not grieve over Homer's blindness, for it could be no misfortune in the presence of such inward visions.

The most essential thing is that Homer's epics have been preserved, thanks to the unflagging exertion of the most gifted nation on earth. In the earlier period, the Homeridae of Smyrna deserve great credit. They are not to be regarded as a family but as a guild of men who pursued one and the same art and hence had worshiped one hero whom they set up as their head and from whom they derived their name.

According to the account given by Aelian and now commonly accepted, Lycurgus on his travels in Ionia had found that the single sections into which Homer had been broken up were being recited there. He gathered up these separate parts and brought them to Greece, where Peisistratus later had them put together into the *Iliad* and the *Odyssey*. Onomacritus, among others, is supposed to have assisted in this task. He and his fellow workers clearly toiled conscientiously and sought with commendable critical piety to preserve only the authentic old material. Still, one may wonder how much genuine old material was discarded and how much new added when the two epics were divided into twenty-four books each.

To judge the composition of the *Iliad* correctly we must note that, whereas the *Odyssey* is peripheral concentric in structure, the *Iliad* is linear, presenting the events in their temporal sequence; hence, we cannot expect from it the tension found in drama or the frivolous suspense common in modern novels.

Composing in the manner of a continuous relief must have been for the bards and their audiences a delight they could hardly get enough of. To be sure, inconsistencies occur, and seams showing unhappy inventions and intrusions are visible; however, the poem received its final form so long ago that our criticisms pointing out these defects come too late. No Delphi rules the nation in the *Iliad*, no Dorians undertake migrations, no Ionic metropolis is mentioned, no Bosporus, no cavalry as part of the army, and no Corinth ruled by wealthy tyrants.

Pre-Homeric bards must have shaped nearly every motive, arranged the material in good order, and determined the character of the individuals quite firmly before Homer gave them ripe perfection. Not initial fumblings but consummate skill characterize the *Iliad*, and the *Odyssey* too, wherein a few more or less whimsical imperfections are completely nugatory.

For us the entire and true proportionality of the *Iliad* consists in the relation between the earlier parts detailing the inadequacy of the great heroes and the later parts presenting the tremendous power and passion of Achilles whose greatness, once he bestirs himself, towers over everybody and everything.

From the very beginning, the successive events alternate most artistically: the dissension in the assembly, the embarkation of Chryseis, the purification of the Achaean host, the mission of the heralds to Achilles, his talk with his mother Thetis, Odysseus in Chryse delivering up Chryseis. Only an age ripe in spirit and the art of poesy could have produced such scenes as that of Helen at the Scaean Gate, where the poet discreetly refrains from having her questioned about Menelaus. In the oldest version of this scene, Helen pointed out the Achaean heroes, so that the Trojans could find out who they were individually.

In the fifth book, essentially dedicated to Diomedes, the tempo increases, beginning with verse 144. The hero dispatches four pairs of Trojan brothers, kills Pandarus, wounds Aeneas, captures his horses, and hits Aphrodite. A somewhat striking inconsistency is that Zeus, devising evil, terrifies the Trojans with his thunderbolt at the end of book seven, while in book eight everything turns out favorable for them.

Homer took great pleasure in describing fighting and was incessantly recounting some battle or other, even some that had been fought long before his time. The technical precision with which he described the manner of wounding and the place where the armor was pierced reveals the interest he could take for granted in his audience. Some modern readers have little understanding for Homer's views, and suppose such battle scenes should have been omitted. But it does not follow that a passage is expendable just because it can be omitted without leaving a marked lacuna; moreover, excising the battles would not lay bare the oldest form of the poem. We should allow antiquity its delights even though our own tastes, dulled by piquancy and propaganda, may have different preferences.

We might ask ourselves whether our perceiving certain passages as dispensable does not argue forcefully for their artistic beauty and propriety. Likewise, we may criticize certain other passages later Greeks found fault with who only read Homer, but never heard him recited, and hence had only an uncertain notion of epic quality. It is dangerous for us to apply our notions of what is dispensable to these passages, for the epic poet even in Homer's time was a great artist and in sovereign control of his material. When he retarded his narrative by interweaving conversations, we must allow him his artistic economy.

Episodes like those of Glaucus and Diomedes in book six ought to be regarded similarly; the interruption of the action by dramatically superfluous but epically beautiful passages like the duel between Ajax and Hector with whom, as the reader knows, gods and men but especially the poet, are so concerned that they will both survive; the conversation between Idomeneus and Meriones, and the first part of book fifteen dealing with the gods at great length and finally sending wind-swift Iris with a message to Poseidon. In the midst of a violent debate, Nestor, who at the quarrel of the leaders had already drawn attention to his former deeds, gives a long-winded account of a war between Pylos and Arcadia in which as a young man he dispatched Ereuthalion, the lord with the iron club; later on he narrates the whole Elian war, and Phoenix likewise relates his whole former life.

The demeanor of the individual characters reveals unerring artistic certitude and convincing truth. One need only observe the nuances between the two Atreides as limned at the slaying of Adrestus and the abundance of individual personalities described for us in a single battle as in that by the ships.

The multitude of images also serves the linear composition and the constantly shifting lights and shadows of the battle scenes. It is wondrously charming when the dense clouds scatter and suddenly the sunny mountain peaks and headlands appear.

We are also reminded of certain gripping passages as when Diomedes says to his opponents:

> Unhappy the parents whose sons encounter my strength. (Il. 6:127)

or:

> Draw near that soon you may fall in the snare of destruction. (Il. 6:143)

Indeed everywhere we meet persuasive power, beauty, and suppleness of expression, applying to everything from thunder to flattering compliment, which Hector accords even to his team of horses.

The serious and tragic mood enveloping the whole second half is of the

highest epic art. This part has no episodic material except the new shield
of Achilles in book eighteen and the purposefully long-drawn account of the
funeral games in honor of Patroclus. Like the second half of the *Odyssey*,
it presents a more complicated and profound psychological development
culminating in the dissolution of Achilles' wrath into sorrow at Hector's
death. The funeral pyre of Hector at Troy closes the *Iliad*. Homer refrained
from adding the death of Achilles; hardly any poet since then would have
cared to do so.

The scene at the end of the *Iliad* in which Achilles yields the dead body
of Hector to Priam is of deliberate artistry. The store of events leading to
the overthrow of Troy was as old and complete as Homer's treatment had
made them. That the *Iliad* does not also contain at least the content of the
Aethiopis, i.e., the death of Memnon and Achilles, can only be attributed to
poetic skill of the first order. An extraordinary sense of proportion determined that and perhaps also the feeling that nothing could excel the scene
of Priam and Achilles in the tent. The premonition of Achilles' inevitable
death pervades the *Iliad*, so that its fulfillment is unnecessary.

Finally, we draw attention to two later poetical developments adumbrated in the *Iliad*: the chorus of the drama and bucolic poetry. The chorus
speaks *as one*, as in the sentence *Thus one would speak*, expressing the
thought of many. The shepherd appears here for the time being as a mute
witness of nature, as for instance when far off he hears the roar of two
streams where they join in a gorge or when his heart is joyful on a windless
night as the moon gleams and the stars shine. Someday he will find his voice
in Greek poetry.

In comparison with the *Iliad*, the *Odyssey* is obviously the later poem,
for it indirectly relates to the *Iliad* and avoids matters already treated in it.
Here, as in the *Iliad*, the first half is essentially epic and forms the basis of
the second half, which verges on the dramatic. But the peripheral concentric structure of the *Odyssey* contrasts strikingly with the linear structure of
the *Iliad*, for it has running through it a twofold story: the wanderings of
Odysseus and the deeds of the suitors in Ithaca, which flow together in a
crowning catastrophe.

The poem obviously went through many transformations until, under
the shaping hands of a poetic genius, it finally attained the majestic harmony
it now has.

No reasonable ground exists for doubting that this poem was Homer's;
indeed, it is much harder to suppose a second poet of his rank could have
existed. He was more mature and more sure of himself than at the time he
created the *Iliad*. He most likely became an old man, and it is well to remember that other Greek poets, especially Sophocles, retained their full poetic

Achilles bandages Patroclus

powers into extreme old age. He now mastered all the means of the highest epical art so well that he could transmute his epic into dramatic art.

Despite its consummate art, the *Odyssey* patently reveals that it arose in relatively early days of Greek history; this is shown by its limited geographical horizon veiling in myth everything west of the Grecian isles.

The surest hand has ordered everything into a grand artistic whole. Homer did not begin with Odysseus' departure from Troy but arranged matters so that the beginning was near the denouement; it is but a short stretch of time from the island of Calypso to the slaying of the suitors. Book one opens with the gods in counsel assembled, briefly discussing the hero on Ogygia and divulging their plans.

The first four books deal with Telemachus, the suitors, Penelope, and Telemachus' journey to Nestor and Menelaus, giving a broad and beautiful exposition with many related mythological elements and ending with the suspense of the suitors in the boat lying in wait for Telemachus. Not until book five does Odysseus step into the foreground.

At the bidding of Hermes, Calypso has to let him go, and after infinite hardship he arrives on the island of Scheria. The three following books present his reception by the Phaeacians, beginning with the meeting of Nausicaa.

In its earliest traditions, this part has no doubt a rather shabby scene shot through with elements of fable; in its present form it deftly shows Odysseus not only recuperating but also revealing himself.

This whole Phaeacian existence is portrayed in pleasing golden colors, mainly to provide a background for Odysseus to narrate his story, for it forms a frame around the marvelous tales covering books nine to twelve, wherein he narrates his harrowing experiences. In earlier versions, the bard may have put them at the beginning, but these experiences are much more touching when told by the half-rescued hero himself.

This whole episode is put in the most appropriate place conceivable. Here is released in one stream everything that might have marred or retarded the dramatic quality of the epic structure and all the grotesque mythical elements that might have distorted individual motivation and characterization. One might say that the whole fabulous world of the sea-farer is gathered in this one person.

As emphasized in book one, the rancor of Poseidon is the cardinal motive on which the unity of the first half of the *Odyssey* is pivoted. Undoubtedly this is quite an ancient theme, as may be the case with the whole Cyclops story. It may well be that Homer was the poet who had Odysseus hurl his second taunt at the blind Polyphemus, against the warning of his men, and then reveal his name, thereby largely occasioning the woes that befell him and his shipmates. According to the poet's unexpressed assumption, the mere mention of an unnamed man would not have enabled Polyphemus to wail to his father Poseidon with very much point.

The second half of the *Odyssey* is structured much like that of the *Iliad*. The poet could have brought everything to an end rather quickly if he had wanted to. In its oldest form the end probably did come soon.

Instead, the poem breaks up into a variety of episodes. In the course of a good many conversations, the poet through a variety of devices prepares the way for the catastrophe. These conversations do not always advance the story but they do reveal the characters more fully. By way of example, we need only refer to the conversation between Odysseus and Telemachus in book sixteen.

The longer conversations reveal character and hint at future events, as book fourteen, devoted to Eumaeus and to the two fictitious tales of Odysseus, illustrates. In book fifteen, Eumaeus gives a circumstantial account of his early years.

The aim of the poet is to establish the guilt of the suitors as fully as possible, so as to justify the pagan yet humanly understandable vengeance Odysseus takes on them. This guilt grows gradually on all sides until it hurls the guilty to terrible destruction. It exemplifies *hybris* and the ruin it entails.

Therefore the whole wretchedness of Ithaca has to be presented; the listener is to learn with increasing indignation how many are involved in the crimes and how deep the wickedness has gnawed.

The chief purpose of book sixteen is to embitter the listener. In it he learns about the misery of Laertes, the number of the suitors, the foreknowledge of Odysseus that he will be maltreated, the secret conspiracy to kill Telemachus, and the former kindness of Odysseus toward Antinous and Eurymachus, two of the worst of the lot. The more patient and restrained Odysseus is, the more smashing will be the vengeance. Odysseus can restrain his yearning in order to put his wife to the test. His wife and the people of Ithaca will recognize him when he will have taken his revenge and rightfully assumed his sovereignty.

In the meantime, beginning with the narration of Odysseus to the Phaeacians, the figure of the hero has filled the listener with ever greater interest and gripped him with its compelling magic. In his earlier career he was one among sundry great men, a firm character but still in company with Achilles, Agamemnon, and Ajax. Now he steps out of that general context to become a sharply molded personage, representative of the Greek individual most familiar to Socrates. He is one of the two best known figures of antiquity, indeed the ideal of the Greeks, not just at some age or station in life but the ideal as such, and this without any frills but in one bodily contour, alive and nimble.

His four monologues during the shipwreck, while swimming in the sea and on reaching the shore, introduce him and show that he does not lose grip on himself even when battling the stormy waves. His wonderful address to Nausicaa reveals another aspect of his character. And now the woes of the much-enduring hero give depth to the whole first half of the epic; the most frightful accounts of his suffering would be well-nigh unendurable did they not come from the mouth of one who had survived.

We call to mind his conversation with the shade of his mother Anticleia who had died of grief for him; she gave him heart-rending accounts of Ithaca, the afflictions of his wife and his father and the gloom hovering over his homeland. She pined away for him, for Odysseus is the kind of person for whom one may grieve oneself to death. One may also recall his most gruesome moment, as he himself calls it, when he saw six of his men in the jaws of Scylla, shrieking and stretching out their hands to him for help as she snatched them up and devoured them.

No harm is done if the listener takes Odysseus for a bit of a braggart, as when passing dread Charybdis he gripped onto a fig tree and swung from it like a bat until at last the great whirlpool spewed up his mast and keel. When he tirelessly spins a yarn about his past life, Athena smiles and says:

Not even in your native land do you give up telling lies. He relates a very pretty tale of his life to Eumaeus, which here and there approaches his actual life so closely that the feeling he puts into it is genuine.

Before his identity is known, he now and then interjects an impatient and somewhat vehement reproach into the complaints of others about conditions in Ithaca, asking them why they put up with them. But to be able to keep silent is kingly; accordingly his words have a solemn ring when he says to Telemachus: *If you are really my son and of my blood, then tell no one that I am here,* etc.

This Odysseus is the center around which the other five main characters are grouped: Nausicaa, Penelope, Telemachus, Eumaeus, and Eurycleia. They cannot have achieved their full development until after the character of Odysseus is finally established in its supreme maturity. The later Greeks could not have produced a Nausicaa or a Penelope. As to Eumaeus, what an epic figure he is! He is removed from all idyllic elements. He and Eurycleia, although slaves, have become persons in their own right and oppose the wanton robbers.

The vengeance is to be final and complete. Among the suitors some are deliberately portrayed as better, others as worse; yet all are headed for their doom. One of them, called Amphinomos, is a thoroughly decent fellow and Odysseus tries to warn him, but all in vain. His triumph over Irus shows Odysseus in his full and secure majesty; he slings his tattered knapsack over his shoulders and resumes his seat on the threshold.

The conversation Odysseus carries on with Penelope in book nineteen is a most exquisite instance of epic retardation, designed to analyze the two chief characters more fully before the denouement and before Penelope recognizes him. Odysseus relates matters increasingly nearer the actual events and his true personality shimmers more and more clearly through the mask. Penelope is more and more shaken, but despite all her lamentations his eyes betray no more emotion than if they were of horn or iron. In the famous foot-washing scene, where Eurycleia recognizes him and he grips her by the throat, he might well be less harsh, but he is justified when his heart growls in anger at the lecherous maids.

The grand finale comes in books twenty to twenty-two, involving a great many characters of the *Odyssey*. The whole action visibly heightens and speeds up. At the beginning of the last banquet an ominous tension is in the air. After Telemachus defiantly reproves the suitors and Ctesippus hurls a cow's hoof at Odysseus (book twenty), Penelope's marriage is discussed for the last time. Theoclymenus relates his ghastly vision and the incident of the great bow takes place. Since no one else could even string the bow, Odysseus asks to try his hand at it. Circumstantially, it is described how he twangs the string so that it sings like a swallow, and how Zeus sends down a thunderclap. And then the shot.

Now Odysseus sheds his rags and the last scene begins, that of the savage, frightful, but imposing revenge, whose only parallel is the fall of the Nibelungs, exceeding in forcefulness everything else in the whole poem. Odysseus crowds all he has to say to the suitors into seven gripping verses; then begins the battle whose single episodes, motives, and development are pure and perfect art.

The hero acts as lord and king that he is, without hesitation or deliberation. The realism displayed in describing the various details of death, including the jerking of the feet of the hanged women and the execution of Melanthius, suggests that Homer may have witnessed similar occurrences.

Books twenty-three and twenty-four contain disputed and interpolated material. Penelope's dawdling caution in recognizing Odysseus may be an ancient and genuine trait. That she sleeps through the best thing that ever happened to her, much as he does on his return from Phaeacia, is also quite an authentic touch. The final victory over the rebellious Ithacans is dubious, as is the scene where Laertes let fly his spear. But magnificent is the conception of the final behest by Zeus, accompanied as it was by a flaming thunderbolt, granting the Ithacans forgiveness of the evil they had caused themselves, so that concord and peace might reign again.

The whole treatment of the *Odyssey* is so masterful that interpolations can be detected at once. Odysseus is plainly speaking for Homer when he says:

> I told you all that yesterday and it is odious
> To repeat a tale already plainly told.

So, when tedious repetitions occur, like the speech of Menelaus in book seventeen and various items in the scene in the underworld in book twenty-four, or when needless parallels occur of matters already told, like the second Melanthus scene in book nineteen, we may safely exonerate Homer from them. It is quite different with set phrases like:

> And they put their hands to the savory banquet,
> But when desire for food and drink had been stilled,
> Downward plunged the sun and shadowy grew the highways,

or when a man starts out in a chariot

> He cracked his whip and the willing team flew on its way

and many similar phrases. Such set phrases are genuinely epic and have a truer ring than constantly new turns would have. On the other hand, the

poet well understands the proper way to use variation, as when he appropriately varies the reception Nestor and Menelaus give Telemachus; Menelaus
has to begin talking about Odysseus on his own to avoid repeating the
motive of questioning used in Pylos.

Set expressions are also found in the recurrent epic epithets applied to
gods, men, and various objects. The poet employs them in agitated or pained
speech, even in the most tense moments, to describe and identify matters
carefully: while Penelope is in deepest distress over the fate of Telemachus
she speaks of

> the swift scudding ships that serve
> Men as horses to ride the salt waves and cross the wide water.

And when the suitors are about to waylay Telemachus, the poet does not
spare the listener a description of the ship with its mast, sails, rudder, etc.

Again the poet deliberately interjects past episodes into extremely tense
situations so as to draw them out. Just when Eurycleia notices the scar on
Odysseus' leg and everything is at stake, a circumstantial account is given of
the way he got it on a boar hunt in his youth; all the incidentals that are
included, accounts of situations, banquets, landscapes, and the like, disclose
that the purpose in interjecting this episode is to draw out the tale, thereby
heightening the suspense.

In delineating the individual characters Homer knows exactly how far
to go to enhance the effectiveness of the poem. At the beginning the obvious
procedure would have been to present an enumeration and a description of
the suitors. Instead, he presents them incidentally as time and occasion make
for vivid effect. Antinous and Eurymachus talk most. One gets to know the
names of quite a few of their number in the slaying scene only. To give their
names earlier would clutter the story.

All descriptions are characterized by moderation and serve only to
emphasize genuinely significant matters and often to draw out a tense situation. This is exemplified by the graceful and detailed account of the way
Odysseus got his bow from Eurytus when, at the beginning of book twenty-
one, Penelope opens a screeching door and fetches it out of a storeroom.

One should also observe that the palace and garden of Alcinous are
described barely enough to evoke a pleasurable image; the same holds for the
cave of Calypso, the grotto of the nymphs, and the fresh spring on Ithaca.
Of the many beautiful objects described in the *Odyssey*, we shall mention
the baldric Herakles had for his sword.

Here and there, Homer probably curtails and rearranges material. He
runs over the details of the Circe story in book ten quite rapidly; her house,
her mode of appearing, Hermes' appearance and departure, her oath, every-

thing flashes by, as it were. One gets the impression that there might have been a much longer version. But this brevity is eminently justified and of the right proportion for the *Odyssey* as a whole.

In addition the *Odyssey*, like the *Iliad*, is obliged to catalogue some mythological details now and then, as if the poet were giving brief résumés of much ampler lore at hand. Demodocus introduces the story of Ares and Aphrodite and of the Trojan horse. The underworld scene in book eleven gives the procession of mythical women; that in book twenty-four provides Agamemnon's shade with the occasion to tell of the burial of Achilles.

In contrast to the *Iliad*, the *Odyssey* gives few particulars about the gods and their activities on Olympus; it holds the imagination of the listener more with bird flights and other omens.

The *Odyssey* is not bare of similes though it has fewer extended similes than the *Iliad*, where they are aesthetically indispensable for the numerous battle scenes. We may say the poet no longer needs these purple patches because he enlivens his people and events adequately with his descriptions. However, he resorts to the extended simile when Odyssus comes out of the thicket on the shores of Phaeacia *like a mountain-bred lion,* or when Agamemnon giving fragmentary details achieves an appalling effect by saying that he was killed while banqueting *as an ox is struck down in the stall* and that his men were *slaughtered one by one like swine.*

When Agamemnon tells, in this connection, how Clytemnestra slew Cassandra while he was trying in vain to defend her, and how she turned her back on him, her dying husband, refusing to close his eyes and mouth, Homer gives us an example of the gruesome. In general, though, he reveals his greatness percisely by omitting the repulsive elements surely adhering to the original myths. He also knows where realism is in order. The deeds and sufferings of Polyphemus display realism to the point of being horrible, yet the narrative is effective poetically and indirectly expresses the anger and desperation of Odysseus.

Homer exhibits judicious sobriety in expressing strong emotions. It is the account of the deeds and actions that is to awaken the feelings in the listener; accordingly, Odysseus takes leave of Calypso and of Circe twice without displaying undue sentiments.

The *Odyssey* contains many tender and touching passages. For instance, the jars of delicious wine set in a row in Odysseus' storeroom against his return from toilsome wanderings, the way his men, released from Circe's dehumanizing spell, take his hands and sob quietly for joy, or when he returns to the men left on the beach, how they crowd around him *like calves around their mother* and feel as though they were at home in Ithaca again.

When the Phaeacians put Odysseus ashore in Ithaca he is asleep and so does not recognize his homeland until Athena convinces him by pointing out unmistakable landmarks. While in the hut with Eumaeus he recognizes by the behavior of the dogs that a friend is approaching; it is Telemachus, who graciously bids the stranger keep his seat.

As to the world of the *Odyssey*, we shall pass over its precise geographical details, a subject later Greeks eagerly pursued, although the Ionic bard

Murder of the suitors by Odysseus
Vase painting

had a remarkable knowledge of Pylos, Lacedaemon, Ithaca, etc. Important and significant, however, is the mythical geography. A short distance beyond the known regions, there dwell monsters like the cruel king Echetus on the continent; farther away is the island of Calypso, *the navel on the belly of the sea,* the center of the Mediterranean and the counterpart of Delphi on land.

Aeaea, the island of Circe, the home and dancing floor of Dawn and the rising place of the sun, need not even be thought of as in the east but only as a place where daylight really begins as opposed to the perpetual night in the Cimmerian land. Syria is an island beyond Ortygia *where the turning point of the sun is.* It is highly speculative what *Ocean Stream, Gates of the Sun,* and *Land of Dreams* refer to (book 24:11f.). The short nights of the Laestrygonians imply a glimmering of knowledge about the north.

It is significant that in this view of the world, the farther away from home or the nearer the rim of the world, the more ideal and blissful life became. On the island of Syria just mentioned, hunger and disease are unknown; when people get old Apollo and Artemis carry them away. Happiness clearly marks the life of the Phaeacians. They are near and dear to the gods and from them receive everlasting abundance under gentle skies unmarred by cloud or storm.

In the *Odyssey* one breathes pure sea air free of all dust and dirt. This poem is full of inspired descriptions of ships and voyages. Homer described the raft of Odysseus with astonishingly accurate technical detail. Odysseus

proves skilled in the art of shipbuilding, as a king on an island no doubt had to be; even the ax Calypso gives him is a splendid tool.

To be sure, the raft smashes to pieces almost as ingeniously as it was made, but it is an overpowering storm that does it. His swim to land is almost as formidable as the storm itself. But Scylla and Charybdis represent the most horrible of all mythical horrors. Indeed, as soon as one ventures beyond the bounds of the known, the sea becomes precarious, and beyond Crete

No other land appears, only sky and water.

The last symbolic command Teiresias gives to Odysseus is to avoid the sea, and yet, out of it, death in its gentlest guise will come to him worn out in comfortable old age, surrounded by a happy people.

The *Odyssey* was composed at a time when all other nations were fearful of the sea, except the Phoenicians, but their enthusiasm never turned into poesy concerning either the sea or anything else. Only the Greeks transmuted such experiences into poetry.

2. *Homer and the Greeks*

The poesy of myth enabled all early peoples to live in that which abides and is constant, i.e., in the transfigured image of the nation itself; but the Greeks were especially indebted to Homer for this legacy. Hence, in no other nation did a poet ever assume such stature with young and old. Plutarch says elegantly: *Homer alone has triumphed over the fickleness of human taste; he is forever new and in the happy splendor of youth.*

For the sake of the state, Solon in Athens demanded that the rhapsodes recite Homer in toto, and the Pcisistratidae followed him in this.

But Homer's power became incalculable when he manifestly became the chief source of education for all from youth on. The Greeks were perhaps the only people that instilled in their children an objective and very liberal ethical view of the world, without any theological or political bias, as opposed, for instance, to the Pentateuch and the Shah Namah. Pythagoras, Xenophon, and Plato in the first two books of *The Republic*, resisted Homer much too late to make any headway; thus it was Homer who not only fashioned the gods for the Greeks but in effect awakened or kept alive in them the principle of human freedom. To be sure, other select poetry was used in educating the young; still the *Iliad* and the *Odyssey* were by far the most important course of study.

Homer was the fundamental source for the Greek notions of divinity and humanity in the widest sense; he was their codex in religion, their teacher in military affairs, and in their primary history, which all their geography applied to and all their history connected with until rather late. An uninterrupted critical, aesthetic, antiquarian, and linguistic study of Homer continued through the age of the Roman emperors and deep into the Byzantine period.

Scholars studied his mode of naming things and attempted to elucidate the obscure passages found in his epics. Philosophers and scholars of antiquity found in Homer inducement to compose all sorts of dialogues, treatises, and reflections, as dozens of titles indicate.

To be sure, there were scoffers like Diogenes who marveled at grammarians who claimed to fathom the sufferings of Odysseus but understood not their own; still, preoccupation with the myth remained a fact. A specific indifference to the non-mythical and non-Homeric world asserted itself, and in this respect the bard came to be a dilatory element in the nation, causing men to adhere to the past as the typical and to care little for precision of detail. Had the individual poleis not been interested in their origins, their racial composition, and the history of their institutions, we should have only the scantiest history of Greece before the Persian Wars.

Later Greek poets had reason to complain, for there were people who pointed to Homer and protested that they had no need of any new poetry. This attitude alone vouches for Homer's enormous influence, evident in countless ways from the perpetual quoting of his verses, especially at banquets, and the philological jests men indulged in, to the gorgeous manuscripts in the hands of the powerful.

The Lagides of Alexandria and the Attalidae of Pergamum vied with each other in promoting the study of Homer and in glorifying him. Ptolemy Philopater erected a temple to Homer in which his statue was surrounded by those of seven cities that claimed to be his home.

Parody and travesty of Homer also deserve being mentioned. These arose on their own among a lively people reacting to the solemn in art, poetry, and even the rituals of worship. The Greek worship practice in general protected itself against these by incorporating pleasure and mirth wherever possible. Its solemn moments, however, were not immune to parody; Alcibiades, for instance, aped the Eleusinian Mysteries.

Homer was ineluctably the first poet to fall a victim to parody, because parody, in order to succeed, has to burlesque what is best known, thus getting the greatest possible number to join in the laugh.

The comic effect infallibly derives from the contrast between the grave old form and the light, new, ephemeral content, as when the Homeric figures and manners are travestied in the *Battle of the Frogs and the Mice* (*Batrachomyomachia*) or when his epic manner of speech is applied to any trivial subject whatever.

Later literary assertions that this or that person may have originated parody are almost worthless. It may well be that Homer was parodied even to his face. At all events, later Greek speech and writing sparkled with incessant allusions to Homer, consisting often of a single word which everyone caught and completed, or full-length quotations sometimes cited with comic variations. Whoever, for instance, set fire to a manuscript, said:

Draw near, O Hephaestus, for Thetis has need of you.

Thus Plato when he burned his tragedies, and thus Metrocles when he burned the lectures of Theophrastus. In the dialogue of Protagoras, the Platonic Socrates, at the gathering in Callias' home, could not refrain from hastily parodying the underworld scene in the *Odyssey*. The Greeks quoted Homer vastly more than they did the tragedians.

In time, parody developed into a separate form. Hipponax was already a famous parodist. In the fifth century the comic poet Hermippus produced a whole body of poetic parody. During the Peloponnesian War, Hegemon of Thasos enjoyed a wide reputation for his parodies; presumably he inserted new topical names and events into the Homeric text so that superficially this new material had a rhapsodic ring. His *Gigantomachy* so charmed the Athenians that they laughed most on the day when news of the Sicilian disaster arrived. It is well known that Epicharmus, Cratinus, and Aristophanes made brilliant use of parody in parts of their comedies.

Around the time of Philip of Macedonia, there flourished besides Euboeus of Paros who vilified the Athenians, a certain Matron who was surnamed the *parodist*. In his *Symposium of Xenocles the Orator*, he applies the Homeric idioms, epithets, and even whole verses to a current subject, thus creating one of the most harmless and elegant products of parody. In the third century, the Cynic Crates parodied the elegies of Solon in addition to Homer.

3. *The Homeric Hymns*

The Homeric Hymns, deriving from various periods, contain five longer ones: the Delian Hymn to Apollo, the Pythian Hymn to Apollo, the Hymn to Hermes, the Hymn to Aphrodite, and the Hymn to Demeter. These are independent poems, whereas the smaller ones are usually preludes, such as the rhapsodes customarily sang before other songs dealing with the heroic world. The longer ones were no doubt recited at festivals, but they were neither ritual poems nor temple hymns and are quite different from the lyric hymns of the Aeolic as well as the choric poets. These hymns are rather a branch of epic poetry, rhapsodies and narrations taken from heroic legends.

The two hymns to Apollo and the one to Demeter were evidently composed in the tradition of the Delian, Delphian, and Eleusinian temples and were recited at festivals there. The Hymn to Aphrodite was probably composed for the court of a prince in the vicinity of Mount Ida; that to Hermes seems to have grown out of the poet's own sheer delight. At any rate, these are lay poems glorifying the gods; these and similar poems, in addition to Homer's epics and Hesiod's *Theogony*, may have contained the most important instruction the Greeks had on the manifestation of their gods.

The fact that this poetry was designed to be recited at festivals conduced to its limning the gods as Panhellenic and beneficent. Even though the hymns we have are the only ones quoted in ancient literature, they may be merely a small portion of the former store of hymns, for it is quite conceivable that this species of poetry, its content universally known, was regarded as far more dispensable than the heroic epics and hence fell into oblivion, especially after lyric poetry and drama began to present the myths in their own fashion.

As to particulars, we shall draw attention to the lovely picture of the rhapsode and the maidens singing hymns in the Delian Hymn to Apollo. These Delian maidens, servants of Apollo, and the rhapsode sing praises to Apollo, Leto, Artemis, and to famous men and women of antiquity. Moreover, they can imitate the sound of the voice and the dance rhythm of any human, so that everyone hearing them supposes he is hearing himself, *so well their harmonies join.* Then, the rhapsode addresses the maidens thus:

> Think of me hereafter when a son of earth, a toilworn stranger, asks you who the sweetest singer is that sojourns hereabouts and who delights you most. Then all of you should answer: "A blind man dwelling on the slopes of steep Chios and his songs will ever remain the sweetest." And we shall carry your fame as far as we roam on earth to inhabited cities, and men will believe us, for what we say is true.

Perhaps the maidens of Delos owed their songs to the rhapsode himself.

Of the preludes, the Hymn to Ares has the character of an invocation, consisting initially of epithets addressed to the god. This can be hardly the song of a rhapsode, and yet the form, reminiscent of later pseudo-Orphic hymns, may be ancient, going back to temple rituals. Most of the invocations in it are very beautiful and poetic, especially the prayer at the close. The Hymn to Artemis is a splendid prelude, as is the Hymn to Athena, the others being fine old specimens, too.

The preludes interpret in a striking way how earth and sea, mountains and woods, express their awed delight at the appearance of the gods; they remind one of the devotional preludes the Italian improvisators produced in the fifteenth and sixteenth centuries. Hymn thirty, to Earth the Mother of All Things, represents a remarkable parallel to the opening lines of Lucretius. This hymn glorifies Mother Earth with almost the same expressions Lucretius applies to Venus.

4. *Cyclic Poets, Rhapsodes, and Later Epic Poets*

These poets are called cyclic because they constantly tried to link their poems with those of Homer so that all these works would form one single cycle. These poems were blindly ascribed to Homer; fairly accurate information, however, has enabled scholars to classify them and assign tentative authorship to some of the poems.

The cyclic poets gave material preceding but mainly following the *Iliad.* Arctinus, in his *Aethiopis* and the *Sack of Troy,* and Lesches in his *Little Iliad,* treated of Penthesilea, Memnon, the death and funeral of Achilles, the madness and suicide of Ajax, Odysseus before the sack of Troy, Philoctetes, Neoptolemus, the sack of Troy itself, and the departure of the Greeks from Troy.

Stasinus of Cyprus, in his *Cypria,* gave a long account of events preceding the *Iliad,* beginning with the procreation of Helen. The *Returns* by Hagias of Troezen related the adventures the Greek heroes had on their homeward journeys after they had sacked Troy; the *Telegony,* by Eugammon of Cyrene, was a continuation of the *Odyssey.*

There were also a *Thebaid* or Thebais cycle, the *Epigoni* of unknown authorship, and an *Oedipodea,* a *Theogony,* and a *Titanomachy.* According to Proclus, this cycle included the myths from the nuptials of Uranus and Gaea to the death of Odysseus at the hands of Telegonus.

Arctinus of Miletus lived at the commencement of the Olympiad system of reckoning, Lesches of Mytilene at the eighteenth Olympiad, Stasinus and Hagias at some unknown period, and Eugammon in the middle of the sixth century. In addition, the cyclic poems of Hesiod deserve brief mention, the so-called E(h)oiae, which in turn were associated, in a much discussed way, with the catalogue of women.

It is not known when poets ceased adding to this epic cycle; probably one of the Alexandrian scholars was the last. In this cycle the nation found those traditions that portrayed most imaginatively its deep spiritual life. These poets came upon the tradition of the gods and heroes still in a fluid state and committed it to writing as a kind of folk revelation; out of this treasure mine numerous dramatists and painters extracted their topics for generations to come.

This cycle contained not only pre-Homeric material but also collateral legends and variants of the Homeric incidents. It is also to be noted that those who collected and redacted these myths were lay people, a goodly number of them, each deviating from the others, and attaching their own names to their works.

Later the cyclic and their related poets were regarded as full-fledged writers. Apollodorus, for instance, who had their writings before him and made excerpts from them, cited as follows: *He who wrote the Thebais, he who wrote the Alcmaeonis.* These poets may well owe their survival to such citations, for it seems they faded from the memory of the rhapsodes rather early, only Homer and Hesiod persevering on their lips.

The rhapsodes were indispensable in keeping alive poetic works, including Homer, even after his works had been committed to writing and subjected to criticism, for public libraries were still nonexistent, and the complete works of a poet like Homer were cruelly expensive. In a sense, the rhapsodes were the successors to the bards (*aoidoi*); they competed at Panathenean Festivals according to rules and gave recitals at banquets and other occasions, the recitals consisting of separate poems chanted in medley, as the term *rhapsode* suggests.

They probably had a wide and varied repertoire and thus disseminated poets already assured survival in written form. We know, for instance, that Simonides of Zacynthus sat on a chair in the theaters at Athens rhapsodizing the poems of Archilochus, and that living poets having occasion to present their poems before people assembled as at Olympia were wont to hire professional reciters since this art required a strong and practiced voice.

Whereas only scholars took notice of the cyclic poets, the rhapsodes kept Homer alive and for this reason were called Homerists (*Homeridae*), even during the Diadochi period. The wicked Cassander was an ardent admirer of Homer and knew most of his works by heart. Demetrius Phalereus had the rhapsodes recite Homer in the theaters at Athens, no doubt with painstaking accuracy. Regular recitations of Homer might have been generally desired in Athens. In the large theater at Alexandria the comic poet Hegesias recited Hesiod, and Hermophantus recited Homer.

At first blush one might assume the mantle of the epic to have passed mainly onto the shoulders of visual art, for such art alone was able to bring forth a constantly new form of beauty and to give the myths perpetual youth in painting and reliefs. But after the spontaneous period of early poetry there followed, as already suggested, a period of literary skill and craftsmanship, and in accordance with laws supposedly derived from the primordial there arose of necessity a derived, a secondary literature which in its way is still rich in traits of what preceded and which alone has given us knowledge of those traits.

It is impossible to trace the development from the spontaneous song to the formal class of poetic literature in its details, but it is certain that for some hundreds of years the hexameter was the foremost meter the Greeks used in their poetry, that in general the recounting of events was the main refined diversion of the people, and that single tribes and cities provided an inexhaustible abundance of myths and legends.

Consequently there arose a steady stream of epic compositions; since their interest lay primarily in the content, these epics dwindled when the logographers collected and condensed the legends treated in them. In fact, this whole body of epics vanished, including even the *Heraklea* by Peisander of Camirus, the only work the Alexandrian scholars had admitted into the canon beside Homer and Hesiod, and the *Thebais* of Antimachus from the time of the Peloponnesian War.

The large number of the known titles alone is enough to show the popularity of these works. Since prose developed relatively late, the hexameter in vogue for centuries was used much for narration, forming a hybrid genre halfway between the epic and the chronicle, and also in philosophical writings by Empedocles and Parmenides. It may be only by accident that we know nothing of contemporary historical events cast into epic form, as attempted in the drama and found in Serbian epics.

Granted that the force of myths crowded contemporary history out of poetry, still, we know little of former history utilized in epics, even though it had become legendary or filled with emotional appeal. Apart from the Persian Wars, Greek history provided less rewarding material than Roman history did. For unlike Lucan and Silius, Greek poets had no world empire to glorify, only their poleis.

We should like to have more information about Rhianus of Crete, a historical epic poet of the Alexandrian school of the third century, who dealt with the Second Messenian War, later rewritten by Pausanias who was drawing upon the historian Myron for the First Messenian War. He was a prolific epic poet, and in addition to the Messenian works he wrote a *Heraklea,* an *Eliaca,* and a *Thessalica.* It may be thought that he had excellent popular models at hand and had rather spoiled than improved them.

The epic was destined to be replaced by other poetic forms (quite apart from the visual arts) when the nation had attained other, more immediate modes of expression, even though a subsequent revival of the epic as an art form of literary learning remained altogether possible. Within its main substratum, the myth, there grew up two competitors for the epic, namely, that branch of higher lyric poetry represented by Stesichorus and Pindar on the one hand and the whole body of tragedy on the other, and within tragedy in particular the epic parts: the choruses, as in *Agamemnon,* presenting the sacrifice of Iphigenia, and the reports by messengers, as in *Ajax* and *Oedipus at Colonus,* which contain narrative material in a new and gripping form. Once the drama has taken over, the epic loses its virginity.

5. Narrative Poetry of Alexandria

The later Greek epic deserves a glance if only to convince oneself how hard it had become to achieve anything novel or brilliant in Homer's field. The two chief Alexandrian representatives are Apollonius of Rhodes and Callimachus. We shall begin with the first, the Argonaut poet, who lived at the time of Ptolemy Euergetes and Ptolemy Philopater.

Apollonius sought above all to get the sound and the ring of Homer into the structure of his hexameters, but being a mediocre poet he failed to fuse his solemn elegance or psychological and rhetorical descriptions with the somewhat crude, primitive motives of his material into a concordant artistic whole. He also betrays the loss of genuine feeling for myths prevalent in his age: he tried in vain to eke out the meager figures of his chief gods and heroes with nauseous sentimentality.

His subject was a geographical itinerary beset by tricky rocks and shoals, which cropped up in the *Odyssey* but which Homer happily avoided. Instead of pruning away the clutter gathered from everywhere including colonial poetizings, he really crammed his epic with most disparate and extraneous subject matter. His enumeration of heroes reeked with mythological and genealogical lore. A general shortcoming of his treatment was that later he was unable to keep the many famous characters occupied on the journey.

Amid the delicate handling of the material this shortcoming strikes the reader in the face, whereas in older, naïve improvisations he was less conscious of the rougher spots. When Apollonius introduced his personages he differentiated and characterized them finally and imagined that was all there was to it.

Commentaries show that Apollonius—somewhat beyond his due—was looked upon as a classic, and the learned Roman P. Terentius Varro Atacinus translated him rather freely into Latin and the poet Valerius Flaccus reworked the material into an epic.

Callimachus, the head librarian at Alexandria during the time of Philadelphus and Euergetes, was the older contemporary of Apollonius and like him a poetic antiquarian. He was a prolific writer whose best works, the elegies, have perished; his hymns in imitation of the Homeric Hymns have survived to demonstrate how song can degenerate into a mere literary category.

He was essentially concerned to imitate carefully the language of Homer, his religious and geographical erudition, and his pervasive liveliness, but his vehement sham animation and his meager talent come off poorly. In vacillating between the epic and the elocutionary, invocatory hymn, he appears to be reviving an ancient mode extensively used in the Homeric Hymns to Apollo; in these hymns he could not forgo telling the god what he (the divinity) had done, thereby implying that he knew more about it than the god himself did.

Yet the Homeric invocation did not spring from sentiment but from the situation, for while chanting the hymn the singer faced an image of the god. The writing poet Callimachus proceeded with his invocations as Scottish preachers do, who squeeze a whole sermon into a prayer, and supposed he could infuse life into his poems by his incessant apostrophes which he thought were ablaze with poetic fire.

His first hymn depicts the birth of Zeus, the story of his youth, and his choosing to direct the kings of earth, and is decked out with all sorts of pedantry and repeated addresses to the god. The second, to Apollo, begins with an affected theophany and weaves into an account of Apollo's activities the founding of Cyrene, the poet's birthplace. The third, to Artemis, is a stale counterpart of the Homeric Hymn to Hermes, an example of misdirected erudition.

In it Artemis has to do all kinds of things while a mere child; she has to entreat Zeus for her whole future mythological paraphernalia, order her weapons from the Cyclopes, etc. In the fourth, to Leto, Callimachus utilizes her wanderings to display geographical knowledge much as Apollonius does in the Argonauts; he closes the hymn with a formal excursus on the Hyperboreans.

Apollo, as pertly forward as Artemis in the third hymn, vaticinates in the womb of his mother, doling out instructions to Leto. With a clumsy parade of erudition and rhetoric, Callimachus in his fourth hymn enumerates all sorts of places dedicated to special gods. At the end, he lavishes a deal of flattery on Ptolemy Philadelphus by saying that Apollo had not wanted to be born on Cos, an island destined to glorify Ptolemy in the future.

The next, on the Bath of Pallas, not being an epic poem, hardly belongs in the same class with the others; in Doric distiches it resembles an elegy as many things in Ovid do. It describes a consecration ceremony in connection with the myth of Teiresias being blinded because he saw Pallas taking a bath. The sixth hymn, to Demeter, also Doric, contains one myth tolerably told about the vengeance the goddess executed on Erysichthon for chopping down sacred trees.

6. Bucolic Poetry—the Late Epic

Nevertheless, it was possible even during the Alexandrian period for a highly gifted poet to create, by novel and happy manipulation of myths, resplendent individual scenes in which were stressed tender sentiments, opulent realism, bucolic moments, and also humor. This was Theocritus, somewhat older than Callimachus and Apollonius, yet belonging to the time of Ptolemy Philadelphus.

Three of his narrative pieces deal with the myths of Herakles; they are of uneven quality and surely not fragments of a Heraklean epic but independent compositions. The *Herakliskus* (Little Herakles) presents a lively and lovely sketch of young Herakles—the episode of the snakes, the prophecy of Teiresias, and the subsequent nurture of the youngster.

Herakles Slaying the Lion, mutilated at the beginning and at the end and composed not in the Doric but epic language, is a poem of 281 verses relating in prolix but crafty manner the wealth of Augias, the arrival of Herakles at Augias' residence, and the story of the slaying of the lion as told by Herakles to Phileus, the son of Augias; this poem deviates considerably from the usual manner of Theocritus, but could still be attributed to him.

The Cyclops is an idyll composed almost entirely of a plaintive monologue addressed by Polyphemus to Galatea, as reported by a mythical personage. *The Epithalamium of Helen* is almost wholly a nuptial song sung by twelve Laconian women. The *Dioscuri* is a regular hymn in the epic, the Homeric sense, as evident from the prelude and especially the postlude, but is interrupted nevertheless by a dialogue in alternating lines.

The bucolic poetry of Theocritus likewise is still predominantly epic, insofar as it presents actions and situations in monologue and dialogue. His bucolics are based on the songs shepherds sang in Sicily and in lower Italy; these almost certainly derived from the earliest settlers on the island and from Greater Greece and were still found in our century in the form of *carmen amoebaeum* (responsive song).

It may well be that the peasants and shepherds, in addition to popular songs, ritornels, had their hymns to the gods and also their singing contests which grew naturally out of singing ritornels in alternation and setting up arbiters to judge. The ritornels, love songs, and popular singing contests most likely expressed rather well what the people felt and thought about things. When the learned poets turned to country life, they found a new poetic form virtually ready-made. The use of the old hexameter for everything expressed in verse is quite ancient and genuinely pastoral; bucolic poetry also has its *caesura* characteristically after the fourth foot.

In Sicily, where shepherds in quite early times had created a minor body of myths and an ideal type in Daphnis, bucolic poetry took its rise quite early too, reputedly under Stesichorus of Himera; thus a great poet and master of choral lyric occupied himself with this facet of poetry, though we have no inkling what he did with it.

Living in Sicily during the fifth century, Sophron depicted the everyday life of the common people in mimes composed of dialogue in Doric prose and thereby contributed to the shaping of bucolic poetry. These dialogues were of such merit that Plato is known to have derived pleasure from their study. Theocritus is supposed to have modeled two of his most important genre pieces portraying city life on Sophron, the *Pharmakeutria* [the Spell] and the *Adoniazusae* [the Women at the Adonis Festival].

Whatever the bucolics of Stesichorus may have been, at all events this species of poetry came into flower as a reaction against the contemporary effeminate and bombastic verse of a later somewhat overwrought and blasé period, after the myths had been pretty heavily grazed. The crux of the matter is that a distinguished poet like Theocritus came along and applied his hand to this new material.

Although singularly competent in the epic, he may have felt that the heroic epic and the myths had seen their day and so he took from the actual songs of the shepherds what he found useful as a background to evoke the loveliest nature poetry. Although rustic life had been commented upon since Hesiod in didactic verse, Theocritus apparently raised the despised poetry of helots to refulgent honor at a time when only hothouse poetry and epigrams were being composed.

The bucolic idyll is above all not a village tale but a situation which after a few words of introduction takes shape in speech and song, the speech portraying the picturesque, the song the emotional quality of life, both of them employed as monologue and dialogue. While in the *Pharmakeutria* (the Spell) the words are only spoken, not sung, the first idyll contains a solo sung at the request of another person, the third is a serenade consisting of ritornels, and besides the spoken dialogue as generally found, idylls five and eight present actual singing contests.

The most charming idylls may be those where the shepherds celebrate their own or others' moods as in the seventh, where responsive singing gives way to the successive rendition of whole songs, or as in the first, where the languishment of Daphnis is most aptly and perhaps genuinely presented from the shepherd's point of view in the hyperbole of Hermes and Aphrodite coming to comfort him and at whose death plants and animals are involved. At least these are not mere rhetorical hyperboles.

From these songs filled with emotion a gradation leads down to the playful, the risqué *carmen amoebaeum,* and the plain dialogue. The danger the poet faces is that amid the mythological insertions the dialogue and the life of the shepherd may easily turn into a mere specious cloak.

The successors, at that, are in danger of becoming all but pedants; so Bion. Excessive descriptive insertions can topple, too. The description of the carved mazer fits quite properly into the first idyll of Theocritus. The long-winded description Moschus gives of Europa's basket with all the stories painted or embroidered on it is much more questionable.

These bucolic poets would like to follow individual elements in Homer. In Moschus, Persephone and her nymphs at Enna, and Europa before her abduction, clearly recall the influence of Nausicaa and her maidens. The sweet slumbers and prophetic dreams brought by the morning form a beautiful beginning for this second idyll of Moschus.

Learned epics were produced under the Roman emperors and on into the Byzantine age. The Orphic *Argonautica,* composed by the pagan poet Nonnus after Christianity had taken over in the fifth century, and *Hero and Leander* ascribed to Musaeus at the beginning of the sixth century, betraying imitation of Nonnus, are two of the works that have survived.

Eudocia, wife of Emperor Theodosius the Younger, was a special benefactress of the epic and highly honored the epic poet Cyrus. When she left the court and went to Jerusalem, he felt himself threatened and became bishop of Cotyaeum in Phrygia where he lived on into the reign of Emperor Leo. Here and there poets continued to turn out Argonauticas and Thebaids; preoccupation with Homeric studies kept the epic smithies hammering away until quite late.

7. Didactic Poesy (Hesiod)

How far back into antiquity go the laws and lore that various peoples have had regarding rhythm or the form of song? Solemn rites and usages handed down presuppose that rhythmical language was old among the Greeks; Delphi couched its oracles mostly in hexameters. But the Greeks, at least in historical times, never had a caste of teachers and especially not of a priestly-political character to impose any poetic forms. However, didactic poetry among the Greeks embodied something else, namely, rhythmical proverbs and precepts dealing with peasant life and, in a larger sense, the gnomic (aphoristic) field as a whole.

The name Hesiod may be an appellative, i.e., a generic designation; at any rate, the Greeks were convinced that a definite ancient poet by that name had existed who, although consecrated by the Muses, was a secular teacher of his nation, answering to the life and views obtaining at that time. They regarded Hesiod's work as highly important and probably based their notions of the poet on the various passages where clearly a specific person is speaking at a definite place.

Hesiod is at least as old as Homer. The question arises: How must one conceive of the Boeotian people and then how of the entire Hellenic race that listened to this poetry and memorized it, thus preserving it, most likely long before it was recorded? First we shall apply this question to *Works and Days* and answer it with the suggestion of Otfried Müller that at that time the Greeks had no contempt for the banausics, and rustics had not yet become politicians. This Boeotian peasantry likewise preserved a body of poetic lore which, until relatively late, it regarded as Hesiodic.

Hesiodic poetry is subjective and in this sense the polar opposite and complement of the objective poetry of Homer. In the *Theogony,* the poet tells in detail how the Muses called him to Helicon and consecrated him; in *Works and Days*, he exhorts almost constantly in his own name, and the myths he narrates (Prometheus, Pandora, the five races of men) are tendentious, serving as moral guides. The purpose of the mythical narratives, animal fables, maxims, etc., is to drive home the main thought. Hesiod does not set out to extol the life of the country or the feelings of the peasants. Their life is hard, and the farmer lacks the leisure of the shepherd; the poet also complains about the weather at Ascra. In truly Spartan fashion Cleomenes observed that Homer is a poet of free men, Hesiod one for helots.

Müller rightly understood that the higher trait binding this poetry together and elevating it above the didactic is the religious element in it. The decrees and dispensations of the gods advance justice in the life of man, ordaining work as the only road to happiness and so arranged the year into seasons that each may have its dues and impose appropriate duties. Beginning with its opening myths, this whole body of poetry is shot through with pessimism.

It is noteworthy that Orientals express their hortatory and aphoristic writings in the form of priestly legislation, and that in spite of all its ostensibly religious purpose *Works and Days* is altogether a lay poem, the private composition of a poet or, if one prefers, of a peasant. Hesiod does not want to be a king like a Solomon or a pseudo-Solomon.

Another question is how he brought his poetry to the people and whether he himself was a bard. When he appeared at the singing contest at the funeral rites for Amphidamas of Chalcis, he must have been regarded as one. We may presume the art of the bard to have been involved in his praises of Amphidamas and his ancestry and similarly wherever he composed epic material, as in the *Theogony*, if he is the author after all, and in the myths at the beginning of *Works and Days*.

It is significant that the hexameter was the verse commonly used to express popular ideas, rules, and admonitions. As to its style, the poem is permeated with ancient naïveté all the way through. It has the beginnings of a style, though of a primitive one that has not yet matured. Hesiod is far more archaic in his manner than Homer.

The text of *Works and Days* as now extant is, to be sure, quite fragmentary. The complete version must have been in perfect harmony with popular conceptions, for otherwise oral tradition could not have preserved it. The arrangement of the parts in the version we have is quite garbled. At the end are found aphoristic statements about the kind of work various days are suitable for. These verse statements were mnemonic reminders current on the lips of people, though no specific poet was known to have composed them.

Even though the Boeotians were not convinced that the *Theogony* was by Hesiod, and though in content it differs markedly from the *Works and Days,* it shows all kinds of affinities with it nevertheless. The *Theogony* is also didactic and its author is truly a teacher of his nation. In any event, we are dealing here with some Boeotian poet, whether Hesiod himself, or one of his descendants, or one of his school, who established with his work a third species after the epic and the hymn: the cosmogony, inseparable for the Greeks from the theogony, which presents a system of causality producing maturer and more perfect forms through procreation.

It is difficult, and in most cases impossible, to do justice to the author as a thinker and a poet. One can never be sure what antecedents he drew on. The Greeks constantly put Hesiod on a level with Homer, mentioning his name or reciting him with the same marked respect. They thought highly enough of him to believe that he had composed the whole work; he himself stressed his inspiration by the Muses, the real source of his revelations.

At the very least, the several parts of the *Theogony* are by an artist highly skilled in representing vast primeval events, at times only adumbrating them in somber forms (as for instance Earth), stirring and manifesting themselves as half-conscious and half-unconscious powers or as some beings of the darkness becoming conscious in a dream. An inchoate splendor reigns here, similar to that in the *Edda.*

The poet certainly must have achieved a powerful effect by reciting these passages much as Homer did by reciting his underworld scenes. He and perhaps he alone filled the greatest need of the nation, for no subsequent didactic composition created anything so vivid or of such elemental power. Whereas later works are literary and designed for smaller audiences, the *Theogony* is a profoundly comprehensive and intimate expression of the spirit of the nation for which it speaks.

The poet expressed the folk soul of the nation, and yet his images of the children and grandchildren of Night must have been novel and striking, much as the following race of Pontus: Nereus and Nereids and a whole ruck of monstrous kin: Graeae, Gorgons, Echidna, Chimaera; then follow Tethys and Oceanus and their progeny: fresh water, streams, and springs.

There should be mentioned also the mysterious birth of Hecate and the secret birth and rescue of Zeus. Quite incidentally and as something presumed known to the hearers, we learn about Prometheus matching wits with Zeus at Mecone, whence follows Prometheus' theft of fire and Zeus's vengeance through Pandora. Whether a later addition or not, the Titanomachy is grandiose, particularly the uproar of primal elements until chaos is ablaze and the Titans are finally fettered in Tartarus. The rest of this part is spurious, having the ring of mnemonic verses.

Among the philosophers who wrote in verse Xenophanes, in addition to his elegies and historical poems, wrote an epic *Concerning Nature* which he recited at banquets and elsewhere. In verse, as opposed to the prose of the Ionians, he elucidated the inspiring fundamental concept of the Eleatics, the theistic pantheism of *the one and the many*. Parmenides, who may have been his student, also used hexameters to express his doctrine of being in all of its abstractness.

The title of his work is also *On Nature;* he introduced Dike (Justice) as his teacher and as a revealer; his introduction before the Dike section is exquisitely impressive.

The work of Empedocles of Agrigentum, who flourished in 444, is also *On Nature.* He was the last to use this powerful form of expression associated with myths; most of the extant Orphic and Pythagorean fragments attributed to him are late and in all respects doubtful. His central philosophical doctrine denying the principle of creation and annihilation and affirming the principle of change and development is vividly picturesque. In addition he has, much as has Lucretius, a number of figures of speech executed in great detail, like those of the lantern, the painters, and the water clock.

The sheer habit of using hexameters, the practice of reading before groups, the use of hexameters in mnemonic verses, the desire of scholars to excel as poets, and the ease with which hexameters could be tossed off brought forth all sorts of compositions in this verse form. Of course the urge to instruct was in no way as strong in these later didactic writers as it was in Hesiod, nor did they speak to the whole nation as he did.

Whether they were trying to popularize science to meet a demand need not be ascertained. At any rate, everybody knew that in addition to these poetic works, claiming to transmit a body of knowledge, there existed another tradition that was careful, scholarly, and serious. Quite remarkably, besides these poets, there are writers being mentioned who, conversely, treated the myths not in epic verse but in prose; thus reputedly did Aristeas of Proconnesus in his *Theogony,* Dionysius of Mitylene in his *Argonauts,* and others.

Nicander of Colophon was a poet of some stature; his *Heteroiumena* (Metamorphoses) gave Ovid the idea for his poems. In his *Theriaka* and *Alexipharmaka,* the subject of many commentaries, he inaugurated the poetry of medicine. A follower of his was Marcellus of Side in Pamphylia, at the time of Marcus Aurelius; he produced a medical work in hexameters, comprising forty-two books. Nicander, the author of a lost *Georgika* (a poem on agricultural matters), which Virgil is supposed to have drawn upon occasionally, was also the finest of the poets of husbandry (the *geoponici* and *georgici*).

Hunting and fishing were celebrated by the *cynegetici* and the *halieu-tici;* Athanaeus lists them down to Oppianus. There were also geographies written in verse. In the time of the emperors, Dionysius the *periegete* (cicerone) composed a versified history of the world. The *Mosella* by the Roman poet Ausonius is the best work of this kind.

And now, at last, versified cookbooks. They originated in Sicily, where Mithaecus, mentioned by Plato, composed a work on native cookery, and Epicharmus wrote comedies of which three-fourths of the extant fragments deal with eating. Here Archestratus of Gela or Syracuse, a contemporary of Dionysius the Younger, traveling about widely to gather information wrote his *Hedypatheia,* i.e., gastronomic rules and descriptions of all sorts of eata-bles, in the earnest, didactic manner of Hesiod and Theognis. Others imi-tated him. There was a poem on fish pickled in brine, which Euthydemus of Athens attributed to Hesiod.

A certain Numenius is also mentioned as the author of a poetic work on the art of cookery, and also a Timachidas of Rhodes who treated of similar material in eleven books done in hexameters. As mentioned above, Matron, the parodist of Homer, composed a famous symposium. In the days of Dionysius the Elder, the dithyrambic poet Philoxenus, a celebrated gourmet and adventurer, wrote a symposium not in the epic but dithyrambic form, to say nothing of other authors of whom it is uncertain whether they wrote in prose or verse.

These didactic poets, as far as we know them, ever and again came forth with items full of great beauty, which tell us that we are in the pres-ence of a sensitive and perceptive nation manifesting this sense abundantly even on commonplace subjects.

Chapter Ten

MUSIC

If we ask what facts and concepts we have to discard from modern music to gain a fair notion of Greek music, we get this answer: The people did not sing out of books and so were able to move about freely while singing. Moreover, we must give up the view that our musical scale is the one and only system of harmony.

The distances between tones are fluid and variable, and thus we must be able to conceive of other scales and tone intervals than ours. Hence, we may have to relinquish our notions of harmony and polyphonic singing arranged for several voices. We must also abandon the idea of constantly coming up with new melodies and even that of thematic recasting.

As for musical accompaniment, we have to transport ourselves out of the modern world with its brass bands and drums and banks of fiddles, tooting and drumming our ears to death, to say nothing of all the locomotive whistles and car horns.

The ears of the Greeks must have been exceedingly sensitive, as their prosody amply testifies, when gut-stringed instruments played only by striking with the fingers or plectrums [thin ivory pieces] were audible in gigantic theaters seated to capacity, or when cithara players were featured in theaters, or flutes and lyres served as martial music among the Spartans.

The people had a fund of old, traditional melodies, called *nomoi*, something like the Irish tunes, essentially variations of a basic type, some of which were distinguished by special rhythms. The names of thirteen popular flute melodies played as dance tunes come down to us from late antiquity; the same source gives a list of songs according to trades or occupations as sung by people while grinding grain, or while bathing, by women weaving or spinning wool, or nursing babies, by the reapers, by the peasants toiling in the fields, or by people trampling out grain; according to tradition the singing of pastorals was invented by the Sicilian shepherd Diomos. There were songs for special occasions like the wedding song and the dirge, others in worship of specific gods like Demeter and Persephone, Apollo and Artemis; others were named after a loving or beloved being. Here, too, belongs the *ailinos,* i.e., a mournful dirge for Linos [a lost youth]; this name was at times also applied to music of a gay mood.

It may well be that those songs named after occupations and occasions represented now a class of songs in which new words were improvised to a fixed melody, now a class in which songs given specific names had both fixed words and melodies, though this would not exclude all changes in the wording. Often occasional texts must have been improvised for accustomed tunes. Aristophanes speaks of serenades; unhappily, these are mere names to us, and we would like to know to what extent they represented popular songs in Greece. Do we have improvisations here perhaps somewhat akin to the Italian *ritornello?*

Music closely linked with the lyric is certainly as old as Hellenism and at all events as old as its rites of worship. Their musical instruments derive from primeval times and have mythical origins (cf. Pindar, Pyth. 12, 19 where, after Perseus slays the Gorgon, Athena hits upon the flute to mimic the wailing sounds of the snakes). However, a focal point of the most intense interest, the welding together of lyric, music and dance did not take place without a special development. Not until quite some time after the epic did the lyric attain the highest artistic form.

The rhythm of the hexameter was strikingly clear and appealing, and in the hands of Homer this verse form produced marvelous beauty and liveliness. The Greek words, joined with the tone, permitted endless variations our ears are hardly capable of perceiving, a world of meters and strophes.

The linking element between these two arts and also dance was metrics, which we puzzle out of texts as best we can. Only a proportioned scale and articulated intervals make a tone language possible, and a universally valid tone system could assure this world of sound forms Panhellenic standing, but creating this required a great musical genius.

This man was Terpander of Lesbos, the *charmer of men* as his name signifies, *who gathered the various melodies as they naturally developed in different regions according to local moods and customs and arranged them according to rules of art into a coherent system to which later Greeks clung, however extended or sophisticated its later development. He invented the seven-tone scale in which these tones follow sequential rules and form a musical unit,* a fact he expressed by increasing the number of the lyre strings from four to seven (O. Müller, *Literaturgeschichte* p. 267).

Hailing from Lesbos, Terpander served as an intermediary in music between Asia Minor and Hellas; he is the originator of a most significant development continued by Olympus, Thaletas, and Sacadas, and later by Philoxenus and Timotheus. It is characteristic that the Greeks almost immediately introduced the music agon.

When the Spartans introduced the music contest at the Carnean festival in honor of Apollo, Terpander carried away the crown of victory, a decisive event, for Terpander later became the lawgiver of music in Sparta and also won the first prize four times in musical contests at Delphi. Sparta and Delphi were the first to stage this kind of music agon. Even if these stories about Terpander rest mostly on invention, they still show what great importance was attached to his appearing at these festival agons. Also, the names of Olympus and Sacadas appear similarly associated with the Pythian festivals.

The melodies of these masters were called *nomoi*. They were named after their composers; so some were called Terpandrian *nomoi,* others Polymnestian *nomoi,* etc.; some were given specific ethnic designations as the Boeotian or Aeolic *nomoi* of Terpander, and others were designated by their meter or musical character as trochaic, orthian, etc. In addition, the Greeks distinguished three genera of scales of music—the diatonic, the chromatic, and the enharmonic, the last of which employed quarter tones. The subdivisions or modes of the genera are called *tropoi, harmoniai,* and also *tonoi* by Plutarch; these modes include the grave Dorian, the swelling Phrygian, and the soft Lydian.

After Terpander, the Ionian and Aeolian modes were added; Anacreon used only the three old ones. To these five were afterward gradually added ten more attributed to various men. To understand how all these modes could survive side by side we simply have to assume that not only the tonal but also the auditory system of the Greeks was different from ours.

In any event, Greek music did not have harmony in our sense, for it lacked the triadic component; their instruments probably played only the melody. Perhaps we could say that they stressed the rhythmical element more than the melodic. But it is altogether possible that we are wrong in this—just as we may well be wrong in many another point regarding this music "without surviving sound."

Terpander set hexameters to music, including excerpts from Homer, for voice and lute, and also composed preludes of this kind. He also worked with many different kinds of meters. We shall not try to determine whether he devised a system of recording notes or whether his melodies were transmitted orally until recorded in the fourth century.

According to Alypius, later times knew of an older system of recording

Marsyas playing the flute for Dionysos
Vase painting

instrumental music with hooks and a few letters of the alphabet, and a later system of recording vocal music made up of letters only. Even in the fourth century B.C., the musical notations were suitable only for indicating pitch, the time intervals being apparently determined by the quality of the word syllables.

Olympus of Phrygia made the lute (cithara) equal in rank to the flute; he invented the enharmonic genus or scale with its energetic and spirited rhythms, in which arsis and thesis have a three-to-two relation. The flute afforded greater freedom. The tones of the flute could be multiplied more easily than those of the lute, especially since ancient flute players were accustomed to playing on two flutes.

Olympus (660–620) was the first to compose melodies for flutes, chiefly to revere the gods. They were mostly impetuous and passionate melodies of mourning, like the one in the Lydian mode he played at Delphi in honor of Pytho, slain there by Apollo. He also composed melodies that ranged from the quietly cheerful, to the enthusiastic, to the enraptured.

He may have been no poet himself, simply playing the flute without recourse to the word, as his only form of expression. In his time, the flute was regarded as the Dionysian instrument, the lyre as the Apollonian. In addition to the *nomos* of Olympus, there was Pythian flute music without song as played by Sacadas at Delphi. However, at the first Pythian festival *aulody*, i.e., singing accompanied by flute playing, was presented. This *aulody* was abolished even after Echembrotus the Arcadian musician was crowned for it, because it made the listeners melancholy. *Aulody* remained a favorite musical entertainment nevertheless, especially for rendering hexameters and elegiac distichs, to which it was first applied by Clonas, the inventor of this technique.

Another creation of this time was the *nomos* in three parts by Sacadas, in which the first strophe was set to the Dorian mode, the second to the Phrygian, the third to the Lydian. The impression he made on the nation was so profound that his melodies later competed with those of Pronomos of Thebes when Messene was being rebuilt to the sound of flutes played by Boeotians and Argives.

We shall omit other instruments like the syrinx, the *sambyca* invented by Ilycus, the *magadis*, the *crembalum*, and others. Though wind instruments later were as common as today, the absence of percussion instruments kept the range of tone color to quite moderate proportions.

Just a word about the combining of the flute and lyre attributed to the school of a certain Epigonus at some indefinite time and about the effects later achieved by the massive use of these instruments. Athenaeus reports that at the festival procession of Philadelphus a band of six hundred men took part, three hundred with gilt lyres and golden crowns. Nevertheless, the human voice joined with instruments enjoyed an advantage over mere instrumental music.

The human voice was most active in the sumptuous profusion of choral songs deriving from rites of worship. Here the Greek words of the song must have combined metrically and melodically with the tone in a manner we can hardly imagine.

The rise of the choral ode is linked with a musician who like Terpander came from abroad, Thaletas the Cretan, who had been invited to Sparta during the second half of the seventh century to restore peace among the citizens in the turbulent city. According to an anachronistic legend, he is also supposed to have been the teacher of Lycurgus. His Cretan predecessors might just as well have belonged to the solemn and dignified cult of Apollo as to the orgiastic cult of Zeus with its wild, exuberant dance tunes and the Curetes beating their cymbals and shields.

In Sparta, he perfected the system of music inaugurated by Terpander; he produced especially paeans (songs in praise of Apollo) and *hyporchemata*, i.e., portrayal of mythical events by rhythm and symbolic dance gestures. For this purpose he employed, besides his Cretan tradition, also the music and rhythmics of Olympus. Thereby he enlivened the paean; under his influence, the *hyporchemata* must have become even more blithe and sprightly.

Sparta became a center of the dance for both sexes. At the gymnopaediae boys imitated the movements of wrestlers and then shifted into the wilder Bacchic dances. Musicians of this school, especially Thaletas, developed the *pyrrhic,* or war dance, a favorite of the Cretans and the Lacedaemonians. Thaletas fashioned hyporchematic compositions into *pyrrhics* in swift and swooping rhythms; likewise Hierax of Argos, a composer of famous melodies, composed a dance tune representing the *pentathlon,* while another master of that period, Xenocritus the Locrian, is reported to have composed a special Locrian or Italic key and dithyrambs based on material from the heroic myths.

We can hardly imagine what a multitude of these choral songs there existed. If a polis had occasion to send a mission to some renowned divinity to offer, tell, or ask this divinity something, it sent, apart from the regular ambassadors, a choral group, if it could afford to do so, with a song composed of new words and a new melody, the so-called *prosodion,* to be sung at the altar. Choruses of boys were often sent to agons at festivals and to famous temples with offerings.

In time, however, wealthy cities did not display ritual sumptuousness so much by having one chorus sing various pieces involving several melodies as in having a number of choruses appearing one after the other. These songs were chanted for centuries not from music sheets but by repeated practice and by playing instruments, probably the flute. At all events, music had a large popular following.

Every male was required by law to engage in music until he was thirty. The children learned first the hymns and paeans to the gods and heroes of the country and then the (modern) melodies of Philoxenus and Timotheus; every year, the boys and youths danced circle dances to these tunes played on flutes in Dionysian fashion.

At social gatherings, responsive singing was in common usage; since everyone learned to sing, no one dared to refuse. In addition, the young people were trained to sing marching songs (*embaterions*), accompanied by flute playing and by marching movements, as well as to perform yearly dances, clearly very artistic ones, in theaters. There were also choruses of young women; all this because in that harsher age music seemed indispensable to making life more genial.

As indicated earlier, all this preoccupation with choral singing and music from childhood on must have given the people a musical bent and to the individual harpists, flute players, and others, a certain skill. In spite of lacking musical triads, variety in instruments, and adequate musical notation, they achieved a high order of excellence in music, even though it did not rank among their most important interests in life.

In this context it is fitting to say something more specific about the dance, representing a prodigiously rich facet of Greek art. Scholars are agreed that dancing originated in the mimic art, which substantially is the origin of our dances, too, but we shall not touch on them. The Greeks did not go in for group dancing so much as for individual gesturing which comes rather natural for the southern races and reaches its peak in artistic pantomime.

The Greeks were born with an aptitude for rhythm and with a capacity for mimicry expressing itself in the movements of the whole body. This combination of a flair for rhythm and capacity for mimicry constantly recreated the dance; the Greek audience could also be relied on to have a fine sense for interpreting pantomimic arts.

In his *Deipnosophists,* Athenaeus gives all sorts of picturesque bits, some of which he himself hardly understood, others which he misinterpreted, as the notion that sculptors had gone about observing the gestures and movements of the people as a whole, choosing the most graceful and noble for their works, whence these gestures and movements were introduced on dance floors and from there to the *palaestra.*

We shall first consider some dances that were quite widespread. Some of these were named after their places of origin, some after specific rituals, others are mimetic like *pouring out corn, cancellation of debt, the owl,* etc. One dance widely known was the *pyrrhic* (weapon dance), which was regarded as a military exercise and taught even to five-year-old children in Sparta, where it remained popular longest; another was the *gymnopaedike,* danced by naked boys which was a representation of the *palestra* [wrestling] exercises and the *pancratium* [wrestling combined with boxing], and the *hyporchematike,* danced and sung alternately by men and women. The hymns and paeans were sometimes accompanied by dancing, sometimes not.

Dancers were also trained for specific functions in the rites of worship; indeed, all choral poesy and music were associated with choric dances. Dancing accompanied every consecration ceremony performed in a mystery ritual; Orpheus and Musaeus, both excellent dancers, also promoted this art.

The drama really took its rise from the Dionysian choric dance, with which much of the artistic development of the dance was later connected, like the *emmeleia,* a stately tragic dance, the *sikinnis,* a dance connected with the satyrical drama, or the *cordax,* a vulgar dance of the old comedy. Aeschylus is reported to have outlined many new dances and to have taught them to his choral dancers (*choreutes*).

In addition, there was the artistic dance by individual performers. There was also dancing in step by ball players; indeed, this ball game was itself almost a dance found already among the Phaeacians. Those who played on instruments and perhaps those who sang began in the early centuries to dance along with their performances. We are told that the ancient harp players kept their heads fairly quiet but moved their feet briskly.

Dancers were hired to perform at symposiums; in Xenophon's *Banquet of Philosophers,* a couple of children came in and danced, and after the guests had imbibed they danced, sometimes rather coarse dances, even ugly old people taking part. In contrast to men of equal standing in Rome, men like Pythagoras and Socrates danced even when sober, the former to keep healthy and limber, the latter because it exercised all his limbs, as he customarily explained when he was occasionally surprised dancing.

During the time of the Roman emperors pantomimic performances became quite popular, as is best evidenced in Lucian's *de saltatione.*

Having given the arts of music and dance a brief look, we may inquire what significance they had for the Greeks and what force the Greeks thought they exerted in their lives.

The might and majesty of music derive in part from its divine primeval origins, as mentioned before. Plutarch says that in every respect music inspires awe because it was invented by the gods; generally, however, Apollo was regarded as the originator of music. It is remarkable that all the authors who wrote on this subject attributed an ethical significance to music.

The Orphics and Pythagoreans regarded music as having purificatory and therapeutic virtues; Pythagoras himself is reported to have effected physical and mental cures by means of his rhythms, songs, and incantations. Even Theophrastus is reported to have said that music heals infirmities of body and mind, and to have enumerated at random fainting, anxiety, insanity, sciatica, and epilepsy.

The chief healing instrument was the flute, and according to this same source Aristoxenus, a student of Aristotle's and a great musician and music theorist, healed an insane person by playing the flute after trumpet tooting had put him into a still greater frenzy.

No doubt the presence of virtuosos at music agons held at festivals was in early times absolutely essential for the success of these contests. In connection with Arion, Herodotus depicts the stately and impressive stage appearance of these masters, as he himself must have witnessed them.

When Greek sailors, murderers of a fellow Greek yet lovers of music, had decided to kill Arion in order to rob him, they permitted him at his request to stand on the afterdeck (obviously so that he could be free) and dressed in his full professional costume to take up his lyre and play a lively tune (the *nomos orthios*) before he leaped into the sea.

When a lute player was scheduled to appear on a theater stage, everybody thronged to hear him so precisely on time that an enemy could plan an attack on this occasion as well as on that of a popular assembly. The famous Persian general Memnon used the lute player Aristonicus of Olynthus to have a count made of the people of the Bosporian cities while he performed there.

A certain Alexander, the commandant of the garrison in Aeolia, hired the finest virtuosos of Ionia, the flute players Thersander and Philoxenus, and the actors Callipides and Nicostratus, and announced a great theatrical program. Then, when the people from neighboring cities had filled the theater, he surrounded it with soldiers and barbarians, holding the men, women and children for high ransom.

Greek audiences must have been accustomed to sitting very quietly while listening, for as mentioned above, it is a mystery how a stringed instrument plucked with the fingers or struck with a plectrum could be heard all over a large theater.

That writers began to treat of music quite early indicates how important this art was in Greek life, whereas of sculpture they took no notice for a long time. Plutarch notes that most of the Platonists, the ablest Pythagoreans, and also grammarians and harmonists had commented on the old music and its decay. The famous peripatetic Aristoxenus of Tarentum was a versatile writer on music; his *Elements of Harmony* in three books has survived, giving a theory of music, although his works on rhythmics, musical instruments, the history of music, and similar themes are known only by their titles and in fragments.

We can easily understand why philosophers occupied themselves with this subject if we reflect what a magical charm music had exercised over the Greeks, though from our point of view it was imperfectly rendered. A unique relationship is here involved, found apparently nowhere else in the whole history of civilization, namely, the intimate relationship of music to education and the state. We have seen how carefully Sparta officially assured itself of having music.

The Greeks were firmly convinced that music had a political aspect; the *locus classicus* for this is Plato's *Republic,* book III, section 10 ff., where he severely scrutinizes the kinds and rhythms of music to be allowed in his ideal state. In that same context, he proceeds to generalize on the conditions of life and identifies beauty with goodness, ugliness with evil; then follows his discourse on policing art, necessary in his state for the proper nurture of the young, the chief element of which was music because its rhythms and harmonies penetrate easiest into the inward part of the soul and dwell there longest. In another passage (book IV, section 3), he says that, since changes in music draw in their wake the greatest changes in the state, the guardians of the ideal state should build their fortress on the foundations given by music.

Such statements suggest that the Greeks were extremely sensitive in an area of art where the Occident, even in the southern parts, today appears dull; they enable us to understand how responsive the Greeks were to all art and especially to the periodically recurring Dionysian frenzy.

Above all, as Plato explains, the different genera of music should not be intermingled. Hymns, dirges, paeans, dithyrambs, and lute melodies should respectively preserve the peculiar character appropriate to them; when an occasion demands one kind of melody, it should be used, not another. As in the good old days, not the unmusical rabble but only the cultivated people who have listened attentively in quiet surroundings to a whole piece should be allowed to judge of its canonical propriety and what penalty, if any, the inappropriate use of melodies may entail.

Commenting on the tendency to cling to a traditional achievement and to oppose every whim for changing melodies and rhythms, Plutarch says it is not for naught that melodies were called *nomoi* (laws). Thus the old music limited to a few strings could maintain its simplicity and dignity with a purposeful abstinence, for the artists must have known about ampler means, and the new composers in that early period were very restrained and kept within bounds of the beautiful. The poleis that watched most assiduously over their laws—Plutarch mentions Sparta, Mantinea, and Pellene, and Plato Sparta and Crete—long held strictly to the old music.

The story about Timotheus of Miletus, who for increasing the number of his lute strings from seven to eleven had his lute taken away and hung up in the Skias rotunda, best expresses the resistance to musical innovation. But the Spartans were too late with their conservatism; from the end of the Peloponnesian War on a theatrocracy, as Plato called it, ruled in Sparta to the detriment of poesy and of the whole intellectual life in Greece. The audience turned from a silent into a clamorous one, as if it knew what was excellent in music and what not. Had it only been a democracy of free men! But the presumption that everybody knew everything became the rule, and as a consequence the populace became so impudent as to judge in matters of taste.

The poets themselves were to blame, for they exceeded propriety with

their Bacchic frenzy and voluptuousness, and mingled hymns with threno-
dies, paeans with dithyrambs, imitated flute tunes on lyres, in short, mixed
everything into a hodgepodge and ignorantly maintained that music really
had no system and was best judged by the listener's enjoyment whether he
was possessed of any taste or not.

At any rate, poesy no longer played a dominant role in music which no
longer was either manly, divine, or pleasing to the gods but effete and garrulous. As a consequence, instrumental music began to rule the roost, and it
is reported that beginning with Melanippides flute players no longer
received their pay from the poet and thus were not dependent on him or on
the composer.

No doubt another critical development was the increased emphasis on
virtuosity; as the individual actor expected to win fame and fortune from
pantomiming or dramatizing solo parts, so the individual musician hoped to
achieve fame and wealth.

This development was irresistible. Though an artist was initially ridiculed for his innovations, he could take comfort from the prediction Euripides made to Timotheus when he too was similarly scoffed at, that the public would soon be groveling at his feet. As to this deterioration which he
deplored, Plato has an Athenian describe it as far advanced and incurable;
Aristoxenus, the first historian of music, writing in the second half of the
fourth century and already quite a *laudator temporis acti* (praiser of a bygone
age) says: *Since audiences have degenerated into barbarians and the popular
music has greatly deteriorated, too few of us remember what music once was.*
(Athenaeus, XIV, 31).

Chapter Eleven

POESY IN OTHER THAN
HEXAMETER MEASURES

1. General Remarks

There may have been a time when, besides the epic and the two species of poetry Hesiod represented, the Greeks had only folk songs with refrains. Following this mythopoeic, religious, seasonal, and festival art, the lyric arose as a spontaneous creation, not like the poetry of Occidental nations that at the very least had Latin church hymns as models. The elegy may well have appeared as a great innovation, even as a kind of debasement.

Modern lyric poetry contrasts most sharply with the Greek, recognizing hardly any set limits or laws and seeking to escape discipline for pleasure. Greek lyric poetry on the other hand was, by its connection with singing and conviviality, with dancing and instrumental music, bound to detailed standards of composition and performance, being thereby protected against sublimation into nothingness.

Our discussion of Greek poetry does not claim to be a clearly arranged literary survey; we shall deal with poesy only as a free expression of life and as a cultural force in the nation. The individual states and social castes took part in many ways, now here, now there, now stressing this aspect, now that. Beginning with the epic bards, poetry fell into all sorts of hands but remained a high art nonetheless, its forms commanding the utmost respect.

It was a long time before the old poetry gave way to new forms, this event occurring only after all imaginable contents had been poured into the old forms. Greek poetry grew slowly and consistently, each order giving way when its season of fruition was over. No foreign literature, no religion with foreign imagery, interrupted this development; hence we shall proceed in accordance with the development of the various forms.

A large number of poets enjoyed renown from the outset, and though their works were topical and involved in contemporary affairs, their names endured. Complete collections of their works were made early, and it is a misfortune that apart from Pindar and the tragedians so little has survived. Later Greeks possessed these works intact and consciously treasured them as significant cultural developments.

Poetry accorded with the life of the individual as well as with that of the nation; it was not faced with a division into the educated and the uneducated, being accessible to every freeborn Greek. Its original source was the body of myths known to rich and poor alike, as were the rites of worship; yet it remained a sublime art.

2. *The Elegy*

To be sure, the old popular and religious poesy had favorite forms of various kinds, but until about 700 B.C. the hexameter was the only acknowledged art form and everything was made to fit into this meter; Hesiod also bowed to it.

The Greeks were slow in developing new forms and faithfully retained whatever was excellent in art. They did this with two forms that rose almost simultaneously, the elegiac and the iambic.

The elegy is built on the pleasing alternation of the hexameter with its counterpart, the pentameter, which is called *elegeion*, whence the poem got its *elegia*, for any type of poetry derived its name from its metrical pattern and external form. As soon as several metrical schemes were available, poets chose a form with the most delicate regard for the respective sentiments and the mood of the soul.

Such an elegy was sung, not just recited; it was accompanied always and only by the flute. The foremost occasion for presenting elegies was at banquets, especially at the end during the festive part (*komos*). It could deal with any emotional mood, being by no means limited to the dirge and love laments. Some event or circumstance may have aroused hope or fear in the poet and moved him to express reproach or give counsel. The elegies that have survived are given to exhortation slightly tinged with aphorisms; they are smooth and lovely, not grandiosely elliptical as some later lyric forms are.

Remarkably significant fragments have survived from the earliest period, like Callinus' fine *Call to Fortitude*, Tyrtaeus' *Lawfulness*, and his *Exhortations*. These are impressive poems designed to be recited to soldiers on campaign, on an evening in camp after the paean, by a soldier specially skilled in this art who might thereby earn an extra portion of meat. Laconism permitted no patriotic effusions but did allow these somewhat stylized elegies.

Archilochus praised warfare in his elegies, charming fragments of which have survived, among them the lighthearted Ionic prototype of Horace's *relicta non bene parmula*. [A shield relinquished is no protection.] He also treated of love, the delights of the banquet, and sorrow for a friend who died; an elegy like the one on his friends drowned at sea was probably delivered at the funeral repast commemorating them.

When Ionia succumbed to the Lydians, this eminently Ionian form of poetry turned more to celebrating love and enjoyment. It is Mimnermus who marks this transition; in addition to writing poems dealing with war he specialized in erotic elegies. Most of his surviving fragments lament the brevity and frailty of life, reminding one of Koheleth (Ecclesiastes), and calling upon us to enjoy ourselves against the dark, uncertain background of life. Later, Solon expressed all aspects of his stirring life in the elegy, before and after his lawgiving, in the most varied moods of appeal, warning, reflection, and joy.

Theognis of Megara is an enigmatic poet. Fourteen hundred of his verses have survived; much of this material is fragmentary and the order of its arrangement disputable. One may get the impression that many of these pieces, though they seem to be fragments, were really composed as short maxims. Such poems read like fragments, as do parts of Hesiod's *Works and Days*; the explanation of this mode of writing may be that often his bitterness found adequate expression in a distich, thus snipping the elegiac thread.

Some of his poems to the gods are elegiac in nature and may be preambles to elegies. Then, his distiches filled with jealousy and melancholy addressed to his young friend Cyrnus could almost be called a poetic epistle, which arises almost spontaneously as soon as the person addressed is not present and not involved in any passionate relation with the poet.

Some of his convivial pieces were no doubt genuine banquet addresses. The following are characteristic: his poem acknowledging that he was drunk, that in which he seeks the mean between nothing and too much, those dealing with the Persian Wars, e.g., his prayers for preserving the jovial life of Megara, his address to wine, his poem on the gift of wine, his apology, his resolution to revel while life lasts, his proposal to make a pause at the banquet, and his series of distiches.

The erotic verses, beginning with verse 1,231, are certainly in part his, being either fragments or complete versions of elegies. In any event, most of these poems are ancient and different from others of this class in the Greek Anthology.

Xenophanes composed a lovely elegy for a banquet in which he expressed the hope that the guests would make it safely home without help.

Critias was the first to give a poetic catalogue of things, a rhetorical adulteration never found in the older epic; he would list a number of inventions naming the regions where they originated to the point that Athens, the victor at Marathon, was the inventor of pottery—offspring of clay, the potter's wheel, and the oven. Much more elegant is the fragment in hexameter he composed on Anacreon. It may well be that the inner necessity of the elegy was already disappearing.

To compensate for the lack of inner resources, Antimachus resorted to itemizing, as in his famous elegy on his deceased Lyde, crammed with all sorts of misfortunes taken from mythology. Parody appeared at the latest with Crates, one of whose parodies on Solon has been preserved.

Of the Alexandrian elegists we shall mention only Alexander of Aetolia, one of the poets of the Tragic Pleiad, whose elegiac fragments are in somber tones, and Callimachus, preserved in small though numerous fragments, whose writings Ovid characterized with these well-known words: *quamvis ingenio non valet, arte valet.*

The elegy experienced a revival in Alexandria as a favorite literary exercise, but real life was put into it again only by the Romans, who found in it a perfectly congenial form of expression. Tibullus and Propertius composed individual, spontaneous elegies; even though they had learned the technique from the Alexandrians, their originality is indubitably their own, for they derived their strength not from Hellas but from their own nation.

3. *The Epigram*

As indicated above, the genuine, living elegy, the creation of the *train-trailing Ionians,* appears to have run its course rather early, but this did not keep poets from continuing to turn out untold scores of elegies. Then the mood for brevity took over, turning elegies into epigrams and, to the extent that they were convivial, into so-called *scolia.*

We must bear in mind that the epigram took its origin from the elegy. It did not, as the term itself suggests, take its rise from inscriptions on tombs, monuments, or votive offerings. The epigram is short and sharp, whereas the elegy is decidedly unhurried. Early Greek epigrams did not have to have that sudden, surprising fillip at the end; in time epigrams actually inscribed formed a literary species in stone and bronze. The epigram, having a Protean character, extended its span from memorial and votive inscriptions to untrammeled comment on all sorts of topics, particularly to love, satire, and convivial pleasures.

Simonides of Ceos, the older contemporary of Pindar and Aeschylus, was the first poet to become famous for composing epigrams, and precisely in him, skilled in the elegy, celebrating those who fell at Marathon and Platea, the relation between these two modes of writing is apparent in that many of his so-called epigrams represent all the essential later shadings.

He composed the famous inscription at Thermopylae:

> Stranger, if ever you come to the Spartans, bear them this message:
> That we are lying here, faithful to their commands.

As here, so elsewhere the epigram is seen in all its pristine strength.

Various personal epigrams of his are intimate and lovely, like the distich on the tomb of a murdered man and the one in which a dying daughter appeals to her mother to bear her father another child.

Several of his distiches on victors at musical contests would give in briefest compass the place and kind of agon and the name and country of the winner; others, on works of art, might contain the name of the artist without further elaboration, or again, would praise another and add a highly prosaic statement of the fee he received.

Besides inscriptions on tombs and votive offerings Simonides also did epigrams of a droll and derisive character; he even wrote a scornful epigram on the death of his enemy Timocreon, parodying the epitaph on his tomb.

After this brief look at the versatile Simonides we mention in passing the epitaph Aeschylus wrote for himself with its allusion to Marathon; the unexcelled epigram of Euripides which, addressing the Sun, asks whether he has ever seen anything like the death of a mother and her three children in one day; and the epigram of Plato who, converting the epitaph into a *jeu d'esprit*, composed witticisms and epigrams on love, indulged in plays on words, and created two nature images anticipating fully the style of the later Greek Anthology.

Now we shall turn our attention to the chief store we have of the epigram, the Anthology. The epitaph plays a big role here. The relation to the dead was perhaps all the more intimate among the Greeks just because they were so hazy about the hereafter. The headstone cost little since it required no architectonic shaping or trimming, so the poor servant girl received an epitaph if she left behind a memory to be cherished.

Such epitaphs required no famous poets, although they gladly did some to see their names chiseled in enduring stone; even the common people of Hellas could hit upon fine and fitting expressions to ease their sorrows;

form and meter were no hindrance to these people, for they knew much of Homer by heart.

These epitaphs are especially significant for their veracity and candor. While looking calmly at their own still empty graves, these people expressed sorrow for their deceased friends, wailing and lamenting without restraint in the face of destiny, feeling no necessity to express resignation before the sufferings life can inflict.

On the other hand, they candidly praised the good fortune of such as fared well, and gladly noted the pleasures they had enjoyed, reflecting clearly, for our benefit, the trials, tribulations, and joys of everyday life in those distant days.

Relatively early, conjectures were made as to whether famous men would be found among the blessed and whom one might meet there, even though the actual pagan heaven took shape rather late. Hades, naturally, took up a lot of space, and though the Greeks talked little about meeting friends there, they liked to imagine that mother and child would be fondly reunited. On the other hand, some Greeks denied all possibility of an after-life.

The epigram is inexhaustible when, grounded on the elegy, it makes use of erotic, symposial, and satiric subjects. Here its natural predisposition for antithesis comes into play; the form of the distich is itself congenial to this juxtaposition of opposites, for it can sing with lyric sweetness or snarl with wit and scorn by allusively matching opposites. It can flash images or it can sting; in time it took over, among many other functions, also that of Archilochus' iambs.

To achieve with it a comic effect was made easy by its beautiful and solemn form which constantly recalled Homer and the elegists, contrasting incongruously with the content when the latter was of a diametrically opposed variety. The epigram naturally indulged heavily in plays on words, sometimes to the point of repulsive indifference. Satire liked to don the cloak of simulated vindication. *They say you have dyed your hair, O Nicylla, when really you only bought it raven black.*

In addition to this form of the epigram, used we know not how frequently for anonymous invective against individuals, there stood another, likewise derived from the elegy, used for detached gnomic reflections on life and the world. This gnomic epigram passed judgment on a host of matters dealing with life, destiny, and morality, mostly impersonally but sometimes with reference to some name. Lucian made excellent observations in epideictic sentences such as the following:

> Eros is not the cause of the trouble but rather the wanton
> Lusts of the human heart lurking behind the god.

The epideictic epigram expressed, briefly and beautifully, a moral maxim, i.e., an observation drawn from life or a reflection on morality, clothed in the form of an exhortatory address of the poet to himself or to another, as when Lucian foretells to another the fickleness of his fortune. Then it may be a little incident or anecdote tossed off with a didactic touch, sometimes resembling an outright parable.

These epigrams delight especially in piquant little incidents drawn from animal life: a mouse wants to eat an open oyster, whereupon the oyster claps shut; a swallow fetches a cricket, a compeer in song, to feed her young; a hen that froze to death while sheltering her chicks causes a poet to reflect that Procne and Medea in Hades should hang their heads in shame.

Epigrams brought out many subtle antitheses by way of comment on actual events. One of the loveliest of this kind is that of Euenus in which Ilium says: *The ashes of time have consumed me, but in Homer I still have my being and my gates of bronze.* Indeed, these epigrams speak out pointedly to the glory of Homer and other poets.

They also record exclamations of readers and give expression to adroit mythological inventions, as for instance when Mnemosyne, listening to Sappho, feared that mankind would get a tenth Muse. To this epideictic genre belong finally the epigrams containing riddles not put in the form of questions but so describing something that one should be able to guess what it is.

4. The Iambus

The harsh iambus, serving from its beginning as a vehicle of invective, cut athwart the pleasing grace of dactylic poetry in the seventh century. It may serve as an apology for this form of Greek invective if we say that this harsh, punitive tone is in order if it stems from a grand and noble concept of what ought to be. We shall not attempt an artistic or moral vindication but simply grant that abuse heaped by one person on another became a species of literature. We know of no other ancient people who had anything like it; later, the Provençals devised something akin to this in their *sirventes*.

The iamb was more closely related to the comical quality of ancient poesy than to the lampoons which were customary at festivals and religious celebrations and were imitated in Aristophanes' *Frogs*. Taunting and mocking were called *iambus*.

This form was introduced into literature by Archilochus of Paros, a poet whose characteristics we can hardly make out because only a few of his iambic fragments fit into the general pattern. Later literati may not have cared to quote him. Archilochus has a highly important place in the history of poetic forms. His meters are the iambic and trochaic; in the iambic the shorter syllable precedes, in the trochaic it follows the longer syllable.

Both meters are light and rapid, the iambic serving to express wrath and bitterness, the trochee being a mean between the iamb and the elegy (likewise cultivated by Archilochus), had less nobility and spirit than the elegy and was therefore better suited for common, everyday subjects.

The iambic verse had three dipodies forming a trimeter and the trochee had four dipodies forming a tetrameter. These meters maintained themselves consistently as normative forms for certain kinds of poetry. Archilochus perfected these metrical forms so that no essential improvements had later to be added.

As for the mode of delivery, iambic verse was not sung, at least not in our sense of the term, but rather chanted by a rhapsodist. The stringed instrument invariably used since Archilochus to accompany the recitation of iambic verse was the triangular *iambyke*.

Archilochus held fairly faithfully to the tone of common life, often using coarse expressions which tempted later grammarians to record them, and his followers dragged in all sorts of trivia from everyday life, especially eating and neighborhood gossip. In this context, we may note that shortly after Aristotle the rhythm of popular speech approached the iambic meter.

If we inquire why this gifted maligner had such a profound effect on his own age and on succeeding generations, the answer may be summed up in saying that among the poets he was the first uncompromising realist, taunt and mockery always ready on his tongue.

The followers of Archilochus were Simonides of Amorgos, given mostly to gnomic verse, of whose works one pessimistic fragment and a general satire on women have survived whereas his individual invectives are lost; then Solon, whose excellent political iambs sound as though they might have come at least in part from a tragedy, since their content could well have been given in the elegiac meter; neither his iambs nor his cheerful, jovial trochees, so far as tradition tells, contained any personal invective; finally Hipponax, the creator of the deliberately ugly *lame* tetrameter, having a spondee in place of the final iamb; he was as venomous as Archilochus and wrote, besides, social satires wherein he realistically depicted life from its frivolous and shabby side.

In time the iamb became a means to express everything imaginable, as did the hexameter and distich. Gnomic sentiments were put almost exclusively into iambic verse, especially after the trimeter had become the verse of dramatic dialogue and been given a sententious turn by Euripides and the newer comedy. The trimeters of the Cynic Crates exemplify this later gnomic application.

5. Comment on Lyric; the Aeolic Lyric

Before proceeding to the higher forms of the lyric we shall try to answer the question as to why the poesy, music, and dance of the Greeks constituted an integral part of the history of their culture. We may adduce the following.

From the very beginning these art forms were conceived of as a part of the life of the gods and as gifts from the gods to men. They were considered to be the property of the nation, or at least of a whole polis and not just of the educated class. At any rate, they were public property.

Their cultivation, of old a prerogative of the *Aiodos* [itinerant singer of songs and poetry] was taken up by the rhapsodist, but the nation as a whole continued to manifest its vital concern for the preservation of the traditional body of myths and especially Homer. Later, when the use of the hexameter had become a matter of derivative learning, a matter of the art and craft of "literature," the custom of reciting in public was widely continued nonetheless.

We must recall the long and intimate connection between poetry and music. All transmission of these arts and traditions was by word of mouth. In addition to the rhapsodists' chanting to small groups, public recitals at festivals of all sorts were a large-scale activity; and even when recitals were taking place only before social gatherings, still they afforded poets popular renown. Elegiac poets especially enjoyed wide and enduring fame.

The rise of a rich, vibrant, and multifarious store of lyric poetry is a phenomenon the cultural historian can trace from the seventh century on. Lyric poetry most probably took the stanza from the old folk songs. No doubt folk singers hit on the stanza form by repeating melodies.

From its very beginning lyric poetry developed along two main lines: the lyric of the Doric choral song and the individual lyric of the Aeolians. The choral ode was developed by the Dorians in the Peloponnesus and Sicily, whence it spread over all Greece. These odes were sung by choruses that moved rhythmically while they sang, thereby helping the eye to grasp the most complicated structure of the stanzas. The chorus moved forward while singing the strophe, back while singing the antistrophe, and stood still while singing the epode.

The rhythmical structure of the odes varies exceedingly; their mood is exalted, and their content nearly always of a public nature. Divine festivals, weddings and burials, and celebrations in honor of public figures or winners at agons were occasions calling for the singing of these choral odes, which consequently avoided personal and private motives and stressed public and official motives to be shared by many.

By contrast, the Aeolian lyric flourished in Asia Minor and especially in Lesbos. It was recited by individuals who accompanied themselves on a lyre or some other stringed instrument and went through appropriate and dignified movements. These lyrics were composed of a series of like verses or of short melodious stanzas often of three similar verses followed by a dissimilar one as the Alcaic, Sapphic, and other stanzas, all uniform and without any epode. The rhythmical structure of these stanzas varied but little. The thoughts and moods expressed were the concern of the individual, even where the state was involved.

As far as we know, Aeolian lyric poetry began with Alcaeus of Mitylene. We would like to know whether he really created the form of the ode. Antiquity knew songs of his in a partisan vein, others that were exhortations to battle, to drink wine, to make love, and also hymns which, as far as hypothetical reconstruction can tell, appear to have been heavily influenced by the epic.

Fragments of his poems in various stanza and verse forms reveal him as a poet of rare force and fire, like the lovely fragment wherein he portrayed his house as an armory, or the one that summoned men to drink upon the death of the tyrant, which Horace imitated in *Nunc est bibandum* (Let us now drink). The passionate feelings and emotions expressed in his poems will ever vindicate him as a poet, for of such stuff are genuine lyric poets made.

Alcaeus addressed Sappho, his contemporary, with these words: *Dark-haired, pure, sweet-smiling Sappho, I would speak a word with you but may not.* Athenians later regarded her as a woman of easy virtue because they no longer understood her spontaneity and the freedom women enjoyed in Lesbos and also among the Dorians. She never named the youth she loved and praised in her songs. Phaon is sheer fiction, and her leap from the cliff into the sea is a late fabrication.

She was an accomplished artist, as were also her rivals Gorgo and Andromeda, and a teacher of her younger girl friends to whom she addressed a few of her songs, for musical accomplishment and gracious demeanor were refinements prized above all others in that society. When a beautiful relief presented two women with musical instruments who instead of playing on them are embracing each other, then we may regard this as portraying the actual relations between women touched by the muses.

Wedding of Peleus and Thetis
Vase painting, British Museum

Of the few compositions by her that have survived, the glorious song to Aphrodite is the most complete. In antiquity, her lyrics alone filled nine books, and she also wrote epigrams and elegies. Catullus' *Vesper adest* is an adaptation of her hymeneals, partly in hexameters. Erinna, a friend and student of hers who died young, composed a poem, *The Spindle,* in three hundred hexameters.

About 540–520 B.C., there flourished Anacreon, an Ionian of Teos, of whom O. Müller wrote:

> In him the spirit of the Ionian tribe, having lost all its profounder purpose, views life as worth while only if it is adorned with conviviality, wine, women, and song; he shows none of the Aeolian fervor, being wholly taken by the pleasures of the moment.

Anacreon and Ibycus lived at the court of Polycrates, and after the latter's downfall, Hipparchus invited Anacreon to Athens. He may have had still other masters and protectors. His poetry is replete with references to Polycrates and his love for boys with whom he wished to be young.

He also wrote poems to hetaerae; he composed a savage satire on one Artemus whom a lady by the name of Eurypylae had preferred to him. Its language is closer to that of everyday life, the rhythms are looser and freer, and the stanzas more unruly. He devised the short Anacreontic verse predominant in lyrics imitating him.

It is hardly credible that the personal song of the Greeks came to be silent after Anacreon, because there was no age when the soul would not break forth in song. Our greatest loss is that we possess so little of the most famous lyricists. If only we had even the later and second-rate ones whose very names even are not known to us!

Finally, individual lyric poetry includes as a distinct genre a type of drinking song characterized by a considerable range of musical freedom and hence called *scolia,* i.e., crooked or bent poems. Men were not yet exposed to boredom by the toasting at convivial gatherings; the lyre or myrtle twig was handed to persons from whom one could expect a song or pithy saying. The convivial song became a separate category of poetry consisting generally of short stanzas whose rhythms varied but remained essentially Aeolic.

It is likely that participants at banquets often improvised these drinking songs, though some of the greatest Aeolic poets were famous for composing them, beginning with Terpander who, according to Pindar, invented this genre. The *scolion* of all *scolia* is the charming *Drink with me, be young with me, love with me, and wear a garland with me; be mad with me and sober when I am sober again.*

Here we get a glimpse of life overflowing with pleasure and charm, and we may be glad of the hints that have survived, the few fragments of the loveliest songs the Hellenes ever sang, enabling us to surmise what a wealth of the most beautiful things of all times may have perished.

6. *The Choral Lyric*

The choral dance or circling dance accompanied by song was common among all the Greeks from their earliest days. The Dorians were especially devoted to this dance, accompanied for a long time by a simple musical refrain like the song the Elean women sang to Dionysus, or the Olympian victory song with the *Hail, O beautiful in victory.* Divine festivals, victory celebrations at athletic agons, weddings, and funerals always occasioned hymns of various kinds: the processional hymn (*prosodion*), the choral hymn to Apollo (*hyporchema*), the maiden song or song sung by maidens (*partheneia*), the hymn of praise (paean), the wedding song (*hymenaeus*), and the dirge (*threnos*).

With the enormous growth of music, including rhythmics and metrics, at the hands of Terpander, Olympus, and Thaletas, who likewise stressed the dance, this whole class of songs expanded considerably. To be sure, only remnants have survived, but the lavish contributions made by both the polis and wealthy individuals for these performances gives us some notion of the effort that must have gone into music.

The musical performances were all put on a competitive basis. In Athens, the choruses of the *phylae* competed with one another, and *choragy* (defrayal of the cost of choruses) became a duty of the citizens. Every important city, especially in the Dorian Peloponnesus, had its chorus teachers whose lifework consisted in assembling and training choirs.

And so, in addition to the old popular songs that continued, there developed a wealth of art forms in each of the special categories enumerated above. The art of metrics came to realize its almost limitless powers in poetry, music, and the dance. Of course, we have specimens of only the first of these three.

The line of choric poets began with Alcman, who flourished in the second half of the seventh century. According to legend, he was a Lydian brought as a young slave to Sparta and there freed. In music he had Terpander and Thaletas as predecessors but he also made it clear that he created new compositions.

He did not, like Pindar, use the choir merely as an instrument but spoke of it, to it, and with it, having it even use the plural forms pertaining to "we." He composed choral songs of various kinds to celebrate gods and men; the largest surviving fragment is a *partheneia,* a song to be sung by maidens. He also composed love songs meant to be sung by individuals playing on lyres. He made use of various kinds of verses and stanzas; his dialect was the Spartan Doric.

Alcman was followed by Stesichorus, a citizen of Ionic-Dorian Himera in Sicily but of Ozolean-Locrian descent. The most important innovation attributed to him is the wholesale introduction of epic material into the lyric. By doing this he filled a great need, for the choral lyric of whatever sort could not in the long run dispense with the myths and yet escape monotony; it had to draw on the epic tradition. Thus we find that Stesichorus dealt with the myths of Herakles, Pelias, Meleager, stories of the Theban and Trojan cycles, and other poignant historical events.

A number of Stesichorus' fragments are supremely beautiful, like Clytemnestra's dream of a snake and the marvelous verses telling how Helios gets into the golden chariot of the sun and journeys to the other end of the world. In the hands of Stesichorus these myths take on a heightened, a lyrical existence. To be sure, since he made the praise of individual figures his object, he treated this material rather freely, especially on occasions when he appears to weave himself into these myths.

Arion, from the city of Methymna on Lesbos, cultivated and developed

the dithyramb, in itself a very ancient form of poetry, by introducing into
the choral song at Corinth utterances of Dionysian excitement, which always
stood for jubilant mirth and wild sorrow, thereby giving the choral song an
artistic and even majestic tenor. His odes were sung by circling choirs, i.e,
they moved in a circle around an altar, accompanied not by the flute but by
the lyre, for Arion was the greatest of all lyre players. Not a scrap of his
dithyrambs or hymns has survived. The poem to Poseidon is falsely ascribed
to him.

Ibycus, a poet of Rhegium during the second half of the sixth century,
was a wandering poet who together with Anacreon shared the hospitality of
Polycrates in Samos, celebrating in song the boys the tyrant loved. He must
have had much in common with Stesichorus though his love songs are the
only poems of his we know. To judge by the fragments, some of them singularly beautiful, it was likely that myths such as those of Ganymede or
Tithonus woven into his love songs gave them the necessary consistency and
enduring freshness.

Simonides of Ceos was a many-sided and reflective poet rather than a
lyrically inspired one. He lived on his native island as a chorus teacher,
spending much of his time in the *choragium* [place for training choral danc-
ers], beside the temple of Apollo. He was highly respected by Hipparchus of
Athens as well as by the men of eminence in Thessaly and was so influential
with the tyrants of Sicily that in 476, on the Gelas River, he was able to
mediate peace between Hiero of Syracuse and Theron of Agrigentum.

He was awarded an official commission to commemorate the heroes of
the Persian Wars with inscriptions and elegies; he also won many victories
in music contests. Incidentally, his muse was the first to sell her talent for
money. He was the first of the choral poets to perfect the victory ode
(*epinikion*); we may add that statues to victors also became customary from
about 540 on.

His victory odes were probably quite similar in sense and structure to
those of Pindar, for they too lauded mythical heroes and praised victors of
contests, applying general reflections and sententious observations to the situation at hand and passing mild, humane, and easy Ionian judgments on
moral matters. One of his charming fragments is a dirge Danae sings to her
slumbering son Perseus.

Simonides' art was not sublime like Pindar's but it was more touching.
He reflected more on the impermanence of life but praised the hereafter
less than Pindar did. He etched his thoughts more finely and diversely than
Pindar, making his mode of expression more pliant and pleasing.

In his epigrams as in his choral songs Simonides was perhaps the first
among the poets to employ the antithesis which was to play so large a role in
later rhetoric.

Bacchylides, the son of Pindar's sister and a student and rival of Pindar at the Sicilian courts, was a graceful and elegant poet rather given to the praise of wine, women, and the charms of private life. He shaped everything, even his erotic and lovely convivial songs, into choral odes. He is by far the most lucid of the choric poets, and yet his beautiful paean on the benefits bestowed by peace might be put more appropriately into elegiac form; his lovely fragment extolling the rousing effects of wine on the imagination is composed in simple four-line stanzas approaching the gentle, genial tone of the Ionic elegy.

Apart from the impossibility of getting a proper conception of the accompanying music and *orchesis* (art of dancing in the chorus), our knowledge of this choric poetry is fragmentary because we have only a bundle of victory odes (*epinikions*) from the pen of Pindar, a poet renowned in antiquity for his contributions to several branches of lyric poetry, and the most sublime poet that ever celebrated occasional topics.

Pindar was born in 522 B.C. and lived for over eighty years. Though possessed of a weak voice he devoted his life exclusively to music and poesy, a pious man who loved the gods and was beloved by them, and as a choric poet he was also a great theologian, something no priest of that day was. His victory ode gives us an insight into the great social significance of choral lyricism.

It was an acknowledged high point in his life when an athlete or other contestant won at Olympia, Delphi, Nemea, or Corinth, receiving a short ode in his honor, and upon returning home was honored with a longer ode. As for the poet, he was rewarded liberally enough for compositions of this kind to feel tempted to give them priority over his other endeavors.

Pindar wished to spend his life only with men who had won victories, at the same time enjoying a reputation for wisdom among all the Hellenes. Naturally, he was mainly concerned with those who were rich enough to pay him and the chorus; consequently Pindar esteemed possessions. According to him the wealthy man adorned with virtue had command of the future, i.e., of the world hereafter, and though the best of all things is water, the prerequisite substance of our physical existence, the goodliest possession of all is gold.

As to the content and mode of composition of his victory odes, Pindar deliberately refrains from depicting the agonistic victory, which would have made for insufferable monotony, and celebrates the victor himself. Only his longer odes, elaborated at leisure and detailing the victor's genealogy, kindred, household gods, native country, etc., adequately illustrate his artistic skill.

He derived an appreciable advantage from celebrating the victor's whole family. But he drew upon the myths to provide substance to his poetry, thereby injecting a strong epic element into most of his odes; but shunning the leisurely narrative method of the epic, he proceeded to limn with bright, swift strokes those aspects of a myth which helped to develop a specific thought. These myths were associated with the victor either through his divine or his heroic ancestry, with which, incidentally, every Greek nobleman at that time was provided.

He knew no restraint in praising song; his loveliest tribute is the beginning of the first Pythian ode. Furthermore, he valued his odes in direct proportion to the significance of the victories they celebrated; he created their artistic counterweight as it were, and rounded out thereby the good fortune of the victor.

The sublime solemnity of his odes stands between us and the recognition of self-promotion, as for instance, *There is but one glass that mirrors the deeds of glorious contests, Mnemosyne* (the goddess of memory, mother of the Muses) *and her songs*, or, *Now wind is most needful for man, and now rain water, the daughters of Nephele* (cloud), *but if with great effort a man distinguish himself in an achievement, then honey-voiced songs celebrate him, the footing for after-fame and assured pledge of high merit.*

He praised his own worth loud and long, something that would not always sit well when choirs sang his odes in foreign lands, but he brought it off as long as people took him at his word.

He turned with vehemence on those who envied or despised him, calling them foxes and cawing crows feeding far beneath him, the eagle. Now and then he resorted to a caustic ending (e.g., Pyth. 2, Nem. 7).

Occasionally he clothed a drearily prosaic topic in the most dignified pomp and then dropped wooden words in the midst of it. For instance, to indicate that the time of a festival was nearing he said: *Zeus . . . your seasons circling in a dance to the colorful strains of the lyre have sent me hither a witness of the noblest contest;* or, in support of the honor of a victor: *I who am neither bent on wrangling nor bold in strife bear witness under a towering oath, and the sweet-voiced Muses will grant me leave to speak.*

Each *epinikion* has its own individual structure, no two being fashioned on quite the same pattern. Though his odes are generally taken to be either Doric or Ionic, some are Lydian. Pindar himself said that one of his poems was Lydian in melody and manner. This one, an ode to Asopichus of Orchomenus, has a special and delicate sweetness; it shows how, by making a deft and winged presentation of a charming legend like that of the Graces, one may create a poetic composition out of almost nothing.

In a momentary flash, Pindar is able to evoke the most marvelous effects and often his manner of dwelling on a myth is almost hypnotic. He is a poet of great stature, despite his shortcomings which we need not try to varnish over, especially where beauty is so abundant. Still, the quality of his poesy is uneven.

Apart from his fame, Pindar must also have enjoyed a certain notoriety among the Greeks; otherwise Aristophanes would not have been able to refer to him in connection with the solemn poetic dolt introduced into *The Birds*. His works must have been collected early. The victory odes may have survived because their antiquarian nature afforded the Alexandrians most opportunity to display erudition. This antiquarian cast saved Apollonius and Lycophron from oblivion while others have perished.

If we compare individual lyrics with the choral odes, we shall find Alcman's four hexameter lines incomparably more heartfelt and enjoyable, indeed better than anything else by Alcman with the possible exception of the fragment on the nocturnal rest of all nature, which however is nothing more than an enumeration.

Sappho above all others showed the superiority of the simple stanza over the intricate Doric one for expressing deep feelings and emotions. We would give all of Pindar, or what we have of him, for the song to Aphrodite. Hauntingly touching also are her fragments to the Depth of Night, ending with *but I am lying alone,* and the poem to the plain, untutored woman wandering unknown and forgotten in the underworld forever because she plucked no roses by the Pierian springs.

Though the world has suffered its greatest losses in Sappho and Alcaeus, still Anacreon is extraordinarily lucid and lovely, especially his fragment to Dionysus, beseeching the god to prosper his love for Cleobolus, the fragment to the youth with the maidenly looks, and the one to Eros who tossed him a purple ball and urged him to sport with a Lesbian maid, albeit she could not brook his white hair.

As natural charm speaks out of these fragments, so triviality plagues the choral lyric, and pedestrian poets especially plumped into this most difficult form. The period of great art was also the period of frequent misuse of these dignified modes, and Aristophanes satirized these poetic bunglings.

We have just mentioned the rattle-pated poet who, appearing in *The Birds* to help found the Cloud-Cuckoo-Town, patched up verses from Pindaric reminiscences. A little later in the play Aristophanes brought on the stage Cinesias, a dithyrambic poet of Thebes, and satirized him mercilessly for wanting to waft himself up into the clouds, the true home of his art. Also, Strepsiades, in *The Clouds*, declaims shreds and tatters taken from the dithyrambic poets.

All choral lyrics impress us as essentially and necessarily labored because this form forced poesy into an unbearable strait jacket. But since scarcely a third of this genre of poetry has survived, as already indicated, it appears to us now somewhat like the rind of a squeezed lemon. Even the choruses of Sophocles have such an infinity of strained or difficult expressions that we must of necessity conclude that choral music and rhythms posed well-nigh insuperable difficulties even for him.

How lyric poetry fared from the fourth century on is altogether obscure. The Greeks never used lyric poetry for purposes of written communication, nor did they produce the poem written in loneliness. For them, the lyric was and remained linked with the fortunes of music, virtuosity, and recitation

Ganymede and Eros
Two-handled vessel, front and back views

generally, and these fortunes can hardly have been favorable in the course of events the dithyramb brought about.

Soon after Pindar the *epinikion* must have fallen into desuetude because wealthy victors disappeared, and privately commissioned wedding songs and dirges can hardly have fared better. The *prosodia* which a chorus chanted when approaching a divinity, and other ritual songs, newly composed for each occasion in earlier times, were probably now drawn from older poets when new songs, as Lucian testified, overtaxed the resources of a community, at least for his period (Demosth. Encom. C. 27).

7. *Tragedy*

The whole field of subsequent drama owes its dignity and significance essentially to the dignity and significance conferred on it by the Greeks and especially the Athenians. The crux of the matter is that the drama was not created merely for pastime or pleasure, which would have kept it a minor diversion, but as a part of a highly important cult of the polis.

The development of an art is influenced by the manner of its origin. It must be stressed that the attempt merely to imitate life is not enough to produce tragedy; such a procedure might produce at best only a certain farcical parody of the external events of life, namely, comedy—if the gods be propitious.

Greek tragedy points unmistakably to an altogether different source involving a different kind of mimesis. Originally it was not the actor nor the dialogue but the chorus that comprised the core of the drama, and since the Greeks held to the chorus with characteristic tenacity, transforming it only gradually, it maintained its dramatic role alongside the dialogue. Aeschylus, whose plays presuppose a large number of mute supernumeraries and fanciful settings, divided the conversation among several actors only strikingly late.

We shall never be able to retrace all the individual steps in the rise and development of the drama. It is almost as if all the evidence of earlier stages in the development of the drama had been carefully wiped out. Without the all-pervading presence of a "divine breath of life" the drama could never have achieved the monumental standing which made it and let it continue to be the concern of the whole people: it developed out of the great Dionysiac ecstasy.

Drama came out on a grand scale in a grand setting. It was a deliberate and specific achievement. The Persians and the Jews, indeed the peoples of the Orient as a whole, had no drama because they may not have been able to sustain the tense antithesis contained in the drama. Indian drama, developing out of the Vishnu ritual and music, came later, having many analogies to Greek drama and was perhaps directly influenced by it.

Why did the drama not appear immediately after Homer instead of taking ambiguous routes, since the *Iliad* as well as the *Odyssey* have their dramatic qualities? And why did it appear in Athens instead of in Corinth or Miletus, for instance? It is almost astonishing that the stage had to wait three hundred years even though the epics had so many dramatic elements in them. But the original and decisive impetus necessary for this creation stemmed from the worship rituals of Dionysus and the feelings and emotions they generated.

Out of the music and out of the choral odes there arose as out of a flower bed a gorgeous, somewhat strange blossom: the drama, dedicated at first to Dionysus, then to the whole body of myths. Only after these surcharged emotions and impulses had touched the soul of Greece did she create this highest form of artistic endeavor.

Conversation and dialogue, which the Greeks had ample opportunity of practicing in the popular assembly and in the courts of law, were found in Homer in amazing abundance and perfection. The forcefulness and rich nuances of direct speech are manifest all through the Homeric Hymn to Hermes; drama did not exceed it.

Another important constituent was the tradition of worshiping the gods dramatically. The mimetic element had been present in different rites of worship from days of old. The *hyporchema*, developed long since, was a choral hymn which was enacted mimetically by different persons stepping forward out of the chorus.

And finally there was the essential element of a myth already represented in endless variations in epic, hymn, and the visual arts but now demanding its ultimate and definitive realization.

Moreover, if we consider that these plays were staged only at Dionysus festivals, that is, so infrequently that people would desire to witness longer poetic products, and if we consider the general character of Greek art which preferred throughout clear and well-defined forms thereby putting the mind accustomed to them into a definite mood, cramping the creative spirit yet protecting it against vagrant fancy, thus making possible under the most favorable circumstances the creation of free and beautiful products within the bounds of a strict artistic order, then we shall understand what is not at all self-evident, namely, that Attic drama could become the foremost category of Greek poesy and be recognized as such.

According to Aristotle (*Poetics* IV, 12), tragedy originated with the authors of the dithyramb. The dithyramb was a choric hymn in honor of Dionysus which choirs had been presenting regularly since Arion; there were mirthful and jubilant songs of this name celebrating the coming of spring; on the other hand, there were also hymns of lament, and the city of Sicyon, for example, had these hymns lamenting not Dionysus but Adrastos, probably an ancient nature deity. The first step toward the drama seems to have been taken when the chorus leader, representing either Dionysus or his messenger, told of the life, especially the sufferings of Dionysus, during which time the members of the chorus posed as satyrs, whether in joy or in fear.

We do not know when or by whom myths and persons other than those of Dionysus were introduced into the drama at Athens. At any rate, during the time of Peisistratus, Thespis introduced a great innovation, an actor, as opposed to the ordinary members of the chorus; this actor played successive roles in different masks, posing as Dionysus, Pentheus, or as a messenger in a tragedy of Pentheus.

Still, Thespis held on to the chorus and its dances as the chief components. In later generations people treasured and performed these dances of which this Thespian drama consisted. The dialogues were pushed into the background and thus became merely occasional interludes in reality providing the chorus with material and the opportunity to create dramatic effects. Thespis borrowed the trochaic tetrameter from poesy at hand as others later adopted the iambic trimeter.

Phrynichus, 512 B.C., still had only one actor playing successive roles, including those of women. Choral lyrics still formed the main part of his dramas. His *Phoenissae* had two choruses: one of Phoenician women, the other of noble Persians. Choerilus of Athens and Pratinus of Phlius, a Dorian living at Athens, were especially famous for their satyr plays; both flourished after the close of the sixth century.

However, when and how did the Attic state begin to concern itself seriously with drama? Dionysus festivals with bands of Bacchic revelers were most likely celebrated on the initiative of merrymaking individuals, but the state must have assumed responsibility for the choruses until it finally commissioned poets to take charge. Before 500 B.C., there must also have been in existence some sort of permanent wooden seats for spectators.

Poets attempted to use historical events as dramatic subjects relatively early in the development of the drama, but they soon abandoned these attempts. The heroic achievements of Athens in the Persian Wars, with emphasis on the merits of Themistocles, formed the topical theme of the *Phoenissae* just alluded to; Thespis also staged a drama, *The Fall of Miletus*, for which the Athenians fined him a thousand drachmas because he had reminded them of their own misfortune. Later, Aeschylus composed *The Persians* and *The Women of Aetna*, and much later, in the fourth century, Theodectes, who otherwise dramatized subjects from myths, wrote *Mausolus*, an occasional piece dealing with an orator and a tragedian.

These were only isolated attempts. Poets shunned historical topics because these demonstrably moved spectators rather severely; and for that matter, myths shut their golden vaults again, after having unlocked them for a brief while for drama. Moreover, *The Persians* by Aeschylus, the only play we have on a historical subject, affects one somewhat like a mythical subject set in a drama because it has a foreign setting and a strange tone, i.e., it is detached from the realistic world, being a fictional Persia with but few aspects taken from the real life of the East.

The poets compensated for the exclusion of historical drama by introducing repeatedly lofty patriotic sentiments and political interests of the day. In the *Supplices,* Aeschylus enjoined eternal friendship between Athens and Argos, and in the *Eumenides* he clearly alluded to the fate of the Areopagus.

The invectives Euripides hurled at Sparta in his *Heracleidae* and *Andromache,* and the way in *Supplices* he has Theseus enforce burial of the dead soldiers against Theban opposition, are well known. Tragedians and orators vied with each other in exploiting these patriotic themes.

The tragedians seem to have virtually ignored the non-heroic, non-mythical past. With his *Cresphontes* and *Temenus* Euripides reached back to the Dorian migration, but during the height of the classical period no drama dealt with Solon and Peisistratus, Cylon, the marriage of Agariste, Periander and his house, Aristodemus, Aristomenes, *et al.* The Greeks left the historical drama for the modern world.

This limitation saved tragedy a great deal of travail. Our modern education is not oriented toward history, not even our national history, as Greek education was oriented toward its heritage of myths. The modern audience has to exert itself more to appreciate historical tragedy, which has grown to be more complex than Greek tragedies.

We demand a wealth of detail, interpenetration of plot and subplot, and a multitude of characters gradually developed in the course of the play. In modern plays the confluence of events and development of the characters is made to mount up to the climax with a view to creating the greatest suspense. Hence we find so few excellent historical tragedies. Many, like Goethe's *Egmont,* exist only for the sake of some gripping scenes.

Greek tragedy may have avoided historical subjects because it could hardly have achieved the stage realism they required; consequently Greek tragedians enjoyed the great advantage of being able to forgo a lot of exposition on which our playwrights have to spend so much time and effort. The modern playwright loses concentration in the presenting of political and other distracting details; the Greek myths did not require this dramatic discursiveness. The whole setting within which the incidents occurred in a Greek drama was a part of the common culture; the entire life and layout in a royal residence, for example, was standardized.

But in the end Greek tragedy could no more continue without changes than the Greek temple could, and there is no necessity that Greek tragedy as it was should have sufficed for all times. In the first place, the myths were not inexhaustible; moreover, psychological complexity and variety have a right to exist though perhaps less tangibly on the stage, which aims at realistic and full-rounded treatment of the characters, than in the novel.

A rich variety of nuances in the dramatic action and character portrayal was desired in Greek tragedy already during its most flourishing period, as is evidenced by Euripides who also takes the spectator on the stage. But it was not more than an attempt and a beginning. Delicate and complex character development was not pursued because it would have overtaxed Greek classical drama; realism in Greek comedy was also much more modest than in its modern counterpart.

To get a just comprehension of Greek tragedy at its highest development we must bear in mind that it strives to present neither a lifelike, full-length portrait, nor its external physical details, for it is the high point of a Dionysian festival and its mood, and is thus given over, root and branch, to ideal representation.

Hence the dignified splendor of the dress worn by both the chorus and the actors, of whom there were two after Aeschylus and three after Sophocles. These actors filled all the roles of a play. They wore high-soled shoes, exaggerated headdress, and cotton wadding in their clothes to increase their size and dignity; they also wore distinctive masks to represent the different characters. Mute supernumeraries and assistants supported them in goodly numbers, likewise in gorgeous dress.

Once the chorus began to enact other than Dionysian characters, it dropped the satyr masks except for satyr plays.

> Since the Greeks were accustomed to preserve and cultivate all older forms of poesy that had some individual and characteristic quality in addition to the newer forms that grew out of the older, in time they developed the satyr drama and joined it with the tragedies so that finally three tragedies ending with a satyr drama formed a dramatic cycle called a tetralogy. (O. Müller II, 38.)

Doubtless it was not always easy to create a wild and ribald satyr play from the myths and to fit it in with the dramatic treatment. Furthermore, since it is undeniably risky to draw many general conclusions from the single extant satyr play, Euripides' *Cyclops,* which is a pleasant farce, many things must perforce remain obscure.

Suidas said that Pratinus, the rival of Choerilus and Aeschylus, was the first to write satyr plays. Was there perhaps a time when satyr plays were just left to farcical improvisation and therefore not committed to writing? According to the second *Vita* of Euripides, there were only eight satyr plays among his ninety-two plays; this species may have gone against his grain. Sophocles, too, appears to have composed but few. Who saw to it that satyr plays were regularly performed?

The content of these plays may have been similar to the comic exploitation of the gods in middle comedy and also similar to the Sicilian comedy of Epicharmus. Often Hercules was the main comic character, presented as an egregious glutton. To the Aeschylean trilogy of *Laius, Oedipus,* and *The Seven Against Thebes* was joined the satyr play called *Sphinx,* and to the Oresteian trilogy the play *Proteus,* probably a jest at the expense of Menelaus who went vagabonding about, leaving his brother in the lurch and returning much too late to deliver or avenge him. Anyway, these mirthful concluding pieces trimmed the tragedies with a pretty border.

Equipping the actors and chorus was a matter dependent on the localities where the plays were performed. That drama was a unique expression of a religious festival is here of the greatest importance, for it involved a whole polis and required a gigantic expense for its performance. After the wooden seats in Athens collapsed under the spectators in 500 B.C., the large theater of Dionysus gradually arose at the foot of the Acropolis, and other Greeks followed this example.

At the time of the Peloponnesian War, the Peloponnesus and Sicily had some exceptionally fine theaters. The vast size of these theaters, used also for other festivals, popular assemblies, and the like, and providing a kind of census of the citizenry [since all citizens attended], was appropriate for only a certain style and to that extent limited the range of these theatrical performances. The size of the audience determined the size of both the theater and the gigantic proportions of the stage performances.

Essentially it was the chorus that determined the design of the theater; accommodations made for the chorus demonstrate this optically, for two thirds of the audience had to look at the stage sideways while all could see the chorus equally well. In the center of the orchestra was an altar-shaped platform (*thymele*), the venerable point where the drama and the worship of Dionysus came to a focus.

This was originally the Dionysus altar around which the chorus danced as it sang dithyrambs; it had in time become the center of the orchestra and served as the chapel of a hero (*heroon*), a terrace with altars, a burial site, or whatever need demanded. Beyond the orchestra was the scene building serving among other uses as a backdrop for the elevated stage immediately in front of it. The stage was relatively long and narrow with steps leading up to it at either end. The actors impersonating heroes were distributed with their followers along this stage.

When an actor was meant to come on stage from some distant place, he did not come from behind but entered the stage coming up the side steps; those out of the city itself or other nearby place came up the left, those coming from the country or from far away, up the right steps. In general, the stage was the courtyard in front of a palace or the space before a royal tent or simply some public place. Poets had to take these matters into careful consideration, and even comedy writers representing everyday life had to adjust themselves accordingly.

The wall forming the backdrop had three doors, the middle one leading to the royal apartment, the doors on either side to guest chambers, women's quarters, sanctuaries, prisons, etc. It must have been possible to change the setting as implied in the *Eumenides* of Aeschylus and the *Ajax* of Sophocles. This was accomplished in part by *periaktoi*, revolving triangular screens set on either side of the stage, indicating the location of the scene. If scenes inside the rooms or quarters were to be shown on stage, then an *exostra* was shoved or an *eccyclema* rolled forward onto the stage.

Machinery for hoisting people or gods up or letting them down to the stage, or for enabling them to descend below the stage (Charon's steps) and apparatus for simulating thunder and lightning were all available. Already at the time of Aeschylus famous artists like Agatharchus painted stage scenery and decorations. We are credibly assured that the great poet had had a hand in all these developments.

But all this splendor falls short of modern stage demands, a realistic and delimited scene. The classical stage also lacked modern lighting and the effects attainable by it; its stage decorations were sparse and symbolic as in *Ajax* and *Philoctetes*. The Greeks got their theatrical illusion from a totally different source.

It was certainly not easy to project the voice to all parts of this theater, and the incongruity between the voice and the thickly padded and richly adorned actors must have struck others in antiquity before Lucian. We do not know whether the masks helped to amplify the voice; the actors managed by sacrificing all subjective gestures, using only stylized postures, and by speaking or chanting in a slow, unvaried monotone, which must have sounded very strange.

Incidentally, it was desirable for the actor to have a large physique, a good mind, and a wide cultural background, and so there were never more than a few excellent actors around. Lack of competent talent may partly account for restricting the number of players to three except in *Oedipus at Colonus*. But the Greeks evidently preferred three distinguished actors to a large but uneven company of talkers and hence paid no heed to dramatic desideratum to have at times five or six persons participate in a realistic conversation, just as they paid no heed to any of the other stage illusions in our sense.

It is also to be noted that limiting the number of players reduced the expense of the state in paying the actors' salaries. Though the protagonist, deuteragonist, and tritagonist were not known as individual actors today are, they were adequately distinguished for the Greeks by their change of costumes and masks.

Over against the actors stood the chorus, originally composed of forty-eight members, then reduced to twelve, and finally increased by Sophocles to fifteen for each part in the tetralogy. As a dithyrambic chorus it circled around the altar, as a dramatic chorus wearing distinctive masks it sang alone or alternated in antiphonal singing and dialogue with the actors.

As it came into the orchestra from the side entrance it sang the *parodos* or entrance song explaining its motives for coming on stage. Once in the orchestra it sang *stasima* between the episodes, usually when the stage was empty, during the respites which the play more or less frequently provided. It also rendered lively little songs and dances to express joy or exultation when roused to emotion by some sudden turn or event in the play.

Also while the scenes or episodes were being enacted the chorus would sing a *commus* to express deep emotion, and when passion had risen to an unusual pitch the actors might suspend dialogue to join with the chorus to create an even more powerful effect. At times the chorus would divide, one part singing with lyrical rapture, another engaging in dialogue, depending on the exigencies of mood and feelings.

It is to be assumed that upon occasion the chorus only gesticulated, while at other times it moved in concerted dance motions. Presumably it was accompanied by harps, lyres, or flutes.

The parts of the dialogue taken by the players are divided into the prologue preceding the *parodos,* the episodes separated by choral odes, and the *exodos,* the episodes and *exodos* being really the main parts of the play. From time to time the actors on the stage joined in the choral singing. Apart from the *commus* in which the two actors carry on a musical dialogue with the chorus, they sang duets and even longer arias, the so-called *monodies.* Euripides loved these latter especially and composed them without rhythmical repetition, i.e., in the manner resembling the later dithyrambs.

The anapaestic system was used especially by the chorus in the *parodos,* its formal entry, and also occasionally at the end of a choral ode, to soften the transition in dialogue. One can hardly imagine them sung to a regular melody or spoken as normal speech; they were probably rendered in an irregular chant, the so-called *paracataloge.*

In the older period, the dialogue of the actors as well as that of the chorus, represented here by its leader, was cast in trochaic tetrameters, which were also used for longer scenes in later tragedy, whereas the extant tragedies are mostly in iambic trimeters devised by Archilochus for other purposes. The iambic style in Aeschylus is dignified, somewhat heavy, and touched with archaisms though in others, following him, it approaches the conversational tone.

Actors liked to indulge in long speeches which the chorus may have interrupted with two to four choral verses. The poets also disposed of the shorter speeches with great art, intensifying the tone with the so-called *stichomythy* in which the actors conversed in alternating *distichs, stichs,* or *hemistichs* (half-distichs, single verses), resulting in a dialogue in allegro, presto, and prestissimo.

The long and complex exposition of Euripides' *Ion* is a conversation purely in alternating *monostichs*. Even when all three actors were on stage, usually only two conversed with each other. In a long scene in *Orestes* in which Orestes, Pylades, and Electra are present all the way through, first speak Orestes and Electra, then Orestes and Pylades, then Orestes and Electra, and finally all three together. This will suffice to explain the poetic structure of the tragedies.

Now we may investigate the poet and his position. First, almost all the great dramatic poets were poets or playwrights by profession. In order to stage a drama a poet applied to the *archon eponymous* or *archon basileus,* and if the archon had confidence in the applicant he assigned him one of the choruses that rich citizens coveting honor gathered together, supported, and equipped in the name of the phylae.

Poets, whether tragic or comic, were brought up in the tradition of chorus masters (*chorodidaskalos*); they taught their choruses all the dances and songs appearing in the plays, much as the choral and dithyrambic poets trained their choirs. The dramatic poet also had to direct the players, who were paid not by the *choragus* (chorus leader) but by the state and assigned by lot to the poet unless he had actors regularly attached to him.

The state paid the poet a fixed sum for directing and staging a play. Now tragedy, much as choral activity as a whole, had become subject to competition, and the *choragus* to whose chorus the judges awarded the victory received the prize. During the earlier period tetralogies composed of three tragedies and a satyr play were adjudged as one unit. Sophocles dropped the composition of tetralogies and began composing individual plays which could have been staged separately, and other poets followed him in this practice.

The judges appear then to have judged each play separately. They were sometimes influenced by the plaudits of the spectators, for surely audiences at tragedies must have behaved at times as the audience reportedly did at the staging of Aristophanes' *Clouds,* when the people clapped and cheered enthusiastically for this or that poet to get the vote of the judges.

This pressure from below may help account for the few victories Euripides carried away—five out of ninety-two plays—which is out of all proportion to his popularity among the cultivated public. Considering the inferiority of most victors of that time, this fact is hard to understand for subsequent generations which preferred him to all others. It seems the office of the judges must have fallen into strange hands much too often.

Plato's *Symposium* teaches us that the poet crowned with victory might, together with his choral dancers, hold a celebration, offering a sacrifice, at which a large crowd, invited or uninvited, might be present. The *Symposium* confirms something we learn elsewhere, too, that poets wrote either tragedies or comedies but not both, for Socrates, awake with only Agathon and Aristophanes as they passed the wine goblet from left to right, maintained in the teeth of universal practice that comedy and tragedy were really appropriate to the same writer. At any rate, a notice in Suidas tells us that Ion of Chios, living in the fifth century, staged both comedies and tragedies. If this is accurate, he is alone in this accomplishment, for otherwise the stock in trade of comedy is to ridicule tragedy.

It is simply amazing how long these poets lived and were creative, some of their best creations, like those of the Venetian painters, belonging to their declining years. In the course of sixty-two years, Sophocles wrote 113 plays. At first he and Euripides appeared only every three or four years with a tetralogy, later every two years. As indicated above, these tetralogies no longer formed a single unit.

These poets also did not act in their own tragedies as Aeschylus had in his; Sophocles is supposed to have refrained because of his slight voice. At any rate, the poets did their utmost even after Aeschylus to make their plays succeed. In one of his biographies we read that Sophocles adjusted his roles to the individuality of his actors. The poet was a composer and ballet director to boot, and was always visibly present at the staging of his plays.

What a powerful role tragedy played in Athenian life in spite of—or because of—its presentation at long intervals is demonstrated by the fact that, after Sophocles produced his *Antigone,* he was chosen as co-general with Pericles in a war against Samos, and by the fact that Aristophanes made tragedy along with the highest matters of state the staple of his comedies.

At this point we may touch on the continuing knowledge of these tragedies. The Athenian was distinguished from the rest of the Hellenes by his ability to recite the tragedians and by having his memory stored with poetical and musical items of the dramas as well as concepts of the characters and of the plays as they were staged. The strongest proof of Athenian familiarity with the tragedies is that Aristophanes perpetually alluded to them, which would have been pointless without widespread conversance with the tragedies.

We may have to assume that there was a lot of publicity in connection with this literary activity. Memory artists probably recited these plays to groups on appropriate occasions, and as for the musical aspects, the Athenians probably sang parts of the most difficult *monodies* of Euripides much as Italians sing snatches of arias.

In discussing the style and treatment of material in the tragedies we shall begin with the poetic significance of the chorus, originally the sole, then the main part of the tragedy but reduced in time by a series of transitions we can no longer retrace to a kind of frame around tragedy. Originally the chorus consisted of representatives of the Dionysiae; later it became a group of individuals related to the locale of the play, ranging from the Oceanids in *Prometheus* to the sailors from Salamis in *Ajax*.

According to Aristotle, the task of the chorus is to serve as an emotionally involved spectator not perceptive enough to resolve the dramatic conflict but of sufficient insight to give the play a measure of reflective balance in emotionally shattering moments. The modern notion that the chorus was an *ideal spectator* whose observations were meant to guide and dominate the audience is not fully correct, for the chorus participated emphatically in the drama from the very beginning.

Actually, the chorus rarely intervened overtly in the dramatic action. The Argive elders personified by the chorus in *Agamemnon*, who were so loquacious about their age and so persistently obscure in speech, attempted to intervene but after taking counsel remained thoroughly divided and after drawing their swords on Aegisthus were dissuaded by Clytemnestra.

Sophocles evinces unerring tact in the use of the chorus, for whenever his chorus attempts to take action, it is shown as unsure of itself or deluded, but sublime when it limits itself to sweeping discourses on the laws governing life. Sophocles does not cling to the notion that the chorus may consist of elders or maidens or any other group exclusively, having them perform as such from time to time, but he treats the chorus alternately as a real or an ideal component of the drama, but even in the latter case he is not content to cast it merely in the role of an *ideal spectator*, but always as something greater.

With Euripides the chorus had no longer a mediating and tranquilizing influence, but was either a confidant or accomplice of the protagonist, or performed the role of a narrator of events that happened earlier in a dynasty, or in a campaign. In *Ion* the chorus was anguished by its knowledge that Creusa had mixed some poison; in *Medea, Iphigenia in Tauris, Helen,* and others, it was a confidant; in the *Troades* it was a fellow sufferer almost to the point of being comic.

In the last-named play, the odes on the wooden horse and the capture of Troy are quite beautiful, and the second ode in *Hercules Furens,* a remarkably long ode by no means inferior to Pindar, recounts all the deeds of the hero given up as lost and believed to be in Hades. In *Hecuba* the chorus elaborates in much detail how it was surprised at its toilet by the Greeks overrunning Troy. Other choruses often indulged in lamentations, as, for instance, the chorus in *Hippolytus* which, after the departure of Phaedra, chants variations on the theme *Oh would that I were far away.* Other choruses advanced only general reflections or Athenian sympathies and antipathies, just as the characters in the drama do, forgetting its own task.

As for the action of tragedy, we shall begin by cursorily disposing of the preliminary questions of fate and catharsis. All the latter-day talk about the idea of fate in the tragedy of the ancients in contrast to ours seems to us so disconsolately superfluous because it reflects the notion that ancient drama was bent on inculcating the view that no one could escape his fate and that this wisdom—actually a truism running up and down the highways and byways in those days—was the essence of tragedy.

Several kinds of fate have to be distinguished: (1) blind necessity, which may be virtually synonymous with the will of the gods, who are frightfully envious and vengeful; (2) conditional necessity as in *Oedipus,* where a chain of events is contingent on antecedent events—this and that would not happen unless something or other had occurred before—; (3) ancestral guilt, compounded from generation to generation by revenge upon revenge.

The high art of tragedy, brought out especially by Sophocles, interweaves the characters and actions of human beings into fate in such a manner that the spectators see this fate as ineluctable and the myth as in a sense vindicating itself. The decisive element determining the chain of events is not the external occurrence, the visible destiny, not what the spectator has long known by heart, but the inner quality of the people involved, the way their characters develop and the way they touch the spectator's heart. Oedipus at Colonus is thoroughly wretched, and yet through his very wretchedness he is transfigured; Prometheus in his downfall takes the full sympathy of the spectators with him, as Ajax also does. The more empty and perilous earthly things appear, the more malicious the gods at times seem to be, the grander and the more magnificent the characters of the protagonists appear.

The vindication of destiny by no means implies the guilt of the respective protagonists, and the stale cliché that the tragic outcome is due to some guilt is to be rejected thoroughly and completely. In the first place, the Greek did not regard actions undertaken from selfish motives as necessarily entailing guilt; hence, the Greek poet and spectator saw and judged guilt differently from the way we do; hence, too, an individual may have been guilty, but fate by no means always seized upon this guilt, and that is ultimately the crux of the matter.

In his *Agamemnon,* Aeschylus heaped all sorts of blame and guilt on Agamemnon, and yet it was not these at all that destroyed him. Iphigenia's death is a mere pretext for Clytemnestra, and Aegisthus is not an avenger of the many Argives lost by land and sea; he can only avenge his father on the son of the man actually guilty. In short, Aeschylus does not adjudge Agamemnon guilty. Sophocles had to make Oedipus vehement and passionate so that the spectators would find his fate bearable, but his fate does not depend on these qualities in his character any more than Antigone's fate depends on her incorrigibility and inflexible will, moving her to scorn all gentle means after Creon had thoroughly roused her spirits.

We shall touch briefly on Aristotle's famous definition (*Poetics,* VI, 1):

> "Tragedy, then, is an imitation of an action that is serious, complete, and of certain magnitude; in language embellished with each kind of artistic ornament, the several kinds being found in separate parts of the play; in the form of action, not of narration; through pity and fear effecting the proper purgation of these emotions. [By 'language embellished' I mean language into which rhythm, harmony and song enter. By 'the several kinds . . . in separate parts' I mean that some parts are rendered through the medium of verse alone, others again with the aid of song."]

The interpretation of these statements is in dispute; Goethe conceived of the catharsis as applying only to the characters of the tragedy, not to the audience. At all events, it would be erroneous to suppose that some end beyond poetry, i.e., some moral purpose, was intended. Nevertheless, Aristotle intended the aroused emotion of fear or compassion somehow to touch and transfigure the emotions of the spectator.

One of the most striking differences between the ancient and modern drama is that the action in ancient drama is exceedingly restrained in relation to the wealth of inner motives and of narrative details. The chief reason for this is that the actor, stilted on high soles, all padded out and a mask over his face, was unwieldy and not able to act but only to speak. So, in *Oedipus at Colonus,* Antigone is merely led out amid the comings and goings and speechmaking on the stage; remarkably little direct action, such as fighting, murder, or other violent activity takes place on the stage, with the rude exception of Ajax' suicide, fastening Prometheus in irons to a rock, and a few things like that.

Had their technique permitted it, no doubt the Greeks would have presented visually many events they could only narrate. Decisive here was not aesthetic diffidence toward anything not immediately concerned with the inner strivings of the heart, as latter-day critics have contended; nor was it the wish, as Horace said, to spare the audience bloody and stunning drama, for the poets staged the crudest and most atrocious acts possible.

Not only did they frequently bring corpses on stage; in the *Libation Bearers,* Aeschylus showed even Agamemnon's bloody garment, and in the *Bacchae,* Euripides had the fragments of Pentheus brought on stage. Moreover, he had the rent and slashed Hippolytus make his gruesome appearance on stage and even sing a monody while dying.

We would do well to discard the idealistic notion of aesthetic abhorrence and bear in mind that it was rather practical difficulties that had stood in the way, for even walking about on *cothurni* was precarious and vehement action could easily make one tumble, as legend tells us Aeschines did while playing the role of Aenomaus and pursuing Pelops. The suicide of Ajax may have been not altogether easy and safe. Moreover, the vast Greek theaters severely hampered any desire to act in a natural manner. Euripides, who had a strong realistic bent, was unable to overcome the stylized dignity imposed on him by the theater.

The Greeks centered the dramatic interest not on external action but on the motives; they developed the inchoate feelings, reflections, and decisions, seeking to compensate for stage mannerism by detailed narrative realism. In *Agamemnon,* Clytemnestra goes into frightful details in telling about the murder of her husband: how the death rattle in his throat gasped out little sprays of blood which refreshed her as Zeus's rain refreshes sprouting fields in spring; and in *Antigone* the messenger narrates how Haemon, having driven his sword into his side, threw his arms around Antigone and gasped out a swift stream of blood on her pale white cheek.

The terrible description the messenger gives in *Medea* of the death of Glauke and Creon suggests likewise that, if the listeners' ears were thus maltreated, the spectators' eyes would have been dealt with no more delicately had it not been for the limitations imposed by the theater.

Rather than stage actual events, a peculiarly fervent narrative style, quite different from that of the epic, was developed to make known the catastrophe and the events preceding it. These reports were rarely made by the main characters, but generally by messengers or other secondary players who spoke as eyewitnesses to on-stage characters with a view to arousing them to near frenzy.

In this respect, all three tragedians produced masterpieces. An extraordinary achievement, though, is the messenger's report in Euripides' *Bacchae,* telling of the frenzied bacchantes on Mount Cithaeron, which is really not so much a report as a splendidly colorful and circumstantial description composed with poetic rapture and empathy. It is as though he were giving his utmost to praise and transfigure the mystery of the Bacchic frenzy.

It is generally accepted that myth was the substratum of tragedy. Though different poets handled the myths with considerable freedom, they remained nevertheless a permanent fulcrum for tragedy, the lack of which is one of the main shortcomings of modern drama: the suspense inherent in the events themselves and in their consequences. When the same myths were made use of time after time, much as were the motifs of the libretti of eighteenth century Italian opera, they became so well known that the spectator was not held by mere suspense and expectancy, as in the horror drama formerly popular in the Parisian playhouses, but by the pity and terror the dramatist evoked with his creative treatment of soul-shattering material, thus ever anew giving a sense of wonder.

By renouncing suspense and stressing the most elegant style in dialogue and the most exquisite artistic rendering, the Greeks accomplished something repeated only once during a period of great art. During the Middle Ages and the Renaissance, painters did their best work when portraying the best known stories, those of Jesus and Mary, presented over and over, hundreds of times, in contrast to those legends intelligible only when explained.

We have already noted that familiarity with the myths on the part of the people entailed unique advantages for the poet, enabling him to shorten his exposition when composing a tragedy. Aeschylus, writing unitary trilogies, had to do an exposition for only the first play, the second having its exposition in the first, the third in the second. In all his extant plays, Sophocles gave artistic expositions of the background.

Euripides, on the other hand, appears to want to save time and effort by having one of his main characters or a divinity give a prologue setting forth the myth the play is based on. He gets directly to his tale of woe. What with his contemptuous treatment of the myths, he could hardly have taken any other course. His procedure was a rude convenience rather than a real exposition. The use of one of the main personages betrays a certain dramatic indifference; Plautus, Terence, and Shakespeare do better by having a special individual deliver the prologue.

These prologues, at times tediously long-winded and dealing with occurrences that take place later in the play, correspond to the *deus ex machina* in so far as they save the poet some dramatic elaboration. Here we might also point out that, quite in contrast to the newer tragedy which is governed by the laws of suspense, the older tragedy often shattered the suspense in mid action. Since the plot depended on the myth and was therefore well known, it could be presented with appropriate simplicity.

The suspense ceased, for instance, in the middle sections of the Aeschylean trilogies, while reflective observations with all their multitudinous woes were carried on and on. Aeschylus even revealed the identity

of Orestes and Electra at the very beginning of the *Libation Bearers*. Sophocles was the first to construct an Electra play in which the recognition was
delayed until the last third of the play. He also showed in every possible way
that Clytemnestra deserved death, whereas Aeschylus presented only lamentations, descriptions, songs, and sacrifice.

When we reflect upon the intrigue, conspiracy, deception, and secret
machinations attempted in the older tragedy, we see how childish they were.
How utterly simple, for instance, are things in the *Libation Bearers,* where
Electra at the tomb identifies a stranger by fitting her foot into his footprint,
no doubt a genuinely old saga trait. The audience is also quite plainly told
how Aegisthus will be led on and killed; the only touch of intrigue in the
plot occurs when the chorus deceives the nurse, who thinks Orestes is dead,
persuading her to get Aegisthus to come without a bodyguard.

Already the ancients noted that the Aeschylean drama did not have
many complications and *peripeteias* compared to the newer tragedies, which
included Euripides, and that Aeschylus was more concerned with the dignity
of his characters than with villainy, the gratifying and the sententious, all of
which he regarded as unsuited for tragedy. We need not discuss how ancient
drama, so lacking in complications, compares with modern drama.

These plays lack variety as well as suspense. Keeping the action tied
down to one place tends to make for monotony. Oedipus at Colonus, for
instance, never once leaves his spot on the stage until he walks away to meet
his death, and other protagonists do likewise. Instead of the external incidents of life we might expect to find in a play, Greek drama stressed the
inner conflicts, vividly illuminating these in their minutest transitions. In
Greek drama psychological truth overshadows what in our sense is dramatically real and probable.

A scene like the one in which Clytemnestra works long and hard to get
Agamemnon on his return to alight from his chariot and walk on the purple
rug into the palace would be quite impossible today; Aeschylus portrayed
Clytemnestra's dissembling by having her receive Agamemnon with a display of affected pomposity.

Of the three unities, that of time comes about more or less by itself and
is actually rather a fact accepted than a rule observed. The unity of place
could also be manipulated somewhat freely: the *Eumenides* begins in Delphi
and continues in Athens; the first half of *Ajax* takes place before the tents of
the heroes, the second half on the seashore with underbrush in the background. Regarding unity of action as well as action in general, the poets
were quite free, and that even before Euripides. It sufficed for the action of a
tragedy to have logical coherence or confluence toward a unifying purpose;
indeed the more proper expression might be unity of interest. Euripides was
the first to combine unrelated plots in one play.

Many plays derived their unity of action from the myths and from the sequence of scenes they necessitated, especially when, as in *Oedipus at Colonus,* the protagonist never left the stage.

Still, Greek drama includes masterpieces of the first rank, like *Oedipus the King* by Sophocles. Here, in scene after scene, the spectators see the inexorable approach of destiny before the participants themselves do. The rejection of the prophetic warning, which leads secondarily to the king's growing suspicions—in absurd concatenation—of a whole series of innocent men; his false sense of tranquil security, an exceptionally powerful dramatic technique arousing sympathy in the spectators for one believing himself still happy, and the final horrible awakening to the truth—all these show mankind's tragic blindness to destiny.

How gripping it is to watch Oedipus relentlessly pursue the hunt for the murderer, *as though Laius had been his father!* In fact, nearly every word he utters bears witness against him. But the poet who gave us this exceptionally unified and convincing tragedy also gave us *Ajax,* whose hero takes his leave in the middle of the play though he continues to influence and affect the spectators as an echo and a shadow to the end, and Herakles in the *Trachiniae,* to whom the whole play keeps drawing attention but who puts in his appearance only toward the end of the play after Deianira has committed suicide.

Euripides often strings incidents together rather aimlessly and makes his action a shifting about of motley scenes, thus destroying unity, with the result that the drama as a whole is hard to remember. Furthermore, he irks the audience by repetition, first discussing a matter, then letting it happen, and finally reporting that it has happened. His tragedy *Troades* aims to dazzle the spectator with its variety and its series of scenes presenting the capture of a city; still, the last act and some choral odes have exquisitely beautiful passages. But any building up to a climax amid this universal outpouring of woes and lamentations is unthinkable, and at the end of the play named after her, Hecuba is exactly as she was at the beginning.

The poorly constructed *Hercules Furens* also vexes the spectator by having two catastrophes overtake the family of the hero, the first through Lycus and the other through Herakles himself, who earlier had given every promise of delivering rather than destroying.

What Euripides lacks in powerful passions, which vitally support dramatic interest, he makes up in a rich variety of events on the stage and through complications of dramatic action. Sometimes he achieves his dramatic effects by the splendor of his stage displays, by panoramic prospects, etc. At the end of *Orestes,* Helen appears transfigured in the air; the first impression of the *Phoenissae* is that it presents a beautiful spectacle.

But besides this delicate sense for the external effects, Euripides is often indifferent to psychological probabilities and improbabilities. Although *Helena* has some beautiful parts, it is from the beginning an unfortunate subject. To have Menelaus travel about for years with a phantom Helen without his detecting it is mythically acceptable but psychologically implausible; it is patently difficult to sustain this illusion on the stage as a realistic mode of human conduct. This myth is too crude for dramatic purposes.

Menelaus then finds the true Helen in Egypt while the phantom Helen disappears into thin air. If only this phantom Helen could have been brought on the stage! Unhappily, the play only gives reports about her as about so much else, thereby weakening the characters and the dramatic effect. One also pities the chorus with its otiose wailing and lamentation.

Although Helen gives the captured Greek women hope that they will return home, they remain in Egypt; at least not a word is ever said about their release. Here too we have an *élan généreux* without any consequences. Finally, the Dioscuri have to appear as *dei ex machina* to restrain Theoclymenus from inflicting a bloody vengeance on his own sister for permitting Helen to escape. Moreover, the prophecy of the Dioscuri that Helen would be famous as a goddess and that Menelaus would find a home on an island of the blest is by no means foreshadowed by their characters in the play.

The *deus ex machina,* a subject introduced when we discussed Euripides' *Helena,* is a device Sophocles also resorted to when he had the deified Herakles intervene in *Philoctetes.* Euripides used this device in about half of his plays, mostly his later ones; in a few he used it so as to remove any possible remaining doubt, as for instance to assure some dynasty future dominion. In such instances the *deus ex machina,* like the prologue at the beginning, emphasized more forcefully the connection between the play and the myth.

The god could very well be replaced by another prophet, even one that had been severely punished like Polymestor in *Hecuba,* who foretells the curse that will strike the victors.

This *deus ex machina* need not always bring about a reconciliation. In the *Bacchae,* Dionysus leaves Cadmus and Agave deeply afflicted though promising Cadmus future reign and finally both of them a home in the islands of the blest. The purpose of this celestial intervention is to sever the knot and to restore legal authority, as in *Orestes,* where Apollo dispenses a highhanded but nonetheless viable justice, and especially in *Hippolytus* where, but for the intervention of Artemis, the innocence of the hero would remain unknown. When a poet can get out of an impasse of his own contriving only by such a device, the result is not drama but a misuse of power.

As to the construction of the tragedies, closer study, especially of the later ones, has gradually laid bare some secrets and concealed virtues that are barely discernible on the stage but which must have exerted a subtle influence nevertheless. In some of their plays, Sophocles and Euripides, for instance, put a scene of the main dialogue in the middle and divided the rest of the scenes equally, one half leading up to, the other half away from, the keystone scene, thus creating a kind of pyramidal symmetry. No human eye could see this pattern, nor could a human ear hear it, and yet it is demonstrably present. There are further elements that have not yet been explained but which nevertheless mark the supreme artist.

In our examination of the characters in the tragedies we shall limit ourselves for the time being to Aeschylus and Sophocles. The ideal nature of their tragic heroes strikes the eye at once. They are all figures drawn against a background of gold; in Aeschylus' *Agamemnon* even Clytemnestra and Aegisthus partake of the ideal, she by covering the deed with every possible reason that sophistry or passion can adduce, so that if one fails another will surely suffice.

Eteocles in the *Seven Against Thebes* is an outstanding ideal figure, and in *Antigone* the two sisters are likewise ideal characters even though they differ in their views because Antigone insists on burying her brother. Only the servants, like the watchman in *Agamemnon* and the nurse in the *Libation Bearers,* have any traits of common life about them.

Sophocles abandoned to their fate those characters we should call evil, like Creon in *Antigone,* representing the highest degree of blind infatuation, the Atreidae in *Ajax,* Odysseus in *Philoctetes,* and others. Though Sophocles would have known how to derive evil purely from the depths of selfishness, these characters are still not villains; they partake of the ideality surrounding everything related to the mythic and heroic world. They speak with a strong sense of "justness," and at times express profound sentiments. In their dialogues, to be sure, they deliberately withhold things with a view to deceiving, but they still have no bad conscience.

Apart from the fact that the Greek was permitted a wide range of action, none of these heroes had to have feelings of guilt, for the gods themselves drove men to evil, and evil was prophesied by oracles and predetermined by destiny. In Aeschylus, the concatenation of deeds binds the action together into a trilogy. Hence these tragedies have no Iago, no Richard the Third, no Franz Moor. Not until Euripides do we find characters that might have a bad conscience, though they do not, being rather self-possessed knaves and rascals.

Moreover, Aeschylean tragedy is unique in staging only supernatural beings as in *Prometheus.* This drama is rimmed by a colossal mythic horizon consisting of crags beyond the seas on the faraway purlieus of the world, and contains descriptions of the mythical characters that bewail Prometheus, and of the journey that Io makes over the earth, vivid accounts of storms, of the underworld, and of tremors of the earth, etc., all vividly portraying a primeval state.

And the victims of Zeus, the one riveted to the crag, the other driven about over the earth, are brought on the stage in a scene that even today overcomes the reader with amazement and fills him with a sacred awe. Prometheus, mighty and great, knows the past and the future; Io, on the other hand, moves unsteadily amid an inchoate world of intuitions and in the end falls into a muddled delirium.

The real guilt of Prometheus is that, although he knew better, he nevertheless helped Zeus in his rebellion against Cronus, as his mother Themis also did. Then he befriended the race of man which Zeus had decided to destroy, and this act provoked the spiteful wrath of the ungrateful Zeus. But the Titan knew a secret that gave him power over Zeus, namely, the frightful consequences of a possible marriage between Zeus and Thetis.

The public knew this, too, because in Pindar's *Isthmia* VII Themis blurts out the whole story, for the gods and men are mutually dependent on each other and Moera rules over both. To what extent these themes derive from Aeschylus is something we should like to know.

Of the secondary characters, Cratus with his sneering tone toward Hephaestus, and Hermes with his caustically bitter words against Prometheus particularly impress the reader. All the others speak to Prometheus with a certain tactful deference. Zeus is in high dudgeon against them all and extremely powerful to boot. Prometheus remains insolent toward everybody, even toward the minor Oceanids as at the departure of Io, though they remain faithful to him to the end where, in a sublime and lucid strophe, he draws a picture of the gigantic processes of nature as he sinks out of sight.

In *Agamemnon*, Aeschylus made use of one of those metaphysical devices, as Manzoni did in *Promessi Sposi* with Fra Cristoforo and Federigo. Even Shakespeare was unable or unwilling to use the supernatural implied in the ghost of Hamlet's father or in the witches and ghosts of *Macbeth* as the pivot of a whole play, as Aeschylus did with Cassandra by turning the supernatural into something sacred. After the whole first part of the play has overflowed with evil memories and dismal premonitions, Cassandra makes her appearance as personified prophecy and ties the whole piece together; the spectators in Aeschylus' day still believed sufficiently in Cassandra to be deeply moved. In her grandiose manner she describes the characters of Agamemnon, Clytemnestra, and Aegisthus by animal similes, and as a clairvoyant looking through the walls of the palace she foretells what is about to happen, knowing the past from the banqueting of Thyestes onward as well as the future vengeance to be wreaked on Aegisthus and Clytemnestra, her last sole comfort as she goes toward the palace and says: *Enough of life!*

While the poet did not intend to conceal the evil that Agamemnon did, he regarded him as personally innocent nevertheless and as expiating the blood guilt of his forebears. But he presented Clytemnestra as the acme of abhorrence and duplicity without ever raising the question whether we can endure the spectacle. To him she must have seemed just as he presented her: raving in scornful triumph over Cassandra.

And withal she is not free but a tool, and knows it. *The terrible spirit of vengeance* (Alastor) *of the evil host Atreus has clothed itself with my powers,* she says, *and executed Agamemnon, requiting the lives of the children of Thyestes with the life of this man.* In the end she would gladly give her wealth and power if only the curse of alternating murders were transferred to some other house.

But now Aegisthus comes in and gloats over the vengeance that has struck down the son of Atreus, who had slaughtered his half brothers and fed them to Thyestes, their father and his. After a heated dialogue between Aegisthus and the chorus, interrupted by a mollifying speech by Clytemnestra counseling that no more blood be spilled, the people return to their homes. She adds that what she and Aegisthus did they did under the lash of necessity, struck by the wrath of the daemon. After another exchange of invectives between Aegisthus and the chorus, Clytemnestra concludes: *And now we rule!*

With the reminder that Aeschylus described with the same simplicity the great god Apollo of the *Eumenides,* the protector of the city in Eteocles, and the defender of the nation in Darius, we shall now turn to Sophocles. He was a poet who set out, as far as possible, from psychological and human premises having perennial validity and effectiveness.

Furthermore, Sophocles developed his characters and situations to the uttermost and exhausted them to the fullest so that his dramas present completely coherent truth. The ancient world marveled at his character creations, sometimes, as his *Vita* says, accomplished by a mere *hemistich.* The main character was emotionally exploited to the full. To do this, he shortened the part of the chorus and made the tritagonist (third character) indispensable, thus providing for a confidant where needed, or for a contrast to the protagonist, like Chrysothemis in *Electra* and Ismene in *Antigone.*

Characters like Ajax, Philoctetes, and Electra are very richly endowed. Whereas Orestes is the main character in Aeschylus' *Libation Bearers,* Socrates cast Electra in the main role and let her clandestinely save Orestes after Clytemnestra has turned him out. Antigone is a sheer product of the creative imagination to whom in Euripides only Iphigenia (*Iphigenia in Aulis*) fairly compares.

Particularly powerful is Oedipus in *Oedipus at Colonus,* whose counterpart in modern literature might be Calderon's *El Príncipe constante*. Oedipus starts with a plain expression of misery and keeps heightening his lamentations as each of his daughters and Creon and Polynices enter, until finally a sublime sense of consolation comes over him and a preternatural discernment enables him to lead the way.

This treatment of the myth is fraught with danger: as Sophocles makes the mythical element give way to general human qualities and consistently accentuates their inner truth, a conflict arises with the raw, old, static theme of the myths. This conflict becomes perceptible in the slaughter of the animals in *Ajax,* but particularly in the story of Nessus in the *Trachiniae* and already in the prologue where Deianira tells of Achelous, the river god, wooing her in his baroque transformations. In *Antigone* an incongruity exists between the primitive motif of killing a person for performing funeral rites over the body of a brother and the psychological subtlety of the narrative.

In Sophocles, fate is so intertwined with character and action that to the spectators it appears as inevitable, not because they know the myth by heart but because it is a part of the inner nature of things. As indicated above, the only exception is *Philoctetes,* which psychologically defies the ending prescribed by the myth: Neoptolemus, in contrast to Odysseus, is so touched by the sufferings of Philoctetes that he is ready to take him home. Then Herakles appears as a *deus ex machina,* the only instance of this device in Sophocles, to proclaim the laws of destiny.

Sophocles was probably attracted to this subject as to Ajax by its pathological content. He exploited these sufferings to the full, achieving a climax in the breakthrough of compassion in Neoptolemus. Sophocles was more interested in exhausting this aspect than in a harmonious conclusion.

Euripides, too, exploited the sufferings of some of his characters almost in a Sophoclean manner, Medea and Hecuba for example, though Hecuba's gentle pleading and her subsequent shocking vengeance are hard to reconcile. But *Iphigenia in Tauris* and *Iphigenia in Aulis* are fine and lovely pieces in which the pure and noble heart of a maiden finds a way out of great difficulties created by the contentious passions of men. The free and firm decision Iphigenia makes to sacrifice herself has rightly been called divinely inspired.

Theonoe in *Hecuba* is a similar figure. The chaste and saintly Hippolytus is a rather peculiar young man who is perhaps the more intriguing on the stage because so few in Athens were like him. Ion for that matter is a similar figure. The counterpart of these good characters are the depraved, the crazed and atrocious women, Phaedra and Creusa, in addition to Medea. Hermione in *Andromache* has also a monstrous streak in her character, revealed especially in her dialogue with Andromache, where we are not sure but that she may be right in the Greek view of things.

Orestes and Electra
Interior of a drinking cup

Euripides liked to let women be the source of passionate deeds and of boldly laid plans for the fulfillment of which men are useful. In his later years he produced the *Bacchae* with the splendid figure of Dionysus treading the boards in this his last, glorious tragedy.

In discussing Euripides' treatment of his materials we saw that he liked to alter them somewhat highhandedly; he also permitted himself considerable freedom in the delineation of character. In itself this would have been all right. However, he did it out of subservience to the Athenian tendency toward realistic variety in preference to the purely mythic view and out of subservience to popular sentimentality and practical rhetoric.

Sophocles characterized the realism of Euripides by observing that, whereas he himself presented human beings as they ought to be, Euripides presented them as they are. Unhappily, Euripides depreciated his characters by making them inwardly worse than their external appearance would suggest. Not only did he make skinflints out of Ixion and Bellerophon, a common wench out of Helen, a silly ass out of Menelaus, a malefactor out of Orestes, etc., but he brought on stage episodes of everyday life that were rather shabby, for example, in *Electra* he married the heroine to a peasant, and in *Hippolytus* he had the chorus report in all solemnity that a washer-woman had talked Phaedra out of her passion.

Hence Aristophanes perpetually harped on Euripides' failure to respect ideality in general. And, indeed, he does have something akin to German painting of the fifteenth century: rather repulsively realistic characters drawn against a fairly golden background of tragedy. Whereas Sophocles dealt with the character as a whole, Euripides at times exploited the feelings of the character to the utmost detail, going even into material aspects, as in the scene of the *Phoenissae* where Jocasta welcomes Polynices with a lugubrious catalogue of woes she has endured in exile.

Telephus, wounded by Achilles, he brought on stage dressed in rags so as to arouse compassion, and in like manner also a number of kings, a device Aristophanes ridiculed in *The Acharnians*. He made his women noble and affectionate as often as he made them horrible, and he brought even children on stage to arouse sympathy, having a man behind the scenes chant words for a child on stage. Euripides did not succeed in evoking sympathy out of the inner depths; otherwise he could hardly have been as crude as he was in *Orestes*, which is only a chaos of egotistic passions.

For Euripides the myth was often only a background against which to present personages of his own time to orate in impassioned situations. At times his plays seem only a rostrum to air contemporary Athenian reflections on matters human and divine. As suggested above, he preferred to forgo contemporary events but compensated by discussing political interests of the day. He was especially fond of imitating the rationalistic methods of the Sophists, particularly Anaxagoras. Of his philosophical pieces one was named *Sage Melanippe*, as distinguished from *Melanippe Bound*, and Helen's apology to Menelaus in the *Troades*, a paradigm of bold sophistry.

There is a genuine Euripidean touch in the way Eteocles and Polynices plead at length before Jocasta and she in turn recapitulates and refutes their arguments. The poet might have been especially proud of this episode, which escaped Aeschylus in his *Seven Against Thebes*. Euripides betrayed his speculative bent even in the poesy criminal Polymestor who, after describing the gruesome manner in which the Trojan women blinded him and killed his sons, could not resist making a concluding generalization about women for which Agamemnon takes him to task.

Jocasta's tirade in the *Phoenissae* referred to above is full of sententious pronouncements. It is quite likely that it was because of this characteristic that Socrates preferred Euripides to the other poets. For he must have sensed that he had here a potential device for making philosophical thought accessible to the masses.

It was precisely this speculative element in Euripides which appealed to later periods, including the Byzantine. When the chorus had disappeared and the dramas were no longer staged but used merely as models of declamations, the sense for the dramatic having been lost, the sententious dramas must necessarily have been regarded as the best.

Euripides attached to his characters certain qualities which we must term purely arbitrary. The reconciliation of Ion and Creusa (a woman believing she has the right to do anything), brought about by the discovery and recognition of certain signs, strikes us as rather nugatory because in the course of time the characters have lost so much interest that we hardly care whether or not they will ever be happy again.

One of the worst dramatic violations was to suspend a character by madness not growing out of his own inner development but sent by some wrathful divinity. An instance of the legitimate use of madness we find in *King Lear* where Lear the madman, Edgar simulating madness, and the court fool are juxtaposed in sharp contrast.

If Athena had not crazed Ajax in Sophocles' tragedy, the leaders of the Achaean hosts would have killed him treacherously anyway to get Achilles' weapons; still, Ajax' madness is meant to show how a vehement heroic character turned into a frightful monster, a transformation necessitated by his whole nature. Conversely, in *Hercules Furens* the madness motif is altogether specious, however grandiose it is to have Iris introduce Lyssa, the specter of Madness.

Here, at the very pinnacle of his labors, having fulfilled his duties and even saved the lives of his loved ones, Hercules is changed into a madman at Hera's behest and turns murderously on those he has just saved, only to come to reason again and deepest sorrow. Euripides minutely depicted the pathological symptoms of this action: how Hercules shook his head, rolled his eyes, moaned and bellowed. The obvious exploitation of pathos at the end is somewhat shocking, as when Hercules desires to see his dead children once more and embraces "his" father Amphitryon, the status of whose fatherhood is very ambivalent throughout the play.

Amid all this, Euripides enjoyed a mounting popularity among the Greeks, a result not at all disappointing to his expectations because he had steadily hoped to achieve it, despite his earlier failures to win prizes. The fascination Euripides exercised on his contemporaries is indicated in a story Plutarch tells of the victorious Siceleots, how they avidly shared small passages of his plays they had learned from captured Athenians, many of whom they supposedly spared for the sake of their knowledge. (Plut. *Nicias*, 29 ff.)

Euripides may owe his later reputation chiefly to the splendor of his language, apparently having applied to art the language of the most cultivated circles in Athens, which is more lucid and intelligible to us than that of his forerunners. But it is also most significant that he has safely weathered the attacks Aristophanes made on him in his *Acharnians, Thesmophoriazusae,* and *Frogs.* Aristophanes especially satirized the rampant realism of that time but not sustained by the Attic theater; he further charged that Euripides did not create his characters out of inspiration but had pieced them together out of the gossip of the times and the shreds and snippets of the current culture.

Aeschylus [as a character] in *The Frogs,* in contrast to Euripides, presented a kind of wild magnificence. He declares that the task of the poet is to ennoble mankind and that by leaving a generation inspired by heroic sentiments he fulfilled his task better than Euripides did. In spite of all the apparent respect accorded to Aeschylus, Aristophanes would surely have treated him quite differently if he had been alive.

It is hard to believe that comedy, making it its business to ridicule tragedy, was not at least in part responsible for the decline of tragedy. Comedy, with its scorn, also presumed to school the people better than the pathos of tragedy could. This decline and ruin of tragedy is perfectly obvious after the fourth century, and we should profit by examining the reasons for it as far as we can.

The practice of staging tetralogies at the Lenaeas and Greater Dionysias continued, and the abiding popularity of plays by the three great tragedians is well attested. There were always a goodly number of tragedians of ephemeral fame. Prominent among them were the descendants and relatives of the great tragedians like Sophocles, the grandchild of his illustrious namesake, who first competed in 396, winning twelve prizes in his career; also Astydamas, the great-grandson of Aeschylus' sister, who is said to have composed 240 plays and to have won fifteen prizes. However, none of these poets were truly great; hence they were quoted so little that they might as well never have existed. There was probably a good reason why nothing survived after 400 B.C.

The chief reason may be that this species of drama could be exhausted relatively quickly. Through all its days ancient drama was subject to the inherent limitations of having to confine itself to universal and public events because staging a play was such a gigantic undertaking, requiring such a great expenditure of effort, such a sumptuous outlay, and the attending to such a multiplicity of details that the drama had to be relevant to the whole community. It could not convert itself into an exhibition for the wealthy, the highly cultivated, or those with special moods and interests, i.e., it could not resolve itself into a specialized genre more modest in its material demands yet poetically still of exceptional merit. This drama was limited in the type it could produce, and once it began to deteriorate there was no halting it. For the whole setting of tragedy with all its requisites was so grandiose that once the soul no longer fully animated the body everything threatened to topple.

In order to remain universal, tragedy could no more discard the myths than comedy could its buffoonery and shallow intrigues. All historical events would have been too local, too temporal, and somewhat unintelligible in other cities; the Greeks had taken a fling at historical tragedies and rejected them once and for all.

The myths themselves were not inexhaustible, and Euripides had already used up a major part of what could be used. An impasse had been growing which could only lead to decline: the opposition on the one hand between psychological and dramatic refinement, beginning with Sophocles and Euripides, and on the other the crude and harsh events in the myths, often hardly amenable to dramatic development.

The absence of first-class poets also tended to undermine tragedy. Those who came to the aid of tragedy were mostly ambitious dilettantes. Aristophanes' *Frogs* suggests that a rapid increase in dilettantism was taking place; when Herakles asks whether after Euripides Athens no longer has any lads composing tragedies, Dionysus replies that she has thousands who can outbabble Euripides by miles. In *The Birds* a philistine boasts in a barber shop that his son has a talent for tragedy as others have for rhetoric.

Sometimes parents dedicated their sons to tragedy in their childhood. These plodders probably attached themselves to Euripides as the most recent great influence available even though he had anticipated them in so much. In their hands, in Plato's judgment, marvelous and sublime tragedy catered merely to the pleasure of the spectators by presenting sensual delights and omitting the useful lessons of hardship.

The agonistic character of the drama deteriorated to the point where the true office of the judge ceased. In the old Hellenic view it was the office of the judge to pronounce impartial judgment as an expert regardless of the cheers or boos of the spectators. Earlier Greek drama was rated by judges unswayed by popular applause, but later the Sicilian and Italian custom obtained whereby the spectators pronounced judgment by raising their hands. This practice of awarding prizes by public approval no doubt became increasingly more doubtful and ambiguous.

To provide new material, late tragedy must have relied heavily on the exploitation of erotic motifs, though stylistically it must have been largely given to casuistic sophistry. Euripides had given vogue to casuistic dispute in dialogue or longer speeches; Agathon is said to have been fond of antitheses in the manner of Gorgias and to have made them the staple of his style.

Now the stage was taken over completely by oratory, and the plots of dramas were arranged to provide opportunities for set speeches.

In the fourth century rhetoric paved the way for tragedy on more than one occasion. Severe critics, like Plato in his *Gorgias,* found that if melody, rhythm, and the poetic meters were removed, only prose would be left but this would have sufficed for the masses: in the theater the poets played the part of orators. And finally, even among later writers of tragedies, this rhetorical element was not inexhaustible; anyway, in the mastery of this art Euripides had no peer.

In time all the world could afford the enjoyment of dramatic art. During the fourth century in Attica—and who knows where else—traveling troupes performed tragedies at the Smaller or Rustic Dionysia in the *demes;* this we learn from the oration *On the Crown,* especially in section 262, where Demosthenes chaffs Aeschines for his shabby life as a strolling player. During the fourth and third centuries the Greeks must have erected numerous theaters, though we have barely an idea what was played in them.

At the time of Aristotle stardom among the actors gave them a higher social standing than that accorded the poets. Polos, during the time of Demosthenes, exemplified the kind of tricks an actor could resort to for effect by bringing on stage while playing the title role in Sophocles' *Electra,* not an empty vase purportedly containing the bones of Orestes but an urn actually containing the bones of his son, who had recently died, and lamenting loudly and earnestly over them. This story speaks for itself; one would like to know whether this whole macabre business was not spread by rumor all over Athens before the performance.

In time a single actor was playing a whole tragedy. When no traveling troupes were available a single actor had to do this to give outlying cities a notion of tragedy, and of course he had no chorus trained to sing the Attic odes. The single actor was reciting the several dialogue roles consecutively, and almost certainly he sang the monodies, since it is known that audiences were eager for them, especially those by Euripides, and choruses were almost certainly not available.

In pantomimes, i.e., in excerpts giving only the bare outline of a tragedy, an actor was mimicking all possible roles to musical accompaniment. The actor who boasted to Demosthenes that he could earn a talent in two days on the stage might have been a mime.

8. *The Old Comedy*

Aping the serious side of life for humorous effect must be as old a practice as the serious moments themselves, and clownishly burlesquing the events of everyday life must have been one of the earliest means the individual had of triumphing over others.

The comic element in Greek poetry is genuinely old. Apart from the antics of jesters and burlesquers, it had long been present in epic and lyric poetry as a distinct trait. We need only call to mind Homer's Thersites, Polyphemus, and Irus and the old custom of parody as well as the poetry of Archilochus elevating the lampoon to a species of poetry the form and content of which must have greatly influenced comedy.

But neither the antics of jesters and burlesquers nor the urge of one polis to mock at another would have given rise to comedy if the Dionysus cult had not provided the appropriate occasion. Comedy could arise only in competing with tragedy in the same theaters, in performing for the whole polis, and in making use of a ready chorus—and thus only could it develop into the gigantic public buffoonery achieving sublimity while representing the ignoble and the ludicrous.

The Smaller or Rustic Dionysias, festivals marking the close of the vintage season, were intimately associated with the rise of comedy. The principal part of this comedy was the *comus,* a lusty revelry devoted to drinking, dancing, and singing. During the carousal period of the *comus,* men and women were wont to exchange clothes. This festival included a procession in which men masked and crowned with flowers and herbs carried a phallus to the accompaniment of a special song, a custom of which we get a notion from Dicaeopolis in Aristophanes' *Acharnians* when he makes a truce with the Spartans and returns home to participate in the Rustic Dionysia. After the special song the crowd of people jeered at the first person they happened to meet.

Ancient lyrical comedy of this sort is supposed to have survived later in many places alongside of fully developed comedy. Somehow masked characters carrying on a dialogue and making dramatic gestures developed out of, or attached themselves to, these mirthful doings. But comedy long remained *an obscure pastime of unbridled country folk, not dramatized by any poet or sponsored by any archon.*

There is a fairly well-confirmed tradition that comedy first took shape in Megara, noted for its wit and passion for drollery. But Aristophanes suggested that this Megarian comedy was content with stringing together coarse, ludicrous episodes; it was more a ribald farce, akin to that of the burlesquers, which was vulgar instead of comic. There was a connection between bawdy farce and the Sicilian comedy of Epicharmus caricaturing the gods and certain social classes, to which we shall return later.

Whatever its origin, it is certain that without Athens and the large theater the old comedy would not have existed; there comedy took on a new purpose and significance. The main question for us is: When did the archon make the chorus and the spacious theater available? Probably around the beginning of the fifth century. It seems it was during this period that the oldest writers of Attic comedy of whom we have any record appeared. In a fragment, Ecphantides boasts that he deviated from the Megarian form. And the course charted by the early comic poets was followed by the illustrious line of comic poets during and after the Periclean age: Cratinus, who died in 410 in extreme old age; Telecleides; Hermippus, whose fine fragment portraying preparation for war Athenians preserved; Eupolis, who began in 429 and continued until toward the end of the war; Aristophanes, who wrote under a pseudonym from 427 to 424 and then under his own name till 388; Phrynicus after 429, Plato 427 to 391; Pherecrates; Leucon; and finally, by way of transition to middle comedy: Diocles; Phylillius; Sannyrion; Strattis; and Theopompus.

A great deal of information about these poets has come down to us, and the plays of Aristophanes, the only ones that have been preserved, enable us to surmise many details about their works, though the restoration of a lost comedy from a title and a few fragments is not only harder than restoring a tragedy, where the established myth may be of help, but is in most instances absolutely impossible.

Comedy, as we know it from Aristophanes, had in common with tragedy the stage and the orchestra; the three, occasionally four, masked characters; and finally the practice of competing for prizes. The dress of the actors in comedy differed considerably from the dress in tragedy, the former having been thoroughly baroque. In place of the *cothurnus*, the *sokkus* was in vogue because in comedy the actor had to be nimble. Sometimes the masks were made to resemble recognizable persons, though the maskmaker was afraid to make a portrait mask of Cleon for Aristophanes' *Knights*.

Comedies were not performed as tetralogies but as single plays. The chorus contained twenty-four members, twice as many as the Aeschylean chorus; it danced the wild and indecent *cordax* instead of the solemn *emmelia* of tragedy. This chorus sometimes divided itself into contending halves and performed so that the spectators could surmise strange adventures and imagine the human figures taking on the shapes of the animals they represented.

Aristophanes had choruses of wasps, birds, and clouds, and other poets had choruses composed, according to their titles, of goats, griffins, ants, nightingales, bees, centaurs, sirens, or airy spirits. This art of personifying impersonal objects indicates that the chorus enjoyed a freedom not found in the poesy of any other nation; it was a totally new element.

Comedy had an immense wealth of metrical variety. The dialogue was mostly in loose iambic trimeters but also in longer verses cast in both iambs and trochees and in the famous anapaestic tetrameters. The *parodos* and *stasima* were far less important parts in comedy than in tragedy, serving mostly to demarcate the scenes.

On the other hand, during a main intermission in comedy, the chorus came forward once or even twice to deliver a *parabasis,* a choric element not found in tragedy but implicitly important in comedy. The *parabasis* accompanied the movement of the chorus which stood at first before the altar, facing the stage, and then turned about and faced the spectators.

The chorus began the *parabasis* with a song in anapaests or trochees, then recited the main body of the *parabasis* chiefly in anapaests, ending in a coda of shorter verses to be spoken in one breath, presenting the personal views of the poet on poetry, politics, and other matters. This recital constituted the *parabasis* in the narrower sense.

Sometimes we find a second *parabasis* attaching to the first, giving the main message; the chorus chanted a song, usually in praise of divinity, then as a rule sixteen trochaic verses containing a humorous charge against the polis and its people, the *epirrhema,* and finally repeated the *epirrhema* and lyrical strophe as the antistrophe.

The *parabasis* is unique in the history of poesy. When the poetry of other nations, as in the thirteenth century or in the Renaissance, discussed literary themes or the relation of the poet to his audience, it did so in a separate poem or at the beginning of a canto, an epic, and the like; otherwise a poet would at most indulge in an occasional jibe or witticism. The Greeks went further even in their choral lyrics. The poet spoke from and to the chorus and was too easily tempted to speak on behalf of himself, though limiting himself to a few phrases or verses, without causing a break in the continuity.

But in the *parabasis* the poet removed the comic mask to converse leisurely with the spectators, telling about his own personal concerns in the anapaests and then, after a brief address to the divinity, giving advice on political and other affairs in the lyrical strophes and *epirrhemas.* The aesthetic effect can be argued pro and con; perhaps it served a purpose to interrupt the comedy from time to time by an extravagance.

The *parabasis* included: a) purely personal concerns between the poet and the audience, self-praise and comic boasting even in connection with the great king, what he as a poet was and wanted to do, and what he in general had accomplished for comedy, reproaches heaped on the public for discarding its aging poets and harangues addressed to the judges; b) whole tirades of slander directed at private citizens; c) exhortations, mostly of a political character, addressed directly to the public without any bearing on the rest of the play; d) the chorus speaking in the *parabasis* behind its own mask while the poet was speaking alternately in his own name. In other words, the comic chorus being one of the most supple creations poesy ever produced, was everything imaginable and changed its mood and meaning to fit any and all circumstances.

Now and then the chorus was made up of members of some social standing, as in the *Thesmophoriazusae,* the *Ecclesiazusae,* and the *Lysistrata,* three plays dominated by women. On the other hand, Aristophanes was pretty hazy as to whom *The Clouds* represented; he himself occasionally asked who they were. In *The Frogs,* he took great liberties with the chorus made up of initiates who appear to be only part of the population in the grotesquely foreshortened hereafter. They were blessed souls of the dead who were initiated somewhere while on earth, i.e., the natural and inevitable chorus in the hereafter. But then the poet turned the chorus into a jolly host of Bacchic revelers and finally into whatever he pleased.

The festive precedents of the whole Attic drama, the ineluctable ideality of the choric element, of the music and the whole surroundings, and finally the natural reaction to caricature enabled Aristophanes to introduce now and again passages occasioned exclusively by his sense of beauty. This explains how the old comedy of the Greeks could at any moment break into an ideal style, which is a feat beyond the powers of our ordinary stage plays and our comedies.

We ask ourselves what impression it made when the chorus comprised only clownish personnel. In *The Clouds,* a magnificent tone sweeps through the beginning of the anapaestic tetrameter where Socrates invokes the air, the ether, and the venerable goddesses, the clouds, be they on Olympus, at the ocean, or gathering waves of the Nile in golden vases, to hearken to his prayer and accept his offering. Then followed the lovely choral ode of the clouds rising from the sea, moving over Greece, and surveying Attica; then, after a filthy interruption Strepsiades could not suppress, they proceeded to give a companion piece to the celebrated description of Colonus in *Oedipus at Colonus.*

To be sure, the shapes of the clouds were not comic but resembled those of mortal women; in the meantime, however, Socrates had defined them as the patronesses of trickery, fraud, boasting, and lies, and even so he had them utter sublime verses. As a matter of fact, Aristophanes may have given vent to his great poetic genius at any point.

Very beautiful also is, in his *Birds,* the proclamation of the hoopoe to his wife the nightingale, whose melodies were to press aloft to the throne of Zeus, while Phoebus as well as the rest of the gods were to join in the lament. Here poetry suddenly soars up to the Olympus that has just been ridiculed. Though Eirene, Opera, and Theorie, the three allegorical figures in *Peace,* are represented by elegant wenches, they are still meant to be ideal.

Without doubt the second half of *Peace* was largely calculated to rest on these lovely mute creatures.

We shall just mention in passing that in Aristophanes the gods have to submit to the most impudent treatment.

The action in Aristophanes is usually simple and direct and proceeds without a hitch, as does the founding of the city in *The Birds*. Little retarding comic episodes may be found there but no counterplots, no main and subordinate plots crisscrossing each other.

Though Aristophanes slandered Euripides for excesses, he exceeded him in his passion for litigation and forensic proceedings. Not all his speeches for prosecution and defense are as remarkably fair as are the just and unjust speeches in *The Clouds*. The long-winded speeches by the sausage-seller and the Paphlagonian, composing a goodly part of *The Knights*, strike us as tedious, as does also the dog trial in *The Wasps*. The trial between Aeschylus and Euripides in *The Frogs* is somewhat long, though there is more action in *The Frogs*, at least in the first part, than in the others.

Even without much action a lot of variety was introduced by having characters in different masks appear successively on the stage and take their cues from the main actors. Thus in *The Birds*, in addition to the heralds, messengers, and slaves, there appeared one after another a priest, a poet, a soothsayer, a geometer, an inspector, a dealer in decrees, and later a parricide, Cinesias a dithyrambic poet, and a sycophant.

The Acharnians hinges on a single motif in which Dicaepolis has three samples of peace sent to him, doubtless in bottles, of five, ten, and thirty years duration, and choosing the last, he enjoys it together with his people. All other action occurs around the market place to which the Megarian, the Boeotian, the informer, the husbandman, and Lamachus repair; the royal ambassadors, Pseudartabas and the Thracian had already appeared in the opening scene.

The Wasps is similarly constructed; various dramas made use of a soothsayer and a sycophant. Aristophanes played so loose with the unity of time that he had to bridge the lapse of time with a choral ode or, in later works, with a dance. In *The Acharnians*, Lamachus, who had just gone out to war, is brought back wounded after an interval of only fifty verses, and in *Plutus* the whole action in the temple of Aesculapius, which Cario reports immediately afterward, has to be thought of as taking place during the interlude between verses 626 and 627.

On the other hand, there is an appealing turn in *The Knights*, where the two slaves steal the oracle from the sleeping Paphlagonian and learn that he is to be succeeded by a sausage-seller, and are able in the next moment to give a fiery welcome to a sausage-seller who just happens to walk by.

In the *Peace*, the dung beetle which Trygaeus uses to soar aloft is a parody on Pegasus Bellerophon rides up into the sky in a Euripides drama. For that matter, in one of Aesop's fables a dung beetle had already flown up to the gods. The mortar in which War personified wants to pound the cities to a pulp, the two missing pestles Brasidas and Cleon, recently killed in action, and the Goddess of Peace tossed into a pit with stones on her, are palpable allegory, proverb, and picturesque folk speech which, however, require a firm hand and a sound controlling intelligence.

We remember the following quixotic paraphernalia: the gigantic compass and ruler with which the geometrician Meton wants to survey the aerial city in *The Birds,* the two ballot boxes (urns) the dealer in decrees carries in with him, the parasol Peisthetaerus is asked to hold over Prometheus, and the thinking hut of Socrates in *The Clouds.*

An inexhaustible treasure trove, always available for action and character, was Hades, the setting of *The Frogs.* In his *Golden Race,* Eupolis had the shades of Solon, Miltiades, and Aristides discuss Cleon's management of the Peloponnesian War. The passage preserving this information informs us that rhetoricians, in treating of conversation among the shades, called it "phantom poetry."

As to characterization, the main personages were caricatures in the original sense of being surcharged and exaggerated, just as their costumes, farcically conceived and fantastically concocted, had no resemblance to anything in real life. These characters were not meant to be probable, or types, like those of the newer comedy, but simply buffoons, often quite individual, at times even ideal buffoons. Only the subordinate figures, merely representing an occupation or function, were presented realistically: the landlady, the sycophant, the soothsayer, and above all the slaves.

The Frogs has something quite unique, namely, the personification of poor theatrical taste. A derogatory abstract quality is personified in a concrete person, Dionysus, whose divine attributes are in no way challenged. Aristophanes simply let the god of theater stand for the disposition of the public to be entranced by its Euripides and to quote him on every occasion. Therefore, with Aristophanes as with Rabelais, we must beware of too precise identification, as if this or that personality were always the same one. Farce has large prerogatives and glides into all sorts of postures, shapes, and relations.

Figures in farce are not only perpetually metamorphosing but may at any moment speak and act realistically in their ostensible original capacity: Dicaepolis and Trygaeus as landlords, Cario and Xanthus as slaves, Strepsiades as a wretched philistine, Dionysus as a god. The poet must be able to treat his characters as he pleases if he is to achieve his artistic goal: to put Athens into a grotesquely comic mood and at the same time to judge it.

The finest and best characterization of the Athenians is supplied by Peisthetaerus and Euelpides of *The Birds*: the former personifies the boastfulness of the Athenians who are, however, able to deal with any situation and to improvise the most astounding kinds of existence. One need but observe the rabble-rousing harangue in *The Birds* to understand the extent to which demagoguery once dominated and was to dominate again in Nephelococcygia.

This harangue exploits every possibility of the situation and shows how self-assured the Greek was in other, more real-life situations. Every clever Athenian could recognize himself and his ilk in this aggressive and shamelessly grotesque insistence on one's legal rights. Euelpides is his goodnatured, credulous companion who chatters steadily, recounting his little woes; though he is completely loyal to Athens, he joins Peisthetaerus in boasting even against the gods.

In all his individual utterances hyperbole is used as an essential means to achieve comic effect, even when it is a matter of portraying someone absent like the great king in *The Acharnians*. It takes eleven years for an embassy to travel to this great king and return. It reaches his residence in the fourth year, but he has gone with his military forces to the mountain range of gold to perform a royal defecation. Parody, i.e., mimicking a serious or tragic passage in a trivial or comic context, implies literary criticism and turns the speaker into a caricature, as happens to the pawnbroker in *The Clouds*. The whole caricatured existence of comedy in turn tends to produce comic sallies.

Other periods of history have left satiric self-portraits but none so grandiose and concrete as that of Aristophanes' comedy. Such sublime buffoonery accompanying an inner and outer crisis like that of the Peloponnesian War is unique in history. It was no doubt an unusual period of maddened frenzy. Athens developed gradually its immense riches of political arrangements, civil and judicial forms, culture and customs; everything was *a priori* agonistic in concept, arranged for outstripping and surpassing competitors.

This agonistic aspect took on an increasingly public form; hence the conflict between superstition and atheism, between the dominion over an empire and the crisis overtaking it, finally ending in a life-and-death struggle on the high seas, between genius and lunacy interlaced with each other. Still, a great number of significant and even great individuals developed in these circumstances: the greatest artists, poets, philosophers—Thucydides, Alcibiades—all this in the midst of pestilence, hunger, and war.

To collect all these myriad facets into the focus of a huge concave mirror was the task of comedy. Poetry had been accustomed to realism, i.e., to seize upon the external details, since the days of Archilochus; and comedy seized upon details large and small, aided by a colossal fantasy which magnified them into grotesque reality. At the same time, comedy possessed a wealth of splendid art modes and ideal components. It was able to mingle rapture and ridicule.

And there was an Athens that enjoyed placing its eyes at the focus of this mirror. Whereas the French Revolution would have lopped off the head of anyone who cast the slightest doubt on the value of its passionate enthusiasms or dared to portray them as grotesque, Athens lived her mad life, desiring to know how she appeared in the eyes of her great poets and allowing them a high degree of independence in their views, often no doubt minority views. At the same time, these comic poets were also balanced against the tragedians and spurred on by competition with them.

During the war, Aristophanes espoused the cause of peace. But whether it was wise to come out so strongly for peace, as he did in *The Acharnians*, in the spring of 425 B.C. before a favorable peace could have been negotiated, is debatable. The continuation of the war was by no means due to Cleon alone, and in Lamachus Aristophanes derides one of the most capable and devoted soldiers of Athens. Fundamentally Dicaepolis is just a vulgar philistine, motivated purely by the comforts and enjoyments of peace without any notion of the higher blessings.

In *Peace*, negotiations for peace are carried on and concluded and peace celebrated, and at the same time a popular view of the causes and progress of the war is put into the mouth of Mercury.

In *Lysistrata*, the poet fell into his former error, for at that time the Spartans were in Decelium, allied with the Persians, and without the slightest reason to sue for peace as the messenger does in this play. Since only the most unfavorable peace could have been arranged at that time, *Lysistrata* was politically as inopportune as could possibly be.

We need not interpret these views on the part of the poet as a wish to secede; his peace sermons always carried away a majority of the spectators. It must also be noted that in his accounts of events leading up to the war, as in *The Acharnians*, he did something no modern playwright could do in wartime: blame his own Athens as sharing in the war guilt. But he cleverly managed to plead for the good Athenians as opposed to the bad ones who sought wealth by trading with the Megarians.

Even if the poet's yearnings for peace are of doubtful value, still his sounding the alarm in *The Knights*, in 424 B.C., at the dangers besetting democracy, is a truly imposing warning. The Paphlagonian servant who has his lord Demos fully in his power is Cleon, but the sausage-seller outwits and outsharps him: a true picture of the democratic process of replacing bad leaders with worse.

As long as they could, comic poets like Aristophanes, Eupolis, and others, opposed the demagogues, a stand with which the majority of the spectators probably sympathized. The feud Aristophanes waged with Cleon took real courage and also entailed consequences for the poet. Cleon had already complained to the council about *The Babylonians,* one of Aristophanes' first plays, for allegedly exposing Athens to ridicule at the Great Dionysia in the presence of foreign ambassadors, though actually for blows dealt him in the play; then, after his complaints to the council remained fruitless, Cleon had the theater police give Aristophanes a sound thrashing after the staging of *The Knights,* admittedly strongly partisan, though the poet evened the score in the secondary *parabasis* of *The Wasps.*

The Birds is of the highest beauty. Performed in 415 B.C., this play avoids the anxious subjects of the times, the mutilation of the Hermae and the Sicilian expedition, in order to develop in Peisthetaerus a more general image of the Athenian especially as a colonizer and empire builder. As to his political views expressed in later plays, particular interest attaches to the compliment which Aeschylus is made to pay Alcibiades in *The Frogs.*

The *Ecclesiazusae* comically portrays Athenian democracy as feeble and feckless and roundly thwacks the political utopias of the philosophers.

We shall not try to determine the degree to which comedy served the welfare of the state, or in what way its massive personal invective tended to turn able minds from public life and state offices, a phenomenon so characteristic of the following century. The Athenians had to choose and wanted their comedy as it was, being entertained by it in a wonderfully ingenious manner. Not until the fourth century did the demos forbid personal masks.

Since Aristophanes indulged in so much filth, what shall we think of him as a man? It seems well to regard him as neither a pillar of society nor a worker of iniquity. Nor will he ever be made into a saint, either.

Aristophanes leveled the merciless thrusts of his wit particularly at the theater, the other comic poets and tragedians, and also the dithyrambic poets; indeed, he condemned their admirers to the central pool of the underworld, individual actors along with the spectators. He frequently quoted from the tragedians with comic transmogrification. Without the *scholiasts* the point of view of many of these would be lost on us; even so, we are often left to surmise their topicality. The best instance of this sort of spoofing is in *The Birds* where the rhymester indulges in Pindaric solemnity and is finally driven to beg in this style.

Precisely this literary criticism, however invaluable in revealing the degree of interest and participation in poetry, is one of the weak aspects of comedy. It is an infallible sign that poesy is beginning to decay when it takes to literary criticism and draws its life from it, for poetry cannot long continue on this fare. It was a stroke of good fortune for Aristophanes that he had such a royal victim as Euripides to pluck limb from limb, but he could no more dethrone him than he could Cleon. That so much clever ridicule could not turn Athens from Euripides attests to the independence of Athenian taste.

In *The Frogs,* the agon between Aeschylus and Euripides remains on a high level as long as they limit their mutual accusations to generalities, but it sinks to bathos beginning with verse 1119 where Euripides starts to criticize the individual openings of the tragedies of Aeschylus, who later repays him tit for tat. After they have parodied one another's manner in the choruses and monodies, one is amused by the rather puny conceit of fetching a pair of scales and letting the two tragedians spout their verses into respective pans.

Since Dionysus still hesitates to render a decision, Pluto comes in to force him to, and only after the poets have given their opinions on Alcibiades and political questions does Dionysus take Aeschylus and leave Euripides sitting there. Finally their merit is decided not on their poetic excellence but on their attitude on partisan political questions, Aeschylus having voted for Alcibiades, Euripides against.

When Dionysus summons Euripides to engage in the agon with Aeschylus, Aristophanes gives a very fine reason for leaving Sophocles out of it; in fact, Sophocles, who honors Aeschylus in this play, is treated with dignity even though in *Peace* he is said to be so stingy he would put to sea on a hurdle for an *obolus.* Aristophanes attacks Euripides mercilessly from every side, and in addition to the literary criticism he evinces so much venom in slandering Euripides on private affairs that one is tempted to regard Aristophanes as guilty of mean envy.

There is no extenuation for this personal abuse of Euripides, and also of Agathon, in the *Thesmophoriazusae,* where parody is compounded with denunciation. Aristophanes' moral indignation at Euripides is simply preposterous.

As for the ridicule Aristophanes heaped on Socrates in *The Clouds,* the fact remains that, despite the good-fellowship between them in Plato's *Symposium,* Socrates in his *Apology* named *The Clouds* and its writer specifically among the causes of his ruin, and indeed those who accuse him of searching into things above the earth and making the worse appear the better cause constitute the earlier and more dangerous accusers. He says to the judges: *Those who hear a man spoken about in this fashion will believe that he is an atheist. . . . These accusers established your prejudice when you were boys.*

The last drama of Aristophanes is *Plutos,* a most graceful piece. Save for a single antiphonal section it has no choral parts—the *Ecclesiazusae* already had no *parabasis*—and hence in its form it is no longer to be counted with the old comedy, though it is not typical therefore of the middle comedy. We have here a masterly dramatization of the conflict between Plutos and Penia (Wealth and Poverty), with man's complex egotisms. This drama does not deal with Athens, the polis, or with a moment of its development, but with the world at large and with a universal moral problem.

9. The Middle Comedy

The so-called middle comedy flourished roughly from 380 to 330 B.C., its chief practitioners being Eubulus, Anaxandridas, Alexis, and Antiphanes. It revived the custom of mocking at certain social classes, an ancient comic motif thrust into the background by the overpowering political preoccupations of Athens that had shaped the old comedy. During the middle period, the Megarian element appears to have come to the fore again, ribald farce to have joined with a comic treatment of divinities and amorous episodes so as to form a substratum.

Earlier we spoke of Megarian farce. It is supposed to have cultivated the art of ludicrously aping certain occupations and social classes, for instance the occupation of the family cook. Epicharmus, a generation older than Aristophanes and dwelling mostly with Hiero at Syracuse, is supposed to have developed the comic potentialities of this Megarian farce. He poked fun at the foolish and ridiculous behavior of the common people, making his comic characters peasants, drunkards, or social parasites. His comedies included philosophical reflections, not only moral but also metaphysical. Just how these reflective passages fitted into his plays remains an enigma.

His plays drew heavily on the myths, moving the whole world of gods and heroes to a rather lower sphere. They pictured the gods from the stolid and priggish point of view of the common man, stressing the most vulgar instincts and urges. They portrayed a gluttonous Herakles, a wedding feast of the gods, a banquet at which Hera and Hephaestus quarrel and are conducted by Dionysus back to Olympus, inebriated. In short, he was as disrespectful to the gods as Aristophanes was in *The Birds*.

The transition from Sicilian comedy, with its ridicule of social classes and its jesting at the expense of the gods, to middle Attic comedy was accomplished much more easily than that from the old Attic comedy to middle comedy. Uncongenial developments were sapping the vitality of the old comedy. Aristophanes' scoffing at the state, its representatives and crises had become impossible; the people were too exhausted and wretched to bear up under the caricature which may be fitly applied only to great subjects. Besides, many able people had grown weary of politics.

Although a state decree mentioned at various times was in force against the use of personal masks, it did not stop the practice of venting personal malice by ridiculing people under their own names, or of satirizing entire social classes. In addition to these, all sorts of victims of city gossip, chiefly philosophers, orators, tragic and epic poets, also foreign rulers, were made a laughingstock in comedy, and once a comic poet began satirizing some individual, others chimed in.

Middle comedy has no definite trace of the chorus and consequently no *parabasis*. In the later plays of Aristophanes, the word "chorus" wherever found between the scenes without a choral ode of any sort merely indicates an interlude by a flute player or a short dance. Comedies were still performed at the Dionysus festivals, but in view of the large output of comedies, in all probability the performances had to take place at intervals in between these festivals. It is likely that the production of comedies was turning into a business.

It seems that comedy, in its search for new material, found it in stories of love and seduction. Anaxandridas was allegedly the first to exploit these themes; on the other hand, the assertion persists that Aristophanes in *Cocalus,* one of his lost late plays, had employed abduction and subsequent recognition and other motifs common in Menander. Middle comedy exploited erotic motifs in plays not dealing farcically with the gods, and even sometimes if they did; it differed from the new comedy by more frequently parodying literature, satirizing social classes, and utilizing mythological themes.

To judge by the titles, middle comedy must have indulged heavily in a subject frankly dubious in itself, even without Aristophanes, namely, that of burlesquing the gods. The *Amphitryon* of Plautus is the only play that gives us some adequate idea of this comedy. If this play is really an imitation, then the original may well have had many pleasant comic scenes, like the one where Hermes, by virtue of his omniscience, bemuses Sosias about his own identity and then, by sharing some of his mysterious knowledge, convinces him that he, Hermes, is Sosias.

The rest is simply offensive, especially the shameless bewildering of Alcmene, in consequence of which she sleeps with two men and sorrowfully protests against having done so. She refuses to admit—she cannot admit—that she is guilty of this act, while the howling rabble knows that it is true.

Though the titles may suggest more than the plays contain, many piquant titles suggesting considerable Athenian realism indicate that the

Silenus with a bacchante
Interior of a drinking cup

newer comedy excelled the old in satirizing social classes. Fragments preserve rather charming genre pictures like the one Athenaeus preserved from the *Olynthians* by Alexis, wherein a beggar woman tells that they are five: her husband, the beggar; herself, the old woman; a daughter; a younger son; and the buxom one, probably a daughter she wants to prostitute; and how they alternately go hungry and grow more and more wretched. The main value of such passages is that they give us insight into cultural history.

Colorful boasting was also found as when a fellow describes the perils he and his table companions were exposed to: *Our dinners consist of sharpened swords, our salads are burning torches, and for dessert our servant brings us Cretan daggers, etc.* Gross exaggeration, however, no longer played the large role it once did in the old comedy. In passing, we may mention that, according to the many examples in Athenaeus, a favorite device of these poets was to have their characters pose riddles and answer them without any perceptible connection with the main action of the comedies, it being merely a kind of wit the Athenians fancied.

These comic poets enjoyed parodying the tragedians, but above all they enjoyed travestying the philosophers. Epicrates of Ambracia presented a scene in Plato's academy wherein the whole student body wrangle over the question whether a pumpkin is grass, an herb, or a tree, until a Sicilian physician ridicules them for it. When they become angry, Plato calmly counsels them to meditate further upon the matter.

In Antiphanes occurs a taunting tirade at the Sophists in the Lyceum, i.e., the Peripatetics, for their distinction between being and becoming, which sounds like a parody on the logical expositions of Hegel. Furthermore, various fragments of Antiphanes and of Alexis gibe at the paltry life of the Pythagoreans who did not enjoy wine or anything animate but would eat a dog that had been killed and was therefore inanimate.

They seem to have left the Cynics in peace, perhaps because they feared their viciously sharp tongues. At any rate, the ridicule leveled at philosophy shows how important philosophy had become in Athenian life; moreover, it no longer paid to satirize the state, and since the philosophers in their treatises railed at each other more witheringly than the comic poets did, we really cannot feel very sorry for them.

It is fortunate that the middle comedy as well as the old and the new appear never to have attacked the visual arts; Scopas and Praxiteles had the good luck to be ignored by them, perhaps in part because they dwelt permanently in Athens.

Over against all these things the oddly important place occupied by the cook, eating and good living as a whole, is exceedingly significant. Because the poets could take this taste preference for granted in their audience, they talked so unconscionably much about eating and drinking. We have numerous quotations of this kind from Eubulus, Alexis, Antiphanes, and Anaxandridas, i.e., from the most respected comic poets of their period. Anaxandridas, for instance, portrays the half barbarous and grotesque banquet served when Iphicrates married the daughter of Cotys, king of the Thracians. Alexis tells about a glutton who burst like a storm upon the market and bought up all the fish as soon as they were for sale in the stalls.

The comic dramatists also made game of Misgolas whom Aeschines, the orator, described as always having about him youthful harp players both male and female. In his *Aesop*, Alexis told a story, perhaps handed down from the past, of a discussion between Aesop and Solon in which Solon said that innkeepers watered their wine not to make money but to keep their patrons from suffering headaches.

Epicharmus, the ancestor of middle comedy, also provided the most important precedent for it, namely, the parasite who now became a stock figure. Alexis created Chaerephon, a parasite who hunted up free meals at whatever exertion. Whenever a dealer in cooking utensils rented a pot, Chaerephon was right there to inquire who was preparing a banquet, so that he might crowd in first, even going as far as Corinth to sponge a meal. Antiphanes even wrote a comedy entitled *The Parasite*.

A *prestissimo* in Mnesimachus gives us a spate of words which a cook has his slave deliver to young men taking riding lessons in the agora, to entice them to his local inn. Sixty different foods were enumerated, and this whole speech was to be rattled off in one breath, a task more strenuous than any corresponding tour de force in Aristophanes. From the literary point of view one must admit that these excerpts contain a lot of good comic material.

10. *The New Comedy*

Middle comedy gave way to the new comedy about 330 B.C., which next to the bucolic poetry of Theocritus, is the final artistic achievement of Greece and is graced by such illustrious names as Menander, Philemon, Diphilus, Poseidippus, and Apollonius of Carystus.

The creator of the new comedy, or at least the poet who more than any other held the entire later antiquity spellbound, the author of 105 plays, was Menander of Athens, the nephew of Alexis, a student of Theophrastus, and a friend of Epicurus and of Demetrius Phalereus. Though he had won only eight victories because Philemon was more popular in tone, he did not succumb to the blandishments of Ptolemy Lagus who tried to lure him to Alexandria. He died at fifty-two in Athens where he had enjoyed *gentle and refined pleasures in moderation* as Epicurus had recommended, though these included his living with *hetaerae,* specifically the soulful Glycera and the high-spirited Thais.

The magnificent statue of Menander seated, now in the Vatican, portrays him as a somewhat middle-class though exceedingly intelligent person, a man whose external good nature concealed a sly roguishness within.

The numerous fragments of Menander and especially the Roman imitations give us a much better notion of the new than we have of the middle comedy. Plautus and Terence knew this kind of comedy not as texts perused in a study but as a living tradition. To be sure, the Romans dealt freely with the originals, not shrinking from combining two plays into one.

From the Roman imitations we know that, as a rule, the scenery in the new comedy presented a rather long street lined with houses where the characters in the play lived, with occasional public buildings, shrines, etc., between them. The costumes corresponded to those worn every day by the various social classes. Though masks could have been discarded to get the advantage of facial expression, they were retained, for in essence the new comedy did not strive for individual characterization but for the typical.

The only step the new comedy took toward individualization was to increase the number of the different types of masks. On the whole, these were comically grotesque, only those for women being at times charming. The chorus was completely eliminated. Flute players and dancers made up the interludes. The lines were probably delivered in a loud and rumbling tone as in tragedy.

The setting of these plays was mostly in Athens of the Diadochi. Even after Chaeronea and after the Lamic War Athens remained rich and politically not impotent, though it no longer displayed the glorious spirit of past generations, having turned in part to the philosophers and rhetoricians and in part to the enjoyment of private life.

Even though its scene was Athens and the association of ideas evoked thereby is gratefully acknowledged, the new comedy did not concern itself with this specific Athens but with universal human themes. Athens' national, political, and religious interests were resolved into a philosophy of live and let live. Comedy made use of the various social classes as well as the several professions and trades, especially in drawing the secondary figures of the parasite and above all the cook, who now really came into his own.

The new comedy continued to jeer at the philosophers and to parody tragedy, a subject it could gradually have laid aside. Occasionally, by way of reviving a motif of the old comedy, it indulged in personal invective. The central emphasis of this comedy, as it has been among all nations under similar circumstances, was on flirtation and love affairs. The soul of the play consisted now of intrigue and suspense, of tying the knot and unraveling it within the scope of probability.

The burden of the play was carried by those members of the play whose characters determined the action and who, through their complete lifelikeness, were meant to arouse the interest of the spectators in relatively even balance for and against the central theme. The satirizing of social classes was now secondary compared with the artistic development of this intrigue.

To judge by Plautus and Terence, the stage presented only a limited section of life, characters, and possible combinations of intrigue appropriate to them. The females were monotonously uniform and quite insipid for want of a more sensitive emotional life; they were merely *hetaerae*, now gentle and congenial, now sly, base and greedy, though these latter qualities were no great drawback.

In addition, there was the strumpet, the slave of a procurer. If a lover bought her freedom, such a woman could become a *hetaera* and could also get a husband. To get married she only had to prove that she was born free but was carried away into slavery; the ransom covered the moral incongruence so that the *hetaera* could achieve marriage, probably her goal.

Stingy fathers wanted to break up the relations between their sons and the *hetaerae* but succumbed to temptation themselves, and so rivalry between father and son was a fairly common theme. Parents and older people enjoyed little respect in those days, mostly because they did not respect themselves. These characters, as well as the youthful lovers, were rather stereotyped; profound character analysis such as found in Theophrastus would be too much to expect.

The main character and generally the promoter of the intrigue was a slave who, thanks to the general laxity of morals, had managed to assume a position of no mean importance. He spanned the moral spectrum from the good at one end to the bad at the other, now benevolent and kindly, now selfish and egotistical, always recognizable by two qualities: his wealth of useful information and his effrontery, i.e., vanity at his being in control of the outcome.

The new comedy took over the device of two slaves of two gentlemen. They carry on intrigues, serve as confidants, and imitate on a vulgar level the doings of their masters. We shall also mention the officer who is not a citizen but a homeless, semibarbarian mercenary. He is the "great warrior," with a parasite of vastly superior intelligence, and is always gotten the better of by any cunning slave. He also excmplified the continuation of social satire found in the middle comedy.

The new comedy tried to outdo the middle comedy in satirizing both the cook, whom we meet in all kinds of variations, and the whole business of cooking and dining. We learn to know the haughty cook who preens himself on his scientific culinary knowledge and on being a student of Epicurus, declaring that all cooks are ignoramuses except himself and two colleagues who still perpetuate the art as taught by Sicon, the master chef. Sicon was thoroughly versed in nature and taught his apprentices astrology, architecture, and strategy.

A cultivated cook made his culinary art the mother of all culture. Another posed as the cook of the new school whose founder discarded sharp spices, which Cronus himself had used, in order to spare his guests the embarrassment of tears, sneezing, and drooling. He knew how to cook for youthful revelers, toll collectors, aged people, or any others. He had developed practical physiognomy to be able to spot good patrons.

Other cooks talked in a purely mythological style, or on the least occasion would spout poetry. A gentleman complained that the cook he had hired talked in Homeric idiom only. That cooks were arrogant toward poor patrons was as natural as that a boastful master chef whom one hired with his whole kitchen crew terrified everybody with his insolent conduct.

In this new comedy everything was in the hands of chance. These playwrights rather frequently used the device of recognition between adults who had been lost, kidnaped, or exposed in childhood and sold as slaves or threatened with this fate. They also overworked the theme of mistaken identity and allowed base deception and vulgar subjects to pass as comic. It is an open question whether the principle of *ridendo castigat mores* [ridicule chastens morals] was operative in these plays. At best they might have taught people to shun folly.

Whereas Euripides had members of his cast recite his prologues, Menander had allegorical introductory figures do it. Menander resembled Euripides not so much in his characterizations as in his complication of incidents, sententious expressions, and philosophical reflections. Many of his aphorisms have been preserved because they are among the most elegant general reflections ever made about life.

Menander's diction and mode of expression have the graceful, even temper of the cultivated mind without any burlesque; whenever Plautus indulged in burlesque, he borrowed it from Epicharmus or made it up himself. In antiquity the elegance of Menander's style was universally recognized.

Though the Attic spirit and sense of form were further refined in later drama, still we must acknowledge that the old comedy and tragedy of Athens are unique, unequaled, and irreplaceable by anything else under the sun, or by anything since created by mankind. The new comedy, on the other hand, could be duplicated in every literature; it is merely a matter of sprightly art, moderate observation of life, and detachment from serious national concerns.

11. *Alexandrian Comedy and Farce*

The history of the theater in Athens is obscure. We know that playwrights there tried to produce every species of drama, including the satyric. All we know about Alexandrian comedy comes from scattered reports, and these tell only about satire cast in dramatic form and about outright farce. The so-called *gay* tragedy that arose during the time of Ptolemy Lagus belongs in the general category under consideration; it does not seem to have dealt humorously with gods and mythical personages but to have travestied tragic episodes of the myths. Machon of Sicyon is the only surviving name of comic poets who staged their plays in Alexandria. Otherwise it was Athens that set the tone for comedy and that remained its principal center.

In the time of the Diadochi, Dionysiac drama reigned everywhere, at the courts and army camps as well as in cities. Wherever Greeks went and wherever they could afford it they built theaters, and there large troupes of Dionysiac artists, who had their central headquarters in Teos, performed the plays, even though the *choragus* and the agonistic element had disappeared from the theater.

The Dionysiac artists also helped to perpetuate the new comedy, though in time only through their most renowned representatives. Farce may have played a big role too. If in the Orient, from the shores of the Nile to the Tigris and the Indus, any one thing held the Greeks together, it was the theater. Delight in dramatic spectacle was something every Greek was born with, and as drama was the unifying influence among the Greeks, so the Orientals were instinctively fascinated by alluring subject matter, such as mythology and art. The unbridled theatrical impulse may well have been the standard and banner of the widely scattered Greeks.

During the period of the Roman emperors when only the iambic parts of the tragedies were still being performed, it seems that full-fledged comedies were staged at least during the first two centuries, though from the third century on they were dislodged, mainly by pantomimes. In his description of *Paris on Mount Ida* (Metamorphoses, Book X), Apuleius gives us the liveliest impression of the splendor these mimes may have had.

PART IV

ON PHILOSOPHY, SCIENCE,
AND ORATORY

Chapter Twelve

ADVANTAGES AND OBSTACLES

In turning to a discussion of the science and philosophy of the Greeks we shall not attempt to give a history of these subjects, but to present their relation to the Hellenic spirit, beginning with a look at the Near East.

This area was far ahead of the Hellenes in accumulating knowledge. Egypt and Babylon possessed a polymorphic civilization vastly older than that of the Greeks, and when we consider that for ages these countries had been surrounded, threatened, and even invaded by greedy barbarians, like the Hyksos, and had to be constantly on the alert for self-protection, we must admit that we are faced with a colossal achievement.

Here we are concerned with the earliest massive aggregations of human power, and for the first time in history these nations may have made it their purpose to acquire knowledge. Powerful priestly castes were entrusted with this task and by consistent and concentrated exertion succeeded in amassing a truly great amount of material. The Phoenician civilization was the first offshoot of the Middle Eastern and nearest or most accessible to the Greeks.

Not until relatively late did the Greeks manage to organize a state, and then not one but many; hence they found it impossible to develop a caste of scholars or scientists. They possessed, however, a strong "Hellenism" which inhibited all foreign borrowing, and when they did borrow, as from the Phoenicians, they Hellenized their take so that it was hardly recognizable as such.

The peculiarity of their language gave the Greeks a tremendous advantage in the development of science as well as poesy. It appears as though the Greek language had already virtually contained the future of philosophy within itself; it is infinitely pliant to thought and thus became its transparent veil, especially so for philosophical thought. Greek as a language is brilliantly capable of detaching itself from the world of particulars, a language correctly designated as a practical dialectic and for this reason exceedingly creative of philosophical idiom and notations.

As to the assumption that the greatest and most decisive ideas may have originated in Egypt, one ought to consider whether the old Egyptian language was capable of expressing a non-pictorial idea, or of an unimpeded flow of abstract thought. The Semitic languages are far inferior to Greek. To translate Aristotle into Hebrew would certainly be impossible; even the Arabs had no philosophy before they had the Greek models. Only the Asiatic Indians and the Germanic peoples had languages intimately suited to philosophical discourse.

The earliest Greek philosophers—Empedocles, Heraclitus, and others—personified abstractions or gave mythological names to philosophical concepts. But philosophy soon created its own language, partly by defining the meaning of hazy general and intellectual terms abundant in the language and partly by making copious use of the ease with which Greek can form abstract substantives. The Greek language could easily create a compound word—or get along by combining a verb or a noun with a preposition—for expressing a new concept, and could convert neuter adjectives and participles into nouns for designating new elements, principles, etc.

Moreover, Greek had gerundives available, and its verbs provided an endless wealth of designations and nuances of all kinds for expressing qualified and unqualified concepts. Further, it had the capacity of nuancing the meaning of verbs by turning infinitives and other language elements into nouns merely by adding an article. This plastic facility entailed the temptation for philosophy to content itself with abstractions and neuter nouns, on the supposition that it had thereby already understood the facts and had mastered the principles.

The Greek language used the same word (*kakon*) for ugly and for evil; it had no definite word for self-confidence, but in spite of these and other shortcomings one must admit that Greek was not simply a philosophical instrument one gradually acquired but embodied philosophy as it did conversation capable of the most delicate intellectual shadings. The Greeks were able to distinguish and designate parts and wholes, the particular and the general, without in the course of the process sanctifying words or worshiping them as ossified entities. Sharply defined terminology did not bear enslavement as a corollary.

Whenever a philosopher and his school developed a technical style, another would set up a school next to him and develop his own new mode of thought and expression; here, too, the agon prevailed.

However the Greeks may have analyzed particulars in the world of the intellect, they always managed to find a vivid expression for it. The Greeks could easily change over from particulars to generals and from generals to particulars. Consequently, they could view the whole process of thinking and of thought as detached observers and develop logic and dialectics; in turn oratory and sophistry gave the Greeks their eloquence.

In addition to their language, the Greeks had uncommonly fine philosophical endowments; not this or that degree of accomplishment marked the Greeks but their capacity for coming to grips with any and all kinds of intellectual problems. Moreover, the inherent weaknesses of their religion were conducive to their philosophy. This proclivity for rigorous rationalization may arise in the presence of a strong religion as in India and Islam but then only as a heresy in a limited group. Since no restraining force or organization obtained in Greece, philosophical thought could proliferate at will.

The absence of an all-powerful priesthood that might have merged religion and philosophy into a rigid system was of paramount importance and decisive for the Greeks, as was also the fact that religion did not foster a priestly caste which, as the guardian of faith and knowledge, might have pre-empted the purlieus of thought. The Greek philosopher was neither dependent on any social grouping nor was he limited to any official class or required to meet any specified standard of education which might have imposed itself upon his thought.

From the very beginning, philosophers emerged from the most diverse surroundings, being acknowledged as wise men according to a kind of self-evident consensus. It was really the nation as a whole that determined the philosophical status, and since intellectual activity was accessible to all and sundry, not only to the free-born but also to the slaves and Hellenized barbarians, the community of thinkers was quite large. In fact, anyone who had access to philosophy could take part in it. Celebrated philosophers were in demand as teachers everywhere, and instead of combining into castes they set up competing schools.

But with all its advantages, philosophy was heavily handicapped from the very outset by the myths. After the Greeks had naïvely lived through that period which later seemed to them heroic, the myths persisted as the glorification of that age, in enduring serenity. This refulgent body of ideas hovered like a vision over the nation, which felt that it was the rightful heir of these past glories as it fancied them.

For some time, these romantic ideas supplanted rational philosophy with a strongly pronounced philosophy of living; they supplanted knowledge by assuming its primal form, containing within themselves all nature, the lore of the earth and history, as well as religion and cosmogony in a marvelously symbolic raiment.

Held and preserved by a stabilizing form which was the most glorious poesy, these myths constituted the romantic youth of the Greeks. They lived on wherever Hellenes dwelt, and even among barbarians, as long as the ancient world endured, even if at the end only as a science, a collection, or a comparative study. Their lasting expression may be found in art and poesy where they keep on sending up new shoots. Interpreted, allegorized, and intellectually refuted, this body of myths, rival and deadly enemy of philosophy that it was, nevertheless endured. And yet it had to be overthrown if thought and knowledge were to thrive freely. This break with the myths took place only gradually and was never fully accomplished.

Chapter Thirteen

THE BREAK WITH THE MYTHS

If we look at the personages who first gave rise to a world of thought which was independent of the myths without, however, setting them aside, we find that before philosophy came into being in Ionia, the garments of wisdom were woven of maxims (gnomic utterances), and seven famous men were celebrated for their labor at this loom. Thales, Pittacus, Bias, and Solon are included in all the rosters; the other three are variously given as Cleobulus of Lindos, the Spartan Cheilo, Pherecydes, Anacharsis, even Epimenides, and others. Later, when the Greeks could not stand the idea of a sententious tyrant, they replaced Periander of Corinth, the Greek Solomon, with Myson, an obscure Spartan.

The wisdom of these seven men showed itself predominantly in statesmanship. In the opinion of Herodotus, only Thales went beyond practical considerations; he was likewise the founder of Ionian philosophy. Herodotus said further that Thales had predicted an eclipse of the sun and had divided the Halys River into two channels, which made him a sort of wizard. The other six were called wise because of their political acumen.

The Greeks conceived of these seven wise men as semilegendary types. Although their life span spread over a period of a hundred years, myth-making fancy could assemble all seven of them at Delphi or at a symposium given by Periander in Corinth. The stature of their reputation is well indicated by the mythical story of the golden tripod fished out of the sea which, according to a Pythian oracle, was to be given to the wisest man, not the most pious. Beginning with Thales or Bias, it made the round of all seven, though none would retain it. Finally it was dedicated to the Delphian or Ismenian Apollo.

The sayings attributed to these seven wise men were recorded in gold letters on the walls of the temple at Delphi. We should like to know when, how, and by whom this audacious piece of propaganda was perpetrated. Their surviving aphorisms are contained in several collections; among them are not only gnomic sayings but also sententious answers (*apophthegmata*) and anecdotes. There are also short proverbs, mostly of an ethical nature, the most important being a number of laconically brief and obscure ones, not always flattering in tone or content. Here we find the saying: *The majority is evil.*

The gnomic element is, of course, much older, being plentifully represented in Hesiod's *Works and Days*. The Spartans with their laconic expressions remained on the gnomic level. Here the Greeks met with the Orient which, excepting India, never passed beyond the gnomic level, i.e., beyond individual ethical insight, and at all events, not beyond the parable. Out of all this ethics as a system could not be developed.

Parallel with the seven wise men and occasionally showing a kindred spirit, marched a line of men difficult to subsume under one predicate, but perhaps "eccentric saints" will do. As indicated above, the exceptional speculative capacity of the Greeks was preconditioned among other things by the slender metaphysical tenability and the countless inconsistencies of the popular religion, which was obviously inadequate to account for the world, too weak to coerce mankind to accept its explanations, and could never lead to any ethical precepts.

This Greek religion had not fallen prey, as a number of Oriental ones had, to a subverting priesthood. The processes that produced the system of the Brahmans, of Zarathustra, of Moses, etc., were impossible in Greece, or at least they were never accomplished. Hence any highly endowed individual could evolve religious ideas and clothe them in mythical imagery so that they could become part and parcel of the popular religion.

Indeed, it was more difficult than we suppose to discard the myths which for a long time had been the sole mode of expressing anything and everything. The men to accomplish this task were the Apollonian men whom we mythologize on our own and then perceive as rivals of philosophy just coming into existence. They diffuse a marvelous splendor by their rigorous regimen (*askesis*), their inspired mood, their purification ceremonies, offering to suffering Hellas the hope of atonement, partly by miraculous deeds and partly by their doctrine of metempsychosis. Tradition turned these men into supernaturally endowed creatures of fantasy and so into mythical figures able to leave their bodies at will.

In addition to individuals like Epimenides of Crete, Aristeas of Proconnesus, and Pherecydes of Syros, who had held the most disparate views, there were not only Apollonian but Dionysian Orphics forming for the first time a grouping or sect exploiting a mood, as may be inferred from those named above. Along with their vegetarianism, asceticism, and belief in metempsychosis, these Orphics had a literature erroneously joined with the name of Orpheus; they evolved their own cosmogony and assured men a blessed state hereafter through purificatory rites.

Their vegetarianism may have derived in part from their belief in reincarnation. They felt that their most important mission was to call the Greeks to repentance, to regard the body as a tomb of the soul, and to strive for liberation from the cycle of births; for them life really began only after the escape from this mortal coil. At any rate, Orphism strove to be a new and special religion. How far its specific content was disseminated is unknown.

The shimmer of myth veiling Epimenides and other men like him envelops the great Pythagoras in a haze so thick that it prevents our seeing this historical figure with any degree of accuracy. Marvelous tales about Pythagoras derive from relatively old sources. An ancient writing, allegedly from his own hand, told of a trip he had made into Hades and asserted likewise that he could remember four previous incarnations in which he had borne the names of Aethalidas, Euphorbus, Hermothimus, and Pyrrus. He was also credited with the power of bilocation and according to a persistent story was seen on the same day in Metapontum and Crotona.

He must have been born at Samos around 570 B.C. He appeared in Italy around 532 and died in 497, three years before the revolution in Crotona which drove out his followers. That he journeyed to Egypt would also seem to be true. Such a journey was not a particularly adventurous undertaking during the time of the twenty-sixth dynasty when Naucratis still existed there as a Greek city. Still, gaining the confidence of that most genuine Egyptian, the priest, must have been beset with considerable difficulty.

The passage in Herodotus telling us that the so-called Orphics and followers of Bacchus were really Egyptians and Pythagoreans clearly shows that the Pythagorean and Egyptian creeds had somewhat similar elements just as the Orphic and Pythagorean rites were so similar as to be confused. We shall not try to establish whether he reached Babylon or not; there is no good reason to doubt that he did. He must have had some communication with India too, for his doctrine of metempsychosis is far more suggestive of India than of Egypt.

The foremost legacy Pythagoras left to the Greeks was this new religion and the system of ethics based on reincarnation and linked with asceticism. He was less a philosopher than a religious reformer who, at a time when the anguish of existence weighed more heavily on man than before, taught that earthly life was to be endured as a penance for evil deeds committed in previous incarnations and that, after the cessation of this life, man would not lie in the grave like a mute stone as Theognis had thought but, after purification, would be reborn in ever new forms. Only the pious person who was consecrated in secret ceremonies and who throughout his life followed the sacred usages and ascetic practices could finally escape from the cycle of ever repeated births and deaths.

Pythagoras founded a fellowship in order to propagate this hope of immortality. Like the Orphics he, too, regarded the body as a tomb or prison house of the spirit, which was of a higher, heavenly origin. We are not expressly told whether he taught that the spirit, after its transmigrations through many bodies, would achieve extinction as its reward, or whether, as Plato and Empedocles hoped, the spirit would be absorbed into the divinity; its immortality, however, suggests that Pythagoras held the latter view.

Consistent with the view that the spirit was penned in the body *for punishment* was the belief that it had to endure the shades of the prison house until liberated by the divinity, lest it fall into even greater affliction; hence the Pythagoreans developed a dread of suicide and inculcated an attitude of patient long-suffering while awaiting death in old age.

We do not know how the past was mirrored in Pythagoras' mind and what sort of relations and associations beckoned to him there; hence we should not just dogmatically toss out of court without any hearing the account of his four previous lives. The same holds true for the reports of his power over animals. We are told that he had a long conversation with a furry bear, after which it returned to its native woods. A splendid steer with which he had been friendly was cared for at a temple in Tarentum into its extreme old age. An eagle is said to have swooped down out of the sky and let him pet it, etc. Most likely these stories reflect the view that he recognized human souls in animals.

It is uncertain whether Pythagoras adopted his doctrine of metempsychosis from the Orphics, as the ancients believed, or they from him. It may be most relevant to say that metempsychosis took its place among the Greek ideas because there was no one to hinder it. At all events, Pythagoras made such a deep impression with it that wherever the belief in immortality took a new or seemingly new upsurge, the Greeks immediately thought of Pythagoras. For instance, the Getae had a rather peculiar belief in a hereafter, independent of Greek tradition. The Greeks explained that Zamolxis, really a god, had been a slave of Pythagoras and upon returning to his people, had proclaimed to them the belief in a happy state hereafter.

Of the philosophers before Plato, Empedocles of Agrigentum firmly and clearly taught that the soul pre-exists and is punished by migrations through men, animals, and plants. Even though he was not a Pythagorean, a sentence of his reads: *I have been a maid and a boy, a lamb, a bird, and a fish in the sea.*

Of all the things Pythagoras acquired in Egypt, the land of mathematics and especially geometry, the knowledge of mathematics was of the most far-reaching consequence. Linked intimately as it was with his teachings and mathematical as well as musical research, it largely determined that the nature of Pythagorean philosophy would lead to a mathematical and musical conception of the world instead of meandering like Orphism into bogs of monstrous theology.

Now, the theory of numbers developed by the Pythagoreans is, indeed, a controversial subject, and how much of it is to be ascribed to the master is uncertain. But the fact that Pythagoras had made mathematics one of the basic disciplines of his teachings is incontrovertibly established by the testimony of Aristotle who said that the school of Pythagoras antedated Empedocles, Democritus, and others; what was practiced so early must obviously trace its origin to the master himself.

It appears that in the world of numbers Pythagoras purposely mingled different things together. He must have conceived of numbers as analogous to forces and number relations as analogous to thoughts. He must have associated certain thoughts with unity and plurality, with straight and crooked, with the holy number four in relation to the holy number ten $(1 + 2 + 3 + 4 = 10)$ and then suddenly drawn his listeners from these numbers into the sublime. His doctrine had not only a moral but also an aesthetic side: the circle was to him the fairest of figures, the sphere the fairest of solids, and hence he maintained that the earth was a globe, which was a remarkable assertion at a time when the earth was variously described as an ellipse or as a round disk.

Furthermore, he declared that musical notes were numbers and vice versa, thus making numbers the basis of music. Finally, he ascribed geometrical figures to the elements: fire was pyramidal, air icosahedral, etc. Reducing the moral, intellectual, and material world to numbers wrought havoc in Hellenic life. And yet this attitude of mind passed on to later thinkers, and ever since geometry and mathematics have remained the foundations of all science.

But all this served only as the groundwork for his system of the universe (cosmos). Either Pythagoras himself or his school achieved eternal glory by being the first to remove the earth from the center of the universe. Though this school devised the incomprehensible notion of a counter-earth and a central fire, at least this system could lead to an earth turning on its own axis.

To the Pythagorean school falls also the distinction of having been the first to divide the soul into intellect, affect, and reason; animals possessing the first two, only man having also reason. We cannot tell what part of this insight derives from the master and what from the pupils.

Had this system of teaching been pure philosophy, women would have had no part in it and most likely would have been flatly excluded. Instead, we find women, too, in the movement, like Theano, the master's wife, and Damo, his daughter. These took a lively interest in the profoundest scientific problems. The women who soon flocked to this movement succeeded in keeping out all concubines. Unless all appearances are deceptive, the doctrine of the transmigration of souls accounts for the Pythagorean view of the equality of the sexes in the noblest sense. Likewise, the sage may have honored women as the mothers of the future generations.

Insofar as imagination can penetrate the legendary haze surrounding Pythagoras, his personality must have been signally imposing, indeed Apollonian. With his distinguished countenance, wavy locks, and white robe, he would make his appearance, a man altogether majestic in bearing. His whole being radiated friendliness without a touch of moroseness.

First he taught a few, then gathered a larger number about him, and finally there was a whole city that listened to his words. His method revealed careful reflection. The tradition that for the first five years the students did not get to see the master must mean that he employed his more advanced students to instruct the beginners. These students respected the authority of the master above all. If something was introduced with the words "as the master has said," no further proof was needed.

Pythagoras did not read his lectures and was wont to introduce his discourses with the formula: *By the air that I breathe and the water that I drink I will permit no one to dispute my words.* Thereby he wished to indicate that his followers should first of all keep silent, reflect, and strive for inward composure. The statement that he did not divulge his doctrines we have to take in a relative sense. The Pythagorean ethic and doctrine of metempsychosis were taught openly, whereas his scientific system was kept secret, not because Pythagoras regarded knowledge as unfit for mankind but because he thought it was better to exercise caution and to try to spread knowledge gradually, lest willful reaction retard its growth. On this account, the Pythagorean school used a method of instruction necessarily symbolic and solemn.

The teachings of Pythagoras did not deny the existence of the gods, being to that extent orthodox. Still, the traditional religion did not suffice for him because it could not explain the mysteries of the universe, and the gods had difficulty unburdening themselves of the disgrace heaped on them by poesy, especially Homer's *Iliad*. His only recourse was a protest of aversion: he said he had seen Homer and Hesiod among those suffering the direst punishments in Hades. That he held the gods in sincerest esteem is shown by his reverent attitude toward prayer: he said he would never presume to ask the gods for any gifts, leaving such matters completely to their discretion.

A lavish worship of the dead, associated with necromancy, superstition, and spook stories, had hitherto been prevailing at Crotona and Megapontum. Pythagoras, with his doctrine of metempsychosis, might well have come into conflict with this cult and in order to exercise a purifying influence introduced one of his own which was far more dignified than much divine worship in Greece at that time. It may be said that his cult and comprehensive teaching were conducive to metempsychosis.

It would be most important to learn what his new and lofty ethics linked with metempsychosis consisted of. The prohibition of eating flesh does not necessarily imply that he believed a man's soul had to work its way up through animal stages in previous existences, even though in ancient times the practice of vegetarianism had rested on this notion. The Pythagoreans of the fourth century observed a number of abstinences and other usages with a view to a happier lot after death. They also wore a distinctive dress.

The asceticism enjoined on them was far brighter and more cheerful than that of the Orphics; it was to keep the members of the fellowship pure and not to sweeten a tainted conscience as in Orphism. Its purpose was really to promote and preserve a frame of mind that would make man worthy of a higher humanity. Hence those of the inner circle were to refrain from wine, to spare their souls crippling agitation.

The keystone of Pythagorean living was to keep one's word so inviolably as to render the taking of oaths superfluous, a remarkable rule of life at a time when perjury cavorted about on every street.

When Pythagoras traveled about, reports tell us significantly, he was announced as coming to a city not to teach but to heal. He must have radiated widely about him a mystic feeling of inspiration. Living as he did in the Greek society of southern Italy, where wealth and luxurious living were the ideal and the highborn gentlemen lived for war and militarism, for the athletic arena and the state, i.e., for the agonistic way of life in the broadest sense, he despised wealth and warned people against inordinate ambition, for those who pursued glory were destined for enslavement.

His followers took his teachings so to heart that they pooled their possessions and formed a communal group, as men usually do only under the impact of an overpowering religious enthusiasm or some other elated mood. He was not cast into the role of a political reformer until relatively late, a fact reflecting upon the political engagement of a branch of later, more worldly-minded Pythagoreans. The other branch joined the Orphics to form a group of superstitious ascetics. Plato, the oldest witness, states that Pythagoras brought about a peculiar mode of living, thus distinguishing himself specifically from statesmen and lawgivers like Solon and Charondas.

In the meantime, the Pythagoreans became a group deviating in vitally important respects from the rest of the Greeks. One may ask whether a group dedicating itself to such a strange mode of living within a polis would not in time become a political issue itself even though the leader wanted the group to stay completely apolitical. Everything had belonged to the polis; then this man Pythagoras came from Samos and through his activity challenged the sole authority of the state. This would seem to explain the political crisis attending his transfer from Crotona to Megapontum and the bloody persecution of his followers after his apparently peaceful death.

Eternal glory redounds to the school of Pythagoras for being the first free association that engaged at once in religious, ethical, and scientific activities. As a body held together by bonds of loyalty, the Pythagoreans were something different from the Ionians and the Eleatics. We know with what a spirit of self-sacrifice they helped one another, how they undertook long journeys to attend the burial rites of a brother whom they had hardly known personally. We are astonished that the effects of the master's teachings were still fresh two hundred years after his death. Such influence could be exerted only by a personality reflecting a strong religious force.

But now the time had come for Greek thinking to work its way to full independence, the time of philosophy proper in its three epochs, named for physics, ethics and dialectics, although the last two had to carry along and nurse the first.

With physics, i.e., the theory of the universe, philosophy introduced itself in spite of all resistance; this is the break with myth; everybody was curious to know. Gradually, however, the nation discovered within itself, too, the power of general reasoning, and this is where ethics and dialectics came in. But the possibility of philosophy was entirely the result of physics, which, as said before, marked the beginning. Whereas for nearly all other nations religion settled the questions of how and whence the world came into being, the Greeks, as soon as they had discarded their myths and gotten over their cosmogonic stammerings, were free to search for first principles.

For Thales the first principle of all things was *water;* for Anaximander, *apeiron,* the limitless (substance), in the center of which the earth hovered like a sphere; and for Anaximenes, *air,* in which the stars move not over the earth but around it.

Heraclitus of Ephesus belongs with these three Milesians and is by far the most important of the group. Antiquity agreed on his intellectual stature, however obscure it may have found his writings, fragments of which continue to offer new insights. He conceived of the universe as a process of becoming and employed *fire* as the symbol of eternal self-renewal.

He regarded everything as in constant flux (*panta rhei*), and strife as the father of all things. He logically assumed a periodic universal conflagration. Indeed, he originated a number of bold and penetrating thoughts, among them that the senses unaided by reason are untrustworthy. He expressed a profound distaste for Homer and his gods and was the first to turn his back squarely on the polis. He concerned himself with problems of universal knowledge and was a citizen of the world.

With their doctrine that all is One and One is God, and with their definition of being, the Eleatics—Xenophanes, Parmenides, and Zeno—opposed the native Ionians. They were fledgling pantheists and, like Heraclitus, in revolt against traditional religion because they sought to grasp the divine essence in its purity. The Eleatic school, like the Ionic, was completely untrammeled in its intellectual endeavors and research. Indeed, unimpeded thought became the indispensable condition of their intellectual activity. Their private wealth and the simplicity of their way of life made teacher and disciple independent, so that they could devote themselves wholeheartedly to their study and research. Already in those early times a universal agon among the philosophers prevailed.

Whether philosophers discoursed on movement, a material principle, or unity and plurality, or number as the Pythagoreans did, or atoms as Democritus did, all these systems were independent creations and not one was a mere commentary on religion. These physical discoveries and intuitions were the first stirrings of thought and research ever made by free individuals, without any priestly coercion or religious interference.

It was no longer necessary to clothe this knowledge in myth or ritual, even though Empedocles' abstract personifications, like Hate and Love, still had a mythical hue. The Ionians, however, spoke about nature because the time was ripe for such ideas. As the mother of many colonies, rich in knowledge of the world and pulsating with cosmopolitan life and the mode of colonial thought, their native Ionia, freed of all religious constraints, must have spurred the philosophers on to reflect as they did, and matters were much the same wherever the Greeks dwelt.

The earliest Ionians, who according to Aristotle did not at all distinguish any prime mover from what they called primal matter (Anaxagoras with his *nous* [reason] being a great innovation), proceeded without any preconceptions. How independent they were in their assumptions is shown, for instance, by the explanation Anaximander gave for the development of individuals, in teaching, among other theories, a gradual transformation from fish to man.

Indeed, the magnitude of the differences in their results marks the independence of these Ionian minds. This holds true for the three Milesians, whereas Heraclitus cast doubt on the testimony of the senses because both the perceiving object and the perceived were caught in a stream of perpetual flux.

To be sure, if for some political or social reason one wished to ruin a philosopher, one had merely to lodge against him an accusation of impiety, in reality only a pretext for some other animosity nearly always stemming from the influence the philosopher wielded over the statesmen of the particular polis. Thus, the enemies of Pericles proceeded first against Anaxagoras because he taught that the sun was a glowing mass of metal, that the moon was like the earth, that sacrificial portents had natural explanations, and because he interpreted the Homeric myths morally and the names of the gods allegorically. Anaxagoras was imprisoned and sentenced to die but instead was banished from Athens and went to Lampsacus where he died. Still, he introduced the idea of *mind* (*nous*) into philosophic thought, even if only as a kind of primal impulse, leaving the rest to natural history.

Protagoras, who had begun his discourse *On the Gods* with the words *It is due to the gods that I cannot know whether the gods exist,* was banished from Athens in 411 B.C., and his books that he had read in the Lyceum and private homes were gathered and burned. Diagoras fared somewhat worse, partly because he had divulged the Eleusinian mysteries; he fled with a reward of a talent on his head but apparently died in Corinth unmolested. Diogenes of Apollonia, who taught that some day the sea would dry up, had to flee for his life. We shall return to Socrates later on.

Generally there was in Athenian democracy a highly conservative insistence that philosophy must not touch the gods, whereas comedy was allowed to make game of them. After the proposal of Diopeithes was enacted in 432 B.C., making it a criminal offense to disbelieve in the gods or to attempt to explain the universe, investigation into nature could be carried on only in secret.

By and large, however, nothing could prevail against philosophy. Xenophanes had already defended his new conception of divinity, his *all is one,* against the popular anthropomorphic and polytheistic religion with this statement: *If lions could paint and make images as men do, they would fashion their gods in the shape of lions.*

Democritus denied the traditional gods and deduced all events out of necessity, which was essentially no worse than the *fate* of popular belief. He asserted that the goal of life should be a serene soul unshaken by fears and superstition. The atomistic school deriving from him paved the way for the skeptics and Epicureans.

However much people might fill the air of Athens with frivolous babble about scientific matters, as Aristophanes' *Clouds* shows to excess, they could not hurt philosophy. The sycophants were continually endangering the life and property of the upper classes anyway, and since men at that time feared death less than they do today, one did not worry excessively about the accusation of impiety. Moreover, most of the accused ducked the charges of godlessness as well as they could, as Epicurus is well known to have done most charmingly by admitting the existence of the gods but denying their rule of the universe.

With all its independence from the ties of traditional religion philosophy first brought about monotheism, not atheism, and finally attained to religion in Neoplatonism.

The polemics against Homer and Hesiod were almost more telling than those against traditional religion, for these poets were the basic presupposition of all Greek life and culture. Beginning with Pythagoras, the philosophers opposed those two poets in the name of a deeper reverence for the gods, whom the Pythagoreans served with punctilious devotion. Moreover, the Pythagoreans built their ethics on religious foundations, quite as if one could retain the many gods after having abandoned the individual myths.

Whereas Pythagoras was supposed to have seen the torments the poets suffered in Hades, Heraclitus said that Homer as well as Archilochus deserved to be thrust and whipped out of poetry contests, and Xenophanes, who combatted the myths with an almost pantheistic notion, composed elegies and iambic verses against Homer and Hesiod wherein he reproached them for what they had said about the gods.

The treatment Plato accords the poets in *The Republic* is well known. Later scholars purported to detect envy of Homer in Plato, who may have looked askance at the myths because he himself had given up composing tragedies as Socrates had given up carving sculpture.

Thinking Greeks everywhere might have begun to outgrow the myths and could have philosophized ethics and dialectics out of physics [nature], but just then sophistry appeared on the scene. This subject merits study by historians of ancient civilization as a social phenomenon. Here we shall merely allude to its position in Hellenic thought and knowledge.

The Sophists offered stiff competition for the philosophers, for wherever they held forth philosophers were in a bad way. We must, however, venture to oppose the usual preconceptions. The Sophists came to Athens from abroad: Protagoras from Abdera, Gorgias from Leontini, Hippias from Elis, and Prodicus from Ceos. They were exceedingly imposing as they spoke at banquets and festivals, delighting the nation and garnering wealth from their fees. The philosophers could not understand why men who taught for hire should have met with such acclaim. We might explain the phenomenon by noting that the ordinary man prizes more highly something he has to pay for than something he gets free.

They settled in Athens, and most illustrious people, men like Pericles and Thucydides, attended their schools and imbibed their learning, an effect presupposing a cause which can hardly have consisted merely of moral indifference.

The Sophists are supposed to have taught that in and of itself nothing is either good or bad, that these qualities depend upon opinion and social agreement, and that about every subject one may assert a pro and a contra. In religion they were allegedly not skeptics but outright deniers, corrupting the Athenians with all sorts of absurdities. But we doubt that people like the Sophists could have brought about such a widespread change of opinion; at most they merely gave formal expression to a mode of thought long since prevailing.

On the other hand, they strove hard and methodically to perfect the art of oratory, to be sure in connection with their doctrine of the subjectivity of all knowledge, hence making one's views about everything depend on persuasion. Moreover, they were up on current philosophical problems, even though they recognized no real objective knowledge but only subjective conception.

Their dialectics, in which paradoxical propositions borrowed from the Eleatics played a significant role, might well have been intellectual gymnastics, and though their formal education lacked depth, and though they could lay no claim to making men better, they nevertheless enlarged mental skills and understanding, for which people were handsomely grateful.

Hippias could pose as a man of encyclopedic ability inasmuch as he appeared at Olympia in an outfit which he had made himself, including the cutting and polishing of the stone in his signet ring. Their most important service was to bring a mass of positive knowledge to bear on an age possessing few books but craving to learn.

If we transport ourselves back into their period, we shall more readily comprehend that they probably exerted an influence similar to that of the Italian Humanists. They had their astronomy and their system of the universe; they had a knowledge of geometry sufficient to enable them to project maps; they explicated poets, taught music, and mastered grammar; they applied themselves to history, archeology, and the comparative constitutions of the poleis, which laid the groundwork for Aristotle's *Politics;* they delved into jurisprudence and studied household management, state government, and colonial organization. Hippias dealt with the science of mnemonics.

In short, even if the famous challenge of Gorgias, to put to him whatever questions one wished, really implied that he would attempt to answer them by logic rather than by drawing on a fund of all-embracing knowledge, nevertheless the Sophists collected a wealth of information which distinctly benefited Hellas. The Sophists were an integral part of Hellenic life and are not to be underrated as they have been.

Chapter Fourteen

THE ART OF ORATORY

Oratory is an offshoot of Sophistic teachings, a phenomenon we shall examine briefly before turning to the philosophers again. Here, too, we must bear in mind above all the power and pliancy of the Greek language in expressing anything one may wish to tell and convey to others, in sharp contrast, for instance, to the Hebrew of that time, and also the great advantage oratory could derive from the many occasions Greek life provided for speaking in private, in public, and at military gatherings. We have no corresponding parallels today.

To our good fortune, Homer has survived. The speeches of his gods and men have an utterly natural power and beauty, and yet they are conceivable only amid an advanced culture deliberately fostered in a polis. This means that already in Homer's time effective means had been evolved for attaining ends or resolving issues by arguing for or against them, and that such speeches were made under severely agonistic conditions, forcing people to consider what it was that made for persuasive eloquence.

It is important to observe that the art of oratory, having its arena in the popular assembly, was a competition in thinking, knowledge and inventiveness. Philosophers may also have been aware from the very beginning that they were in competition with each other and that they would be well advised to study the art of persuasion as did Aristotle, who devoted much of his precious time to oratory and contributed more than anyone else to the comprehension and interpretation of it.

The best sources available for studying this tremendous field are first of all the extant orations. The most important authorities on the history of the development of ancient oratory are *Brutus* and *De Oratione* by Cicero, who had excellent sources and precise knowledge deriving from his own

Greek education. Of the hundreds of systems of instruction, Aristotle's *Rhetoric* and *Rhetorica ad Alexandrum* fortunately survive. The *Rhetores Graeci,* edited by Walz and Spengel, and the exhaustive treatment by F. Blass in *Die Attische Beredsamkeit* [Attic Eloquence] are to be recommended.

The goal of this artistically elaborated oratory, which had an audience relatively unaccustomed to reading but eager to listen because of frequent participation in the popular assembly and the courts, was to make the plausible appear valid. A precious sentiment of Aristophanes acknowledges that *speech lifts a man and gives his spirit wings.*

An anecdote taken from the life of Antiphon gives the most telling example of the power of speech. He had been banished and was living in Corinth where he set up a "consolation booth" with a sign that he could heal the sad and distressed just by talking to them. When people came to him he listened to their tales of grief and affliction and by his soothing eloquence healed their sorrow.

The systematic and theoretical art of oratory could arise only in connection with the development of the democratic courts affording recurrent opportunities for practicing this art. Ancient reports reliably inform us that this timely posture of events first occurred in Sicily when, after the overthrow of the tyrants, many civil claims which had long been forcibly repressed were reactivated in the courts.

We shall not investigate to what extent the philosopher Empedocles may be regarded as the pioneer of oratory. It is, however, certain that Corax, who had been influential under the tyrant Hiero, was a popular orator and attorney at law before tribunals. In 427 B.C., Gorgias the Sophist, of Leontini, went with an embassy to Athens and there introduced the Sicilian art of oratory based on his philosophy which, as noted above, was negative. Starting with Gorgias, for whom Protagoras with his dialectics had done preliminary work, eloquence for a long period of time was the chief study of the Sophists. Gorgias already called himself a rhetor.

Oratory in Athens must have made rapid progress, though only in Athens, where the statesmen had prepared the soil. It was opportune for oratory that since the Persian Wars, tremendous political activity had taken place and two powerful hegemonies had developed.

Furthermore, the orator Thrasymachus evolved a style suitable for practical speeches by replacing the florid pomposity of Gorgias and the stiff dignity of Antiphon with solid periods and more refined expressions. In the midst of this movement, we find men like Critias and Andocides who were neither Sophists nor creators of a new style but merely practitioners of techniques evolved by others.

Finally Lysias, the second great professional speech writer, went even beyond Thrasymachus and deliberately made use of expressions of everyday life, although he was fully conversant with the periodic style and figurative language. In addition to all these developments, Isocrates managed to evolve a style of his own.

The language of politics soon took on a different character. In contrast to the measured demeanor of Pericles or Antiphon, Cleon raved up and down the rostrum, throwing aside his mantle and clapping himself on the hips. Soon professional orators were active in the popular assembly, readily lending their eloquence to introduction or support of whatever proposals anyone might put forward.

In addition to political oratory, the Attic tribunals contributed in large measure to the development of oratory, as already mentioned. It was decisive for forensic oratory that judgments in Athens were passed not as in oligarchies by an official or a small jury impervious to eloquent persuasion but by a large body of jurors selected from among the people and apt to be swayed by an intellectually superior individual, just as in the popular assembly.

Since the parties involved in private lawsuits had to speak for themselves, and any Athenian could speak as a plaintiff in public court proceedings, and since, moreover, the defendant had to speak in his own defense, any litigant lacking competence could hire a professional speech writer to compose a speech for him and then memorize and deliver it before the court. This may have been the primary motive for writing down speeches.

It can be shown that Antiphon was the first such professional who, though he himself delivered no public addresses and never initiated a lawsuit, was one of the ablest advisers of litigants presenting their cases in court or before the popular assembly. It is distinctly significant that forensic speeches of some city in Greece could be of interest and were collected by the hundreds, whereas all the court proceedings of the ancient Orient are of no moment to us. Here, too, a specific way of life is addressing itself to us.

In addition to speeches made before the tribunals and the popular assembly, there was a third category of the so-called epideictic orations. This name derives from *epideixis,* which means a display of ability applied not to a prescribed but to any subject one may choose. This epideictic category, extremely popular and widespread, had various distinct uses. The Sophists cultivated it as a propaedeutic to practical oratory. Sometimes, as in Lucian's *Praise of a Fly,* a harmless theme without political or forensic bearing was developed so as to exemplify the art of narration, but more often a worthier subject drawn from the Sophists' rich store of knowledge was developed as beautifully as possible.

Gorgias' *Palamedes*, a fine example of Greek forensic oration, belongs in this category. At the outset, Palamedes demonstrates the improbability of his having committed an act of treason by showing that it would have been useless, imbecile, and impossible without complicity. Then he gives an orderly account of his past life and the honors he has received. Finally he appeals to the nobility of the heroes who are his judges and proposes that the state keep him in prison until the truth has been ascertained. In conclusion, he refrains from giving a recapitulation as being appropriate only before lesser judges, saying grandly that no one may suppose that the foremost among the foremost Greeks had not paid attention to him and hence did not bear in mind already the plea addressed to them.

Our first kind of epideictic oratory is a kind of speech actually delivered, particularly the panegyric given at festivals; among its ardent practitioners were the Sophists. Prodicus, a contemporary of Gorgias, recited his well-known *Choice of Herakles,* charging an admission fee.

Besides the panegyrics, funeral orations were quite common. In 352 B.C., a great agon of eulogistic lamentations was held in honor of Mausolus. For the sake of acclaim or personal advancement, teachers of rhetoric, often posing as philosophers of some sect or other, found it expedient to deliver their orations in public.

But already in the fourth century epideictic orations, though on occasion valuable and important, were commonly regarded as literary products designed for reading. To this category belongs the lost speech on concord composed by Antiphon, a statesman and namesake of the Sophist, and the *Olympiacus* by Lysias, although he never recited it at Olympia, and also his funeral oration on the Athenians fallen in the Corinthian War after 394, which may be genuine even though it does not resemble the rest of his speeches.

In addition, occasional speeches actually delivered belong in this epideictic genre. The handbook (*techne*) of Dionysius of Halicarnassus, originating at a later date, establishes rules and principles for this sort of epideictic composition. If there were many who did follow these precepts, one cannot help wondering whether the public in the Greek-speaking part of the Roman Empire did not burst out laughing every time it recognized and saw through these commonplaces in a public address.

One may be in doubt whether the fictional speeches composed by the historians belong to the political or epideictic category. Much of the suppressed and late political oratory took refuge in historical writings. Two capital examples—and these must suffice—are the two speeches made by Nicolaus and Gylippus respectively after the Sicilian victory over the Athenians, as recorded by Diodorus Siculus. It is irrelevant to the issue whether he made them up or stole them.

Rhetoric schools, like that of Isocrates, flourished, offering excellent pay to the teachers. These men steadily received astoundingly large incomes, and were rewarded with personal fame to boot, as is evidenced by numerous commemorative statues, the earliest of which was that of Gorgias.

The multitude of handbooks proves at all events that people took a sustained interest in oratory. For the purpose at hand we shall deal mainly with the principles as formulated in Aristotle's *Rhetoric*. This masterpiece, near perfect in execution, presents the art of oratory down to the minutest particulars. It lists and defines the various categories, explaining what they all have in common. It proceeds to treat arguments, drawing heavily on logic and dialectic; then it takes up the what and the how of a discourse; thereupon the structure of speeches and their various parts; and finally the diction, including the subtlest details of beauty, propriety of language, rhythm of the words, employment of metaphors, figures of speech, etc.

In our brief look at the ten Attic orators included in the canon conceivably established by Pergamum scholars in 127 B.C., we shall begin with Antiphon, already introduced as the earliest professional speech writer. In addition to the speeches already mentioned which served as exercises in school, three are in defense of men on trial for their lives. Among them the speech *On the Murder of Herodes* is especially interesting. Probably delivered around 415, it is the oration that reveals the full range of Antiphon's power. His style shows kinship with that of Thucydides, who, according to Plutarch, had studied under Antiphon, as also had Critias and Alcibiades.

The most important work of Andocides is *On the Mysteries*. Here we get to know the individual present at and deeply implicated in the events under consideration. He is actually supposed to have denounced his own father in a mystery trial in connection with the mutilation of the Hermae, but also to have saved him by stating that he could produce the names of many who had embezzled public funds. In this oration, which is quite an exceptional document, he makes some revealing statements on the crime itself.

Lysias was the greatest of the forensic orators. Though born in Athens, his father was a metic from Syracuse, and so the son remained one in Athens. At fifteen he went to Thuriae, a move that turned out to be decisive for his calling as an orator, for there his teacher was Tisias, a former disciple of Corax. After the Athenian debacle at Syracuse and the defeat of the pro-Athenian democratic party at Thuriae in 412, he returned to Athens, and as a wealthy dilettante and Sophist of the Sicilian school, he devoted himself to the cultivation of epideictic oratory.

As a metic he could not himself appear in the popular assembly. Under the Thirty Tyrants his brother was sentenced to drink hemlock while Lysias himself barely escaped with his life. This catastrophe forced him to earn his livelihood as a speech writer, producing an astonishing number of speeches.

Isocrates studied under Gorgias and Tisias, being particularly influenced by Gorgias. He was also an associate of Socrates. His frail body, weak voice, and especially his timidity kept him from the speaker's rostrum in the Pnyx, obliging him to make his living by writing orations for his disciples and for other readers. As a professional speech writer, he thought himself far superior to his rivals, even though he composed a few forensic speeches he later scorned. In his eyes, his rivals compared to him as doll makers might to Phidias.

He was the most accomplished teacher of oratory; his school was the most successful in Hellas, soon having a hundred pupils from all parts of Greece, each of whom paid a thousand drachmas' tuition fee. In his *Panathenaicus*, published in his twenty-fourth year, he expressly declared that he had forgone all other categories of oratory in order to devote all his speeches to the advancement of Athens and Hellas. No doubt he took this patriotic oratory, in which Gorgias was his predecessor, very seriously.

Taking Isocrates at his word, he was not only an orator but also a philosopher, an eclectic, appropriating items from various schools. To what extent he followed Plato it is hard to determine. In time he began to deviate considerably from all contemporary philosophical modes of thought. His supreme skill in oratory will keep his name alive for ages to come, for as the flowing spell of his words enraptured his contemporaries, so it will future generations, moved in heart and mind by a power hitherto unknown in oratory. Without his creative transformation of Attic style, neither Demosthenes nor Cicero would have been possible. Isocrates lacked the thrust of Demosthenes, nor did he strive for it, yet his was the fairest Hellenic diction one can imagine.

Aeschines, the rival of Demosthenes, occupied a uniquely important position among the Attic orators. In his younger years he was an athlete and an actor; later he fell in with Eubulus and was drawn into politics. As an orator he was essentially self-taught but highly talented, singularly personable, and possessed of a clear voice. Allegedly he was the inventor of impromptu speaking. He set down only the three speeches still extant: one against Timarchus, who is said to have thereupon hanged himself, or in any case was imprisoned and dishonored; one in his own defense against impeachment proceedings initiated by Demosthenes; and one against Ctesiphon, to which Demosthenes replied victoriously with an oration of his own. Since all three of these orations are intertwined with the life and career of Demosthenes, the two rivals share a sort of common fame; at any rate, Aeschines enjoys the immense advantage of having left to posterity in his orations materially important historical testimony to one of the most critical periods in the history of Athens. He was a master of creative composition fascinating the reader with its charm.

And now Demosthenes, whose achievements reach the apex of sublimity in ancient oratory. In his youth he had to contend with crooked guardians and so developed an early interest in jurisprudence and rhetoric. Subsequently he became a student of Isaeus, who instructed him in court procedure, civil law, and the art of oratory. He had extraordinary talent but also congenital debilities: inability to pronounce the letter *R*, a twitching of the shoulders, and the like, most of which he overcame by strenuous and sustained exertion. Anecdotes about his self-discipline are probably legendary, like those that proliferate over the centuries about any famous personality.

Demosthenes studied the writings of Isocrates, although he never attended his school; nor did he attend the academy of Plato, probably because the schools of rhetoric and philosophy had nothing to do with each other, being bitterly antagonistic. Among the older masters, he is supposed to have applied himself most assiduously to Thucydides.

He began his career as a speech writer for the law courts. As such, he developed remarkable skill in adapting a speech to the character of the litigant and the circumstances, somewhat like Lysias, although he never swept the listeners along with him as Lysias had done. He displayed his full powers in speeches affecting policies of state, either before the popular assembly or in a state trial.

Demosthenes made artistic oratory not an end in itself, as Isocrates did, but a means to an end, as no less a man than King Philip discovered, who compared the speeches of Demosthenes to soldiers because of their martial force, and the speeches of Isocrates to athletes because they merely put on a spectacular show. After he had slaved and slogged his way to the fore, momentum carried him on ahead of all others, and he became mightier and mightier as time went on and Athens faced the great crisis of having Philip of Macedonia interfere in her affairs.

Demosthenes put forth strenuous efforts to resist Philip in every way possible, and for that lofty pursuit he was well prepared by his unexcelled mastery of the situation based on his insight and his vast knowledge of the laws and the affairs of state. He developed the thrust and power of his style most marvelously in his Philippics and Olynthiacs, which felicitously combine a factual approach with cogent expression.

His thesis was that if the Athenians did not fight abroad to ward off the war, it would march up to their own doorsteps. This message he repeated in ever more striking form. Perhaps he was wrong to arouse the Athenians, weak as they were, against Philip, and surely he would have been well advised to fight to the death at Chaeronea. The aged Isocrates, never so vehement against Philip as Demosthenes was, took his own life there whereas Demosthenes saved his skin, hardly, one might say, to his honor.

It is enough to say that in later antiquity Demosthenes was by common consent regarded as the first orator among the Greeks, as Cicero was the first among the Romans. In his *Encomium on Demosthenes,* Lucian says that the Attic orators were babbling babes in comparison to the musical words, the ringing rhythms, the clear exposition of thoughts, the interlocking proofs, and the hard-hitting delivery of Demosthenes.

We shall mention only the last three orators in this canon: Lycurgus (died after 326), Hypercides (executed 322), and Deinarchus (died after 299).

This magnificent roster of Greek orators is supplemented by an impressive list of Roman orators: the elder Seneca, Quintillian, Rutilius Lupus, Aquila, Rufinianus, and others. In the Roman half of the oratorical empire, the Latins put forth endless effort to achieve effect. But we have as little time to tarry on this matter as on the grand polar complement which all oratory found in the art of the listener (as discussed in Plutarch's *On the Right Way of Listening*).

The time and effort we in our age devote to the acquisition of knowledge, the men of antiquity, among them men of the highest ability, too, put into a study of form. There have come down to us a great number of speeches which had once served the Greeks and Romans as study models. These demonstrate the deep chasm between the ideals of that age and ours. Even if we ask whether our age can really afford to do without eloquence, the fact is we simply lack the time the Greeks had to devote to this art.

We should also bear in mind the historical influence of oratory on Christianity. During the third and fourth centuries, oratory invaded the church, and oratory and dialectic zeal became the masters of dogmatics and shaped the form of the momentous struggles, especially over the second person of the Trinity, which determined the destinies of whole nations. As a matter of fact, oratory and the epigram are the two facets of antique civilization that have survived. After the Greek state, art, gymnastics, even the remnants of their philosophy, either perished or were completely subverted, the Greek tongue still wagged.

This brief look at speechcraft in an era in which it held undisputed sway must suffice.

Chapter Fifteen

THE FREE PERSONALITY

During its flourishing period, what did the Greek state do for science and research? The answer is: it ignored or harried them. As already said, Greece never had a scholarly caste; the polis demanded of its citizens other things than knowledge, and of all ideas the remotest was that the state should institute a school system. The state left the education of the young entirely in private hands. Children learned whatever was regarded as useful at home and in private schools. The state was already powerful enough and could forgo exercising tyranny through the schools.

The polis banished from time to time, or put to death, the thinkers and searchers who, together with the poets and artists, were produced by the great natural endowment of the people. As mentioned before, the danger was especially acute for those attempting to investigate nature and to explain the world as a system of forces and the heavenly bodies as astronomical objects. Men could be haled into court and tried for impiety, and such accusations were frequent and dangerous; though the masses were but little given to fanaticism, they could easily be moved to condemn a doubter in order to ward off the rancor of the gods. The denunciation in Aristophanes' *Clouds* helped to bring about the ruin of Socrates twenty-four years later.

It was dangerous for the inquiring mind of a philosopher to carry on his private quest, for if he withdrew from the polis, it would pursue him as Abdera pursued Democritus, demanding to know what he had spent his wealth on. He is reported to have justified himself by reading to the authorities his *Diacosmus* and *Concerning the Things in Hades*.

Important developments like the break with the myths and glorious discoveries of nature were due to men in whose intellection philosophic inquiry and scientific research could not be separated. For a long time, the

301

only scholars and men of learning were the philosophers; even the Sophists called themselves philosophers. Aristotle was the greatest scholar and the greatest systematizer. Every kind of truth, including material and scientific truth, rested on philosophy.

All intellectual activity owes an absolute debt to philosophy. Untrammeled freedom of thought won by philosophy benefited not only all fields of scientific inquiry, but even in external life it aided greatly in developing the free personality which adorns the researcher.

Never again have free intellectual pursuits, detached from all official schools and institutions and from all obligatory contacts with state and religion, been able to gain so much respect and power. The rise of these pursuits is an important event in world history, carried on and propagated as they were by the sheer drive of men hardly aided by books. Here we see manifesting itself an unusual speculative bent and an altogether new dimension in Greek life.

In the rise of Greek philosophy it was crucial that individuals could propound any kind of doctrine or revelation; and even though there lurked in the background the threat of being accused of impiety, they were not hampered by any sacrosanct union of religion and the state. Furthermore, it was significant that listeners and disciples were at hand who made it worth a philosopher's while to devote his life to intellectual pursuits, with the hope that a student would be sufficiently influenced by the philosopher's personality to carry on his teachings.

That it became customary in Athens after Pericles for philosophers to live with their followers, we learn from the caricature given of it by Aristophanes in the thinking hut of *The Clouds*. Sparta naturally kept out the philosophers, along with the orators, but was an exception. On the other hand, the philosophers to whom Athens largely owed her primacy were not all Athenians. Some, like the Sophists, came from elsewhere: Anaxagoras from Clazomenae and Aristotle from Stagira.

In the cities were places where one could appear and talk with individuals or groups: the stoas, the agoras, the periboloi of temples, gardens and wooded areas with exedrae, etc. Zeno, for instance, taught in the Stoa Poikile, famed for its frescoes by Polygnotus; hence his followers were called Stoics. Other conditions propitious for philosophy were the leisure the polis granted its citizens, the relative ease of life in the southern climate, and the custom of talking and listening inculcated to a high degree by court procedure. Fluency in speech can be taken for granted since the art of oratory and philosophy sprang up together.

If in addition to all this, we consider the variety of the competing philosophers and their doctrines and the constant agon obtaining among them, of which the levee in the house of Callias at the beginning of Plato's *Protagoras* gives us a good notion, then we shall understand that, fortunately for the free personality, no philosopher was able to impose his views on the rest but that all existed side by side.

In this fashion, despite the esotericism of Pythagoras, philosophy became a part of public life. Along with the rather extensive body of knowledge associated with it—we need not think of Democritus—philosophy was almost wholly available to the public, and Greece had an abnormally large quota of people interested in philosophic thought and expression, i.e., craving for a world of the intellect beyond myth and religion.

This receptive society was challenged to think its way step by step through the following: the ancient cosmogonies, the Ionic explanation of the world by principles and elements, forces and atoms; in addition, ethical and political philosophies, the Pythagorean reduction of reality to numbers, the metamorphic identity of God and the universe, the Heraclitean criticism of sense perception, the doctrine of being, the *nous* (mind) of Anaxagoras, the Platonic concept of ideas, and the beginning of dialectics. Not only did the philosophers represent the whole higher order of thought but also the free, nonpriestly, many-sided, and unlimited field and mode of knowledge.

In the midst of all this, athwart the path of philosophy, sophistry made its appearance, recognizing only subjective knowledge and giving free play to opposite assertions and dubious applications to justice and morals. The Sophists left everything to the art of persuasion; they cultivated rhetoric and logic, including paradoxical conclusions. They also took active part in various branches of learning, teaching individual skills and disciplines of knowledge. They disseminated knowledge and formal culture, though of a shallow kind. Everywhere at that time and also later in the schools of these Sophists, we find not merely writers but personalities, and one can imagine the pressure on a man to distinguish himself in a system where he is constantly thrown on the need to achieve effect by his speech.

These Hellenic philosophers also developed a capacity for enduring poverty. The question whether they could in honor accept pay for teaching agitated them considerably. In the older period, the genuine philosophers were generally distinguished from the Sophists by their teaching gratis, but the split over mercenary philosophy continued down into Roman times and likewise the doubt whether a wise man may gather wealth.

This voluntary poverty was naturally greatly alleviated by the predominance of celibacy practiced already by Thales and later taken for granted, except by Socrates, and by Aristotle who wanted to be buried by the side of his Pythias. Only later stoicism proclaimed marriage incumbent on philosophers. How completely detached philosophers were from wealth and luxury we learn from the great number of those who voluntarily relinquished or gave away their possessions or otherwise chose poverty.

In one of his poems, Xenophanes says that at twenty-five he set out and spent his time wandering about for sixty-seven years in Hellenic countries. Though he was driven from Colophon, he must have adapted himself to voluntary homelessness. Heraclitus contemptuously isolated himself from the public affairs of Ephesus, to the disgust of the best citizens, as he himself noted. He threw away his possessions. In explanation he said: *I was searching for myself*, reminiscent of the Delphic *know thyself*. Empedocles of Agrigentum, who was rich, noble, generous, and a public benefactor, scorned all worldly dignity and power. Anaxagoras, of a similar background, withdrew from the public affairs of Clazomenae and from the enjoyment of his great wealth. When asked why one should prefer to live rather than to die, he replied: *To contemplate the heavens and the order of the universe.*

It may well be that he was referring to the heavens as his home, since he felt himself to be in a very special sense not only a citizen of the earth but of the universe. Soon after the Persian Wars he settled in Athens, thus transplanting philosophy there, after which Athens remained the seat and center of this discipline. While sitting in prison following an accusation of impiety, he wrote about the squaring of the circle.

The earlier philosophers and scholars, with the exception of Heraclitus, were citizens and councilors of specific poleis, just as the Seven Wise Men were. The later ones were little concerned with the polis they lived in, treated of the state as an abstract entity, wrote about theoretical politics, and composed utopias.

Abstract thought made for inward happiness, just like Christianity later, providing a refuge from the riddled state. These later sages found the world an alien land, life a temporary shelter, the body a tomb; hence their resigned attitude toward poverty, exile, and other adversities. These philosophers expressed their emancipation from their homeland by their extensive wanderings abroad, undertaken in part for learning purposes and in part for teaching opportunities. Socrates alone felt no need to travel.

They were all bent upon being original; Socrates, for instance, has long been known as such. Each one of them conducted his life in his own fashion, declaring himself to be intellectually sovereign. Each one desired to make his audience, or the people as a whole, intellectually dependent on him, and the ethical philosophers after Socrates even desired to make them better or admirable, something no temple priest at that time aspired to.

Moreover, the philosophers indicated that they were indifferent to the opinions of the world. Democritus is reported to have been self-reliant, desiring to spend his days unnoticed, in contemplative solitude. He went to

Athens, but since he scorned worldly honors, he took pains to remain obscure. He saw Socrates, who was a year younger than himself, but was not recognized. As is well known, Epicurus counseled his friends to pass their time in quietude.

But, upon occasion, it may not have been easy to live in quiet obscurity, for some philosophers exerted great influence from the very beginning. The Athenians hated Anaxagoras and some others with an enduring passion, impelled to it not so much by religious fanaticism as by envy of the social prominence these men enjoyed and the influence they wielded. Plato and Aristotle were so greatly admired that students imitated the stoop of the former and a speech defect of the latter.

But with the accelerated decline of the polis after Alexander, there came a time when the Diadochi, the *hetaerae,* and the philosophers comprised the predominant personalities of their age, and in the second century the philosophers, in addition to their research and reflection, were meddling in politics, appearing in the agora, and engaging overtly in publicity seeking.

Modern historic research had to pay considerable attention to the origin and elucidation of Greek philosophy and hence may have lent the subject a greater importance than it actually deserves. For not much can be gotten from some of these Greek philosophers; if a modern thinker had no more to offer than some of the Greeks, no one would pay any attention to him.

Moreover, Greek philosophy has one inherent limitation which might justify a more modest evaluation of it: it never really came to grips with the question of freedom and necessity in human behavior. It brushed the question now and then, as when Aristotle, reporting that Socrates spoke of the will as not free, proceeded at once to assert that it was. On the whole though, the question was pretty much left to the fluctuations of popular opinion. Atavistic fatalism with its Moera may be the reason why philosophy never expressed itself definitely on this matter. We must acknowledge, however, that the unique, unattainable greatness of the Greeks lies in their body of myths. Later people might have evolved something like Greek philosophy, but never their myths.

The remarkable and decisive contribution of Greek philosophy is that it fostered a free and independent class of people in the midst of the despotic polis. The philosophers never became hirelings or officials of this polis. As we have seen, they withdrew from it by means of self-imposed poverty and self-denial, and despite all solicitations of the polis, of trade, and of oratory, these free personalities redeemed strength and opportunity for contemplation.

In this connection, we shall leave aside all references to the content of Greek philosophy and turn instead to a discussion of the free personality, as found during the ethical and dialectic period, beginning with the singularly outstanding figure of Socrates.

Besides the mythical Odysseus, Socrates is the most widely known Hellene and, seen in broad daylight, the foremost personality in the whole history of the world about whose character and being we are well informed, though not about the details of his life, especially those of his early years. This remarkable figure, rooted in Athens and radiating the most profound influence in the world, was not only a model of piety, self-control, generosity, and steadfastness, but also signally individualistic in his character and activities.

Plato says there never was any other man like him; every other great man of his day could be compared with someone of the past, but not Socrates. The contrast between his outward and his inner life was striking: poor, needy, sustained by friends, yet spending his time from dawn to dusk in the agora, the gymnasiums, and workshops, but also at festivals and banquets; teaching, educating, engaging in maieutics, counseling, ironic, taunting, admonishing, reconciling, and discussing everything imaginable.

Socrates did not set out benches, or seat himself in an armchair, or observe fixed hours, but philosophized jestingly whenever and wherever opportunity presented itself. In contrast to other philosophers, he associated with everybody and carried his wisdom, not as a system but as a mode of thinking, out into the streets. More than anyone else ever did, he popularized the art of thinking about everything and anything.

Even though he took no active part in state affairs, he was a dutiful citizen and soldier because he expected the state to be the main educative influence in the lives of the young people. His only official position was that of a councilor, in 406, when he insisted upon giving the ten generals a fair trial according to law; otherwise he and his followers took a critical stand as regards the state, taking no part in its administration.

He attempted neither to collect nor to impart substantive knowledge as the Sophists did; indeed, his famous claim of *knowing nothing* was essentially a gibe at them. In the *Apology*, he vehemently deprecated being mistaken for Anaxagoras, calling his views, that the sun is of stone and the moon an earth, absurd. It was rank injustice for Aristophanes in his *Clouds* to have saddled him with Anaxagorean unbelief and evil sophistry, an act explicable only on the grounds that at that time already the Athenians were viciously ill-disposed toward Socrates.

Giving up his study of mathematics and his investigation of nature, he sought to arouse an ethical consciousness in man, a difficult enough task which he undertook with his characteristic originality. On his concept of awareness he based his doctrine of virtue, his notion of divinity, his belief in immortality, and his sense of responsibility; thus knowledge, volition, and belief were brought into conjunction as never before.

His views were fundamentally optimistic. He believed that the creating and sustaining gods were beneficent, and pursued this thought teleologically to the point where *monotheism* plainly showed through the thin veil of polytheism.

The Sophists may have pioneered the method of dialectic and logic Socrates used and given this method an impulsion from which he profited, but he alone used it without any ulterior motive. In his Athens which he rarely left, he would buttonhole people in the streets or in the market place. Seeking to make them better in the ethical sense, he stopped people he met to question them, to refute them, and to clarify their ideas.

The Platonic Socrates, no doubt, reproduces the procedure of the historical Socrates fairly accurately. If his collocutor stubbornly defended his improvident views, Socrates would shift the issue, showing it in a different light by a more penetrating approach, in order to baffle him, after which he would leave him to reflect further upon the matter. How this Sophist serving the good filled his friends with enthusiasm is well portrayed by the talk of Alcibiades in Plato's *Symposium,* which along with Xenophon's *Memorabilia* and Plato's *Apology* is the most illuminating sketch we have of Socrates.

On the other hand, we need not marvel in the least that in time all sorts of individuals and factions came to loathe him. Men do not always respond cheerfully to a challenge to improve themselves, since nearly everyone thinks he is already good enough for his station in life. Because of his habit of bewildering people with questions and then walking away to let them think through the problems he had posed, many a man must have taken Socrates for a quibbler and blood brother of the lesser Sophists.

It seems to us that he attached an absurdly foolish importance to the answer Chaerophon received from the sadly tarnished oracle at Delphi which had so cunningly expressed itself in a negation, saying that *no one was wiser than Socrates.* To be sure, he himself interpreted the oracle of the god modestly enough: *Apollo meant that only he is wise who like Socrates realizes that human wisdom is worthless.* Apart from the fact that no one who talks incessantly, not even a Socrates, can spout wisdom all the time and that he bored people with his everlasting analogies, he did attempt to change their convictions by recourse to irony, which is never in good odor since it savors of arrogance.

In his defense, Socrates stressed most vigorously his divine calling in regard to the Athenians by bringing home to them that his neglect of his own household could not be explained in human terms. He also appealed to his own personal *daimonion,* i.e., divine voice which time and again had blocked his path with a warning. We fear that with his appeal to divine inspiration he would, in the eyes of his fellow citizens, have had to yield to every soothsayer.

As it happened, Socrates did in fact become the butt of insults and in the end was done away with, for there was nobody around to treat him with the same irony he had so liberally bestowed on others. Socrates' irony had indeed the power to leave any and all speechless and baffled. It was unfortunate for him, though, that he went about vexing others at a time when the honorable men around him lived in perpetual fear of sycophants and other organs of the polis and hence were not too receptive to his irony. His vexing ways may have antagonized people so that in time when they saw him coming around a corner they would try to avoid him.

In the end everybody was against him: the priests; the old, established patriots, veteran enemies of the Sophists; and all the hangers-on of the newly restored democracy who would not forgive him that some of the oligarchs had formerly been his disciples. And when these three groups had joined forces to bring charges against Socrates, nobody save a handful of his followers would say a word in his defense. No popular movement arose in his behalf. This shows that the Athenians, including the upper castes, had simply become disgusted with him. Moreover, the terrible years after Aegospotami made the people somewhat indifferent to the fate of individuals; they had trouble enough just trying to survive and making ends meet. And even though in his *Phaedo* Socrates condemned suicide, it seems he actually wanted to die. His whole apologia presents the image of loftiest personal sovereignty over fate sustained by a sense of complete rectitude. The conclusion of his defense is truly magnificent. We may well believe him when he says he would find it intolerable to be banished, an exile driven from city to city.

The life and fate of Socrates are easiest to grasp if we imagine him transferred to our own times. First, all who are working to get ahead would hate him; then, all who are faithful to their jobs out of a sense of duty would barely tolerate him; the common folk would admire him to the extent that he got on the nerves of their betters; the powerful and influential would ridicule him; the religious ones would be genuinely anxious to help him atone for his guilt; while the criminals would have nothing to do with him at all. Only a handful of friends would side with him, but no one would put up with his self-praise so conspicuous in Xenophon's *Apology* and *Symposium*.

In any case, he was an incomparably original figure for the Athens of his day, leaving an indelible impression and becoming an ideal of Hellenic life. He will remain for all times a cardinal figure of the Attic world, sublimely symbolic of the free personality.

The Cynics stood for the highest degree of freedom for the individual.

Antisthenes, a follower of Socrates, founded the Cynic school on athletic grounds outside the walls of Athens called Cynosarges, whence the school derived its name. The Cynics did not go in for making man better and so did not incur popular wrath, as Socrates did by thrusting himself upon all and sundry in impenitent Athens.

Whether the Cynics constituted a genuine philosophical school or only a way of life is open to question. At any rate, they scorned logic and physics and limited themselves to ethics. Their central ethical proposition was that virtue was teachable and lasting, and that the foremost virtues were frugality, disdain of pleasures, and inuredness to discomfort. *The good is hardship,* said Antisthenes; to everything else he was indifferent.

Their freedom from want enabled the Cynics to scorn the polis; they were its living reproach. One may hold with Schwegler that this emancipation from duties and obligations constituted an inverted egoism. In any event, those who put themselves beyond the pale of society should not set up social theories. Withdrawal from public affairs was a general trait of the philosophers and the natural reaction against the despotism of the polis. Bruno Bauer says that the decline of the polis enabled the philosophers to breathe freely again, removing an alp, as it were, that was pressing on them.

No coherent doctrine has been handed down from the Cynics, only a mass of anecdotes and some individual traits; though the details of these may be mostly invention, still they no doubt give a fairly reliable impression of this school.

This holds true especially for the main figure, Diogenes of Sinope, the *mad Socrates,* as Plato called him. He is supposed to have been banished from his native city because he or his father had engaged in debasing coin. One need not believe much of this, but it appears not improbable that his development involved a sharp break with his past. He sojourned a while in Athens, in Corinth, and in Thebes. In Athens, a shattered military power when he arrived, he soon became a favorite and nestled into his famous cask in the Metroum.

Diogenes called himself a citizen of the world. He could boast, with great complacency, that all the curses of tragedy afflicted him, for he was *without a city, without a house, deprived of a homeland, a beggar and a vagabond, living from hand to mouth.* Antisthenes, his forerunner, had already uttered all manner of sarcasm at democracy and pride in parochial citizenship.

Everybody laughed when he roundly abused the whole world. It almost looks as if, in the absence of the old comedy, people delighted in his daringly currish mouth.

A strange period of his later life was that following his capture by the pirate Scirtalus, who sold him as a slave to a certain Xeniades in Corinth.

To this Xeniades he presented himself as an independent person, and remained with him. When members of his household and friends wanted to ransom him he refused, probably because he enjoyed his mode of living. Xeniades said that in Diogenes the gods had sent *a good genius* [*daemon*] to his house. He made him tutor of his children, and Diogenes trained them in gymnastics and taught them literature.

In contradistinction to the other Cynics, he appears to have prized literature, though he declared music, geometry, and astronomy to be useless and sneered at plastic art because the statues cost so much.

That in the meantime he got to Olympia is possible. At all events people supposed he had and that he there indulged in his characteristically unrestrained comments. On the day Alexander died in Babylon Diogenes is said to have died from holding his breath. Those who found him in the Craneum gymnasium outside Corinth surmised that he had died *to escape from the remainder of his life*.

It is to be noted that Cynic asceticism, on the whole, was not meant to mortify one's body or wreck one's health. This asceticism was based on no religious motive and was in no way associated with transmigration of souls, something unheard of in all other cults practicing asceticism. It was not meant to subdue the will or to be an end in itself; it was really only a means to free man from fortune or fate and was to that extent a product of Greek pessimism.

Lucian has much to say about the later unworthy Cynics down to Peregrinus Proteus. In Demonax, an eclectic philosopher living as a Cynic, he portrayed the only man whom he honored and that on the basis of a close personal friendship. Born in 90 B.C. on Cyprus, Demonax became a well-known figure in Athens, not only as a philosopher but also as an adjudicator, arbitrator, intermediator, and wit-cracker. He lived without sickness or worry, a burden to none with his modest begging, a boon to his friends and without a single enemy.

When Demonax entered, the chief magistrates (archons) stood up and everybody fell silent. In extreme old age he was wont to enter homes as he liked either to eat or to sleep and was made welcome as a good spirit. When he passed by, women selling bread vied to give him some of theirs, and she whom he obliged by accepting regarded him as a good daimon. Even children brought him fruit and called him father.

Once, when dissension arose at a popular assembly, his mere appearance was enough to silence the disputants; when he saw that they had composed their minds, he left again without saying a word. When nearly a hundred years old and no longer able to help himself, he recited a beautiful verse and abstained from all nourishment until he died, as cheerful as he had been all through his life. The Athenians accorded him a state funeral and mourned him long. Men honored and hung with wreaths the stone seat where he had been accustomed to rest.

Cynic philosophy survived into Roman times, showing that it filled an inner need; it would never have lasted as long as it did had it not answered to something definite in the Hellenic mind and soul.

If we ask where else in Greek philosophy asceticism was found, then the later Pythagoreans come to mind first. Their asceticism was more genuine than that of the Cynics to the extent that it was linked with religious ideas; they regarded the soul as imprisoned in the body and held that one should not let this prison house enjoy any favors.

They had a political purpose in view, namely, to promote the welfare of the state by rearing Panhellenes virtuous in the sense of an Epaminondas. Though they were not sharp-fanged like the Cynics, they must have lived very much as the Cynics did. While the earlier Pythagoreans bathed, cut their hair, anointed themselves and wore white clothes, a certain Diodorus of Aspendus was described as going about dirty, barefoot, and with long, unkempt hair.

The Stoics were moderately ascetic. Zeno, who was said to be too refined for ascetic uncouthness, had ascetic traits nevertheless. A writer of comedies said of him: *He teaches men to go hungry but he still finds disciples*. There was also Cleanthes, who at the beginning had to be frugal but later must have cultivated this quality deliberately.

The hedonism of Aristippus contrasts sharply with the asceticism of the Cynics, for he found the highest good in pleasure and in the enjoyment of the passing moment. The hedonist concerned himself no more with the affairs of state than the Cynic did. Aristippus told Socrates that he would not become a part of any community but would remain unattached wherever he was. Socrates tried to get him to see that he was courting greater dangers by wandering around, but he would not listen. Aristippus drifted a bit too readily to the courts of tyrants and to their sumptuous banquets. Hedonism without money was impracticable.

The philosophers consistently evaded public responsibility in the polis. Plato is as well known for his indifference to public affairs as for his utopias [*The Laws, The Republic*]. The *Theaitetus*, composed by Plato during his middle period, expressed quite bluntly his withdrawal not only from the state but from the whole world around him. In this dialogue Socrates, speaking about philosophers in general, said:

> Not since the days of their youth have philosophers known their way to the agora, nor do they know where the courthouse is or the council chamber, or where the popular assembly is held.

Neither do they hear or read the laws or care for the results of popular voting. The struggle of the political factions for power in the state, the meetings, the banquets, the revels with flute-playing girls—such things they do not think about even in their dreams. As for the gossip of the city, they do not even know that they know nothing of it. Really, only the body of the philosopher is in the city; his mind, esteeming the world lightly, soars about freely, measuring the deeps of the earth and the expanses of the heavens and inquiring into the nature of things, without ever condescending to the world of particulars about them.

How many mental metamorphoses did Plato have to undergo until he could expound the view just given and arrive at that towering philosophical self-assurance which enabled him to demand that in the perfect state philosophers alone and without restraint should rule over an automatically obedient citizenry, and which led him to suppose that his ideal state was attainable? The total picture shows that Plato, as far as his Athens was concerned, kept aloof from matters political and became a utopian visionary with regard to Hellas.

We have earlier observed that the urge to take a hand in practical politics took Plato out of his visionary role and plunged him into Sicilian intrigue where he tried to impose his services as a political and governmental "healer," with the result that some of his disciples, following his example, became tyrannical heads of state. In passing, we shall merely mention that perhaps the ultimate homage a philosopher paid to an oracle is to be found in *The Laws*, where in various passages Plato counseled recourse to Delphi at a time when the Pythian priestess was or soon would be pro-Macedonian.

The Stoa likewise preached that man should care little about the necessities of life and the solicitations of the state. We have already seen that Zeno and Cleanthes to a certain degree lived ascetic lives. Zeno was born at Citium, a Hellenized Phoenician city in Cyprus, where he was a dealer in purple. It is reported that he congratulated himself on the loss of his goods in a shipwreck, for that calamity drove him to philosophy. He studied with Crates, a Cynic philosopher, and also associated with Megarians and Platonists. After having exercised his skill as a Phoenician merchant for twenty years and provided for his modest needs, he set up his own school at the Stoa Poikile. Though he lived a strict and simple life, he charged fees so as to eliminate the press of crowds, it was said.

The chief postulate of the Stoa is that man can and should make himself happy by his own inner resources. Pursuant to this view, the Stoa sketched an ideal portrait of the *wise man* and kept dabbing on colors. However, the Stoa overemphasized the capacity of men, and when challenged to name a wise man was unable to do so. A comic poet taunted: *The Stoics run around looking for a wise man as if one had slipped away from them.*

And when we ask what the wise man should do in relation to the state, the answer is that theoretically he should ignore it; his concern is rather with the world as a whole. Human beings should not be separated into states and cities with their different laws, for all men should be regarded as compatriots and fellow citizens. Only in this sense did Zeno and Chrysippus leave Stoic politics to posterity.

They both evolved utopian schemes which, among other things, provided for having wives in common, apparently an arrangement that forces itself on all those who settle the complexities of life so simply and briefly. In actual practice later Stoics now and then played a very definite role in relation to the state; some helped to overthrow tyrants, and the opposition of the Roman Stoa to the emperors is well known.

Epicurus strove extremely hard to be a man genuinely free. His philosophy had a purely utilitarian purpose, i.e., to serve as a guide to happiness. He called theoretical science useless; natural science was only to free men from terrifying notions, such as evil portents, fear of divine punishment, etc.; indeed, the purpose of all knowledge was only to free man from delusions. The highest goal of life was pleasure, though not physical pleasure but rather a spirit of delight, as well as freedom from mental distress and from physical burdens, whence it follows that the wise man will exert himself more to avoid the unpleasant than to pursue the pleasant.

It is to be feared that few people would be content with Epicurean pleasure properly understood. Epicurus does not deny the gods but relegates them to a lofty interstellar sphere where they live in aeonian blessedness because they do not trouble themselves about mankind. Suicide is justified when a man is suffering unbearably. Fear of death and the underworld is futile: the soul is extinguished at death and death itself is no evil. As for the state, Epicurus esteemed and vindicated it as a contract of mutual protection. He expressed his lack of political ambition in the famous admonition to live in obscurity and to abstain from public affairs, though always permitting those who could not be happy without praise and honor to participate freely in politics.

A distinct mark of his serious and independent mind is his rejection of rhetoric in favor of simplicity. His style was one that called things by their proper names without pompous circumlocution and lordly devices of oratory. In his treatise on rhetoric he demanded absolute clarity. Epicurus signified a swing of the pendulum back from some extravagant mannerisms; for this he will always deserve respect.

Pyrrho of Elis sought happiness in a radical suspense of judgment. *He who remains noncommittal lives in peace without worry, without passion, and without craving, fully indifferent to external good and evil; this imperturbability of mind constitutes happiness.*

If we consider the Greek philosophers and their followers, we shall see that not only was a goodly quota of free Greek minds found everywhere but they also transcended the boundaries of nationality, race, and social status.

Anacharsis the Scythian was the prototype of the barbarian philosopher. Tradition reports that he wrote to Croesus: *I have no need of money; it is enough for me to return to the Scythians a better man.* He is said to have been killed by his brother with an arrow when on a hunt, after his return from Greece, at the behest of the king because he tried to introduce in Scythia the Eleusinian Mysteries and Greek education in general.

Later, Mithridates, the son of Rhodobates and hence a Persian prince, belonged to the circle that greatly admired Plato; he commissioned Silanion to make a statue of Plato and had it set up in the Academy. Zeno of Citium had to submit to being called *this little Phoenician* by Crates. Menippus the Cynic was also of Phoenician descent. A Babylonian called Diogenes was attracted to philosophy by Zeno, and in the fourth century Dionysius the Megarian, Herillus, a disciple of Zeno, and Cleitomachus, the disciple of Carneades, were genuine Hamitic Carthaginians who merely assumed Hellenic names. The name of the last one was Hasdrubal. At first he philosophized in his mother tongue in Carthage, going to Athens only when he was forty years old, where he became the successor of his teacher and a diligent author.

While philosophers of Greece were themselves of mixed national origin, the Hellenic nation was represented in time by Greek philosophers in remote Oriental countries. So Archidemus the Athenian went to the kingdom of the Parthians and founded a Stoic school in Babylon. The recollection of the journeys the earliest Greek philosophers made to Egypt and Asia may have prompted the Greeks themselves to imagine that philosophy had its roots among the barbarians.

Many slaves of the most varied origin became philosophers, presumably because a philosopher could easily teach a talented slave. Whereas a freeman, however superb his natural endowments, often did not take to philosophy, or gave it up when the whim took him, the slave who may have been bought because he was obviously gifted, was obliged to stay and submit to the training. His emancipation and the inheritance left him by his master did the rest.

Thus Diagoras was a slave of Democritus, who reportedly paid him ten thousand drachmas because of his outstanding talents. Bion of Borysthenes in Scythia was reared by a Sophist and made his heir. Pompylus, the slave of Theophrastus, and Perseus, the slave of Zeno, later became renowned philosophers. Menippus the Cynic is supposed to have come as a slave from Phoenicia to Greece. The situation was different with Phaedo who, coming from a respectable Elean family, fell into slavery through the mishaps of war and was ransomed by Alcibiades or Crito at the urging of Socrates and thus saved from a menial life. The most celebrated late instance of a philosophizing slave was Epictetus.

As to women in philosophy, we have already mentioned those in the Pythagorean school. Two of Plato's pupils were women, Axiothea of Phlius and Lastheneia the Arcadian. Arete, the daughter of Aristippus, was also his pupil and the teacher of her son, who was therefore called the *mother-instructed* (*metrodidactus*). There is something special about Greek philosophy contrasting sharply with Greek culture and its preconceptions; it embraces the whole of mankind as its field of inquiry.

The slander philosophers vented against each other is one of the more repulsive traits of the Greek character and cannot be reconciled with the perpetual preoccupation of philosophers with ethics and virtue. Defamation, being a fettered limb of the free personality, as it were, reduced the agon to vulgar strife. Fanaticism, as a rule exceedingly rare among the Greeks, infested their philosophers and, however unpleasant it is, it should not be overlooked.

This malicious quality of the philosophers may have furnished the occasion or pretext for the contempt later visited on philosophy. In the early days of the Roman Empire several schools of philosophy were still extant; at least some sophisticated orators still paraded the colors of philosophy. Students memorized the several systems but came to see that many of the postulates and conclusions were mutually exclusive, and that all the labor bestowed on this field apparently yielded only husks.

People began to learn about the animosities philosophers harbored toward each other's way of life and especially about the intense hatred of the later Stoics for the Epicureans, whom they portrayed as dangerous to the state, claiming they denied the gods or at least their providential care. This violent feuding destroyed what little respect people still had for philosophy. And so in his *Icaromenippus, A Carousal or the Lapiths,* and elsewhere, Lucian, personally satisfied with Cynicism or only certain aspects of it, could deride the catch phrases and conclusions of all the philosophical schools as well as their exponents. But without the accumulation of satire following Timon's *Silloi,* there could have been no sustained mockery as found in Lucian.

The philosophy that followed, namely *Neoplatonism,* was already theosophy, i.e., essentially religion. During the second century A.D., the sentiment in the Roman Empire was no longer that a man could live in poverty and freedom because he was a philosopher, but that if a man was too poor and incompetent to help himself he posed as a philosopher.

We shall touch briefly on the external aspects of life among the philosophers. Above all, a place to forgather was necessary, a place to teach and to house libraries and collections. As is well known, Plato used the Academy, i.e., a gymnasium outside Athens not far from Colonos Hippias, or rather the adjacent property which he had acquired. Here he built a house and that shrine of the Muses where Speusippus later set up the statues of the Graces. The structure called the exedra was also there.

Henceforth the philosophical schools in Athens became formally recognized institutions. They had their *scholarchs* who regularly succeeded one another, and they had their own meeting places retained from generation to generation and an endowment or foundation which might be increased by donations; the income of this endowment went to the *scholarchs*.

But one is well advised to imagine all these things and especially the locality on a rather modest scale. It sufficed to have a place where to meet regularly and to store the books and collections. An anecdote tells about the simplicity of life obtaining at Plato's Academy. According to one variant, Plato had said: *You are eating for tomorrow rather than for today.*

The most frequented of all schools was the Lyceum, founded by Aristotle during his second stay in Athens, at a gymnasium surrounded by groves traversed by footpaths. We do not know whether or not he had to get permission from the city of Athens to whom the gymnasiums belonged. Since he was a metic he could not own any real estate. Theophrastus, supposedly with the help of Demetrius Phalereus, purchased a grove at the Lyceum. But it was in the gymnasium itself that, according to report, Aristotle held rigorously scholarly (*acroamatic*) lectures for a limited circle of disciples in the morning, and popular (*exoteric*) lectures in the evening, dealing especially with rhetoric and political science, for a more general audience.

We are told that Theophrastus had two thousand students, perhaps an overstatement when we consider the many philosophers teaching in Athens, and the length of time the students were attached to these schools, even though hardly one tenth of them became professional philosophers. A place often mentioned later was the garden where Epicurus, after 306 B.C., taught and cultivated friendship, which for him was a genuine experience.

A famous story tells that when Aristotle was near death he asked for some wine of Rhodes and of Lesbos, and having tasted each said, *The Lesbian is better,* and so appointed Theophrastus of Lesbos instead of Eudemus of Rhodes as his successor. His school continued for a long time in Athens, even though he left it *lest the Athenians commit a second crime against philosophy*. Under the Diadochi the Peripatetics achieved fame mainly by their commentaries on the works of the master.

After Alexander the schools and systems were fairly numerous. In addition to those of the Academics and Peripatetics, which continued to flourish, there were the Stoa, the Epicureans, and the Skeptics, each sharply contrasting with all the others. In every one of these philosophical schools the succession of leaders was carefully recorded until quite late. The testaments of the philosophers themselves provided the means necessary for continuing the management of their institutions.

Thus Theophrastus willed his gardens, the tree-lined walks, and all the houses on his property to ten students specifically named, provided they would assemble there to study and philosophize as a group. They were to hold this estate as a sacred precinct and be buried there, as he was, with simple ceremonies. The Peripatetic Lycon willed his garden to his disciples.

Particularly noteworthy is the truly classic testament of Epicurus, whereby he bequeathed his garden, acquired for only eighty minae, and all that pertained to it in perpetuity to his school. His house he willed to his pupil Hermarchus, who had grown old with him in the study of philosophy and succeeded him as the head of the school, and to those who would study philosophy with Hermarchus, as long as he lived. Furthermore, he left revenues to provide funeral offerings for his family, for commemorating his birthday, for the whole school to hold a celebration on the twentieth of each month in memory of Metrodorus and himself, for commemorating his brothers on a set day in the month of Poseidon, and for commemorating Polyaenus in the month of Metageiton. Finally, he stipulated that some slaves should be freed and some money set aside to help provide the necessities of life for all the needy among those who had studied with him.

The state interfered in the affairs of these schools only once. In 305 B.C. a certain Sophocles proposed an enactment providing that the heads of all philosophic schools had to be approved by the city council and the popular assembly, threatening with death all who refused to comply. Thereupon all philosophers left Athens, but returned when a certain Phillion accused Sophocles of illegality and the Athenians revoked the law and fined Sophocles five talents. This was done especially so that Theophrastus would return with his numerous students. Thus it was that Athens once tried to coerce the philosophers. We should note this most remarkable incident carefully, for it was the one and only moment in its history when Athens suddenly became excessively and impertinently modern in attitude.

Philosophical literature had the immense advantage that the philosophers wrote to express their inmost convictions and not with a view to sales, even though their writings might sell. From its earliest days philosophic writing was voluminous. A comprehensive corpus of philosophic writings has survived, and the titles preserved in Diogenes Laertius and elsewhere number many thousands; the Stoic Chrysippus alone is supposed to have written 705 books.

Many of these works were probably little more than pamphlets and some were probably extensive excerpts copied from previous authors, as was common practice everywhere before the invention of printing. We must also bear in mind that philosophy embraced nearly the whole field of knowledge, including mathematics, natural science, history, and political science, in addition to philosophy in the more precise sense. But in spite of all these considerations, the wealth of genuine and original philosophic writing is astounding.

It is true, these works have been preserved very unevenly. We have almost nothing, for instance, from the voluminous polyhistors before Aristotle, from men like Democritus, that great thinker and searcher whose works would answer many questions if only they had survived. Indeed, his works seem to have suffered systematic destruction, obviously at the hands of his philosophical opponents. On the other hand, we have all the works of Plato and most of the important works of Aristotle.

But here a certain discrimination has to be applied, for the material bearing Aristotle's name, apart from fully worked-out items, include also: first, collections and preliminary studies; second, lecture notes taken by students; and third, excerpts from important works made by others. The later Stoa and Neoplatonism are represented by whole libraries of significant original compositions. But none of the original writings of Epicurus, who was more prolific than Aristotle, have survived. Maybe the later Stoics deliberately burned his works, a misguided endeavor because the many refutations of his works and the enthusiasm of Lucretius have kept his doctrines very much alive.

Antiquity was zealous in recording the achievements of the past. In a series of works Aristotle condensed the treatises of earlier philosophers and from time to time referred to his predecessors. The Alexandrines continued this practice, and apart from Diogenes Laertius, who probably wrote his compendium of the history of philosophy at the time of Septimus Severus, Cicero, Seneca, Plutarch, and also the church fathers contain a wealth of historical information.

We should say a word about the dialogue form in which so many of these works are written. Zeno the Eleatic used the dialogue even before Plato. It maintained itself alongside the systematic form with surprising tenacity, passing to the Romans among whom not only Cicero but much later even Gregory the Great made use of it, reaching into the Middle Ages and far into the Renaissance.

For the Greeks the dialogue form was especially congenial, and as a practical teaching device it is perhaps as old as the *acroamatic* lecture, for the formal dialogue develops thoughts more sharply than any other kind of discussion and hence, as mentioned earlier, philosophy was primarily an oral discipline. Socrates, who wrote nothing himself, may well have stimulated his listeners to write down whatever they could remember of his conversations. This may explain the next step philosophers took in composing well-wrought dialogues.

That Plato and other Socratics worked very hard on the form of their compositions is certain. To master the conversational tone, Plato is said to have studied Sophron's *mimes,* i.e., prose conversations taken from the life of the common people. A tradition reports that throughout his long life Plato kept polishing and filing at his dialogues. Even the impious parody of Lucian as seen in *The Carousal or the Lapiths* is above all lucid and dramatic.

Plutarch, on the other hand, arranged his speeches and arguments in *Amatorius* somewhat awkwardly, permitting irrelevant matter to intervene, and has by and large an uneven style. Then all of a sudden he displayed all his artfulness in *De Genio Socratis,* the contents of which are most interesting. After the preliminary dialogue forming the introduction, he presented the Theban conspiracy against Sparta altogether in dialogues carried on by the main characters, interrupted by philosophical discussions and, indeed, by a circumstantial account of a theory of the transmigration of souls in the form of a vision which Timarchus of Chaeronea is supposed to have had at the oracle of Lebadea, all of which is reminiscent of Tieck and the Romanticists who have their characters indulge in literary conversations between elopements and other adventures.

In any event, the Greeks took pleasure in the dialogue. Even though the dialogue was still assiduously cultivated in the Renaissance, today it has fallen out of favor, perhaps because we no longer take delight in listening to others as men once did. Plutarch once wrote a special essay on *De recta ratione audiendi* [The right way of listening].

Chapter Sixteen

SCIENTIFIC INVESTIGATION

The general education of the Greeks consisted of mastering a common body of accomplishments in reading and writing, and in gymnastics and music, i.e., liberal arts. The high value attributed to this education is evidenced by the fact that the severest punishment imposed on recalcitrant subjects was to forbid them to educate their children. The names of teachers who instructed famous men, like those of the three teachers of Plato, were preserved. We have no evidence that the state exercised any control over the qualifications of these teachers. On the whole, for the education of its citizens, the polis relied on the experiences that life itself provided.

The more ambitious individuals craved something more and found it in philosophy, which, having shattered the myths, provided the means to all kinds of knowledge. The propaedeutic to philosophy was above all geometry but also music and astronomy. Philosophy created the sciences in that it systematized the broad fields of knowledge and skills and subsumed them under its own universal principles.

By inquiring into functions of the state it created political science; by analyzing poetry, which many philosophers studied in minute detail, it created poetics; and by recording its own development it originated the history of philosophy. Contributions of philosophy also included historical, mythological, and antiquarian treatises of all kinds so that one can never be sure where philosophy ended and specialized knowledge began.

As observed before, the one subject philosophy hardly touched was that of the visual arts, and seen in the proper light, this was all to the advantage of the arts.

In this respect Democritus is an exception. This profoundly learned man was born in Abdera in 460 B.C., and is supposed to have lived over a hundred years, until 357. We shall not try to determine to what extent he was influenced by his journeys, real or only alleged, to Egypt, Persia, the Red Sea, and even to the Indian gymnosophists. He certainly studied with the most diverse teachers, including the Pythagoreans. Deeply immersed in his studies, he applied his marvelous talents to grasping intuitively the nature of physical occurrences and to making challenging predictions; in consequence, he impressed his fellow citizens as possessing superhuman wisdom. He was a genuine polyhistor, and of all the Greeks living around 400 B.C. he was probably the man with the most penetrating mind and the widest intellectual range.

His writings included among others the *Great Diacosmus* and the *Lesser Diacosmus,* a special study of Pythagoras, an account of the world, a description of the heavens, works on planets, on anthropology, on physiology, on mathematics, on clepsydras and sundials, on magnets, on medicine and dietetics, on rhythms and harmony, on poetic beauty and the arts of poetry, on agriculture, a treatise on military tactics and strategy, essays on research, on the sacred writings in Babylon and those in Meroë, and in addition to all that a work on painting and apparently one on the vaulting of arches.

Of course we may grant that the Greeks excelled not in factual knowledge but in poesy and art, with which we would be quite content even if they had left us nothing else. But when we consider the obstacles they had to contend with, their scientific merits and achievements, even from a negative perspective, appear remarkably great. We must never lose sight of the competition offered to science by the all-pervading myths, by oratory, and by speculative philosophy. The sacrifices Greek scientists had to make were huge and presupposed an extraordinarily firm determination.

The Diadochi countries were the first to provide financial support and security for scientific endeavors. Before that time every scientist had to collect his own specimens and materials as best he could by prodigious self-denial. These men worked uncommonly hard and were poor; there were no royalties, no consultant's fees, and no regular sources of income for them.

We must also remember that they undertook journeys despite poverty and exposed themselves to grave dangers. Yet they ventured to travel the length and breadth of the Greek world in order to acquire information and new ideas and to meet with other scientists and learn from them. There is no doubt that Pythagoras traveled extensively; Xenophanes, speaking of himself, said that he had roamed about for sixty-seven years; and Democritus reported that of all men in his day he had wandered about the most, seeing the most countries and skies, hearing the greatest number of scholars lecture, and tarried five years with the sages in Egypt.

It is certain that Plato left Athens after the death of Socrates and did not return until he was forty. He too spent some time in Egypt, as later did Eudoxus of Knidos. These men were receptive and willing to learn, not being handicapped by the haughty ignorance of the Orientals which would have prevented the latter, had they ever traveled, from associating with anybody and everybody.

For a long time there were no libraries, and so for hundreds of years individual researchers had to collect the books they needed themselves, often having to copy them, until finally the schools of philosophy and the Diadochi princes offered help. As a result, science did not develop uniformly.

It had been assumed that such philosophers as Plato and Aristotle employed teams of disciples to collect materials, work on problems, and investigate the various fields of knowledge according to a unified, over-all plan, that they knew how to muster the requisite means, that Plato attracted mathematicians and Aristotle bequeathed the continued research in the Lyceum to Theophrastus and Dicaearchus. It would be nice to believe this. But in general each man proceeded on his own, and students and teachers came together pretty much by happenstance.

The lack of communication among the investigators occasioned much needless duplication of effort. Some discoveries were repeated—a waste of energy according to modern notions. One may reply that there was probably a larger percentage of happy people then than now; for no citizen was required to demonstrate mastery of any set body of knowledge, since official careers in the modern sense did not exist. High offices for the execution of the essential business of the state were of short tenure, and offices requiring long-term incumbency were more or less despised as banausic.

As for knowledge of nature and the order of the universe, the Egyptians, Babylonians, and Assyrians, as already indicated, had unquestionably been engaged at it longer than the Greeks, and had consequently accumulated many more facts and more extensive knowledge; for this purpose they had privileged castes and well-endowed priesthoods.

Being able to calculate the relation of the moon cycles to the apparent revolutions of the sun, they could set up a fairly accurate calendar, and they had a sufficient grasp of geometry to make maps. By the wonderfully ingenious Babylonian system, whereby a cube of a cubit in the various dimensions is, at the same time, the basis for weight, they could establish a mathematical relation between linear and cubic measures and weights.

The practice of mummifying corpses gave the Egyptians a substantial lead in anatomy. They also evolved a system of medicine based on essentially correct principles. Besides, those ancients must have had considerable knowledge of practical mechanics, metallurgy, statics, chemistry, and other fields of knowledge.

We shall not deny that the Greeks, directly or indirectly, learned many things from these other peoples; to admit this is no derogation to the Greeks. But let us inquire a little more closely. Does an Egyptian papyrus, or stone tablet of Babylon, proclaim any truth such as that in the statement by Anaximander: *The earth is a body floating freely in infinite space,* or in this one by Anaximenes: *The stars do not move over the earth but around it,* or this by Diogenes of Apollonia: *Many earths have arisen through condensation and rarefaction of air?* The principles on which these Ionians based their world conceptions may have been only rather vague surmises; but even so, it is significant and distinctive that they ventured to state such principles at all.

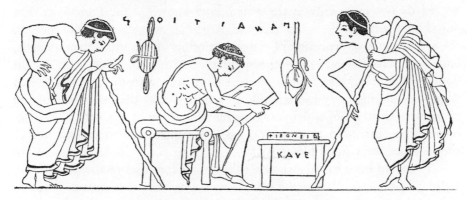

Medical students at a lecture
Measuring cup

In the fifth century, the Pythagoreans gained the grand insight that led scientists to substitute the heliocentric for the geocentric planetary system: *The earth is not located in the center of the universe; it is a heavenly body like many others and not even one of the favored ones; the central position is occupied by a celestial fire which is turned toward the sun and moon but away from the inhabited portion of the earth.*

Heraclides of Pontus, a disciple of Plato, did, it is true, move the earth back again to the center, but he explained the apparent motion of the stars as due to the earth's turning on its axis; he is also supposed to have recognized that Venus revolves around the sun. Then, *circa* 260 B.C., Aristarchus of Samos taught at least hypothetically that the sun was at rest and that the earth coursed around it *by means of* rotation on its axis; and Seleucus the Babylonian maintained outright that the heliocentric system was demonstrably true. Thus the discovery, later known as the Copernican system, was established in its main outlines by ordinary everyday observations.

It appears that Hicetas the Syracusan and Ecphantes, a Pythagorean of undetermined date, were the first to teach that the earth turns on its axis. The Pythagoreans were the first to teach that the earth is a globe on the abstract principle that a sphere is the most perfect shape and that hence the earth has to have this form. (The Stoic in Cicero's *De Natura Deorum*, II, 18, 47, praised the form of the circle and sphere.)

Parmenides was the first to demonstrate mathematically that the earth is a sphere. Aristotle was the first to adduce the eclipsing of the moon as proving that the earth is a sphere; he also taught the uniform attraction of gravitation toward the center of the earth. Archimedes taught the curvature of the sea and Ptolemy confirmed it.

But no power protected this unique knowledge. Alongside all this, the geocentric system, essentially the system later known as the Ptolemaic, won out chiefly because of the authority of Aristotle. According to this system, the earth hovers at the center of concentric orbits of the sun, moon, planets, and fixed stars that are moving around the earth. This Ptolemaic system dominated the Middle Ages. But the saying that a truth once discovered cannot be permanently lost is vindicated here, for at the beginning of the sixteenth century Copernicus, taking his clue from the scattered Pythagorean hints, managed to propound his heliocentric system in defiance of the views of the church hierarchy.

Since we have found Aristotle siding with the reactionaries in science, we may address ourselves to the complaints moderns have raised against him.

One can only say that if Aristotle had to cover all branches of knowledge with the empirical thoroughness he applied to rhetoric and zoology, he would have had to live many lives, but having been granted only one, he filled that one abundantly. He investigated the facts of nature and history more thoroughly and comprehensively than any philosopher had done before him. He was thoroughly familiar with the accomplishments of his predecessors, the Sophists and philosophers as well as the poets. His famous library served him well in these studies.

King Philip and Alexander the Great provided him royally with means and materials, thus making possible his comprehensive zoological studies containing an incomparable wealth of positive knowledge. Thus he came to be the established authority on zoology and botany and was the father of comparative anatomy.

In addition, he had a tremendous knowledge of politics and history, as evidenced by his *Politics*. Furthermore, he was the father of logic, and as such made mankind aware of the pure forms of thinking and of abstract reasoning. In his *Poetics* he created the theory of poetry, and by his *Rhetoric* he became a teacher of public oratory. To all this must be added his knowledge and criticism of earlier philosophical systems and his laying the foundations of metaphysics, which though limited in achievement was at least the first attempt to elaborate such a system.

The structure he set up is gigantic, however one may look at it. Despite his reactionary attitude in the sciences, Aristotle is and will remain in respect to knowledge of the universe, as Dante said, *The father of those that know*.

The Greeks were capable of the most comprehensive empirical investigation once they set their minds to it, but because no polis required either the pupils in a school or the employees of the administration to give proof in public examinations of a certain level of standardized book learning, and since no priesthood sought to protect the minds of the people against superstition and delusion, the Greeks in their system of education were never called upon to master an official quota of facts or to be acquainted with the results of advanced research. These conditions, similar to those obtaining later in the Italian Renaissance, remained unchanged during the Diadochi period and at the Alexandrine school. The Museum at Alexandria was not an institution of learning that required formal examinations, nor did Rome have any resemblance to a China. [Rome, like Greece, did not make a point of the trappings of erudition, in contrast to China, where pedantic examinations were required of civil servants.]

The Greeks enjoyed spinning yarns, and like the hunters today they swapped lies amiably. It is a question whether, for all our reading, education, and emancipation from chimeras and monsters of nature, we are by and large more sensible, or whether we possibly are prone to even more dangerous delusions than were the Greeks.

The more satisfied the Greeks were with their traditional views and myths, the greater appears the stature of Greek philosophers and scholars who were able to transcend common delusions. What a dedicated spirit these investigators must have had, a Eudoxus of Knidos, for example, who wished to go near the sun to determine its shape, size, and appearance, giving his life like another Phaëthon if need be! With such devotion they managed, in spite of all obstacles, to accumulate and record a rather massive body of knowledge in mathematics, astronomy, mechanics, and medicine.

Even the Stoics, holding a fairly low opinion of investigation into geometry and physical science as a whole, founded the traditional system of grammar which, via the Latin grammarians, has come down to our day. Chrysippus invented most of the technical grammatical terms for the inflections and parts of speech. In the end, this one nation with its open mind was to become the eye of all mankind for whatever is worth knowing in the world of appearances.

Chapter Seventeen

HISTORY AND ETHNOLOGY

In the field of history, the ancient Orientals were markedly inadequate as compared to the Greeks. The Hindus were deliberately indifferent to history because they held that the whole external world could be tucked into a fold of Brahma's robe. Though the royal dynasties of Egypt and Assyria had their chronicles, the common people figured therein only incidentally and then as inanimate objects, and alien peoples only as potential slaves and objects to plunder or wreak vengeance upon. Instead of an objective history of their kings, the Persians left a typically transfigured image wherein they rearranged all persons and events in a one-sided way to conform to the Zoroastrian view of the two contending world principles, good and evil.

Among the Jews we find history viewed as a great antithesis, i.e., a theocracy composed of the true Yahweh worshipers on the one hand and all their enemies ranged against it on the other. Their history is a series of indictments, argumentations, and testimonies in a long, drawn-out lawsuit. Only the Phoenicians and the Carthaginians might be regarded not as the models but as predecessors of the Greeks, not only in ethnography and cosmography but also in objective political observations, for they, too, had many poleis and could carry on comparative studies.

They could evolve and apply their objective sense of political and commercial realities and progress to a scientific description of these realities, except of course as the powers that be saw fit to interfere for reasons of state, which is a thing we find it easiest to assume in the case of Carthage.

The Greeks had a panoramic eye and an objective mind, and accordingly wrote the history of their own people and of other peoples as well. They were the first to observe something with detachment, without possessing it or even craving its possession. Since they lived only in poleis, which in turn split into factions, they were able to know and portray each other.

Their ability to observe foreign lands and the events of the past impartially contributed to the everlasting glory of the Greeks, for since then and because of them all civilized nations have had to take notice of all countries and ages. This universal interest we owe to them; we cannot imagine how we might have come to it if the Greeks had not transmitted their mode of thinking to the Romans.

The greatest handicap to careful historical scholarship among the Greeks was not their body of myths, for this they could overcome, but their innate carelessness of precise detail. On the whole, their objectivity was not applied to carefully established facts but to the inner significance of the facts, their general human or national substance, and to making this significance and value as vividly clear as possible.

We have noted earlier what liberties the tragedians took with the destinies and characters of mythical personages. It is important for the historian to bear in mind that the events and traditional conceptions associated with personalities, from the Dorian migration on, were transmitted by word of mouth for a very long time. Thus the tendency to see things from a mythical point of view unwittingly turned historical events into myths. One of the chief differences between Herodotus and Thucydides was that the former drew heavily on hearsay at third and tenth hand while the latter relied on documentary sources and eyewitness reports.

Whereas we, thanks to our education, are bent upon exactitude, recognizing as valid no other basis in our procedures, the Greeks saw and perceived types, and the type is expressed in the anecdote, which is always true for the whole although it has never been true in an individual event. In this sense the first book of Herodotus is eternally true even though not much would remain if the typical were stripped away.

Modern criticism has been able to eliminate some of the anecdotes rather easily by pointing out anachronisms, inaccurate reporting, etc., and yet one would never be able to straighten out everything, as for example in Plutarch, and would not want to either. In addition to the characteristically typical stories that developed spontaneously, criticism is also faced with literary creations and deliberate inventions, a vice demonstrably found in whole schools.

All sorts of people and events are wrenched out of place and made to fit in with Pythagoras: Numa as well as Zaleucus who is supposed to have been his pupil; indeed when the democrats of Sybaris threatened to make war on Croton unless the fugitives from Sybaris were returned, Pythagoras is supposed to have moved the people of Croton to give asylum to the supplicating fugitives. If anyone fell into the hands of the comic poets, like Euripides, he was turned into a fable, as were also his parents and grandparents.

Plato's life is filled with anecdotal elements in Diogenes Laertius as well as in other biographers. Even the facts of his life are embellished with tales, pomp, and witticisms, arousing the most lively suspicions, so that finally nearly every assertion about the philosopher is in dispute. The same holds true for Hippocrates and for the accounts of the different tyrants, how they ruled and were overthrown, and in general for all the stories of conspiracies.

As a matter of fact the vulgate of the Persian Wars as Herodotus found it, especially in regard to the Odyssean wiles of Themistocles and his alleged collaboration with Aristides, appears to be doctored up considerably. The story that the three accusers of Socrates hanged themselves because the Athenians treated them with merciless contempt no doubt reflects what they wished had happened. The traveler with his tall tales should also be mentioned. He trafficked in two directions, bringing tales of exaggerated and contrived marvels from the Orient to the West and transferring and transplanting Greek myths to the East.

Followers of Alexander pretended to find these myths native to the Orient in order to flatter him. They transferred the Caucasus from the north to the Eastern [Indian] Ocean by the simple expedient of naming certain mountains in India "Caucasus" and showed him in the Paropamisus, a ridge of mountains to the north of India, a cave serving as a prison from which Herakles freed Prometheus. They flatteringly compared Alexander himself with Herakles by demonstrating that he had reached as far in his campaigns as Herakles had traveled.

The Greeks reveal a falsifying trait by their forgeries and interpolations. It is highly characteristic that the very first epistle in the later Trojan legend is a forgery. Genealogies and documents were often unreliable: the works of Acusilaus, the ancient Ionic historian, were in their later form a notorious forgery. He supposedly derived them from bronze tablets his father had dug up. Laws and enactments of popular assemblies were casually forged; the latter are betrayed by the garrulous motivations adduced like those of the Athenian resolution to honor Hippocrates.

If we also consider the opposite of forgery, namely, the suppression of authentic dates and documents, we shall get an idea of the difficulties besetting the critical researcher everywhere. Whoever, like Thucydides, sought what is true, first had to discriminate truth from poesy, second, truth from falsification, at every step of the way. And finally, Greek historiography was weak in dealing with events long past but acquired fame in presenting contemporary or recent events.

History (inquiry) in the Greek sense includes in addition to history also local and general geography. The Greeks took up the writing of history rather late but the way they went about it was the soundest imaginable.

They based it on the topography of the individual locality or country, its local myths and antiquities, recollections of all sorts; and the necessary skeleton of their chronology they based on a register—notoriously supplemented by memory—of the Olympic victors, the chief magistrates (*prytanes*) of Corinth, the archons of Athens, the priestesses of Argos, and similar items.

One began with one's native city, the single little state, whose records if any must have appeared more like antiquities than history, then one proceeded with the geography and history of other countries, and finally one interrelated the histories of several countries. But one hesitated long to record the history of the recent past. Only the Persian Wars brought forth events which in their total significance for the Greek nation were comparable to the myths, hitherto the all-absorbing interest of the people.

Hellenic historiography had its beginning in Ionia, and indeed in Miletus, which would have become the teacher of the nations instead of Athens if the enslavement by Persia had not violently cut short Milesian intellectual development. Already in 540 B.C. there existed a prose history of the founding of Miletus ascribed to a certain Cadmus; this work also dealt with the rest of Ionia. Then in 502, at the beginning of the Ionian revolt, Hecataeus, a man of some prestige, began his historical work called now *histories*, now *genealogies*, with this sentence: *Hecataeus of Miletus says: I am writing this as it appears true to me, for the Hellenes recount many traditional tales which I consider to be mostly twaddle.*

Thereupon he studied the tribal sagas of the Greeks and especially their tribal genealogies and must have captured many historical events in his narratives. In addition to the genealogies Hecataeus wrote *Travel Around the World* in which he treated of Europe and Asia in two volumes, drawing on his extensive travels and telling about all the countries Greeks came into contact with. His range of information extended from the Pillars of Hercules to the Indus, and his descriptions of countries were more detailed than those of Herodotus, for they also covered some he did not touch upon.

Charon of Lampsacus pursued the method of Hecataeus. He also wrote annals of his native city and in addition occupied himself with Oriental ethnology. He wrote individual works on Persia, Libya, and Ethiopia, and as a historian of the Persian Wars was a predecessor of Herodotus. Earlier Dionysius of Miletus had dealt with Persian history in his works; and Hippys of Rhegium was the first to write a history of Sicily which also traced the settlement of Italy.

Xanthus the Lydian, who apparently lived until about the Peloponnesian War, wrote an important book on the geography and ethnology of Lydia which, to judge by fragments, must have contained excellent material. His contemporary Hellanicus of Mitylene, still living at the beginning of the Peloponnesian War and the first historical scholar, represented all species of historical composition. Besides writing about his native Lesbos and Aeolia and about Attica, he also composed a work on the Persian Empire and a contemporary history, even though brief, dealing with the events between the Persian Wars and the Peloponnesian War.

These predecessors of Herodotus are usually called the logographers, to whom one could add Democritus (even though somewhat younger) because of his studies in ethnography, as well as others among the early philosophers. While the celebrated tragedians treated the myths in their own fashion, the historians collected and ordered them into some system or larger relationship according to some genealogy or chronology. In connection with all this they also narrated the local history or traditions of their polis, recorded contemporary history, and discovered the geography and history of the Orient. In other words, this pre-eminently talented race began to balance the historical accounts of the world as a whole, having only interest as its guiding principle.

The merit of these historical writings must not be judged solely by their absolute value, their depth and content, and their relative ability to satisfy our curiosity, but also and primarily in view of their having been voluntary creations. We should like to know whether the cities ever paid their logographers a fee or appointed them as municipal historians, whether they ever commissioned them to travel and supported them, and whether they bought books to put at their disposal, or whether the researchers, like most of the philosophers, lived in voluntary poverty. Our impression is that these historians managed almost wholly on their own and that their work required much self-sacrifice.

The same no doubt holds for the cosmographers of the fourth century, the successors in research of Anaximander, Hecataeus, and Democritus. They also had to struggle against the most idiotic conceptions that had gradually become established. Systematic geography owes a great debt to Eudoxus, Dicaearchus, and Ephorus.

Pytheas of Massilia, whose personality and experiences we should like to know more about, interests us especially. He traveled after 340, i.e., roughly at the time when Alexander, also a great discoverer, conquered the world; hence we may suppose that Greeks first arrived at Thule and the Indus during the same years.

His journey took him from Gades around Spain, along the coast of France, to Britain where he appears to have visited the tin country, and then sailed for six days north of Britain to the aforesaid Thule, probably one of the Shetland islands. He established the locality where amber is found and was the first and only witness to distinguish between Celts and Scythians on the North Sea, though he knew nothing of the Germanic tribes. In his work

A Discovery of the Ocean he was the first to relate the moon to the ebb and flow of the tide. He also measured high tides.

In the meantime the people had become literary and inaugurated the age of reading aloud to audiences. Herodotus came and held public readings in Athens, and perhaps also in Olympia.

As to Herodotus, we learn that he was born in 484 at Halicarnassus and in his younger years removed for a time to Samos. Later he helped to drive Lygdamis out of his native city but experienced great vexation and left

Handwriting sample of Herodotus
Laurentian Library, Florence

Samos, probably for Athens. He is said to have joined a colony the Athenians sent to Thurium in southern Italy, where he appears to have written the main part of his *Histories* and to have died in the first half of the Peloponnesian War before having completed his work, for it ends rather casually as if unfinished.

He acquired his wealth of knowledge about the world by traveling to Egypt, Cyrene, Babylon, the Cimmerian Bosporus, to Colchis and the land of the Scythians. Whether he got to Persia is questionable. An ancient report tells us that Herodotus read his *Histories* at the Panathenaean festival and that the Athenians awarded him ten talents.

With an energy that could only derive from a basic urge to know, Herodotus set about his great task of presenting the antagonism between Greece and Asia eventuating in the Persian Wars. To us it hardly seems probable that his *Histories* were designed also to preach a philosophical view, such as that earthly things are transitory, the gods jealous, that contempt for *hybris* brings disaster, etc. We think his only purpose in presenting the colossal conflict which drew the most disparate nations into its vortex was, as announced in his introduction, *to set forth the great and marvelous deeds performed alike by Hellenes and barbarians lest they be obliterated by the lapse of time*. Such an idea would not have occurred to an Egyptian or a Hebrew.

The composition is episodic through the first six books, but after or soon after the Battle of Marathon events follow one another in an unbroken series. He tells the story, now circumstantially (Egypt), now in essentials, of each country as it enters his historical narrative.

His vivid freshness derives largely from his having taken down word-of-mouth stories; indeed most of his narration is so thoroughly conversational in tone that it would be jejune and tedious if he had added borrowings from written sources. Naturally much of his material is not rigorously accurate, most of it having been so conceived as to represent the typical. The first book teems with stories which, though adduced as credible, have all the earmarks of fiction; yet we are inwardly grateful to him for every one of them.

The section from the death of Cambyses to the fake Smerdis with his ears lopped off is genuinely Oriental, but the following parts are Hellenized tales perhaps reworked ten times by the Greeks. Some of the most charming parts of the *Histories* are found in Book One, which has altogether the ring of an oral epic.

Herodotus ascribed to the speakers in his fictitious dialogues a multitude of reasons and motives not as they actually had but as they could have had them, and put his own thoughts into them though failing to give any reports of public speeches. This obtains for most of the reported conversations and discussions of Xerxes with his noblemen (VII, 8 ff., 45 ff.) though not for those of Solon with Croesus.

The account of the Ionian revolt at the end of the fifth and beginning of the sixth book is a masterpiece in conception and execution. Herodotus does not thrust upon the reader but skillfully adumbrates how the Ionians and their character shaped the turn of events. Aristagoras with his map of the world is a striking Ionic figure but still a swindler, even an obtrusive one. And the insubordination of the Greeks, as exhibited before the Battle of Lade, makes the moral causality plain as a pikestaff. If presenting the causal interconnections of events makes an account pragmatic, then the histories of Herodotus prove him to have been a genius of pragmatism.

Regarding his objectivity we have his own characteristic statement about his method: *It is my duty to report whatever people say but I am*

under no obligation to believe it, and this principle applies to my whole book.
He also carefully distinguished what he saw from what he only heard, and
indicated the degree of credibility by saying: *So far I have given my own*
views, my own opinions, and my own inquiries; now I shall report the
Egyptian histories as I have heard them although there will be in this as well
an element of my own views. If we examine the historians of other countries
and see how they are either unable to state things or able to state them only
apodictically, we observe the tremendous advance the Greeks made.

Herodotus was vividly aware of his worth as a Greek, as is plainly
shown in his histories; still he was in no way supercilious in his attitude
toward the barbarians. He respected not only their might and ancient culture, thereby adding to the glory of the Greek victory over Persia, but was
also delighted at finding permanent institutions (*nomoi*), whether they
were praiseworthy or not.

His sympathetic understanding of foreign religions is highly significant.
No doubt experience with the syncretism of divinities and contact with foreign cults in the colonies had broadened the Greek mentality; nevertheless
since Herodotus was the first to treat religion with relative objectivity, he
became the founder of the comparative history of religions and dogmas.
Even though he went about it somewhat uncritically, he sought and surmised affinities and identities of foreign gods with his own, hunting them
out one by one in foreign religions.

He felt no aversion to foreign cultures as such and was glad to learn
that the temples of Celestial Aphrodite on Cyprus and Cythera were trans-
plants of the ancient Syrian temple at Ascalon, and other facts of that nature.
Such data gave him a notion of the temporal origin, development, and
changes in religion. He supposed he knew that Hellenic names of divinities
were really of foreign derivation and that the Pelasgians at first worshiped
anonymous gods, only gradually giving them names, Dionysus being the
latest.

He said that Homer and Hesiod made the genealogy of the gods and
gave them surnames, arranged the worship due them, assigned them their
offices, and described their appearances. He was also of the opinion that the
poets who allegedly preceded Homer and Hesiod really came after them. As
he derived the names of the Hellenic gods, so he also derived the Greek cult
ceremonies (solemn assemblies, processions, petitionary rites) from the
Egyptians, perhaps in the main correctly, for they were of great antiquity in
Egypt and introduced into Greece much later.

But none of this detracts in the least from his great piety for the gods
and for native as well as foreign rites and cults, for those of Samothrace as
well as those of Egypt. And he wanted to divulge only what was commonly

known about these cults and what the context of his account demanded. But even though the results of his studies might be pretty inaccurate in detail, he would still deserve high acclaim for having founded the objective study of religion.

Although the Ionians did noteworthy work in this before him, Herodotus more than any other typifies for us the Greeks in their attitude toward the world at large. The Greeks might regard themselves as different from the barbarians; still they felt themselves related to the whole world and having a common bond in the myths, as the barbarians also had heroes and gods that journeyed in foreign lands.

The belief of Herodotus that the peripheral regions were the world's best part and that Hellas with its wonderfully temperate seasons, and India and Ethiopia, too, with their abundant fauna and tremendous fertility, belonged to those regions, was not so unpardonable in view of the aridity of Persia and Arabia.

Others excelled Herodotus, especially the source whence Thucydides drew his astonishing ethnography of Sicily, the most accurate analysis of racial stratification produced in antiquity.

We do not know when Thucydides was born, only that he died after the restoration of Athens. A scion of a distinguished family and married to a wealthy woman, he employed his means, as his biographer Marcellinus reports, in studying the history of the great war he undertook to narrate, the significance of which he had foreseen before it broke out. He went to great expense to get necessary information not only from Athenian but also from Spartan and other soldiers, ascertaining the truth by the agreement of the majority of the witnesses on both sides.

His culture identifies him as a member of the most elite circles of Athens. He was a follower of Anaxagoras in philosophy and a student of Antiphon in oratory. Gorgias and Prodicus are likewise supposed to have influenced him considerably. As a general on the Thracian front he was given the assignment to relieve Amphipolis in 423, but he had the bad luck to let Brasidas steal a march on him, and even though he managed to save Eion he was banished from Athens—*on a charge of treason!*

Thereupon he resided at various places but mostly at Scapte-Hyle where through marriage he became the owner of some gold mines. Recalled after the war, he went back to Athens where he died a few years later without finishing his project, composed probably during the last decade of his life.

Thucydides limited himself almost exclusively to giving a chronological account of those contemporary events which touched on the gigantic struggle between Athens and Sparta. He knew that this war was the most crucial event in the memory of man and set out to describe it with a dedicated love of truth, not just in terms of apparent findings but going to the root of matters with unbending objectivity.

For this task he had the most thorough grasp of motives, occasions, course of events, and results. One perceives how the clash builds up and becomes inevitable. Avoiding all sensationalism, he calmly portrayed the fatal unrolling of events. While for this purpose he marshaled facts and developed motives in great detail, he rarely expressed a personal opinion and almost never passed a moral judgment; this he reserved for the frightful general chapters (III, 82 f.) where, for once, he renders a true assessment of the moral degeneration of the Hellenes.

Although he had the different personages talk and act in character, he was content to describe them with few words. He discussed only the political implications of Pericles' death, treating them from the loftiest point of view so that his short passage has remained the basis of all subsequent evaluations of Pericles; he severely excluded all personal references to Pericles and was similarly frugal in style throughout his book. Whether his excellent *Praise of Brasidas* is purely objective or reflects his pleasure in having faced a great man in connection with his military assignments is a legitimate question.

The great original contributions of Thucydides raising him above Herodotus and all the earlier Greeks and all other nations is that he subsumed events or phenomena under a universal perspective. At any rate he expressed the general political maturity of Athens, and for us he is the father of judgment on cultural history, i.e., that mode of observing things from which the world simply cannot retreat. Though he may have erred in particulars, he nevertheless blazed new paths for all time to come.

The account of the early history of the Hellenes which comprises the introduction of Book One is a great innovation in that it has all the characteristics of a "construct," and as such it is most significant for the subsumptive method of Thucydides. He began by asking why the frequent migrations from one place of residence to another, and found the answer in the need to withdraw from overpopulated areas and in the ease with which groups could pull up stakes thanks to the scanty agriculture, lack of trade, absence of fortified settlements, and ease of satisfying daily needs.

He recognized that the regions having the best soil (Thessaly, Boeotia, the Peloponnesus besides Arcadia) had to endure the most numerous migrations because, as certain individuals attained to larger possessions and influence, destructive inner dissensions arose and that these regions were at the same time more subject to attack by people from other areas. Attica, on the other hand, owing to its poor soil, was left relatively undisturbed and so retained a stable population. Thus the more rapid and powerful growth of

Athens served to prove that the unequal development of Greek communities was largely due to the migrations.

He observed that the recent cities founded after the rise of navigation were built on shores or isthmuses, whereas the older ones were situated somewhat inland because of piracy. He related the developments accurately: new poleis were founded by groups driven out of other poleis and by dissemination from smaller groups having grown into large and powerful aggregates in new territories, as happened in the case of the Boeotians who had been driven out of Arne in Thessaly.

He also had a marvelous insight into the developments following the Dorian migration, as when he pointed out that with the increase of wealth and revenues the hereditary kingships turned into tyrannies, and that this wealth enabled the development of naval power beginning with the construction of triremes at Corinth, or how difficult it is to get people to co-operate in a large common enterprise, and that just a war between Chalcis and Eretria sufficed to split Hellas into two great factions.

Thucydides was the great historian of his period, even though he omitted much we should like to know and which would be very important for us but was perfectly obvious to him and his contemporaries.

We shall allude once more to the ethnography of Sicily based on exemplary sources and found at the beginning of Book Six.

The personality and determination of Thucydides were clearly exceptional; with Herodotus he raised the general standard of excellence, and we can state that these two famous historians are in themselves two great facts of cultural history. In comparison with them subsequent Greek historians appear as historians of literature rather than of culture.

Still one would have to except Xenophon if only for the first two books of the *Hellenica* portraying the last years of the Peloponnesian War and the period of the Thirty Tyrants so vividly and richly that one could suspect he used notes and materials left by Thucydides. These powerful and glorious sections contrast sharply with the later parts. From the third book on Xenophon gives us a mere chronicle of Spartan power or a journal of Spartan military headquarters. He has so little grasp of the rise of Thebes that he does not even mention the two great Thebans until the end, and then it positively pains him to do so, and he takes no notice whatever of the restoration of Messenia and Arcadia.

We shall just mention in passing that in our opinion the *Memorabilia* and other Socratic writings of Xenophon give, apart from some passages in Plato, the most faithful picture we have of the real Socrates. In his *Cyropaedia* the author strays from the historical facts, using them for propaganda purposes. He depicts Cyrus as an ideal monarch educated on Socratic principles and representing the Xenophontean Hellene antagonistic to Athenian democracy and inclining toward the Spartan way of life as exemplified in the army commander Agesilaus. His straight-faced naïveté apparently betrays no crafty design.

The *Anabasis*, that great prototype of Caesar's commentaries, will always have to be included among Xenophon's distinguished achievements. This work written in the third person, was composed perhaps twenty years after the campaign, obviously from careful notes taken on the spot. In the spirit of Herodotus it unfolds an incomparable series of descriptions and scenes. It is completely artless and stripped of all exquisite eloquence, deriving its effects purely from the events described. Among other passages the assassination of the army commanders is celebrated for its perfect objectivity. One may ask whether anything of equal value in subject matter and presentation alike was found before Xenophon.

We shall give brief summaries of the following authors. Ephorus and Theopompus, disciples of Isocrates, wrote voluminously, the former thirty books covering the period from the return of the Heraclidae to Philip's siege of Perinthus, the latter a Hellenica in twelve books paralleling Xenophon's first books and continuing Thucydides to the battle at Knidos and a Philippica in fifty-eight books recording the history of Greece in the period of Philip of Macedonia.

Callisthenes, in addition to a history of Greece from the peace of Antalcidas to the Holy War, wrote an account of the Asiatic campaigns of Alexander, whom he accompanied to his own misfortune, and likewise Duris of Samos wrote a history of Macedonia down to the death of Lysimachus. Among many other historians three of Sicily should be singled out: Philistus, who wrote a history of Sicily and one of Dionysius the Elder; Athanis, who continued the work of his predecessor down to Dion; and Timaeus, who presented a history of Sicily from the ancient period down to the first Punic War.

Even though all those foregoing works have perished, notices about them and fragments of them preserved in other authors show what tremendous labors men expended on the study of history. This historical literature must have contained some perfectly splendid works. We need but recall, for example, the high regard Diodorus Siculus had for the above-mentioned historians of Sicily, to whom he owed his information about the painful fortunes of his lovely island.

Polybius, the great historian of the second century, so far from being purely Hellenic in his labors, would be inconceivable apart from the rise of Rome. But in spite of all, the reports we get of the historical achievements during this period are very impressive and show that the Greeks were keenly aware of their history and never lost sight of it.

We should also take cognizance of monographs on cities and districts, writings frequently referred to by grammarians and lexicographers. We call attention to *Atthis* (a history of Athens) written in the third century by Philochorus, whose activities must have been astonishingly varied. Marsyas of Pella, a brother of Antigonus and a contemporary of Alexander the Great, wrote a *Macedonica* (a history of Macedonia) in ten books extending from the first Macedonian kings to Alexander's withdrawal from Egypt. A certain Crito of Pieria authored a *Pallenica* giving the founding of Syracuse, a *Sicelica,* a description of Syracuse, a *Persica,* and a work on the *Dominion of the Macedonians.*

The monograph was also beginning to play a role in geography; Polemon and others in the second century achieved names for themselves by giving descriptions of Hellenic localities and landscapes.

In contrast to the writers of these specialized studies we find the synoptic historians. Polybius contrasted these local histories scattered hither and yon with the systematic histories of his times, and in the Augustan age Diodorus Siculus, no great historian but one who had access to excellent sources, composed his *Historical Library,* and Nicolaus of Damascus wrote a *Universal History.* These were the first universal histories ever compiled.

As soon as nations sloughed off barbarism, they had to make permanent connections with the historians of Greece. While we pay heed to the other scientific accomplishments of the Greeks only out of pious respect, since the data of science do not come from the Greeks, we are dependent on Greek historical investigations and on their results and contributions. In general though, the historical investigations of the Greeks impress us with their youthful, refreshing qualities, as do their other scientific activities.

These historical labors are thoroughly independent of foreign models and derive from the joy of self-accomplishment. The Hellenes ever embodied free will and hence have become the standard of excellence for ages to come.

GLOSSARY

abacus: square slab, uppermost member of the capital of a column, supporting the architrave

Achaemenids: line of Persian kings

acroamatic: told orally to chosen disciples only; esoteric

acroterium: an ornament or statue placed at one of the three corners of a Greek pediment

agon (*pl.* agones):   a contest (in athletics or any other endeavor)

agora: a place of a popular political assembly, originally a market place

anadasmos: new distribution of land among colonists

andreia: manliness; valor

anta: pillar or pier, formed by thickening of a wall at its extremity

antibanausic: contemptuous of work and working people

aoidos: itinerant singer of songs and poetry

archon: a higher magistrate in ancient Athens, elected annually

archon basileus: the second archon (see *basileus*)

archonship: office of an archon

asebia: impiety

atimia: dishonor; disgrace

aulody: singing accompanied by flute playing

banausic (*adj.*):   smacking of the workshop or of an uninspired occupation

banausic (*noun*):   a banausic person, a philistine

basileus: king; in Athens the second archon, supervisor of religious service and criminal court

bulaios: giving good advice

cella: the sanctuary of a temple containing the statue of the god

Chimaera: mythological monster

chiton: garment for both sexes, usually worn next to the skin

choragium: place for training choral dancers

choragus: 1. chorus master;
2. citizen who defrayed the cost of a chorus

choregia, choregy: maintenance and training of a chorus, a costly *leitourgia* (which see)

choreutes: choral dancer

339

cithara: a musical instrument of the lyre class

cleruchies: Athenian military colonies set up for safeguarding strategically important points

commus: dialogue in lyrical form

contumacia: contempt of court; sentence *in contumaciam*: sentence in the absence of the accused person

cordax: a lascivious dance

cothurnus: 1. a thick-soled laced boot worn by actors in the ancient tragic drama;
2. the dignified and somewhat stilted spirit of ancient tragedy

coussinet: the convex projection connecting the two faces of the capital of an Ionic column

crypteia: the practice among Spartan youths of keeping the helots under surveillance, and dealing brutally with them

cynegetici: poets of hunting

demos: 1. a Greek city state or province;
2. the people of a state or province

dentil: a small rectangular block in a series projecting like teeth, in a cornice of the Ionian or Corinthian order

depas amphikypellon: goblet with two looped handles

deuteragonist: second actor

diadochi: successors of Alexander the Great, army leaders who fought among themselves for territories of the empire

dipteral style: style using double-row columns

dithyramb: choric hymn in honor of Dionysus

doryphor: spear bearer

drachma: the principal silver coin of the ancient Greeks, of varying value

eccyclema: a machine used to display an interior scene (as dead bodies after a murder) in the classic theater

echinus: rounded molding supporting the abacus of a Doric capital

elegeion: distich

elegy: poem in distichs

embaterion: marching song

emmeleia: stately, tragic dance

emporion: a place of trade, a commercial center

ephebos: young man, 16 to 20, in training for military service

ephor: one of the five magistrates annually elected in Sparta, exercising almost all of the state's executive power

epideictic: primarily designed for oratorical effect or to show the skill of the speaker

epinikion: victory ode

epirrhema: address in Greek comedy spoken by the chorus leader after the parabasis

Erinyes *pl.* (*sing.* Erinys):   avenging spirits pursuing the violator of human and divine law and striking him with madness

eupatrid: member of the aristocracy of ancient Athens

exedra: a room open like a portico, or a semicircular outdoor bench, used for conversation

exodus: the part of a Greek drama following the last song of the chorus

exostra: machine in the background of the stage showing the interior of a house; *in exostra* = in open scene, before everyone's eyes

exules *pl.* (*sing.* exul):   exiles; exiled persons

fasciae: 1. a bandlike ornament of the Ionic order;
2. the three bands making up the architrave

geron (*pl.* gerontes):   a member of the Spartan gerousia

gerousia: council of elders; Spartan senate

Graeae: three sea deities, who had but one eye and one tooth among them, protectresses of the Gorgons, their sisters

gusla: a primitive musical instrument having a round concave body, parchment soundboard and one string

gymnasiarchia: responsibility for maintenance and training of athletes for festival contests, a costly *leitourgia* (which see)

gymnopaediae: gymnastic and dancing festival in honor of Apollo

gymnopaedike: dance performed by naked boys, imitating the *palaestra* (wrestling ring) exercises and the *pancratium* (a contest combining wrestling and boxing)

Gymnosophist: Sect of philosophers found in India by Alexander the Great. They renounced bodily pleasures and devoted themselves to meditation.

halieutici: poets of the sea

heliaea: in ancient Greece, a jury

helot: serf in Sparta

hemistich: half a stich, half a line of verse

Herakles: Greek name for Hercules

herma: statue consisting of a head, usually that of the god Hermes, supported on a quadrangular pillar

heroon: heroes' chapel

hetaeria: in Athens, a political club or party

hexastyle: portico with six columns

hierophant: official expounder of rites of worship and sacrifice

hippeus (*pl.* hippcis):   horse owner; knight

hoplite: heavily armed foot soldier

Hyacinthia: a three-day festival, celebrated by the Spartans in July, in honor of Hyacinthos, son of a Spartan king, and Apollo

hybris: wanton, overweening pride

hyporchema: choral hymn to Apollo

in contumaciam, see *contumacia*

kalokagathia: nobility in character and conduct

Karneia: Spartan festival in August, in honor of Apollo, celebrated at the same time as the Olympic games

kommoi (*pl.* of kommos):   alternating songs of the chorus and a character of
    the scene
krater: a vessel having a wide mouth, used for mixing wine and water
krobylos: a tuft of hair on top of the head or of the helmet

lampadarchia: defraying of expenses for torchlight processions, as a *leitourgia*
    (which see)
leitourgia: an obligation, taken up by, or, more often, imposed on a citizen, to
    finance some public institution as a public service (see *choregia, gym-
    nasiarchia, lampadarchia, trierarchia*)
lesche: public meeting hall
logomachy: a contest in words; a war of words

maieutics: art of midwifery; dialectic method used by Socrates
metempsychosis: 1. passage of the soul from one body into another;
    2. rebirth of the soul after death in another body
metics: residents of foreign birth, who had no political rights, were workers
    and traders
metope: square space between the triglyphs of a Doric frieze
mimes: prose conversations taken from the life of the common people
mina: currency unit, equivalent of 100 drachmas
Mnemosyne: goddess of memory, mother of the Muses
monody: ode sung by one actor in a Greek tragedy
mothax (*pl.* mothakes):   child of a helot brought up in a Spartan family
mythopoeic: producing myths

nauarch: commander of the fleet
neodamodes: newly enfranchised helots
nomos (*pl.* nomoi) (*mus.*):   1. tune, melody;
    2. mode, *e.g.,* the Lydian mode

Olympieum: temple of the Olympian Zeus
orchesis: art of dancing in the chorus

paean: song of invocation or thanksgiving to some deity
Panathenaea: most splendidly celebrated public festival, in the third year of
    every Olympiad
pancratium: athletic contest combining wrestling and boxing
parabasis: choral ode in tetrameters, in Greek comedy
paracatalogue: irregular chant in which the dialogue was carried on
paraenesis: exhortation to valor
parodus: entrance song of the chorus
partheneion (*pl.* partheneia):   song sung by maidens
peculium: property; fortune
penestes: 1. laborer, dayworker;
    2. (in Thessalia) a serf
pentathlon: athletic contest of five events
periaktoi: revolving triangular screens set on either side of the stage

peribolos: courtyard enclosed by walls

perioeci: in Laconia, persons of limited rights who carried on trade and industry

peripteros: having a row of columns on all sides

Persian Wars: the wars between Persians and Greeks, 500–479 B.C.

phratria, phratry: kinship group, clan; subdivision of a *phyle* (which see)

phyle: subdivision of a Greek state

Pnyx: place in Athens southwest of the Acropolis where the assembly of voters was held

polis (*pl.* poleis):   a Greek city-state

populus: the people as a political unit

pronaos: temple vestibule

propylaea *pl.* (*sing.* propylaeum):   vestibule to a temple area of architectural prominence

prosodion: processional hymn

protagonist: first actor and stage director, in Greek drama

proxenia: consulate (office of the representative of citizens of a foreign country)

prytaneum: a public hall in Athens where official hospitality, including free meals, was extended to distinguished citizens

prytanies: executive committee of the council of the five hundred, dealing with the current affairs of government in Athens

psephisma: resolution arrived at by voting; bill

pteroma: colonnade

pyrrhic: warlike dance in which the motions of actual warfare were imitated

rhetra: speech; agreement; decree

rhyparography: smutty picture

sacellum (*pl.* sacella):   smaller temple

scholarch: head of a school, esp. of an Athenian school of philosophy

scholiast: ancient commentator upon the classics

sikinnis: dance of the satyrs

sima (or cyma):   molding with an S-formed profile

skolion: a song, sung to the lyre, which guests at banquets, in turn, were called upon to furnish

skytale: ciphered message

sloka: a distich, two lines of 16 syllables, the chief verse form of the Sanskrit epics

soccus: 1. shoe of the actors worn in Greek comedy;
        2. comic style

sophrosyne: prudence; self-control

stasimon: in Greek tragedy, choral ode between two episodes

stereobate: a substructure of masonry visible above the ground level

stichomythy: in Greek drama, dialogue in alternating lines or sets of lines

stoa: portico of considerable length used as promenade or meeting place

strategos: field marshal; commander-in-chief

stylobate: a continuous base supporting a row of columns

sufi: Mohammedan mystic, possessing nothing and desiring nothing; acknowledges no spiritual head sycophancy: the evil of professional informing

symposium: a banquet or carousal

syrinx: the panpipe, a wind instrument consisting of a series of graduated flutes bound together

syssition (*pl.* syssitia):   the common meal of the Spartans

taenia: a band on a Doric order separating the frieze from the architrave

telesm: 1. votive offering; offering of thanks;
2. talisman

templum in antis: temple whose portico is bordered by antas on both sides, with columns in between

theogony: an account of the origin and the genealogy of the gods

theoricon: in Athens, public money used to provide theater tickets for the poor

thymele: altar-shaped platform in the orchestra

timocracy:

  Plato: a form of government where love of honor is the guiding principle (*e.g.,* in Sparta)

  Aristotle: a form of government where political and civil honors are distributed according to wealth

tribus: a district of the citizens of ancient Rome

trierarchia: furnishing and maintenance of triremes, the costliest *leitourgia* (which see)

triglyph: grooved ornament of a Doric frieze, alternating with metopes

trireme: ancient galley with three banks of oars

tritagonist: third actor

tropaeum: monument commemorating victory

tyche: goddess of fate

tycheum: temple of the goddess Tyche

xoanon: primitive image of wood